Unacknowledged Legislation

Also by Christopher Hitchens

Prepared for the Worst: Selected Essays and Minority Reports

The Elgin Marbles: Should they be returned to Greece?

Hostage to History: Cyprus from the Ottomans to Kissinger

Blaming the Victims (edited with Edward Said)

James Callaghan: The Road to Number Ten (with Peter Kellner)

Karl Marx and the Paris Commune

The Monarchy: A Critique of Britain's Favourite Fetish

Blood, Class and Nostalgia: Anglo-American Ironies

For the Sake of Argument: Essays and Minority Reports

International Territory: The United Nations 1945–95
(photographs by Adam Bartos)

When the Borders Bleed: The Struggle of the Kurds
(photographs by Ed Kashi)

No One Left to Lie To: The Values of the Worst Family

Unacknowledged Legislation
Writers in the Public Sphere

◆

CHRISTOPHER HITCHENS

VERSO
London • New York

First published by Verso 2000
© Christopher Hitchens 2000
Reprinted 2001
All rights reserved

Verso
UK: 6 Meard Street, London W1F 0EG
USA: 180 Varick Street, New York, NY 10014–4606

Verso is the imprint of New Left Books

ISBN 1–85984–786–2

British Library Cataloguing in Publication Data
A catalogue record for this book is available from the British Library

Library of Congress Cataloging-in-Publication Data
Hitchens, Christopher.
 Unacknowledged legislation : writers in the public sphere / Christopher Hitchens.
  p. cm.
 Includes index.
 ISBN 1-85984-786-2
 1. English literature—20th century—History and criticism. 2. Politics and
literature—Great Britain—History—20th century. 3. Politics and literature—Great
Britain—History—19th century. 4. English literature—19th century—History and criticism.
5. Politics and literature—United States—History. 6. Authors, American—Political and
social views. 7. Authors, English—Political and social views. 8. American
literature—History and criticism. I. Title.
PR478.P64 H58 2001
820.9'358—dc21

00-054986

Typeset in 10/12½pt ITC New Baskerville by
SetSystems Ltd, Saffron Walden, Essex
Printed by R. R. Donnelley & Sons, USA

For Salman. As ever.

Allons travailler.
(Closing words of Emile Zola in *L'Oeuvre*)

Contents

Foreword

Writing in response to Thomas Love Peacock, who had said that 'a poet in our time is a semi-barbarian in a civilised community', Percy Bysshe Shelley proclaimed in 1821 that:

> Poets are the hierophants of an unapprehended inspiration; the mirrors of the gigantic shadows which futurity casts upon the present; the words which express what they understand not; the trumpets which sing to battle, and feel not what they inspire; the influence which is moved not, but moves. *Poets are the unacknowledged legislators of the world.* [Italics mine.]

The fate of his polemic *In Defence of Poetry* (which is customarily pared down to comprise only the last sentence of the above paragraph) is not untypical of the fate of radical freelance work in all ages. The magazine to which it was sent, and which had printed Peacock's original remarks, ceased publication almost as soon as the riposte had been composed. Shelley then hoped to publish it in the pages of *The Liberal*, a periodical launched by Byron and Leigh Hunt. But *The Liberal*, too, expired in the grand tradition of noble-minded and penurious reviews. Shelley died long before his essay saw print. His widow, Mary Wollstonecraft Shelley, got it into publication eighteen years after his decease, omitting several of the references to Peacock. Thus, we owe our too-easy familiarity with an attenuated *aperçu* to the belated efforts of the author of *Frankenstein*, who was also the daughter of the authors of *Political Justice* and *A Vindication of the Rights of Women*.

Frankenstein's unhappy creation allows me an easy transition to the following, which was written by W. H. Auden in August 1968. (*August 1968*, following Auden's fondness for numinous dates like *1 September 1939*, is also the title of the poem):

> The Ogre does what ogres can,
> Deeds quite impossible for man,
> But one prize is beyond his reach,
> The Ogre cannot master Speech.
> About a subjugated plain,
> Among its desperate and slain,

> The Ogre stalks with hands on hips
> While drivel gushes from his lips.

This was penned in hot and immediate response, from just across the Austrian frontier, to the Soviet erasure of culture and democracy in Czechoslovakia in that very month. I happened to be in Havana at the time, and on my way to Prague, and was very much struck – without registering it anything like so acutely – by the awful rhetoric and terminology employed by defenders of the Warsaw Pact invasion. The hideous term 'normalisation', a sort of apotheosis of the *langue du bois*, was the name given to the subsequent 'restoration of order'.

Twenty-one years later, the mighty occupation-regime installed by the full weight of *Panzerkommunismus* (Ernst Fischer's caustic word for it) collapsed amid laughter and ignominy, without the loss of a single life, as a consequence of a civil opposition led by satirical playwrights, ironic essayists, Bohemian jazz-players and rock musicians, and subversive poets. Life in the Czech lands, and the Slovak lands too, may since have become much more banal and, so to say, prosaic. But would it be merely 'romantic' to say that Auden, in 1968, had been somehow aware of 'the gigantic shadows that futurity casts upon the present'? 'Moved not', or not so much as moving, he had prefigured the end of a system which depended on gibberish and lies. The sword, as we have reason to know, is often much mightier than the pen. However, there are things that pens can do, and swords cannot. And every tank, as Brecht said, has a crucial flaw. Its driver. Suppose that driver has read something good lately, or has a decent song or poem in his head . . .

Invited recently by the *Los Angeles Times* to contribute to one of those symposia on 'Politics and the Novel', I was asked to name the works of fiction that had had most influence upon me. Novels were specified; even so I should have said 'the war poems of Wilfred Owen'. These are neither novels and nor, in one important sense, are they fictional or imaginary. But I shall never be able to forget the way in which these verses utterly turned over all the furniture of my mind; inverting every conception of order and patriotism and tradition on which I had been brought up. I hadn't then encountered, or even heard of, the novels of Barbusse and Remarque, or the paintings of Otto Dix, or the great essays and polemics of the Zimmerwald and Kienthal conferences; the appeals to civilisation written by Rosa Luxemburg in her *Junius* incarnation. (Revisionism has succeeded, in many cases justly, in overturning many of the icons of Western Marxism; this tide, however, still halts when it confronts the nobility of Luxemburg and Jean Jaurès and other less celebrated heroes of 1914 – such as the Serbian Dimitri Tucovic.) I came to all these discoveries, and later ones such as the magnificent *Regeneration* trilogy composed by Pat Barker, through the door that had been forced open for me by Owen's '*Dulce Et Decorum Est*'. So it's highly satisfying to read again his poem '*A Terre* (Being the Philosophy of Many Soldiers)' and to come across the lines:

> Certainly flowers have the easiest time on earth.
> 'I shall be one with nature, herb and stone',
> Shelley would tell me. Shelley would be stunned:
> The dullest Tommy hugs that fancy now.
> 'Pushing up daisies' is their creed, you know.

A true appreciation of Shelley; to find a dry and ironic use for him in the very trenches. Most of Owen's poetry was written or 'finished' in the twelve months before his life was thrown away in a futile action on the Sambre-Meuse canal, and he only published four poems in his lifetime (aiming for the readers of the old *Nation* and *Athenaeum*, and spending part of his last leave with Oscar Wilde's friend and executor Robert Ross, and with Scott Moncrieff, translator of *Remembrance of Things Past*). But he has conclusively outlived all the jingo versifiers, blood-bolted Liberal politicians, garlanded generals and other supposed legislators of the period. He is the most powerful single rebuttal of Auden's mild and sane claim that 'Poetry makes nothing happen'.

The essays in these ensuing pages were all written in the last decade of the twentieth century; between the marvellous humbling of the Ogre and the onset of fresh discontents. They do not engage with political writers so much as with writers encountering politics or public life. I don't deal exclusively or even principally with poets either, but I have looked for those who try and raise prose to the level of poetry (from Wodehouse and Wilde, to Anthony Powell's ear for secret harmonies and unheard melodies). Another and more blunt way of stating my own ambition is to recall Orwell's desire to 'make political writing into an art'. Sometimes, and less strenuously, I have attempted to show how some artists have almost involuntarily committed great political writing.

The intersection where this occurs is an occasion of paradox, or of epigram and aphorism. One still pays attention when Wilde says that socialism, properly considered, would free us of the distress and tedium of living for others. And one lends an ear when Orwell – so crassly termed a 'saint' by V. S. Pritchett – announces that saints must always be adjudged guilty until proven innocent. Lionel Trilling once alluded to 'the bloody crossroads' where literature and politics meet, and this phrase was annexed by the dire Norman Podhoretz (who is to Trilling as a satyr to Hyperion) for the title of a notorious and propagandistic book. But properly understood and appreciated, literature need never collide with, or recoil from, the *agora*. It need not be, as Stendhal has it in *Le Rouge et Le Noir*, that 'politics is a stone tied to the neck of literature' and that politics in the novel is 'a pistol shot in the middle of a concert.' The openly, directly politicised writer is something we have learned to distrust – who now remembers Mikhail Sholokhov? – and the surreptitiously politicised one (I give here the instance of Tom Wolfe) is no great improvement. Gabriel García Márquez has paid a high price for his temporal allegiances, as have his patient readers. But in the work of Tolstoy, Dickens, Nabokov, even Proust, we find them occupied with the political condition as naturally as if they were breathing. Which is what Auden must also have meant when he wrote, in obeisance to a man whose public opinions he actively distrusted, ('In Memory of W. B. Yeats': February 1939):

> Time that is intolerant
> Of the brave and innocent,
> And indifferent in a week
> To a beautiful physique,
>
> Worships language and forgives
> Everyone by whom it lives;
> Pardons cowardice, conceit,
> Lays its honours at their feet.
>
> Time that with this strange excuse
> Pardoned Kipling and his views,
> And will pardon Paul Claudel,
> Pardons him for writing well.

Nothing is lost, from these verses, in contemplation of the fact that Auden removed them, and many other exquisite poems and passages, from his own canon in a boring attempt to re-establish himself as a man of Anglican integrity. (Also, the rehabilitation of Paul Claudel may take a little longer than he surmised.)

I cannot apologise for the fact that my subjects are almost all English or American or Anglo-American. For one thing, I am mainly English and have no real competence in any other tongue. For another, the Anglo-American idiom is well on its way to being what Kipling and others always hoped for, albeit in a different guise: a world language. A world language, that is, without being an imperial one. (Indeed, at least in some ways, the first to the extent that it has ceased to be the second.) The written record of English literature is also a powerful and flexible instrument for the understanding of British and perhaps post-British society – a point to which I want to recur. While in America, the role of the writer is given exceptional salience by the fact of the United States being a 'written' country, based on a number of founding documents that are subject to continuous revision and interpretation. No clause in the Constitution mandates an opposition party; indeed the whole document is designed to evolve orderly consensus. But the

First Amendment, which places freedom of expression on a level with freedom of (and freedom *from*) religion, grants the writer wide powers. In my graduate class on 'Unacknowledged Legislators' at the New School in New York, which gave me the title of this book, I sought to show how often, when all parties in the state were agreed on a matter, it was individual pens which created the moral space for a true argument. Some chief instances would be Thomas Paine on the issue of independence and anti-monarchism, Garrison and Douglass on slavery, Mark Twain and William Dean Howells on imperialism, and Upton Sinclair and John Steinbeck on the exploitation of labour. But nearer to our own time, there was the disruption by Norman Mailer and Robert Lowell of the unspoken agreement on a war of atrocity and aggression in Indochina. And of course, we have Gore Vidal's seven-volume novelisation of American history, a literary attempt at the creation of what he terms 'a usable past'.

Although admittedly borne around the globe partly on the shoulders of a homogenising American commerce, another way in which English has become a language of universals is the form in which it has been annexed by its former colonial subjects. Here, the critical figure has been Salman Rushdie. Ever since his magnificent evocation of combined partition and parturition in *Midnight's Children*, he has been raising a body of work which, while deeply based in the love and study of classical English letters, truly deserves the name of cosmopolitan. By his experiments with language and dialect and his conscription of musical themes, he has approached the closest to poetry in prose. He is also, in such a way as to make it indissoluble from his other themes, a political writer for an emerging multi-national and (perhaps this needs no emphasis) secular readership. In 1989, just as the Ogre was about to collapse, Salman was criminally assaulted by a simultaneous death sentence and life sentence, a *fatwah* issued by a moribund theocrat. The intervening ten years, in which the forces of mercenary assassination and religious coercion were opposed by the weapons of wit and reason, involved a campaign with which I am extremely proud to have been associated. As I write, it is the discredited mullahs who have to answer to a host of independent and critical literary voices in Iran. Nothing could be more satisfying than this outcome. The *summa* of the published record is a book, originally in French and entitled *Pour Rushdie*, in which almost every writer of worth in the Arab and Iranian and wider Muslim world took Salman's side, and identified his cause with their own hopes for emancipation. This volume was the finest possible repudiation of all the Western conservative elements who claimed to see merit in the Ayatollah's condemnation of blasphemy. 'Is nothing sacred?' *Of course not.* Aptly enough, perhaps, the best defence of Rushdie as a profane and revolutionary writer in the great tradition of Joyce and Rabelais was written by Milan Kundera, literary eminence of the Czech cultural resistance. (It may be found in his book *Testaments Betrayed.*)

'One Balzac', Marx is supposed to have said, 'is worth a hundred Zolas.' Many of the writers discussed here have no 'agenda' of any sort, or are conservatives whose insight and integrity I have found indispensible. I remember for example sitting with Jorge Luis Borges in Buenos Aires, as he employed an almost Evelyn Waugh-like argument in excusing the military dictatorship that then held power in his country. But I had a feeling that he couldn't keep up this pose, and not many years later he wrote a satirical poem ridiculing the Falklands/Malvinas adventure, while also making statements against the junta's cruelty in the matter of the *desaparecidos.* It wasn't just another author signing a letter about 'human rights'; it was the ironic mind refusing the dictates of the literal one. And Borges, too, helped English evolve as a global idiom . . .

George Eliot is my Balzac in this instance. I spent a good deal of the 1990s attempting to understand the role played by lying and corruption and demagogy in American democracy. And here is Eliot in *Romola*, doing all my work for me in her depiction of fifteenth-century Florence:

> There was still one resource open to Tito. He might have turned back, sought Baldassarre again, confessed everything to him – to Romola – to all the world. But he never thought of that. The repentance which cuts off all moorings to evil, demands something more than selfish fear. He had no sense that there was strength and safety in truth; the only strength he trusted to lay in his ingenuity and dissimulation. Now that the first shock, which had called up the traitorous signs of fear, was well past, he hoped to be prepared for all emergencies by cool deceit – and defensive armour . . .
>
> He had simply chosen to make life easy to himself – to carry his human lot, if possible, in such a way that it should pinch him nowhere; and the choice had, at various times, landed him in unexpected positions. The question now was, not whether he should divide the common pressure of destiny with his suffering fellow-man; it was whether all the resources of lying would save him from being crushed by the consequences of that habitual choice.

Later – and this time on Savonarola and implicitly on all spiritual and secular authoritarians:

> No man ever struggled to retain power over a mixed multitude without suffering vitiation; his standard must be their lower needs and not his own best insight.

Finally, and on all forms of totalitarian control, and the way in which they betray their supererogatory nature:

> Looking at the printed confessions, she saw many sentences which bore the stamp of bungling fabrication: they had that emphasis and repetition in self-accusation which none but very low hypocrites use to their fellow-men.

(The last captures precisely the quality of hysterical falsity that led George Orwell to conclude, on literary evidence alone, that the admissions made at the Moscow show trials must have been sham.)

What might now be the tasks, or the opportunities, for the latent political intelligence of literature? The first, I suggest, is to find a language that can match the new world, or new cosmos, created for us by the Hubble telescope and the translation of DNA. We live at the opening of an age where the nature of humanity, and the nature of the universe, can at last be scrutinised and understood without racism or tribalism, and without superstition. (A page of Stephen Hawking on the 'event horizon' is more awe-inspiring than anything in Genesis or Ezekiel.) But we still employ the stilted and faltering metaphors of our pre-history; translating vivid new discourses back into the safe, solipsistic *patois* that we already know. Welcoming the completion of the Human Genome Project in the spring of 2000, President Clinton sounded like a gaping Elmer Gantry when he said it gave us the dictionary our Maker had used to 'create' us. At the present, then, language lags behind reality and behind humanity. Only a handful of authors (Martin Amis and Ian McEwan among them) have attempted to engage on this astonishing new terrain.

I have, finally, a wish for each of my countries. In post-Ukanian Britain, where the lineaments of a secular republic, or perhaps I should say federation of secular republics, are already emerging within the carapace of the *ancien régime*, we shall require something transcendent to replace the exhausted symbolism of the antique. My own semi-serious proposal is that we realign Westminster Abbey, deposing the ossuary of royalism from the centrepiece and re-naming the condescendingly titled 'Poet's Corner'. This would become, not a formal shrine, but a permanent witness to the greatness of English (and Irish and Scots and Welsh) literature. In Oliver Cromwell's memorial cortège there walked John Milton, John Dryden and Andrew Marvell – a more splendid retinue than ever attended the obsequy of any monarch. Whereas the Queen Mother, introduced to the devoted royalist T. S. Eliot, could afterwards recall neither his name nor the title of the poem – she thought it might have been 'The Desert' – that he had read at Windsor Castle. There is an occluded republican tradition in our shared writing, of which Shelley along with Burns and Byron and many others are exemplars. It is time to make it explicit, and to teach it to the children (and, if you insist, to show it to the tourists).

In the case of the United States, we await a writer who can summon every nerve to cleanse the country of the filthy stain of the death penalty. Other priorities might seem at first to make larger claims, but there is probably no single change that would cumulatively amount to more than this one. Abolition would repudiate the heritage of racial bigotry and mob justice while simultaneously limiting the over-mighty state. Every argument of law and decency and precedent has already been skilfully made, against the gallows and the gas chamber and the firing squad and the immolating 'chair' and – arguably most obscene of all – the pseudo-medicalised 'procedure' of deadly injection. But there is as yet no Blake or Camus or Koestler to synthesise justice and reason with outrage; to compose the poem or novel – as did Herman Melville with flogging in his *White-Jacket* – that will constitute the needful moral legislation.

In the course of the decade past, I never even opened any of the books that purported to tell me of the postmodern death (or the relativism or collectivisation) of authorship. Superficial and ephemeral and sometimes sinister, this languid and onanistic tendency was, fortunately as well as inevitably, exhausted before it had begun. Instead, I read and re-read the writers who have allowed me to phrase these imperfect critiques and appreciations, and am grateful for the role they have let themselves play in my own inner life. Perhaps, with effort, we could begin to transcend the pessimistic definition of poetry that describes it as the element lost in translation.

Christopher Hitchens
Washington DC, July 2000

I

'In Praise Of . . .'

The Wilde Side

Generosity is not the first quality that we associate with the name of Ms Dorothy Parker. But she did write the following rather resigned tribute and testament:

> If, with the literate, I am
> Impelled to try an epigram,
> I never seek to take the credit;
> We all assume that Oscar said it.

And so we do. 'Work is the curse of the drinking classes.' 'He hasn't a single redeeming vice.' 'I can resist anything except temptation.' 'He is old enough to know worse.' It's also worth bearing in mind the difference between an epigram and an aphorism. The former is merely a witty play on words (if one can use 'merely' in such a fashion), while the latter contains a point or moral. 'Nothing is so dangerous as being too modern. One is apt to grow old-fashioned quite suddenly.' In what press or public-relations office should that aphorism *not* be on prominent display?

Oscar Wilde's weapon was paradox, and his secret was his seriousness. He was flippant about serious things, and serious about apparently trivial ones. 'Conscience and cowardice are really the same things. Conscience is the trade-name of the firm.' That could have been said by Hamlet, and was indeed uttered by him at much wearier length.

This year marks the centennial of Wilde's greatest triumph and also of his ultimate disgrace. It was on Valentine's Day 1895 that royal and aristocratic London was drawn in a body to see the opening night of *The Importance of Being Earnest*, one of the few faultless three-act plays ever written and certainly among the best-loved pieces of stagecraft in history.

But the moment of greatest adoration was also the occasion chosen by Nemesis. On that very opening night the Marquess of Queensberry, a thuggish aristocrat from the central casting of Victorian melodrama, made a scene at the stage door. Having failed to disrupt the performance, he left a bouquet of vegetables behind him and departed swearing vengeance on the man who was 'corrupting' his extremely corrupt son, Lord Alfred Douglas. So intense was Queensberry in his campaign of defamation that Wilde was led into the greatest mistake of his life – a suit for criminal libel to clear himself of the 'gay' smear, often known in the London homosexual underworld as the vice of being too 'earnest'.

By the end of the year, which featured a trial (also in three acts) during which Wilde had the tables turned on him, the cowardly theatre manager had blotted out Wilde's name from the play's billboards (while continuing to take in record receipts), and Wilde himself was in the dock, indicted not only for committing what Victorians called 'the abominable crime' of sodomy but also for committing it with a member of the lower orders. Bankrupt, humiliated, deserted by his friends and his lover, weakened by illness and betrayal, he became the target for every sort of pelting and jeering and hissing, and was used as a sort of public urinal by a society seeking a vent for its hypocrisy and repression.

I recently made a pilgrimage to the grave of this great Irish rebel, who died in exile in Paris. On his deathbed he did certainly say that 'I am dying beyond my means.' He may or may not, on the other hand, have opened his eyes at the last, looked around the room, and murmured, 'Either that wallpaper goes or I do.'

In Père Lachaise cemetery, among the sort of marble telephone booths favoured by the deceased French bourgeois, one searches for and finds the memorial carved by Jacob Epstein. It has been repeatedly smashed and defaced by philistines, and is the only monument in the whole place which displays a warning against vandalism. An attempted restoration in 1992 could not repair the damage done when some yahoo broke the genitalia off the statue. This lends unintentional point to the inscription on the plinth, which the vandal probably could not read:

> And alien tears will fill for him
> Pity's long-broken urn,
> For his mourners will be outcast men,
> And outcasts always mourn.

We have a tendency to forget that the man who wrote the exquisitely light *Importance of Being Earnest* also wrote the unbearably laden *Ballad of Reading Gaol.*

Picking one's way back to the graveyard gate, one cannot avoid the hundreds of young pilgrims who come, every day, to make a shrine out of the tomb of Jim Morrison. Poems, flowers, candles, scraps of clothing are heaped up to the memory of this lovely boy, cut off in full youth.

> '. . . I am true love, I fill
> The hearts of boy and girl with mutual flame.'

> Then sighing said the other, 'Have thy will,
> I am the love that dare not speak its name.'

These are the only lines for which Bosie will ever be remembered. Mutual flame. Come on, baby, light my fire.

Literature has an unpaid debt to Wilde, and so does philosophy. Take just one example of the former. As the curtain rises on *The Importance of Being Earnest*, we find a rich young bachelor in a fashionable London apartment, playing the piano. He imagines himself alone, and does not notice the butler. On seeing him, he utters the first words of the play:

ALGERNON: Did you hear what I was playing, Lane?
LANE: I didn't think it polite to listen, sir.

Perfect. The action then moves to take in a tyrannical aunt (Lady Bracknell), an absurd romantic and matrimonial skein (Algernon and Jack and Gwendolen and Cecily) that is solved by a genealogical coincidence, a country house, a rural clergyman, a subplot involving a fortune, a happy ending. What do we have here if not the whole fantasy world of P. G. Wodehouse?

Wodehouse almost certainly saw the play as a young man, and went on to give us aunts and butlers and futile young men without ever mentioning Wilde even in passing. Wodehouse had a horror of homosexuality, it is true. But the whole of middle England placed Wilde under a ban for several decades, only occasionally reviving him as a writer of supposedly innocuous drawing-room farce.

The late Sir John Betjeman evokes the hushed conspiracy of silence in one of his early poems, 'Narcissus'. A mystified small boy is told by his parents that he can no longer play with his dearest friend, Bobby:

> My Mother wouldn't tell me why she hated
> The things we did, and why they pained her so.
> She said a fate far worse than death awaited
> People who did the things we didn't know,
> And then she said I was her precious child,
> And once there was a man called Oscar Wilde.

Thus screwing him up for life.

What Wilde knew, and touched, went very deep into the psyche. That great critic Desmond MacCarthy once listed four of Wilde's observations, in this order:

(i) As one reads history . . . one is absolutely sickened, not by the crimes that the wicked have committed, but by the punishments that the good have inflicted; and a community is infinitely more brutalised by the habitual employment of punishment, than it is by the occasional occurrence of crime.

(ii) Man is least himself when he talks in his own person. Give him a mask, and he will tell you the truth.

(iii) Conscience must be merged in instinct before we become fine.

(iv) Nothing can cure the soul but the senses, just as nothing can cure the senses but the soul.

MacCarthy argued that half of Tolstoy's philosophy is in the first quotation, and most of Yeats's theory of artistic composition is contained in the second. Samuel Butler's ethics are in the third quotation, and most of George Meredith's philosophy of love is in the fourth. Hesketh Pearson added that if you read Wilde's dictum 'Every impulse that we strive to strangle broods in the mind, and poisons us' you have imbibed the core doctrine of Sigmund Freud. (And I would add that when Algernon says, in *The Importance of Being Earnest*, 'Really, if the lower orders don't set us a good example, what on earth is the use of them? They seem, as a class, to have absolutely no sense of moral responsibility', he anticipates Newt Gingrich, and the 'welfare reformers', by a clear century.)

Once heard, never forgotten. 'A cynic is a man who knows the price of everything and the value of nothing.' This is not frothy phrasemaking, but serious wit. Not that Wilde scorned the throw-away line, even when it was risky. In the early days of his troubles with the law, he ran into an actor friend in Piccadilly and said angrily, 'All is well. The working classes are with me . . . to a boy.'

Apart from one very scratchy disc made during his American tour, there are no recordings of Wilde in public or in private. But we have it on the authority of some of the great Victorian socialites and conversationalists that he was like this *all the time*. Wilfrid Scawen Blunt, who knew everybody and went everywhere and was one of the great poets of the decade, went to a 'brilliant luncheon' given by Margot Asquith and her husband shortly after their wedding. He could not keep the word 'brilliant' out of his diary entry: 'Of all those present, and they were most of them brilliant talkers, he was without comparison the most brilliant, and in a perverse mood he chose to cross swords with one after the other of them, overpowering each in turn with his wit, and making special fun of Asquith, his host that day, who only a few months later, as Home Secretary, was prosecuting him.'

Yes, quite. There is a revenge that the bores and the bullies and the bigots exact on those who are too witty. Wilde could never hope to escape the judgement of the pompous and the hypocritical, because he could not help teasing them.

I personally find it hard, if not impossible, to read the record of his trial without fighting back tears. Here was a marvellous, gay, brave, and eloquent man, being gradually worn down by inexorable, plodding oafs and heavies. At first, Wilde had it all his own way, with laughter in the court. The grim, vindictive figure of Sir Edward Carson (later to take his Protestant rectitude into the incitement of a sectarian war in Ireland) was the grinding mill, with Wilde the leaping water:

'Do you drink champagne yourself?'
'Yes, iced champagne is a favourite drink of mine – strongly against my doctor's orders.'
'Never mind your doctor's orders, sir.'
'I never do.'

The brutish Carson later asked Wilde how long it took to walk from his Chelsea home to a certain other address:

'I don't know. I never walk.'
'I suppose when you pay visits you always take a cab?'
'Always.'
'And if you visited, you would leave the cab outside?'
'Yes, if it were a good cab.'

That was the last genuine laugh that Wilde got from the audience in court. Not long afterward, Carson, mentioning a certain servant boy, suddenly asked, 'Did you kiss him?' and Wilde incautiously replied, 'Oh dear, no. He was a peculiarly plain boy.' And that was that. Carson seized the whip handle, and never let go.

When he had done, Wilde was haggard and shaken and exposed. He managed one great moment of defiance from the box, in which he gave a ringing defence of 'The Love That Dare Not Speak Its Name'. But the mill was now grinding in earnest, and he was trapped. At the close of the trial, the whores danced for joy in the streets, and mobs were spitting hatred, and dear Oscar was put to solitary work in a red-brick Victorian prison. An ear infection that went untreated by his jailers and an auction of his possessions held by gleeful creditors contributed to his death in penury five years later, at age forty-six. No morality tale could have had a more satisfying ending. There had never been such a victory for the bluenoses and the Pecksniffs since the public baiting of Lord Byron, about which Macaulay famously wrote, 'We know no spectacle so ridiculous as the British public in one of its periodical fits of morality.'

It wasn't only the British public that congratulated itself on the narrow escape from genius that it had undergone. Across the water in Germany, a sinister and twisted physician named Max Nordau had been at work on his book *Degeneration*. It was a powerful, if turgid, screed against what Nordau termed 'Decadentism' in the arts of painting, music, poetry, and sculpture. Nordau's targets were Baude-laire, Swinburne, Zola, and Wilde – above all Wilde. He was not to be forgiven for his blasphemous pleasantries. Why, wrote Nordau splenetically, Wilde even spoke with disrespect of Nature! ('All bad poetry springs from genuine feeling. To be natural is to be obvious, and to be obvious is to be inartistic.')

Nordau strove constipatedly to establish a link between literary and aesthetic 'degeneration' and the sexual, social, and political kind. He was an orthodox dogmatist and authoritarian, who also spoke in the new language of eugenics about the 'diseased' and the 'unfit'. George Bernard Shaw wrote an essay, entitled 'The Sanity of Art', defending Wilde and making fun of Nordau. And that might have been the last that was heard of him. Except that, after a debilitating war and a German defeat, the Nazi movement resurrected Nordau's book and his theory of degeneration.

By the mid-1930s (and we are still talking about the lifetime of Lord Alfred Douglas), German museums and universities and galleries had been purged of the 'decadent', and artists of genius such as Otto Dix had their work confiscated and exhibited in a travelling show of 'degenerate art', where wholesome German families could safely come and jeer. Homosexual conduct, of course, had become punishable even by death. The philistines had really won this time, and were thoroughly enjoying themselves.

The good end happily, and the bad unhappily. That is what fiction means.

Wilde, who did not outlive the nineteenth century (he died in 1900), is nonetheless a uniquely modern figure. If it is safe to say that the work of writers such as P. G. Wodehouse and Evelyn Waugh and Ronald Firbank and Noël Coward is inconceivable without him, then it is safe to say that he is immortal. (Evelyn Waugh's short story 'Bella Fleace Gave a Party' is lifted from a tale of Wilde's.)

More recently, in his *Eminent Domain*, Richard Ellmann, acclaimed Wilde biographer, has argued that, 'invited to dine with Oscar Wilde on Christmas day, 1888, [Yeats] consumed not only his portion of the turkey but all Wilde's aesthetic system, which Wilde read to him from the proofs of *The Decay of Lying*. Once expropriated, this was developed and reunified in Yeats's mind'.

So, rather like Gore Vidal in our time, Wilde was able to be mordant and witty because he was, deep down and on the surface, *un homme sérieux*. May his memory stay carnation-green. May he ever encourage us to think that the bores and the bullies and the literal minds need not always win. May he induce us to rise from our semi-recumbent postures.

First published as 'The Wilde Side' in *Vanity Fair*, May 1995

Oscar Wilde's Socialism

In conversation with Granville Barker, George Bernard Shaw once bragged that the comedy of his plays was the sugar that he employed to disguise the bitter socialist pill. How clever of the audience, replied Barker, to lick off the sugar and leave the bitter pill unswallowed. Of no play in the whole repertory of well-loved drama could this be more truly said than Oscar Wilde's masterpiece in three acts, *The Importance of Being Earnest*. First performed in 1895, to applause that has never died away, it coincided with Wilde's challenge to the infamous Marquess of Queensberry and with his decision to face his tormentors in court. That drama, which also fell into three acts (Wilde's suit; Queensberry's counter-attack; the prosecution of Wilde himself for immorality on the evidence of the first two trials) marked his utter eclipse and decline. In this centennial of Wilde's triumph and ignominy, what can be done to honour his play as it should be honoured?

The Importance is so diverting and witty and fast-moving, and so replete with imperishable characters and *mots*, that it has been a staple of Anglo-American drawing-room comedy for generations. And, despite the cloud under which its author languished for so long (a cloud, as someone once observed, hardly bigger than a man's hand) the play has been deemed fit for even the most demure school productions and amateur fiestas. It is a safe bet that Wilde would have appreciated the joke, because we know that he concealed at least one and – I would argue – probably two subtexts in his brittle dialogue.

The first subtext is of course a homosexual one. To be 'earnest' in Victorian London was to be gay in the slang of the underworld and the *demi-monde* ('I hear he's frightfully earnest') so that one of the coded laughs at least was up in lights in the middle of the most ostensibly moral and bourgeois capital in history. But the game is deeper than that. The two young men who feature as the play's central rivals, Jack Worthing and Algernon Moncrieff, are both portrayed as leading double lives, and as adopting alter egos, in order to pursue their true desires. The name Bloxham is used for a minor character, but those in the know would have recognised Jack Bloxham, editor of a high-risk homosexual aesthetic magazine to whom Wilde had promised *Phrases and Philosophies For the Use of the Young* ('The first duty in life is to be as artificial as possible. What the second duty is no one has as yet discovered'). The magazine, which ran to exactly one edition, was suggestively entitled *The Chameleon*.

Other private or encoded jokes in the play range from the risqué and the nearly obvious (such as the tragedy of young men not turning out to resemble their mothers) to the argot of homosexual tradecraft. The practice of leading a secret life under a pseudonym, known as 'Bunburying', would have had some members of the audience hugging themselves with suppressed glee. 'Cecily', the name given to one of the weightless and vapid society girls, was also gay vernacular for transvestite rent-boys. Looked at in the right way, or played to the knowing ear, even the cloakroom at Victoria Station – scene of the loss of the famous handbag – takes on the charged association of a cruising spot or pick-up joint.

There was originally a fourth act to the play, in which Algernon was taken to Holloway Prison for failing to pay his bills at the Savoy. If that denouement had been retained, the coincidence between art and life would have been almost unbearable. Even as it is, the banter of *The Importance* does throw one shadow forward into the future. When Jack Worthing tells Canon Chasuble that his invented brother has died, and 'seems to have expressed a desire to be buried in Paris', the worthy Canon shakes his head and says: 'In Paris! I fear that hardly points to any very serious state of mind at the last.'

The second of the two subtexts – the socialist one – is less fraught with ironies, and less apparent to superficial reviewers, but is in fact what gives the play its muscle and nerve. In *The Soul of Man Under Socialism* (which had to be published for a time as *The Soul of Man* in order to avoid objections from publishers and distributors) Wilde had subjected the bourgeois order to a merciless critique. In particular, he had shown the Victorian attitude towards marriage as an exercise in the mean-spirited preservation of private property, as well as a manifest-ation of sexual repression and hypocritical continence. In *The Import-ance of Being Earnest*, the same polemical objective is pursued, but by satirical means. Absurd and hilarious dialogues about betrothal, inher-itance, marriage settlements, and financial dispositions are the very energy of the play. Everybody is supposed to marry for money and give up liberty; everybody is constrained to pretend that they are marrying for love or romance. 'When I married Lord Bracknell,' says Lady Bracknell, 'I had no fortune of any kind. But I never dreamed for a moment of allowing that to stand in my way.' It is, indeed, dear Lady Bracknell who continually gives the game away. When she hears that Cecily will inherit a hundred and thirty pounds she declares, 'Miss Cardew seems to me a most attractive young lady, now that I look at her. Few girls of the present day have any of the really solid qualities, any of the qualities that last, and improve with time.'

Her instinctive class consciousness makes her the arbiter of every scene. Inquiring of Jack the suitor whether he has any politics, and receiving the answer that 'I am afraid I really have none. I am a Liberal Unionist', she riposptes, 'Oh, they count as Tories. They dine with us. Or come in the evening at any rate.' Pressing him further on his eligibility and inquiring as to whether his money is in land or investments, she is told, 'Investments, chiefly', and muses aloud:

> That is satisfactory. What between the duties expected of one during one's lifetime, and the duties exacted from one after one's death, land has ceased to be either a profit or a pleasure. It gives one position, and prevents one from keeping it up.

This more or less precisely describes the dilemma of the English aristocracy when faced with the Industrial Revolution, and captures it more neatly than Engels ever managed to. Indeed, one expert on this period, Frances Banks, has argued convincingly that much of the play is also a satire on the Cecil dynasty, whose scion, Robert Marquess of Salisbury, was three times a Tory prime minister in the late Victorian epoch. His biographer was his daughter, Lady Gwendolen Cecil. The two girls in the play are named Gwendolen and Cecily. The Salisbury family motto, just for good measure, is *Sero Sed Serio*: 'Late but in earnest'. And the great family estates were linked to London by a network of those railways in which the landed classes took such an early and profitable interest. In every scene of *The Importance of Being Earnest* there is at least one joke about the railways, with a repeated play on words that depends for its effect on the echoes of 'line' and 'lineage'.

There is little if any strain involved in making these conjectures, because we know that Wilde read the literature of socialism, attended meetings, and kept company with leading socialists such as Shaw (who didn't like *The Importance*, typically regarding it as frothy). Wilde was the only public figure in London to sign Shaw's petition about the Haymarket martyrs. He took an active interest in the rising labour movement, and in the work of William Morris and other leading critics of capitalist utilitarianism. The kernel of his credo, however, is to be found in the offhand remark made by Algernon Moncrieff at the opening of *The Importance*, where he reflects, 'Really, if the lower orders don't set us a good example, what on earth is the use of them? They seem, as a class, to have absolutely no sense of moral responsibility.' Here, in a well-turned aside, is the cruelty and thoughtlessness of all theorising about the deserving rather than the undeserving poor. Wilde never lost his revulsion against sermonising of this kind, and maintained that it was finer to steal rather than to beg; just as it was morally deaf to preach strict dieting to those suffering from malnutrition. It was for guessing at the secret hatred and coldness, which at all times underlay the English profession of charity and moral hygiene, that he made the enemies who rejoiced in his abjection.

Britain was at the time engaged in a grim, self-righteous attempt to hold on to its oldest colony in Ireland. British secret police circles were later to use the weapons of blackmail and moral exposure to destroy two of the bravest spokesmen for Irish independence – Charles Stewart Parnell and Sir Roger Casement. It's unlikely that Wilde's mordant observations about the Empire's treatment of his homeland would have escaped the attention of the prurient. In a tremendously prescient review in the *Pall Mall Gazette* in 1889, he saw precisely why England's hold on Ireland would weaken:

> If in the last century she tried to govern Ireland with an insolence that was intensified by race hatred and religious prejudice, she has sought to rule her in this century with a stupidity that is aggravated by good intentions . . . An entirely new factor has appeared in the social development of the country, and this factor is the Irish-American and his influence. To mature its power, to concentrate its actions, to learn the secrets of its own strength and of England's weakness, the Celtic intellect has had to cross the Atlantic. At home it had but learned the pathetic weakness of nationality; in a strange land it realised what indomitable forces nationality possesses. What captivity was to the Jews, exile has been to the Irish. America and American influence has educated them.

Though this review, too, contained some instances of Wilde at his most aphoristic ('That the government should enforce iniquity and the governed submit to it, seems to Mr Froude, as it certainly is to many others, the true ideal of political science. Like most penmen he overrates the power of the sword'), it demonstrates that he could dispose also of a solid and grounded political intelligence. Within a few years of Wilde's death, the American citizen Eamon de Valera had in effect out-generaled the British Empire. Only this year came yells of anguish from the British Tories as a Republican guerrilla was greeted on the White House lawn, and London (which believed itself to have an exclusive 'special relationship' with the American Empire) gnashed impotently at this reminder of blood debts incurred decades before.

In a similar vein, Wilde reviewed the poems that Wilfred Scawen Blunt published from prison, and announced that the self-righteous Tory 'intellectual' Arthur Balfour had, if nothing else, improved Blunt's style and address as a poet by committing him to jail for his agitation upon the Irish question. Wilde's banter at Balfour's expense was exactly designed to be of the sort that would land him in trouble – Blunt himself noticed the same tendency at a lunch for Herbert and Margot

Asquith, when Wilde teased the entire assembly of the Establishment and won every round – but at least this serves to correct the later picture of Wilde as an epicene dandy whose sallies were confined to the lounge. 'Literature is not much indebted to Mr Balfour for his sophistical *Defence of Philosophic Doubt*, which is one of the dullest books we know, but it must be admitted that by sending Mr Blunt to jail he has converted a clever rhymer into an earnest and deep-thinking poet.' The intention of Balfour and his class, by committing Wilde to jail, was to achieve something like the opposite effect. (Just to increase the *frisson*, it's worth noting that Blunt's volume of poems was entitled *In Vinculis*, later to be the subtitle of Wilde's own prison testimony *De Profundis*.)

We can therefore situate Wilde firmly in the company of the Victorian socialist aristocracy; a radical élite, contemporary with Marx himself, which wrote and acted with great distinction. Its contribution has largely been forgotten, because as George Dangerfield so hauntingly records in his book *The Strange Death of Liberal England*, it was overwhelmed by the First World War that it tried so hard to prevent. I've already mentioned William Morris, who is remembered still as a Pre-Raphaelite and aesthete rather than as an orator and polemicist. Wilde's set also included Blunt, who probably did more than any other single author for the emancipation of the colonies, and who is an honoured figure today in Egypt, India, Ireland, and other former precincts of the Empire on which the sun never set (and on which, as the Chartist leader Feargus O'Connor once remarked, the blood never dried).

One might also mention R. B. Cunninghame-Graham, the friend and inspiration to Joseph Conrad, who rounded off a whole career of travel and writing and anti-imperialist adventure by getting himself elected as the first explicitly socialist member of the House of Commons. In the late Victorian and Edwardian periods, men like this fought to build up an educated labour movement, to win independence for Ireland, and to advance and guarantee the rights of women. The terrible year of 1914, and the attendant capitulation of the Socialist International, put an end to what had been one of the most revolutionary and democratic periods in modern history. From then on, the choice would be made between official and routine Labourism and the disciplined apparatus of Leninism and its mutations. Imperialist war – the outcome of an ostensibly 'liberal' imperium – had very nearly returned civilised Europe to a barbaric state. This does not entitle us to forget a more noble and defeated tradition, in which Wilde, among others, took an honourable place.

I am not employing the terms 'aristocracy' or 'noble' by accident. In all of Wilde's radical writing there is an unashamed belief that those who suffer or dare for freedom are a kind of elect – not the insipid and overbred aristocracy of wealth and property that he lampooned, but an elect nonetheless. Though he was skeptical of organised religion and in most conscious moments considered himself a Hellenist, he employed biblical and prophetic imagery to mark off martyr from mob. Richard Ellmann points out very deftly the ambivalence of his *Sonnet to Liberty*, in which he expressed distaste for those whose anger rose from mere resentment:

> Not that I love thy children, whose dull eyes
> See nothing save their own unlovely woe,
> Whose minds know nothing, nothing care to know –

Yet at the close of the poem, Wilde also distinguishes himself from the Lady Bracknell types who talked selfishly about the 'worst excesses of the French Revolution' and predicted that education for the poor would 'lead to acts of violence in Grosvenor Square':

> . . . and yet, and yet,
> those Christs that die upon the barricades,
> God knows it I am with them, in some things.

Elements of this tension are apparent in Wilde's play *Vera, or The Nihilists*, in which he foreshadowed the coming Russian revolution. He was always to be upset and disillusioned by the failure of this play, which was based upon the true story of Vera Zasulich, a proto-Bolshevik woman who assassinated the St Petersburg chief of police in January 1878. (This action led to a feverish discussion among the anti-tsarist forces about the morality and efficacy of 'individual terrorism', partly because the assassination proved both popular and effective.) And Wilde was a personal friend of another Russian revolutionary, Sergei Kravchinski, who had also shot a tsarist torturer and who lived as a well-liked emigré in London circles. Drawing on Bakunin and Nechayev's *Revolutionary Catechism*, and on his reading of Dostoyevsky and Turgenev, Wilde fashioned a play about propaganda by deed. The hero is beyond doubt Prince Paul Maraloffski, who falls out with the czar and joins the revolutionary conspirators. 'In a good democracy,' opines this prince at one crucial moment, 'every man should be an aristocrat.'

This addiction to paradox, which was always his most penetrating method in any case, led Wilde to state at the opening of *The Soul of Man Under Socialism* that socialism's great benefit would be the abolition of that 'sordid necessity of living for *others*' that was everywhere so oppressive. The effect of this rather flippant-seeming introduction was to peel the whiskers from the face of Church and State, which had bound every citizen into a nexus of obligation and guilt. For Wilde, all talk of 'the masses' and 'the people' was suspect, because these categories were made up of individuals and it was the free development of each individual that counted. He occupied a position somewhere betwen Karl Marx and William Morris; between the idea that labour was something to be transcended and the idea that it was something to be made artistic and enjoyable. Under no circumstances should socialism become the brute collectivisation of existing drudgeries. In an 1889 review of Edward Carpenter's socialist songbook *Chants of Labour*, Wilde wrote that

> Socialism is not going to allow herself to be tramelled by any hard and fast creed or to be stereotyped into an iron formula. She welcomes many and multiform natures. She rejects none and has room for all. She has the attraction of a wonderful personality and touches the heart of one and the brain of another, and draws this man by his hatred of injustice, and his neighbour by his faith in the future, and a third, it may be, by his love of art or by his wild worship of a lost and buried past. And all of this is well. For to make men Socialists is nothing, but to make Socialism human is a great thing.

This was written a hundred years before the fall of the Berlin Wall. Much of it was a statement of desire rather than belief in any case, and later sections of the review betray some misgivings. Of many of the proletarian anthems, Wilde wrote that 'almost any mob could warble them with ease'. Approving Edward Carpenter's sentiment, which was common in those brave radical days, that the masses did indeed have an appreciation of beauty and finesse, he closed by saying:

> The Reformation gained much from the use of popular hymn-tunes, and the Socialists determined to gain by similar means a similar hold upon the people. However, they must not be too sanguine about the result. The walls of Thebes rose up to the sound of music, and Thebes was a very dull city indeed.

It cannot be mistaken to see in this and other Wildean observations a coded plea for the right to live as a sexual outlaw, an eternal dissident and an enemy of the regimented, the 'healthy', and the 'natural'. It was this set of affinities, indeed, which involved Wilde in almost his last polemical battle; one that was to reverberate long after his death.

In 1892 the German author Max Nordau published his book *Entartung*, which translates either as 'Degeneracy' or 'Degeneration'. It was a stern and somewhat dirty-minded philippic against those who led unwholesome lives or professed admiration for unnatural philosophies. The volume was dedicated to Cesare Lombroso, pioneer of racist phrenology and coiner of the pseudo-science of the 'criminal type'. It exuded admiration for racial strength, nature-worship, orthodox manliness, and artistic convention. In identfying the sources of that degeneracy that was sapping the vital fluids of civilisation Nordau made a prime exhibit of Wilde. Claims of genius were merely neurotic, said Nordau, and homosexuality was the greatest degeneracy of all. Wilde, who was by this time being hideously maltreated in an English prison, attempted a feeble defence by pleading that if homosexuality was an illness it should not be punishable but treatable – a sad hostage to fortune. Recovering a little of his old form after his release, he said, 'I quite agree with Dr Nordau's assertion that all men of genius are insane, but Dr Nordau forgets that all sane people are idiots.' Bernard Shaw wrote a riposte to Nordau, staunchly maintaining that here in a new and more virulent form was the traditional superstition that the stock was weakening and civilisation going to the dogs. (Given Shaw's own interest in eugenics, that was quite a strong reply.)

Two historical ironies arise from this little-remembered combat. Max Nordau was, with Theodor Herzl, one of the founders of political Zionism. To this day, the supporters of the ultra-Orthodox and ultra-nationalist forces in Israel refer to assimilated or secular Jews as 'Hellenised' – the worst insult in their lexicon, and one that might have called forth a sympathetic smile from Wilde. Second, Nordau's Jewishness and Zionism did not prevent the resuscitation of his book by the Nazis after Germany's defeat in the First World War. 'Degeneration' became the summary word for everything – cosmopolitan, Mediterranean, skeptical – that the New Order regarded as weak or treacherous in the German character. Those who have visited the exhibitions of *Entartete Kunst* ('Degenerate Art') put on by the Nazis will see the force of the campaign that listed 'pacifism' and anti-militarism along with mental illness, physical deformity, and the mockery of religion as enemies of the state. A parallel exhibition, entitled *Entartete Musik*, had as its poster and advertisement a thick-lipped Negro blowing into a saxophone and displaying a star of David on his lapel.

Wilde's misgivings about socialism – that it would prove humourless, uniform, and hostile to the untamed and the emotional and aesthetic – were to be fully materialised in National Socialism. He might have wished to protest that this was taking the business of paradox too far.

First published as 'Oscar Wilde's Socialism' in *Dissent*, Fall 1995

Lord Trouble

In Berlin in 1892, Max Nordau published his extraordinary book *Entartung*, or 'Degeneration'. Dedicated to the pseudo-scientist and (let me risk a tautology) phrenologist Cesare Lombroso, this dense and lengthy diatribe sought to lay bare the origins and effects of national and individual self-hatred and self-destructiveness. Directed at the languor and amorality of what Nordau was already terming the '*fin de siècle*', it exalted the 'normal', the 'manly', and the utilitarian over the neurotic and the aesthete. Herr Nordau had some unresolved difficulties of his own – he had changed his name from Südfeld or 'Southern Field' to the more bracing and valiant-sounding 'Northern Meadow' – and he was the most militant deputy of Theodor Herzl in proposing a Zionist solution to the *Luftmensch* question, the nagging problem of the enfeebled and deracinated and feminised Jew. (The fact that the National Socialists later borrowed his book and his concept, and staged taunting exhibitions of *Entartete Kunst* and *Entartete Musik*, is not to be charged to Nordau's account, though it would make a fascinating appendix to any study of the relationship between self-loathing and ultranationalism.)

A principal exhibit in Nordau's gallery of the decayed and the corrupting was a man who did not yet enjoy a Continental reputation:

> Decadentism has not been confined to France alone [Nordau had been railing against Baudelaire]. . . . The ego-mania of decadentism, its love of the artificial, its aversion to nature, and to all forms of activity and movement, its megalomaniacal contempt for men and its exaggeration of the importance of art, have found their English representative among the 'Aesthetes', the chief of whom is Oscar Wilde.

Nordau did not recognise Wilde as an Irishman, or understand his outsider relationship to Anglo-Saxondom, but he did take a strong view about the practice of parading down Pall Mall in a doublet, sunflower in hand. ('This anecdote has been reproduced in all the biographies of Wilde, and I have nowhere seen it denied', he snorted.) Moreover:

Phrasemakers are perpetually repeating the twaddle, that it is a proof of honourable independence to follow one's own taste without being bound down to the regulation costume of the Philistine cattle, and to choose for clothes the colours, materials and cut which appear beautiful to one's self, no matter how much they may differ from the fashion of the day. The answer to this cackle is that it is above all a sign of anti-social ego-mania to irritate the majority unnecessarily . . .

Nordau identified Wilde as an enemy of Nature and an admirer of 'immorality, sin and crime'. If Wilde had read the book when it was first published, he might have mocked it gently, as did George Bernard Shaw, for its heaviness or – conceivably – have felt a premonition of the odium that would engulf him when his luck ran out. In fact, he did not refer to the book until he was in Reading Gaol and composing a piteous letter in which he begged for release. In that petition, he abjectly cited Nordau as the authority for considering himself, and his sexual appetites, to be diseased. Thus, he argued, he required cure, not punishment. It was a moment of almost masochistic prostration which makes one wince even now. But then, it makes one wince to read the other letter he wrote from his Reading cell, the long diatribe of resentment that we know as *De Profundis*, and that was addressed to the awful young man who had in effect put him there.

Nordau employs the terms 'degenerate' and 'decadent' almost inter-changeably, and there is perhaps a subliminal connection between 'decadence' and the expiring decade – the low, dishonest Nineties – which he was excoriating. But if Wilde was a proud and warm-blooded decadent, it might be said that Lord Alfred Douglas was a cold and arrogant degenerate. His irritating nickname 'Bosie' was the lisping remnant of a childhood pet-name 'Boysie', and indeed almost every-thing about him might have been designed to illustrate Cyril Connolly's proposal, in *Enemies of Promise*, of the 'Theory of Permanent Adoles-cence'. The greater portion of the British ruling class, wrote Connolly, suffered from arrested development and remained throughout life 'adolescent, school-minded, self-conscious, cowardly, sentimental and in the last analysis homosexual.'

The remarkable book under review – partly remarkable (if I do not sound condescending in saying so) for being written by a young undergraduate still at 'Bosie's' old Magdalen College, Oxford – vindi-cates Connolly at every stage. Born into the Anglo-Scottish dynasty of Douglas, a family with roots that disappear into myth and legend north of the border, Bosie – as I'll have to call him – was chronically spoiled by his mother and brutally dominated by his father, the notorious Marquess of Queensberry. Mr Murray makes a strong case for the existence of a taint of hereditary insanity in the bloodline, and indeed in every published photograph from boyhood to old age the eyes of Bosie exhibit either a manic glare or a stony aspect.

He seems to have been either a troublemaker or a cause of unspecified but guessable 'trouble' even at his preparatory schools, from one of which he had to be withdrawn, and at Winchester – then as now a forcing-house for the future Establishment – he was swift to apprehend the power that epicene good looks might confer on him. One says 'epicene' because his portraits and photographs of the period seem to require the word; however, he excelled as an athlete into the bargain. (Wilde, incidentally, was no drooping pansy either; when challenge or affront demanded it he was good with his fists and – as Bosie's father was to discover – hard to intimidate.) The boy Douglas's chief success, however, was in the editing of a highly affected school magazine called *Pentagram*, to which he contributed much florid hothouse verse.

Wilde's meticulous but rather pedestrian biographer Richard Ellmann once inquired of a gay colleague what it was that male homosexuals actually 'did'. More is at issue here than Professor Ellmann's dogged fieldwork; the old limerick question about 'who did what, and with what, to whom' was to prove decisive at trial and also formed part of Douglas's on-again, off-again assertions of whether he himself was or was not a homosexual. A heuristic parenthesis is therefore necessary. English public-school homosexuality, which has given *so much* to the world of letters, is paradoxically egalitarian. A certain amount of sighing and yearning is pardonable (Connolly was more amused than shocked to find the stern young Eric Blair describing himself as quite 'gone' on a boy at Eton) while kissing can be considered quite ridiculous. Mutual and manual gratification is the rule. The employment of orifices risks the imputation of unmanliness.

Torrid but unconsummated romantic friendships are not by any means unknown. Thus it's of interest to learn that Bosie, having gone like an avenging flame through numberless boys at Winchester, and youths at Oxford, and having had many passionate but platonic friendships on the side, was not introduced to oral sex until he went home with Wilde to the latter's rooms in Tite Street, Chelsea, in January 1892. This was two years after *Lippincott's* magazine had published *The Picture of Dorian Gray*, and Wilde was to discard the original of this story, one John Gray, on taking up with the more beautiful and fashionable Bosie. In 1892, also, Bosie composed his famous poem 'Two Loves', the title of which comes from Shakespeare's Sonnet 144 ('Two loves I have of comfort and despair'). Most people know at least the last line:

> Then straight the first did turn himself to me
> And cried, 'He lieth, for his name is Shame,
> But I am Love, and I was wont to be
> Alone in this fair garden, till he came
> Unasked by night; I am true Love, I fill
> The hearts of boy and girl with mutual flame.'
> Then sighing said the other, 'Have thy will,
> I am the Love that dare not speak its name.'

In the underworld argot of the time (homosexuality had only recently been criminalised in English law) 'shame' was one of the cover words for being gay. Another, amusingly enough, was 'earnest', as in 'I hear he's *extremely* earnest'; Wilde's glee at getting this private joke up in lights over a West End hit must have been extreme also.

Douglas's next poem was – eerily in retrospect – entitled 'De Profundis'. Its opening line ('I love a love, but not as other men') introduces a cataract of self-pity and, no less eerily, touches on a tune 'sung in a prison by the lips of Fear'. Mr Murray has a higher opinion of Bosie's verse than I do, and seems to believe that Douglas might have enjoyed a literary posterity separate from the name of Wilde on the strength of his sonnets alone. He has brought off a minor coup by inducing the British penal bureaucracy to release its file on the poems Douglas composed while serving his own time in prison much later on. Entitled *In Excelsis*, this sonnet sequence displays a great technical virtuosity which in my untutored judgement merely emphasises the narcissism and viciousness of its subject and author. But all this was still to come when Wilde wrote Bosie a highly incautious letter praising his work:

> My Own Boy,
>   Your sonnet is quite lovely, and it is a marvel that those red rose-leaf lips of yours should have been made no less for music of song than for madness of kisses. Your slim gilt soul walks between passion and poetry. I know Hyacinthus, whom Apollo loved so madly, was you in Greek days.

Many a whiskered Victorian father might have bitten clean through his pipe-stem at uncovering such a letter written to his son by a much older man, and the Marquess of Queensberry was a man capable of much more violence at even less provocation. Before he turned up, on the opening night of *The Importance of Being Earnest*, with a bodyguard of thugs and a contemptuous bouquet of phallic-shaped vegetables, he had become quite a hardened disrupter of theatrical events. He created chaos in the theatre on the third night of Lord Tennyson's play *The Promise of May*, because he objected strenuously to the Poet Laureate's hostile depiction of atheists and atheism. (He was, like Wilde, to be 'received' into the Roman Catholic Church on his deathbed.) A man of the ringside and the racetrack, much given to floods of Tourettish obscenity, he liked to taunt his children by denying that he had fathered them and was repaid in his own coin when one of his wives petitioned for divorce on the grounds of nonconsummation. Nobody knew better than young Alfred what sort of man his father was; he had even penned and published a poem of filial loathing – 'A Ballad of Hate' – in the *Pall Mall Gazette*. And yet, and one is always forced back to this: he encouraged Wilde to sue the old brute for libel, agreed not to appear in the witness box himself (an appearance which might well have led to a reversal of fortune for Queensberry), and later made the false claim that he had been willing to risk such an appearance. The remainder of the tragedy is well known, and has been exhaustively set out by H. Montgomery Hyde in his *Trials of Oscar Wilde*. In three short courtroom acts, which horribly parodied his own preferred and per- fected dramatic form, Wilde was shamed in earnest, and ruined, and confined *In Carcere et Vinculis*.

That, indeed, was the original title of his letter *De Profundis*. Murray gives an excellent account of the fate of this dismal missive; the only humourless thing that Wilde ever wrote. Though it was addressed to Bosie, and filled with recriminations grand and petty about everything from love to money, it was given to Robert Ross, who either did or did not forward it to Douglas as requested. Murray leaves the question open; it seems to me quite plain by induction that Ross could not have given the whole manuscript to its intended recipient. If he had, then Douglas and Wilde could not have had their brief and rather affecting reunion and reconciliation at Posilipo after Wilde's release, the same interlude in which the traumatised ex-con, his health wrecked by the deliberate sadism of the British authorities, composed *The Ballad of Reading Gaol*. Not long afterward, Bosie was in Paris with, after the death of his appalling father, money to spend on Wilde. (Wilde reported that the Douglas family was 'in deep mourning and the highest spirits', a game echo of the noble widow in *The Importance* whose hair turns 'quite gold from grief'.) No, Douglas only read *De Profundis* when it was published for all to read in 1905, five years after Wilde's death in Paris. The exposure appears to have been one of the many things that made him ever more cracked, bigoted, solipsistic, and litigious.

The *fin de siècle* came in such a way as to gratify Max Nordau and all the other Puritans and engineers of the soul who were to get their way in 1914. Aubrey Beardsley died aged twenty-six. Ernest Dowson, the poet of combined dissipation and admonition, died aged thirty-three. Wilde himself was to be outlived by Queen Victoria. If Alfred Douglas had expired at about the same time, he might be remembered as a febrile but romantic, or better say romantic and febrile figure. As it was, he lived on until almost the end of the Second World War, wholly absorbed in his own morbid quarrels and justifications.

Murray gives an excellent example of the difference in temperament between Wilde and Douglas. Wilde's tour of the United States was a vast success because he entered into the spirit of the thing, managing without strain to captivate Philadelphia hostesses and Colorado lead miners. Douglas's voyage across the Atlantic, which took place just after Wilde's death, was a dreary fiasco because it was undertaken in a mercenary spirit and executed in a frigidly snobbish one. This was still the time when American money was seeking English cachet; the epoch of the Curzon–Leiter and Churchill–Jerome matrimonial alliances. Douglas decided that he could retrieve his position in this way:

> My idea was that I would marry for her money an American girl who had a superabundance of it, and that she would marry me because I had a title and an historic name, and because I knew, and could easily show her, or anyone else concerned, that, with plenty of money, there would not be the slightest difficulty in getting back again into the social circle from which I was then partially excluded.

But nothing went right; Douglas brought all his baggage of prejudice with him and departed saying that America 'will be a nice place to live in about 500 years time when the people have got civilised and when they have built up a few traditions of conduct and manners'. He wrote a bad sonnet impugning the United States for (the cheek of it) excessive materialism.

Returning to England he did eventually wed a respectable girl named Olive Custance, with whom – and without renouncing his covert homosexual life – he had a son. He continued to produce poetry and became a figure in the world of London literary magazines, giving encouragement to Siegfried Sassoon and Rupert Brooke for, one suspects, something more than their poetic gifts. He might have made a sort of niche for himself, were it not for his maniacal attachment to litigation. Every time anyone wrote anything about his relationship with Wilde, Douglas would sue. He sued, what is more, with all the moralising zeal of a recent convert to Catholicism – a faith he had embraced in 1911 and to which he brought a twitchy fanaticism. Eventually, he was to stand in the court, having accused Arthur Ransome of libel, and suffer the same 'blowback' of evidence that Wilde had had to endure. The judge even ordered the reading of De Profundis. When this was over, Douglas was bankrupt and discredited, deserted by his wife and committed to another long legal wrangle over the custody of his son Raymond, who eventually died in a mental institution.

His rancorous nature also asserted itself politically. He identified with the most extreme faction of the Tory aristocracy in its battle to preserve the House of Lords and thwart the independence of Ireland. Denied a part in the First World War (no regiment would have him),

he played an especially odious role on the home front. The Pemberton
Billing case is now largely forgotten, but in its day it was the British
equivalent of the McCarthy hearings. Noel Pemberton Billing was a
demagogic Tory MP of the extreme Right, who ran a scabrous newspaper called the *Vigilante*. In January 1918, when wartime hatreds and
paranoias and resentments were at their height and when things were
going very badly in the trenches, he published an extraordinary 'stab
in the back' manifesto, asserting that there existed a 'Black Book'. In
this book were the names of those who had been corrupted by 'German
agents who have infested this country for the past twenty years, agents
so vile and spreading such debauchery and such lasciviousness as only
German minds can conceive and only German bodies execute'. The
real target, of course, was the Liberal élite gathered around Asquith
and his rather too celebrated wife, Margot.

Numbers count in this sort of thing, and Billing rode the mood of
xenophobia and spy-mania by claiming that no fewer than 47,000
'perverts' were listed in the 'Black Book'. Some of those so defamed
sued Billing, and Douglas appeared as a witness for the defendant. One
proof of the general sapping of morale, offered by him in evidence,
was the continuing cult of Oscar Wilde, kept up by men like Robert
Ross. When cross-examined he claimed, astonishingly, that his father
the Marquess had only been trying to rescue him from the cult.

Of Wilde himself he said:

> I think he had a diabolical influence on everyone he met. I think he is the
> greatest force of evil that has appeared in Europe during the last 350 years.
> He was the agent of the devil in every possible way. He was a man whose sole
> object in life was to attack and to sneer at virtue, and to undermine it in
> every way by every possible means, sexually and otherwise.

Murray points out that 'during the last 350 years' means in effect 'since
the Reformation'. And 'diabolism', I might add, was one of the charges
leveled by Max Nordau against Wilde, so in this hateful utterance are
combined the influences of an extremist Catholicism and a protofascist
attitude toward deviance.

Despite the efforts of a decent judge to keep order, the mob
atmosphere inside and outside the courtroom prevailed, and Pemberton Billing was acquitted of the charge of libel. On the steps
of the Old Bailey he and 'Bosie' were cheered by the same sort of
throng which had jeered and pelted Wilde two decades previously.
The 'Black Book', I need hardly add, was a complete and deliberate
fabrication.

Anti-Semitism is a classic symptom of the persecution complex, and
it's no surprise to find that Douglas suffered from it to an extreme
degree. In his magazine *Plain English*, in the immediate postwar years,

he acted as a publicist for that other fabricated confection, *The Protocols of the Elders of Zion* (difficult to imagine Nordau approving this move) and authored the then-notorious quatrain:

> How odd
> Of God
> To choose
> The Jews.

This may contain a saving element of understatement. (I forget who it was who replied in the same form: 'Not odd/Of God/The Goyim/Annoyim.') But there was no understatement in his next public allegation, which was that Winston Churchill had acted as the agent of a Jewish conspiracy in plotting to sink Lord Kitchener's ship on its way to Russia in 1916, thus helping to deliver Russia into the hands of 'Bolshevik Jews' and incidentally allowing him to make a killing, with other leading Jews, as a war-profiteer. This time it was Churchill who sued for criminal libel, and Douglas found himself sentenced to a term in prison. There he wrote the *In Excelsis* sonnet sequence, of which number XV begins:

> The leprous spawn of scattered Israel
> Spreads its contagion in your English blood . . .

He dropped the subject of the Jews and their machinations upon leaving prison in 1924 (it was a condition of his release that he not repeat the libels) and turned his attention to literary modernism, writing liverish and forgettable attacks on the Bloomsbury set and subsequently on Eliot and Auden. Murray gallantly traces the remaining years, spent mainly in genteel poverty (much complained of) in a south coast resort-cum-retirement town. Bosie managed to form two late and improbable friendships as his fires burned low: one conducted mainly by letter with George Bernard Shaw and one with Marie Stopes, who lived nearby. He died, having just placed the latest in a long succession of losing bets on a racehorse, in the closing months of the war and of Winston Churchill's prime ministership. In the course of a relatively lucid interval in 1938, during the composition of his memoir *Without Apology*, Douglas had written:

> The thought which has only recently occurred to me is a terrible one. Did my father really love me all the time, as I certainly loved him before he turned against me, and was he only doing what Oscar says in his great Ballad all men always do, killing the thing he loved? Didn't we all three, Wilde, my father, and I, do it, more or less?

The evidence of this book, and of this life, prompts the somewhat more disturbing reflection that some men, at any rate, love the thing that kills them.

First published as 'Lord Trouble' (a review of *Bosie: A Biography of Lord Alfred Douglas* by Douglas Murray) in *New York Review of Books*, 21 September 2000

George Orwell and
Raymond Williams[1]

In Barcelona not long ago, a square near the waterfront was renamed by the mayoralty, of Pasqual Maragall, a member of the Catalan Socialist Party. It bears the title Plaça George Orwell. Not many miles away, in the town of Can Rull, a street was also named in honour of Andreu Nin, the murdered leader of the 1930s *Partido Obrero de Unificación Marxista*, better known to Civil War buffs by its odd-sounding acronym of POUM. The mayor of Can Rull was at the time a member of the Catalan Communist Party.

I choose to regard these relatively small if not minor gestures as something more than a homage from Catalonia. Rather, they constitute a final settlement of a long-overdue account. The full acknowledgement, by both parties of the official Left, of this English dissident and this native hero, represents a victory both for historical truth and for personal courage. As the age of twentieth-century ideology closes, with Stalinism dead and fascism defeated, it is quite possible that only in Catalonia are the schoolchildren taught a full and honest account of that combat, and of those who with their bodies and minds fought, simultaneously and with great gallantry, against the forces that culminated in the Hitler–Stalin Pact and the 'midnight of the century'. This was not at all the outcome that Orwell himself expected. It was his experience in Catalonia that furnished much of the dystopian gloom of *1984*. Reviewing the torrent of lies and falsifications in a later essay entitled 'Looking Back on the Spanish War', he wrote:

> This kind of thing is frightening to me, because it often gives me the feeling that the very concept of objective truth is fading out of the world: After all, the chances are that those lies, or at any rate similar lies, will pass into history ... The implied objective of this line of thought is a nightmare world in which the Leader, or some ruling clique, controls not only the future but *the past*. If the Leader says of such an event, 'It never happened' – well, it never happened. If he says that two and two are five – well, two and two are five.

Both Orwell and Nin were cultural and literary figures, as well as political ones. Both reposed a certain irreducible trust – not a romantic belief, but a trust – in the potential of working people. Both were prepared, when ultimate danger impended, to sign up in a people's army. Both were willing to risk calumny and anathema rather than acquiesce in a lie. Both witnessed to a dramatic and almost unbelievable truth – that the Spanish Revolution was not safeguarded or aided by Moscow, but actually, deliberately strangled by it.

It's worth reflecting on how nearly we were deprived of the testimony that now makes this and other truths into relative commonplaces. Orwell, as is well known, could not get his despatches from Spain published in the *New Statesman* or other organs of the self-satisfied British Left. For trying to give an accurate account of events in Catalonia, he was instead vilified for 'giving ammunition to the enemy' and for undermining progressive morale. For a considerable time, he found it difficult to get his books published – being turned down by editors and publishers as diverse as Victor Gollancz and T. S. Eliot – and most of his literary success is in fact posthumous. Even that, we now know, was lucky enough. He not only survived a fascist bullet that passed through his throat in a Spanish frontline trench, but also a spirited attempt by the KGB (then known as the NKVD) to have him either kidnapped or killed. Recently unearthed documents, from the archives of expired despotisms, give us a sharper picture than has ever before been available.

The internal documents of the defeated Spanish Republic were annexed by Franco's fascists after 1939 and kept in libraries in Salamanca and Madrid. Only some time after the collapse of the dictatorship were they made available to scholars. One tranche of Russian secret police material has thus come down to us by way of General Franco, and is confirmed by subsequent research in the mother-lode in Moscow. It concerns the preparations for a show-trial of the POUM, and for the extirpation of the independent Left in Catalonia. And there is a memorandum, dated 13 July 1937, in which Stalin's glacial eye is trained on George Orwell or, to give him his proper name as well as the name which appears in the files, Eric Blair. He and his wife Eileen, who shared the risk, are described as 'pronounced Trotskyists' and accused of possessing clandestine credentials as well as of maintaining sinister contacts with opposition circles in Moscow. Plainly intended as notes for an interrogation should Orwell fall into the hands of the NKVD, these charges would have been lethal if they could have been brought into any tribunal operating under Stalinist jurisdiction or control. (The couple managed to bluff their way through one near-arrest, and to escape from Spain, in which outcome they were more fortunate than other British internationalists, usually members of the

Independent Labour Party, who were incarcerated or who 'disappeared'.) This story was first related in English by my friend and comrade Stephen Schwartz in an essay written in 1995, and also appears in a somewhat attenuated form in Peter Davison's 1998 edition of Orwell's *Complete Works*. Its significance, and even its existence, has been utterly overshadowed in most of the press by the far less important – and also less new and less concealed – 'revelation' that Orwell, in conversation towards the end of his life, identified to a friend in the Foreign Office the intellectuals and publicists whom he believed to be culpably negligent about Stalin, and about the other forces which had been trying to defame and (though he did not know it) to frame and to kill him, and his wife. The relative expense of outrage and concern on the two disclosures tells us a good deal about the persistence of certain habits among our literati.[2]

As for Andreu Nin, it turns out – as is usual with allegations against Stalin and his followers – that the truth is even worse than one had suspected. In the briefly opened KGB files in Moscow in the early 1990s, reporters from the newly emancipated Catalan Television were able to unearth the 'operational file' on the kidnapping, torture and secret execution of the popular and charismatic leader of the POUM. The resulting documentary film – named 'Operation Nikolai' after the NKVD code-word for Nin – illustrates with a wealth of detail the plans for a rerun of the Moscow Trial in Spain itself, complete with tortured or blackmailed defendants and witnesses, and designed to persuade Western liberal opinion that the charade in Moscow itself had been no fluke. I have no doubt, revisiting the written work of the period, that such a strategy would have met with widespread acceptance among those gullible intellectuals who had already demonstrated such a sincere wish to believe.

The scheme foundered on the simple and extraordinary refusal of Andreu Nin to crack under the revolting cruelty of his interrogators. In fury and disgust, they killed him (or perhaps saw him succumb to his treatment) and, believing that his true whereabouts would always be a mystery, contented themselves with spreading lies and slanders about his defection to the camp of Hitler. As a result of this anonymous and, until recently, unproven heroism, the main body of POUM leaders remained alive. Some of them, like Victor Alba, survive to this day and continue to witness to history and truth. It is as if, in a Catalan microcosm of the twentieth century, Bukharin had not cracked in reality, Rubashov had not given way in *Darkness at Noon*, and Winston Smith had preserved his defiance in *1984*. More credit and honour should be given to this radical determination, than I have so far seen outside the pages of specialist journals.

Nin is well remembered in today's Catalonia not just as the bravest son of the revolution, but as the brilliant translator of *Crime and Punishment* and *Anna Karenina* into Catalan. Having been an early member of the century's first Catalan cultural revival – a revival sent into eclipse by Franco's dire orthodox, Catholic, Castilian policy of nation-breaking – he returned to posthumous literary prominence as soon as the ban on his native tongue was lifted, and now the students of Barcelona read his rendition of the Russian classics as an essential part of their courses in literature. In this, too, there is something satisfying and vindicating. That the genius of Russia should be preserved and passed on, for the rising generation in Catalonia, by one of the victims of Stalinism has a certain – what shall we say? – ironic justice to it. Yeats once wrote, rather fancifully I sometimes think, of a 'Book of the People' in which certain names, once inscribed, could not be erased by any amount of propaganda or brutality or falsification. In one of the cradles of European democratic resistance – the cosmopolitan and indomitable city of Barcelona, which gave us Picasso and Casals and where Victor Serge composed *Birth of Our Power* – the names of Orwell and Nin have survived this most exacting of tests and are now inscribed in a lapidary form that would certainly have astonished both of them.

I should now like to read the opening passage of my favourite among the essays of Raymond Williams; a piece composed in 1958 and entitled 'Culture is Ordinary'. It commences with an evocative setting only a few miles from where we are met today, amid the strange and bookish political economy (and ecology) of Hay-on-Wye, in the ancient county seat of Hereford:

> The bus stop was outside the cathedral. I had been looking at the Mappa Mundi, with its rivers out of Paradise, and at the chained library, where a party of clergymen had got in easily, but where I had waited an hour and cajoled a verger before I even saw the chains. Now, across the street, a cinema advertised the *Six-Five Special* and a cartoon version of *Gulliver's Travels*. The bus arrived, with a driver and a conductress deeply absorbed in each other. We went out of the city, over the old bridge, and on through the orchards and the green meadows and the fields red under the plough. Ahead were the Black Mountains, and we climbed among them, watching the steep fields end at the grey walls, beyond which the bracken and heather and whin had not yet been driven back. To the east, along the ridge, stood the line of grey Norman castles, to the west, the fortress wall of the mountains. Then, as we still climbed, the rock changed under us. Here, now, was limestone, and the line of the early iron workings along the scarp. The farming valleys, with their scattered white houses, fell away behind. Ahead of us were the narrower valleys: the steel-rolling mill, the gasworks, the grey terraces, the pitheads. The bus stopped, and the driver and conductress got out, still absorbed. They had done this journey so often, and seen all its stages. It is a journey, in fact, that in one form or another we have all made. I was born and grew up halfway along that bus journey.

I have come all the way from Washington DC in order to challenge
Raymond Williams on his home ground, so to speak, but it is this
passage and some others like it that make it an honour to do so. One
might quibble here and there – the three repetitions of the uninspiring
word 'grey' may be intentional or they may be inattentive – but this is
a paragraph of great understated power, of a modesty that one hopes
and expects will soon be thrown aside, and also of mingled innocence
and experience. 'The rock changed under us'. There's a good deal of
observant integrity contained in such a terse, shrewd phase.

Although the essay displays evidence of Williams's greatest stylistic
weakness, which was a tendency to tautology ('Every human society has
its own shape, its own purposes, its own meanings. Every human society
expresses these, in institutions, and in arts and learning'), it starts with
a feeling for the land, and for tradition, and broadens out into a
critique of English establishment philistinism. The text is consistently
autobiographical, evincing a strong and confident rootedness in native
heath and in family. 'I was not, by the way, oppressed by Cambridge. I
was not cast down by old buildings, for I had come from a country with
twenty centuries of history written visibly into the earth.'

Unintimidated by ancient cloisters, Williams recoiled from the affectation of what he called 'the teashop', where manners counted more
than culture. He insisted on the struggle against ugliness and crudity,
but he was no Pre-Raphaelite, as this admirable extract shows:

> At home we were glad of the Industrial Revolution, and of its consequent
> social and political changes. True, we lived in a very beautiful farming valley,
> and the valleys beyond the limestone we could all see were ugly. But there
> was one gift that was overriding, one gift which at any price we would take,
> the gift of power that is everything to men who have worked with their
> hands. It was slow in coming to us, in all its effects, but steam power, the
> petrol engine, electricity, these and their host of products in commodities
> and services, we took as quickly as we could get them, and were glad. I have
> seen all these things being used, and I have seen the things they replaced. I
> will not listen with any patience to any acid listing of them – you know the
> sneer you can get into plumbing, baby Austins, aspirin, contraceptives,
> canned food. But I say to these Pharisees: dirty water, an earth bucket, a
> four-mile walk each way to work, headaches, broken women, hunger and
> monotony of diet. The working people, in town and country alike, will not
> listen (and I support them) to any account of our society which supposes
> that these things are not progress: not just mechanical, external progress
> either, but a real service of life.[3]

Far from being any kind of economic determinist, Williams the
admirer of Leavis opposed what one might call the vulgar Marxism of
the Right, which was even then proclaiming (citing Northcliffe rather
than Murdoch) that mass industrial society necessitated cheap and

nasty newspapers and mass media. He saw the exploitative, condescending fallacy that is contained in the notion of 'giving people what they want'. Towards his close, he loops back to his border country roots and says: 'I come from an old place; if a man tells me that his family came over with the Normans, I say "Yes, how interesting; and are you liking it here?"' The peroration calls upon intellectuals to join in the task of reaching and uplifting the decency and humanity of ordinary folk, and of bypassing slogans about 'the masses' in favour of an attention to the people.

Now, if I had been given this text by I. A. Richards in his Practical Criticism course, and asked to analyse it without any knowledge of its authorship, I should at once make the assumption that it was very much influenced by the writing of George Orwell. There is, first, the innate love for landscape and countryside and tradition and for growing things. (I would never notice whether bracken or heather had been 'driven back', and I have no notion what 'whin' may be, but Orwell was a keen student of nature, and could name plants and birds, and had a sense of the lay of the land and also of its Anglo-Saxon underlay.) He had the same sense of being at home in ancient towns and buildings, though he never attended any university. He couldn't stand the 'teashop types' or any form of affectation. His essential Puritanism – in the Cromwellian sense which still leads us to divide our friends between Roundhead and Cavalier – was modified, like Williams's by his view: 'How right the working class are in their materialism.' One might add that his attachment to family, though less happy and confident than Williams's, informed his view that a society could be based on the same principles of solidarity and sharing. Finally, with his essay on Boy's Weeklies and his other reviews of popular taste and its manipulation by press lords, Orwell was 'doing' Cultural Studies before the discipline had a name.

Yet it is a fact that Williams despised Orwell, and devoted a lot of time to misunderstanding and misrepresenting him. In a short book published in 1971, and later in a long interview with the *New Left Review* published in book form in 1979, Williams depicted Orwell as a confected figure, sentimental and naïve about the English class system, and as a moral author of the Cold War and the politics of despair. The waste of effort involved here, and the wasted opportunity, and the peculiar ideological shortcomings that these required of Williams, are (if I may belatedly unmask my batteries) the subject of this lecture.

Williams's latent hostility to his subject is somewhat disguised in the 1971 book, which appeared in the famous Fontana Modem Masters series that in 1971, was a partial expression of the ethos of the *soixante-huitards*. Williams knew, and even acknowledged, that to many of the New Left – I speak both of the old New Left and the new New Left, being now old enough to have been New Left, and young enough to have been Old Labour – Orwell had been an inspiration. But his own acknowledgements were grudging, understated and sometimes – so it seems to me – actually resentful; even envious.

This is apparent from the very first mention of *Homage to Catalonia*. The author of *Keywords*, we may be sure, chose his terms with care. Indeed, we know he did because, with the exception of some stretches of boilerplate politicised *langue de bois*, his prose is relatively exact and precise. (I remember the deft way he criticised the use of the word 'Apocalypse' by certain anti-nuclear writers, pointing out that the word implied revelation as well as awesome ending, whereas a thermonuclear conflagration would involve the second without any element of the first.) At all events, he describes the Stalinisation of Barcelona twice on the same page, first as 'the conflict between the Republican authorities and the POUM' and second as 'Communist–POUM rivalry'. This hardly rises to the level of euphemism. By 1971, a great deal had been uncovered, and also conceded, about the organised repression of dissent in Catalonia by Stalin's agents. The words 'conflict' and 'rivalry' are not just neutral as between the repressive and the repressed; in the context they are a falsification – as if Nin's and Orwell's friends might as well have done to Stalin's police what Stalin's police in fact did to them.

There is another oddity here. Williams was never a Welsh nationalist; but he did have an open sympathy for the survival of Welsh culture and language, and for the long and stubborn struggle that had been necessary to preserve and maintain them. (Of national feeling on the smaller scale he wrote, rather attractively, 'You can be proud without being independent: you often have to be'.) Yet in all his references, unless he is actually alluding to the title of Orwell's book, he invariably refers to 'Spain' and not to Catalonia. What was distinctive in the stoicism and resistance of the Catalans seems to have entirely escaped the bearer of a second identity.

Then there is this. Williams writes that there is more than one view about the May events in Barcelona in 1937, and that 'To move in that area at all is like moving in a minefield'. He goes on:

> Most historians have taken the view that the revolution – mainly anarcho-syndicalist but with the POUM taking part – was an irrelevant distraction from a desperate war. Some, at the time and after, have gone so far as to describe it as deliberate sabotage of the war effort. Only a few have argued on the other side, that the suppression of the revolution by the main body of Republican forces was an act of power politics, related to Soviet policy, which amounted to betrayal of the cause for which the Spanish people were fighting.

Again, one is compelled to observe that this prose is almost bureau-cratic. And, as so often with such prose, that it contains a surreptitious element of pseudo-objectivity. Who, for a start, are these 'historians'? I cannot think of one who has ever described Nin's movement as one of deliberate sabotage. And since when did Williams regard it as his task to endorse a majority of historians, even supposing one to exist? (His paragraph makes plain that this is the view with which he sympathises, though he has a loftily undecided attitude to the second opinion as well.) As for the third view, which is again stated with the maximum of euphemism ('the main body of Republican forces' sounds good; 'sup-pression' is better than murder and defamation; 'power politics' smack of regrettable necessity and 'related to Soviet policy' is masterly in a minor way), it is the only view that serious historians, in Catalonia and elsewhere, now take. Williams might not have read the work of Burnet Bolloten, a Welsh Jew who covered the war for the United Press and later broke with his Communist associates, but he could have done. Bolloten's book *The Spanish Civil War: Revolution and Counter-revolution* is now considered, I nearly said by 'most historians', as exhaustive if not encyclopaedic. But it is remarkable that he seems not to have read Noam Chomsky's vivid and scholarly reflections on Stalinism in Spain, which were published in a volume of his essays that was very much in vogue on the academic Left when Williams was composing his Orwell book.

Two pages later, Williams says of the massacres in Barcelona that they took place 'in the name of the struggle against fascism, and, by most accounts in the name of the true cause of socialism and the people'. This steps across the line that divides pseudo-objectivity from propaganda. 'Most accounts' most certainly do not say anything like that. And the give-away stuff about 'socialism and the people' forces one to the conclusion that Williams – the Williams who joined The Party *after* the Hitler–Stalin pact and whose first published pamphlet was a defence of the 1940 Soviet invasion of Finland – had not by 1971 shed all of his early training in the Stalin school of falsification.

The remainder of the book, which makes some formal bows and motions in the direction of Orwell's 'decency' – also a Williams keyword by the way – is a sly rather than oblique argument that Orwell would have done better to be someone else, and would have been a better author if he had written different, or at any rate other, books. Let me acknowledge the sound points, and also the concessions, that Williams makes along the way. He seizes on Orwell's description, in *The Lion and the Unicorn*, written in the distraught year of 1940, and slightly ridicules Orwell's analogy of English or British society with a family. The passage may be familiar to you:

England is not the jewelled isle of Shakespeare's much-quoted passage, nor is it the inferno depicted by Dr Goebbels. More than either it resembles a family, a rather stuffy Victorian family, with not many black sheep in it but with all its cupboards bursting with skeletons. It has rich relations who have to be kowtowed to and poor relations who are horribly sat upon, and there is a deep conspiracy of silence about the source of the family income. It is a family in which the young are generally thwarted and most of the power is in the hands of irresponsible uncles and bedridden aunts. Still, it is a family. It has its private language and its common memories, and at the approach of an enemy it closes its ranks. A family with the wrong members in control – that, perhaps, is as near as one can come to describing England in a phrase.

I cite it in full because Williams never does, and because this fact becomes important later on. The line about 'the deep conspiracy of silence about the source of the family income' is never quoted by him, because it is tougher and more accurate than the rest of the analogy, and because it echoes Orwell's insistence on remembering the role played by imperial exploitation (a thorny fact which the Communists, a year after 1940, were themselves prepared to play down in the interests of 'national unity' and the brotherhood between Churchill and Stalin). However, Williams does notice that 'a family with the wrong members in control' is too soggy and lenient a description of such a complex and divided society, and makes the further and rather searching observation that no father is ever mentioned. He was in a good position to notice this, incidentally, because his own family and particularly his own father were continuously evoked, for political purposes, in his work, but I had not noticed until Williams called it to my attention that Orwell's image is as free of a father figure as a passage from Wodehouse or Wilde. (A significant difference in the work of the two men is supplied by the fact that Williams revered his father, a railwayman and Labour militant, whereas Orwell disliked his father, who was a chilly and remote colonial civil servant.)

Williams also exposes a certain false modesty in his subject, as when Orwell says of himself that had it not been for the awful pressures of war and tyranny and poverty he might have become a real writer and not what he was forced to become – 'a sort of pamphleteer', as he phrased it. This is the wrong kind of self-deprecation (I speak with feeling, as one who regards 'pamphleteer' as a title of honour) and it is married, in Orwell's essay *Writers and Leviathan*, to a certain archness.

We have developed a sort of compunction which our grandparents did not have, an awareness of the enormous injustice and misery of the world, and a guilt-stricken feeling that one ought to be doing something about it, which makes a purely aesthetic attitude towards life impossible. No one, now, could devote himself to literature as single-mindedly as Joyce or Henry James.

Finnegans Wake was completed in 1939. Nor is this the only rejoinder one might make. Not all of 'our grandparents' were by any means deaf to injustice and misery – one might mention George Eliot and Hardy, as Williams does – and it is peculiar of Orwell, who was customarily alert to the influence of tradition, to write otherwise.

Williams makes another comment which is valid in itself, but which later I believe he misuses:

> It would be easy to say that almost all Orwell's important writing is about someone who gets away from an oppressive normality. From the central characters of *The [sic] Clergyman's Daughter* and *Keep The Aspidistra Flying* to those of *Coming Up For Air* and *Nineteen Eighty-Four*, this experience of awareness, rejection, and flight is repeatedly enacted. Yet it would be truer to say that most of Orwell's important writing is about someone who tries to get away but fails. That failure, that reabsorption, happens, in the end, in all the novels mentioned, though of course the experience of awareness, rejection, and flight has made its important mark.

Before he moves to consummate this and other points, Williams makes another of his lethal lapses into tautology and the obvious by saying, of *The Road to Wigan Pier*:

> But here the political point *is* the literary point. What is created in the book is an isolated independent observer and the objects of his observation. Intermediate characters and experiences which do not form part of this world – this structure of feeling – are simply omitted. What is left is 'documentary' enough, but the process of selection and organisation is a literary act: the character of the observer is as real and yet created as the real and yet created world he so powerfully describes.

I only really met Raymond Williams once, and never had the opportunity to ask him how he thought, in a work of reportage and discovery, including self-discovery, things could conceivably have been otherwise. Yet – as you will see – the idea that Eric Blair somehow metamorphosed into George Orwell, becoming a 'construct' in the process, came to strike Williams as something almost sinister. Without such a metamorphosis, to rejoin with the obvious for a moment, there would have been no 'Orwell' as a character to argue with in the first place.

All these Williams throat-clearing reservations culminate in a full-dress attack on *1984*, which is denounced for being too anti-Communist, for being too pessimistic, and for surrendering to the masochism of betrayal. Williams begins by being mistaken about the sources and inspiration for this novel, which he attributes to the experience of fascism and Nazism alone. It is quite plain, from internal evidence and from Orwell's own writings and correspondence, that it was the Stalin terror (which he had seen early and at first hand in

Catalonia) that provided the raw material for the nightmare of 'Ingsoc'. Writers in Eastern Europe, notably Czeslaw Milosc in *The Captive Mind*, were later to record their astonishment at discovering that the author of *Animal Farm* and *1984*, which they had read only in pirate editions, had not had direct experience of a 'People's Democracy'. But of course, in Barcelona, he had. One might and should add that, as a novelist, Orwell did more than draw on sheer political material. His descriptions of whining masochists and stool-pigeons in *1984*, for instance, seem to me to be taken almost straight from his accounts of sadism and toadyism at English boarding schools.

Williams's error here is even more remarkable, in that he goes on a few pages later to contradict himself directly:

> Ingsoc, it might then be said, is no more English Socialism than Minitrue is the Ministry of Truth. But the identification is in fact made, and has been profoundly damaging. Not in what it says about Soviet society – Orwell's position there was clear and consistent – but in what it implied generally about socialism and a 'centralised economy' . . . By assigning all modern forms of repression and authoritarian control to a single political tendency, he not only misrepresented it, but cut short the kind of analysis that would recognise these inhuman and destructive forces wherever they appeared, under whatever names, and masked by whatever ideology.

So a book published in 1948 – in the face of endless difficulties – should in Williams's view have been a dystopian satire on the form of dictatorship – National Socialism – that had just been defeated and destroyed, rather than on the form – 'People's Democracy' Stalinism – that had just annexed Eastern Europe. Such a book would certainly have been better received by the progressive intellectuals, but it would hardly have forced anybody to face uncomfortable truths.

Williams also appears to have felt – as an unflinching social realist himself – that the novel would have benefited both from being a bit more cheerful and a touch more optimistic. And, for failing in this respect, he accuses Orwell of beckoning on the very future that he warns against:

> It needs to be said, however bitterly, that if the tyranny of 1984 ever finally comes, one of the major elements of the ideological preparation will have been just this way of seeing 'the masses', 'the human beings passing you on the pavement', the eighty-five per cent who are *proles*.

Not content with attributing the views of Winston Smith to his creator – the sort of vulgar fallacy that all students of literature are taught to avoid in their first year – Williams also arraigns Orwell for, as it were, recommending the course of self-abnegation and betrayal that Smith takes when he is finally broken in Room 101. Remember the song at the end of the book? This is how Williams allows himself to characterise it.

> Under the spreading chestnut tree
> I sold you and you sold me.
> He [Orwell] can describe this accurately as 'a peculiar, cracked, braying, jeering note . . . a yellow note,' but still *it is what he makes happen*. The cynical jingle of the rat-race, which in similar forms we have been hearing ever since from the agency offices and parties, leads straight to the rat in Room 101. Of course people break down under torture, but not all people break down. [My italics.]

One rubs the eyes. *Orwell* makes this happen? As early as the Moscow trials, he had noticed that there was something new and horrific and incredible about the abject confessions of the defendants; about the very thing, in short, that caused many people to believe that the same confessions must be true. But to Williams, who doesn't even register this point, the rat in Room 101 is a rodent spawned by the consumer society! As to betrayal and breakdown, it is indeed true that not all the victims succumbed to torture. Andreu Nin did not for one, but Williams had nothing to say about his case except for the insinuation that he might at best have been wasting the Communist Party's valuable time.

The element of bad faith here is made manifest, in my judgement, by Williams's call for a novel about totalitarianism that has a happy ending. Pessimism has its mobilising uses – one of them is the role it plays in the essential and unfinished task of destroying illusions.

I'll end this section by noting a suggestive coincidence. In 1982 in *Harper's* magazine in New York, the neo-conservative critic Norman Podhoretz – perhaps the most unscrupulous man of letters of our time – wrote an essay to prove that Orwell took the American side in the Cold War between the superpowers. He did this by the method of inserting an ellipsis where none belonged, in an extract from Orwell's 1947 *Tribune essay* 'In Defence of Comrade Zilliacus'. As between Washington and Moscow, Orwell had written:

> 'If you *had* to choose between Russia and America, which would you choose?' It will not do to give the usual quibbling answer, 'I refuse to choose'. In the end, the choice may be forced upon us. We are no longer strong enough to stand alone, and if we fail to bring a West European union into being we shall be obliged, in the long run, to subordinate our policy to that of one Great Power or another.

Podhoretz employed the simple expedient of leaving out the whole of the third sentence and the whole middle clause of the fourth one. He continued to do this, in reprints of his dull polemic, despite being advised of the fact that he had been rumbled. Williams, by contrast, chose to omit the second and third sentences. Neither man acknowledged that Orwell drew the conclusion, later in the same year, that the emerging Cold War was a contest between greater and lesser evils, that it did not have to be, and that: 'Therefore a Socialist United States of Europe seems to me the only worthwhile political objective today'. Fighting Stalin and Hitler at the same time was a much harsher business than fending off the crudities of Podhoretz and Williams, but it involved sticking to the same consistent points – even if they were inconsistently expressed – and trusting to the readers to notice who was being honest in the long term, or at all. Orwell, incidentally, never paid his foes back in the same coin. At the very last stage of the proofs of *Animal Farm*, he altered the passage about the blowing up of the animals' hard-built and hard-won windmill. It had read: 'All the animals including Napoleon flung themselves on their faces.' Orwell changed this to 'All the animals except Napoleon'. It weighed with him that Stalin had remained in Moscow during the Nazi advance on the city.

There's a tendency, unremarked so far as I am aware, for Williams's works to end with deflated or inconclusive or even vapid sentences. 'In speaking of a common culture,' he wrote or typed at the end of *The Idea of a Common Culture*, 'one is asking, precisely, for that free, contributive and common *process* of participation in the creation of meanings and values, as I have tried to define it.' What is the word 'precisely' doing in that lame assembly of terms? Check it out – you'll see that I'm right as often as I'm wrong. Anyway, at the close of the Orwell book he wrote, in 1971:

> We are never likely to reach a time when we can do without his frankness, his energy, his willingness to join in. These are the qualities we shall go on respecting in him, whatever other conclusions we may come to. But they are real qualities only if they are independent and active. The thing to do with his work, his history, is to read it, not imitate it. He is still there, tangibly, with the wound in his throat, the sad strong face, the plain words written in hardship and exposure. But then as we reach out to touch him we catch something of his hardness, a necessary hardness. We are acknowledging a presence and a distance: other names, other years; a history to respect, to remember, to move on from.

I can recall thinking, when I read this first, that what was most striking was the insincerity. The sentence about the wounded throat is rather fine, but the rest is either tautology or cant. Of course he is 'still there', even if not 'tangibly'. But how can qualities like frankness and energy be made more or less 'real' – which it has been conceded that they already are, and almost timelessly at that – by becoming somehow 'independent and active'? The hardness, on its own evidence, is neither here nor there. Williams's long withdrawing flannel and flounder in the last sentence, with its presence and distance and other names and years (why not faces?), struck me as a weak way of saying that this example was something to note, perhaps, but also to try and forget.

As it was to prove. In the book-length interview and conversation with Perry Anderson, Francis Mulhern and Anthony Barnett, published as *Politics and Letters* in 1979, there is an entire chapter given over to the promulgation of contempt for Orwell. (The book takes its title in part from a post-Cambridge journal of the same name, founded by Williams and Wolf Mankowitz and Clifford Collins in the postwar period, and consecrated to the rather forbidding idea of a synthesis between Marx and Leavis.) Recollecting this ephemeral enterprise, Williams pays one unintended compliment to Orwell:

> who, then riding high on the success of *Animal Farm*, although now getting really ill, gave us his 'Writers and Leviathan' essay. Then when Collins went to see him in hospital he actually handed over the manuscript of his essay on Gissing and said: 'You are very welcome to this.' By the time it should have appeared the magazine had folded (incidentally inducing a dreadful moment since for quite a long time that essay on Gissing, which Orwell was naturally quite anxious to get back, was lost: it eventually turned up under a pile of someone's old papers).

This glancing mention of Orwell's generosity out of the way, the fun can begin. One cannot always appreciate the answers without being given the full benefit of the questions, but let me allow Williams's first response to stand on its own:

> In the Britain of the fifties, along every road that you moved, the figure of Orwell seemed to be waiting. If you tried to develop a new kind of popular cultural analysis, there was Orwell; if you wanted to report on work or ordinary life, there was Orwell; if you engaged in any kind of socialist argument, there was an enormously inflated statue of Orwell warning you to go back. Down to the late sixties political editorials in newspapers would regularly admonish younger socialists to read their Orwell and see where all that led to.

This is bizarre, coming from the Williams who knew (and had cited the fact) that Orwell had repudiated, in a firm letter to an official of the United Auto Workers Union in America, precisely that misreading of *1984*. It is also bizarre, coming from the Williams who had written and presumably believed, in 1971, that 'the generation for whom Suez, Hungary, and the Bomb were signals for political action looked to him with respect . . . this New Left respected Orwell directly', and who had also asserted (quite perceptively) that Orwell's novels of the thirties were the seedbed of the anti-hero, 'Angry Young Men' works of the English 1950s. Such a piece of double-entry book-keeping – which among other things involves the curiously passive stratagem of judging Orwell by what others choose to make of him – is explicable by one of perhaps two things: a change of heart or a feeling of resentment – even of envy. Williams does not propose a change of heart, at any rate, as his motive. He simply, though pressured somewhat by his questioners, discards the layers of ambivalence that had invested his earlier work:

> The chapter [of the 1971 book] that I would not have missed writing was the one where I discuss the creation of a character called Orwell who is very different from the writer called Orwell – the successful impersonation of the plain man who bumps into experience in an unmediated way and is simply telling the truth about it.

I leave it to any reader to decide whether Orwell among the tramps or the coal-miners took the view, or expected any reader to take the view, that he was 'simply' a camera on the Issyvoo model. Now here comes one of those collectors'-item questions that I promised earlier. Having said that '1984 will be a curio in 1984', Williams's prompters propose the following:

> During the Cold War, the international bourgeoisie had an objective need for extremely potent and, above all, popular works of a blatantly anti-communist direction. Of all the countries in Europe, England was a particularly strong candidate for producing them, because it had no experience of a mass revolutionary movement in the 20th century, the local ruling class was less affected by internal upheavals than any of its continental counterparts, and the social order was the most traditional and stable. It is unlikely to be an accident that it generated the two best-sellers of anti-communist literature on an international scale – Orwell and Koestler. The case of the latter is particularly suggestive since he was himself of course not English. It is always necessary to remember the enormous international resonance of the later Orwell. To this day, for example, tens of thousands of copies of *Animal Farm* and *1984* are sold every year in West Germany, as obligatory texts in the school system. That is not to mention the broadcasting of his catchwords over the various émigré radio networks to Eastern Europe.

To this, Raymond Williams (who was old enough to smile at the ancient Thirties tic about things being 'no accident', and had done so in print) offered this reply:

> The qualification one must make is that the composition of these writings predates the outset of the Cold War – he wrote *Animal Farm* during the period of maximum popularity of the Soviet Union in this country. There was an oppositional element in him which made him the first in the field. The recruitment of very private feelings against socialism becomes intolerable by *1984*. It is profoundly offensive to state as a general truth, as Orwell does, that people will always betray each other.

Well, at least he gave Orwell credit for 'the composition of these writings', which his questioners had thought to be 'generated' by the English-speaking subsection of 'the international bourgeoisie'. He appears to have forgotten that Orwell opposed Stalin and the Soviet Union long before their wartime and postwar popularity, just as his questioners have overlooked the fact that *Animal Farm* was disapproved by the Ministry of Information and rejected by T. S. Eliot at Faber and Faber. (Their inane observation that '*1984* will be a curio by 1984' was itself to become a curio long before 1989.) Nor does he intrude the reasonably obvious fact that Arthur Koestler, regardless of 'upheavals' in traditional and hidebound England, would very certainly have been dead if he had tried to carry on writing in any of the countries affected by the Hitler–Stalin Pact. Orwell would, however, probably have been pleased at the reception accorded his books in any part of Germany – one of the early editions of *Animal Farm* was available only in the Ukrainian language for 'displaced persons' kept in cages in that country, and much of that printing was seized by American occupation forces and turned over to the Soviet zone for destruction. As for the unconscionable exploitation of Orwellian texts by Western or émigré radio networks, we knew long before 1979, from Milosc and others, that the message of these same texts had already been driven home in what *New Left Review* might well have chosen to call more 'concrete' ways.

Williams's obtuse insistence that Orwell magnifies and praises betrayal in *1984* has, I hope, already been answered. When asked whether his view had altered since he penned his 1971 book, he replied decidedly.

> I must say that I cannot bear much of it now. If I had to say which writings have done the most damage, it would be what you call the social patriotism – the dreadful stuff from the beginning of the war about England as a family with the wrong members in charge, the shuffling old aunts and uncles whom we could fairly painlessly get rid of. Many of the political arguments of the kind of Labourism that is usually associated with the tradition of Durbin or Gaitskell can be traced to these essays, which are much more serious facts than *Animal Farm*.

One might as fairly say that, when John Major compared Eric Blair favourably to Tony Blair, Williams was 'objectively' on the side of John Major. I confess, though, that I don't know and cannot guess what may be implied in the idea that these parish-pump observations are 'more serious facts' than the world-historic tragedy satirised in *Animal Farm*. For Williams the Marxist to argue that British social democratic revisionism took its tune from one of Orwell's weaker essays, rather than from Ramsay McDonald or R. H. Tawney, would seem to undergird my suggestion that there is something unpleasantly like jealousy involved in such an a-historical overestimate (as well as underestimation) of Orwell's real-time influence.

I note again that the crucial image – of a conspiracy of silence about the source of the family income – is too strong to have been overlooked by accident. When Edward Said stressed a similar point in his treatment of *Mansfield Park*, nobody accused him of confusing Jane Austen's delicately filiated family relationships with the deep structure of slavery and imperialism.

In the last paragraph of his exchange with *New Left Review*, in which he repeated and intensified his earlier statement by saying 'I cannot read him now', Williams confined his condemnation to the narrow, debatable but scarcely indictable charge that Orwell had changed his mind. 'For example, there was no objective reason at all for the disgraceful attacks he made on pacifists or revolutionary opponents of the war in American periodicals, denouncing people here who were simply in his own position of three or four years before.' What have we here? What we have here is a conscious confusion of categories, allied to an unworthy hint of chauvinism. The American periodical was *Partisan Review*, for all that Williams makes it sound like a sheet produced by Henry Luce. The 'people here' were often those who – sturdy provincials as he makes them sound – did Stalin's work by advocating the partition of Poland, and denouncing the British naval blockade of Germany as an inhuman attack against civilians. That this was also Hitler's work is an equally 'objective' fact, materialised by both Molotov and Ribbentrop in their explicit alliance. So, even if there was no good 'objective' reason for Orwell's attacks, there were some pretty solid subjective ones. As against that, Orwell always defended the right of Indian nationalists to opt out of Britain's war, and showed a lively interest in defending the civil liberties even of the most gullible pacifists. (The British Communists of the time, lest we forget, waited only for Hitler's assault on Russia before demanding the practical equivalent of internment for all those to the Left and the Right who disagreed with their patriotic war aims.)

The recent absurd fuss over Orwell's willingness to 'name names' – the names of those he had already publicly denounced and lampooned – was manured in the soil by those who have never forgiven him for the stubborn rectitude he evinced between 1936 and the time of his death. Notice the way that a lonely, derided, near-bankrupt and desperately ill man is awarded such *power* by Williams three decades later: the power to disrupt the whole movement of those who are on the right side of history; the power to unleash the Cold War; the power to induce despair and to encourage betrayal in the ranks of a people who could look the Normans in the eye. This argues, in the same hypocritical relationship that vice bears to virtue, the realisation that principles are potent, that historical truth will out, and that the fearless individual can make a difference. Raymond Williams had a gift of plain and direct speech, and he never resorted to jargon unless he felt that 'objectively' it was required of him. The Plaça George Orwell, on that Barcelona waterfront, is proof that 'history to the defeated' can still make some amends, and that the masses – as Williams himself so finely stated – are not fashioned for manipulation or drudgery but are made up of autonomous individuals, and that justice is ordinary, though not quite in the way that he thought culture to be, because it is not latent or innate but needs to be decided by struggle and by irony too.

First published as 'George Orwell and Raymond Williams' in
Critical Quarterly, vol. 41, no. 3, Autumn 1999

Notes

1. Raymond Williams Memorial Lecture, delivered at the Hay-on-Wye literary festival, 29 May 1999.
2. The recent publication of Orwell's *Complete Works* (in twenty volumes produced by Secker and Warburg) concludes the argument about his being a 'snitch' or police spy. The entries for 4 March 1949 and 2 May 1949, among many others, show Orwell insisting to his friends Richard Rees and David Astor that 'fellow-travelling' is not to be criminalised. While a petition from the Freedom Defence Committee (FDC) on 21 August 1948 demands that all government employees suspected or accused of disloyalty be entitled to legal and trade-union representation, be permitted to cross-examine witnesses against them, and be allowed to demand corroborative evidence in the case of unsupported testimony from the Special Branch or MI5. Orwell was a sponsor of the FDC and signed this important letter along with E. M. Forster, Osbert Sitwell, Julian Symons, Gerald Brenan, Augustus John, Herbert Read and Henry Moore, among others.
3. I have wondered if this is a sly reference to Orwell's novel *Coming Up For Air*, in which the narrating character, George Bowling, alludes to the misery of the petit-bourgeois housing estates of the 1930s, and sarcastically proposes a statue to 'the god of building societies'. In one hand, this figure would carry an enormous key, and in the other: 'a cornucopia, out of which would be pouring portable radios, life-insurance policies, false teeth, aspirins, French letters and concrete garden rollers'. Either Williams has only a subliminal memory of this passage, or he is again mistaking the voice of the character for the voice of the author. Or else I am mistaken.

Oh, Lionel!

We know from his immense correspondence that P. G. Wodehouse was at once omnivorous and discriminating in his reading (garbage in; synthesis out – a good maxim for any young reader-for-pleasure setting out on life's road). He cited authors as various as Leon Feuchtwanger and Rudyard Kipling, and didn't bluff about a book he hadn't read. And we know that he was excessively fond of the theatre. But he never alluded to the author of these ensuing lines, which come from Act One, Scene One of an imperishable stage moment, when the young master is discovered by his manservant while trying out the piano:

> ALGERNON: Did you hear what I was playing, Lane?
> LANE: I didn't think it polite to listen, sir.

This bit of business, with a line being perfectly lobbed and beautifully returned over the social net, inaugurates a play in which: 1. The butler always has the last, crisp word. 2. Young men stutter cretinously when left alone with the adored object. 3. Country houses ('How many bedrooms? Well, that point can be cleared up afterwards') are an essential retreat from the cares of Mayfair and Piccadilly. 4. Aunts are mythical monsters ('Never met such a Gorgon . . . I don't really know what a Gorgon is like, but I am quite sure that Lady Bracknell is one'). 5. Preposterous rural churchmen are on hand to supply authenticity ('My sermon on the meaning of manna in the wilderness can be adapted to almost any occasion'). 6. Ridiculous matrimonial entanglements of genealogy and dowry lead to a massed chorus of happy endings.

Oscar Wilde doesn't get so much as a walk-on part in Barry Phelps' hearty, upbeat, point-missing celebration of the man he rather tryingly calls 'The Master'. This further omission helps to materialise Alexander Cockburn's surmise that 'Wodehouse's almost pathological prudery in sexual matters, a reticence sublimated in the jocular male partnerships employed in his fiction and the loyal epistolary male friendships of his life, caused him to shy away in extreme nervousness from mention of Wilde.' Phelps touches on this recoil himself, recording Wodehouse's distaste for Beverly Nichols as an interviewer and quoting a letter from Wodehouse to Bill Townend, saying: 'Can you imagine giving lunch to celebrate the publication of a book? With the other authors, mostly fairies, twittering all over the place, screaming 'Oh, Lionel!' This may make George Orwell seem rather naïve for having made the otherwise useful observation that: 'how closely Wodehouse sticks to conventional morality can be seen from the fact that nowhere in his books is there anything in the nature of a sex joke. This is an enormous sacrifice for a farcical writer to make. Not only are there no dirty jokes, but there are hardly any compromising situations.' It's the idea of 'sacrifice' here that seems, on consideration, to be the disputable one.

In this oddly sorted book of facts and reminiscences, Phelps does occasionally contrive to sharpen the outlines of our existing profile of PGW. It's melancholy but unsurprising, and oddly reassuring in view of the foregoing, to discover that Wodehouse's sexlessness arose from a frightful case of the mumps in early youth. So that at least his passivity was not the outcome of any repression or trauma. It enabled, in some fashion, an essential part of him to remain childlike. While this is no psycho-history (no mumps doesn't necessarily equal no Gussie Fink-Nottle) it does help us in considering a possible connection between the knowing and the innocent in modern English comic writing. To take another coincidence which, likewise ignored by Phelps, was pouncable-upon as I came across it: 'Wodehouse also helped C. Aubrey Smith, later Sir Aubrey and a Sussex and England cricketer when Plum was at Dulwich, to found the Hollywood Cricket Club ... The club became the social centre for the British colony in Los Angeles.' That was in 1931, more than a decade before *The Loved One* and Sir Ambrose and the tragi-comedy of Anglo-American manners. (And one might also mention the 'Bide-A-Wee' pet shelter to which the Wodehouses donated a small fortune, to say nothing of the cemetery in which they buried six Long Island pets.) Anglo-American cultural tensions, as it happens, didn't trouble PGW overmuch. He developed a pretty thoroughgoing indifference to England and the English, of a sort which mocks his more roast-beef retinue of affected acolytes. He displayed none of the condescension with which Waugh, for example, approached Anglo-American locutions, and he never scorned to lard his discourse with terms like 'Rannygazoo', 'Hornswoggle' and 'Put on dog'.

Phelps earns his keep by faithfully tracking these entries (many of which went straight from novelty to redundancy to antiquity and are only preserved by 'Plum' having taken notice of them) and other taxonomies and lexicographies: 'Wodehouse invented many phrases, such as 'Down to Earth', which are now so much part of the English language that we assume they are of ancient provenance instead of being only a few decades old. Other examples are 'To have a dash at something', 'Dirty work at the crossroads', 'Foggy between the ears', 'Loony bin' and that splendid back-formation 'Gruntled' ... The *OED* refers to his work 1255 times! Here is a twinge, conveyed among other things by that last exclamation mark, both of what is compelling and of what is exhausting in Wodehouse idolatry. None of the above hits are real chart-busters except perhaps 'gruntled'. ('He spoke with a certain what-is-it in his voice and I could see that, if not actually disgruntled, he was far from being gruntled'), which is drawn from *The Code of the Woosters* yet which Phelps sources as – gawd-'elp-us – a find by Gyles Brandreth and further sources as – gawd-'elp-us again – Pelham Books. The atmosphere of a jolly buff's reunion, complete with painful Drones impersonations and ritual bread-throwing, lies heavy about this work.

As Phelps puts it in his no-nonsense style, having discovered that Wodehouse once spoke well of a Tom Sharpe effort, 'that The Master should commend such bawdy black humour is superficially surprising, given his dislike for anything raunchy, but he must have appreciated that he had met another comic master who could also make the language dance to his bidding.' Well, I mean to say, really. This dance business seems to be on the Phelps brain, since later he avers, or asserts: 'If your criteria for great literature require *Sturm und Drang* with penetrating insights into the human predicament then Wodehouse is not great literature. If those criteria include total mastery of written English, the ability to make it dance to your bidding with a poetic beauty and to any job desired and to give joy to readers across the entire spectrum, then Wodehouse is great literature.'

Golly. So the good end happily and the bad unhappily, because that is what Fiction means and anything else would be too brainy. If Phelps thinks that there is no *Sturm und Drang* in Bertie's confrontation with Sir Roderick Spode and the Black Shorts, he must be a hard man to please. Or perhaps an easy one – he refers twice to a master short story writer called O'Henry and says of Agatha Christie that she is among those 'whose mastery of plot is unbettered and whose use of language to achieve their aims is total'.

There's a reactionary growl underlying all this good clean fun interpretation. Phelps believes that Wodehouse said the last word on socialism in one of his Psmith juvenilia stories – 'It's a great scheme ... You work for the equal distribution of property and start by collaring all you can and sitting on it.' He also defines this as 'satire'. But much more satirical, surely, is Wodehouse in the fine maturity of *Right Ho, Jeeves*, where Aunt Dahlia speaks woundingly of the fabulously wealthy Uncle Tom and having 'just had a demand from the income-tax people for an additional fifty-eight pounds, one and threepence, and all he's been talking about since I got back has been ruin and the sinister trend of socialistic legislation and what will become of us all.'

Wodehouse was here being, among other things, self-satirising. He was, all through his life, absolutely obsessed with money and with the necessity of preserving it from the clutches of the Revenue. This theme permeates his letters and took up much of his time with agents, lawyers and accountants, long surviving his access to prosperity. As is so often the case, the consciousness arose from penury in boyhood and from the crushing disappointment of the cancellation of his Oxford entrance due to a sudden crisis in the family funds. These were all vested in India. 'What made the blow even worse was being withdrawn from the scholarship exam at the last moment. In the face he showed the world young Wodehouse accepted the decision with good grace and clothed it in humour, writing of the rupee – in which Ernest's pension was paid – jumping up and down and throwing fits. 'Watch the rupee' was, he claimed, the cry in the Wodehouse household and expenditure had to be regulated in the light of what mood it happened to be in at any moment. 'Perhaps this supplies another reason for Wodehouse's possible repression of *The Importance of Being Earnest*. Does not Miss Prism say to her pupil:

> Cecily, you will read your Political Economy in my absence. The chapter on the Fall of the Rupee you may omit. It is somewhat too sensational. Even these metallic problems have their melodramatic side.

(The play was first performed in 1895: Wodehouse's Oxford misfortune occurred in 1899.) Phelps strains for effect by writing as if there were a vast anti-Wodehouse consensus, split into two factions. The first faction, one might be led to believe, cannot forgive him for his 'unpatriotic' wartime broadcasts from Berlin. The second faction cannot abide his elitist focus on butlers and wastrels. Thus we are given yet another vindication of 'Plum' for his evident innocence about the broadcasts, and then a story (which I must say was new to me) about Wodehouse being sponsored for his knighthood by the superannuated trade-union bureaucrat Walter Citrine. (Phelps spoils this by foolishly going for unironic paradox and describing the fuddled old carthorse as a red-in-tooth-and-claw socialist.)

The fact is that there are only a few mysteries and controversies left. One of these – a very minor one – Phelps proposes to solve by instructing us that Jeeves (first name Reginald as was revealed by Bertie in a moment of almost unpardonable familiarity) took his name from Percy Jeeves, a Warwickshire fast bowler felled in Flanders in 1916. A second enigma, and one that I should very much like to see cleared up, concerns Wodehouse's motive in giving the name 'Roderick' to both Bertie's chief male nemeses – Glossop and Spode. Evelyn Waugh hung the name Cruttwell on several posturing idiots in his early fiction, and apparently by this means induced a nervous prostration in an Oxford tutor of the same name upon whom he sought revenge. The 'Eulalie' business teaches us that Wodehouse well-kenned the power of humiliating nomenclature. But I still have no Roderick data on which to base a solid speculation.

This is all footnoting. Between Wodehouse and Wilde there is an enormous gulf apparently fixed. Both died in exile, having been meanly treated by a culture that prides itself above all on having a broad and keen sense of humour. Both were vilely baited by the pseudo-lions of a cowardly establishment. Both were tougher eggs than they looked, and both thought the class system an absolute scream. It would be encouraging to think that an unacknowledged, latent tie existed between the louche Irishman and the reticent minor public schoolboy, because only by brooding on such connections can we hope to save the idea of English humour from the drawing-room and saloon-bar conscription that is eternally levied upon it by bland, Loamshire wits like Mr Phelps.

First published as 'Oh, Lionel!' (a review of *P. G. Wodehouse: Man and Myth* by Barry Phelps) in *London Review of Books*, 3 December 1992

Age of Ideology

I was reading Russell Baker's Christmas Day column in the *New York Times*, and taking time to realise that it was his valediction, when a mouse stirred in the attic of memory. Where before had I read such an understated, modest yet replete and satisfied farewell? Where else had I come across the cadences of reminiscence ('I have sat in . . .' 'I have watched . . .' 'I have seen . . .') with which the successful scribbler hangs up his quill? It took me only a short time to 'access', and to reread, Murray Kempton's introduction to his 1994 collection, *Rebellions, Perversities, and Main Events*. I can't say with certainty whether Baker's echoes were unconscious, but I can say that those are the best kind and that they represent the sincerest form of homage.

Those of us who enlist in the apparently pointless but endlessly rewarding occupation of holding up the colonnade take comfort when one of our number is recognised as something more than a mere caryatid. If Kempton had been a column, he would have been Doric – spare and slim and tapering. Welcome and familiar (as a good columnist is supposed to be) at the precinct house and the taproom and the convention hall and the picket line, he could also have passed for a don. Not a don from Brooklyn or Little Italy (though he was able to make himself welcome there, too) but a don from one of the poorer and more racy and intrigue-ridden Oxbridge colleges, with his bicycle clips and Latin and Greek tags and silvered locks and beaming spectacles. I once stood behind Murray Kempton as he was entering a Louis Farrakhan rally at Madison Square Garden, and being patted down by minatory security men from the Fruit of Islam. He explained without condescension that as a veteran attendee, he might have to leave the much invigilated area set aside for the 'White Devil' press and relieve his bladder. The bow-tied young toughs were practically calling him 'Professor' by the time it was over. Now that's a knack, I remember thinking. He's got the Fruit eating out of his hand.

It is as an amateur historian that the Modern Library has so aptly chosen to honour Kempton by reissuing *Part of Our Time: Some Ruins and Monuments of the Thirties*. I say 'aptly' because the spectres of the age of ideology have recently been loosed again, to run gibbering and squeaking through our streets. Even as I write, tomes are in preparation proving that the Spanish Republic and its supporters were the first dupes of Stalinism's grand design. One way of saying that we have been here before is to say that Murray Kempton was there before us.

The key word of the 1930s was 'commitment', and Kempton was able to write with humour but without sanctimony about the absolutist character of allegiance in that period. In his essay 'The Social Muse', he sympathetically disinterred forgotten novels like *The Unpossessed*, by Tess Slesinger, and anatomised the personal frailties and political furies that made for such loyalties and (as night followed day) such 'betrayals'. He may have made the occasional slip – Lionel Trilling was not delighted to be identified as a character in *The Unpossessed* who was more plausibly based on Max Eastman – but he had an instinct for the period and for its style. Here he is, neatly catching another great critic of the decade: 'Some of the writers who supported the Communist ticket in 1932 were gentlemen who detested the values of a commercial civilisation; Edmund Wilson, for example, writing in 1931, sounds oddly like Henry Adams describing Washington after the Civil War.'

It was partly this gift for nuance that caused Kempton to notice, while reviewing the work of Whittaker Chambers, something undeniably authentic beneath the bombast and self-pity. Indeed, it appeared paradoxically as if Chambers had had a real feeling for Marxism, whereas Alger Hiss understood only power and revenge. Kempton was from Baltimore himself and well knew the variant milieus of the Hiss and Chambers upbringings: 'A man's childhood can condition him more than a law of history or what he conceives as the logic of his time.' Before you are tempted to dismiss this as the 'Rosebud' theory of materialism, read Kempton's summary of social insecurity among the shabby-genteel:

> Lanvale Street was in Baltimore's Fourth Assembly District; in one Depression Democratic primary, its residents were confronted with a ballot bulging with Jewish names. In desperation they voted for an alternative candidate whose name was unfamiliar but indubitably old Virginia. They awoke to find they had helped nominate a Negro.

Not only the Baltimore connection puts one in mind of H. L. Mencken here. And then, after this almost lazily atmospheric prelude, comes a shaft of pure acuity:

> Chambers indicates that he very soon lost any disposition to discuss revolutionary theory with Hiss. In his autobiography, he reports only Hiss's admiring comment on the Moscow trials: 'Joe Stalin certainly plays for keeps.' That was a view of things which could hardly offer much meat to an old Bolshevik who grew up in the Communist Party of the 20's when it had a

less limited range of intellectual interests and a faint trace of skepticism about the hero in history.

Such a paragraph simply could not have been written, so tautly and yet so laconically, except by a person with some lightly worn but considerable battle scars. (One pauses to note that *Part of Our Time* was first published in the jittery year of 1955, but that Kempton did not fail to record his own past membership in the Young Communist League.) Whittaker Chambers won in some ways and lost in others, all the while convinced that he had exchanged the winning side for the losing one. Alger Hiss lost in some ways and won in others, almost certainly because he thought he had chosen the camp of victory. It took a real humanist – and a humanist who had at least once applied himself to the dialectic – to bring to bear such a shrewd intuition at the nadir of the Cold War.

All the essays in *Part of Our Time* have in common an unsentimental re-evaluation of the decade, combined with a determination to avoid what F. P. Thompson once termed 'the enormous condescension of posterity'. When Kempton describes the waterfront Bolsheviks of the National Maritime Union or the men and women who had been changed forever by the Sacco–Vanzetti case or that old Socialist-turned-witch-hunter J. B. Matthews, he takes the utmost care to place them in context, to show them in their own words, to accept them at their own highest evaluation. The last two things, of course, very often obviate the need for excessive comment: it is from their own words, as measured against their high aspirations, that we discover the Reuther brothers to be a little smug, John L. Lewis to be an incipient megalomaniac and J. B. Matthews to be a Pharisee. (Incidentally, why do so few national papers today pay a gifted young writer to go out and cover the reviving labour movement?) It was after a close scrutiny of the germinal role of the Pullman workers' union, and also after some study of Bessie Smith and Louis Armstrong, that Kempton wrote the most prescient (for 1955) and the most dialectical sentences in his book: 'We have seen in the past few years, I think, the beginning of a revolution in the position of the Negro in America. It has been carried out by Negroes whose first decisive act was their rejection of the revolutionary myth.'

Not bad for someone whose great-grandfather was author of the 1850 Fugitive Slave Act. Kempton showed a lifelong appreciation for those who could keep money and mouth in an honourable relationship. He detested finks and whiners. His essay on the young men who went to fight in Spain, which is full of mordant words about Communist cynicism, is also full of admiration for one of the party's heroes, Robert Thompson. (Thompson survived Spain, fought in New Guinea in

World War II and won the Distinguished Service Cross. Interviewed in Buna by a United Press correspondent and asked what he did in civilian life, he replied, 'Maybe you won't believe me, but I'm a Young Communist League organiser for Ohio.') On his return to the United States, Thompson was jailed for subversion and severely injured in prison by a Yugoslav detainee who, as Kempton drily phrased it, 'did not know Thompson; he seems to have thought of this as the sort of affirmative anti-Communist gesture which might stay his deportation.'

Did I say 'unsentimental' earlier? Kempton had a pronounced tendency to find the aspect of honour in those who had been brought low. He even became lenient about Richard M. Nixon. (Mario Cuomo once asked Sydney Schanberg of *Newsday* how he could get Kempton on his side. 'Try getting indicted, Governor.') I only ever heard him speak with real contempt of one person – a hungry and unfastidious governor from Arkansas. So I have to suppose, however much it gashes me, that if he were still with us he'd be setting his Quixotic lance in place just about now.

First published as 'Age of Ideology: Murray Kempton on the Thirties' in *New York Times Book Review*, 31 January 1999

The Real Thing

A few weeks ago, his lordship the Earl of Wemyss and March, master of Gosford House in the Scottish county of East Lothian, disburdened himself of Botticelli's exquisite 'Virgin Adoring the Christ Child' for a price of twenty million pounds sterling. Since the buyer was the Kimbell Museum in Texas, there was a fine old British row about treasures leaving the country, irresponsible noblemen denuding the national patrimony, and the failure of the National Gallery of Tony Blair's 'Cool Britannia' to come up with matching funds for the retention of the masterpiece. This is an old set-piece tale in Britain: I remember as a schoolboy at the age of ten being asked to subscribe my pocket money to keep a Leonardo cartoon in the United Kingdom. And the story loses nothing by the addition of a dim and acquisitive Scots peer. But what struck me most about the otherwise familiar newspaper coverage was this. Until the earl decided to realise his Botticelli on the Texas market, nobody knew it was there.

It happens all the time. A culture whose summa is the country house, and a culture to which Empire once afforded numerous possibilities of loot, and a culture furthermore where the eccentric collector is a stock character, is awash in unlocated paintings, manuscripts, and items of furniture. Since the landed and agricultural interest has been in decline for some time – indeed has been making a specialty of its deathbed speech for over a century now – the 'discovery' of a trove is most commonly associated with the need for once-grand dynasties to pay off inheritance or estate taxes, or to get out of debt. Lord Cowdray's family recently raised nine million pounds for these purposes by selling Rembrandt's 1667 'Portrait of an Elderly Man' to the Mauritshuis in Amsterdam. Japanese banks, American galleries, and Swiss pension funds, one presumes, retain professionals to scrutinise old copies of *Country Life* magazine, in the hope of glimpsing a nice canvas in the background of a hunt-ball photograph.

This intersection of the art market, the class system, and what might be termed the English or British character furnishes an ideal locus for Michael Frayn. In his essays and in his plays and screenplays (*Noises Off* and *Clockwise* being notable here) he has raised an edifice of gentle but by no means innocuous satire of his fellow countrymen. His first novel, *The Tin Men*, published in 1965, was a mordant and hilarious account of the last version of 'the New Britain', with mad and manipulative computer scientists, housed in the 'William Morris Institute of Automation Research', being entirely unhorsed by a sudden royal visit. More than one reviewer compared the tempo to that of the young Evelyn Waugh, and indeed a subsequent novel, *Towards the End of the Morning*, is the only fiction set in Fleet Street that can bear comparison with *Scoop*.

Frayn's preferred raw material is the status anxiety, and vulnerability to embarrassment, of the *bien-pensant* middle class. (Together with the late cartoonist Marc Boxer, he has in effect been the chronicler of this anxious and energetic stratum, with its gnawing guilts and worries about private schooling, the environment, and multiculturalism.) At the opening of *Headlong*, we are introduced to Martin and Kate Clay, respectively a philosopher and an art historian, as they set off from mid-bourgeois North London for their uneasily held country cottage. Martin's initial reverie sets his tone as the narrator:

> Where is the country? Good question. I privately think it begins around Edgware, and goes on until Cape Wrath, but then I don't know much about it. Kate's rather a connoisseur of the stuff, though, and it's not the country for her, not the real country, until we've driven for at least a couple of hours, and turned off the motorway, and got onto the Lavenage road. Even here she's cautious, and I can see what she means. It's all a bit neat and organised still, as if it were merely a representation of the country in an exhibition. . . . I share Kate's unease about this. We don't want to drive a hundred miles out of London only to meet people who have driven a hundred miles out of London to avoid meeting people like us.

This passage acts, if somewhat obliquely, as an overture to Frayn's chief theme – which is that of authenticity and the difficulty of deciding it – and also places it in a promising context of social insecurity. At the approach of journey's end, authenticity can be more readily vouched for:

> There's a half-mile squish of mud and shit under the tires where a herd of live cows goes regularly back and forth between meadow and milking shed. Beyond the undergrowth on the left, at one point, is a scattering of bricks and broken tiles, growing a mixed crop of nettles and ancient leaky enamelware. Rusty corrugated iron flaps loose on ramshackle empty structures abandoned in the corners of tussocky fields. Lichen-covered five-bar gates lean at drunken angles on broken hinges, secured with rusty barbed wire. We begin to relax our guard; this is the real stuff, all right. This is what we pay a second lot of bills for.

In general and in the details (the herd of 'live' cows is a nice touch) this again puts me in mind of *Scoop*, and of poor Mr Salter's calamitous visit to the Boot home in remote Somerset. The great secret about the English rural idyll – an idyll most harshly dissipated in Sam Peckinpah's *Straw Dogs* – is that the bucolic scene is very often one of cruelty, surliness, and resentment, rife with inbreeding and inefficiency, and populated quite largely by people who would, had they only the talent or the resources, do anything to sell up and move to the city. (Without elaboration, Martin alludes to 'the lake that collects in the dip by the wood where we found the dead tramp'.) We are, in any case, very swiftly presented with a truly rebarbative example of the squire at his worst. Tony Churt, who calls abruptly on Martin and Kate, 'has the grip of a man who's used to wringing the necks of wounded game birds'. A gun crooked in the elbow, some muddy dogs cringing around his boots, 'an effortlessly landowning kind of voice', and the word-picture is complete. His rather peremptory invitation to dinner at Upwood, the local Big House, is accepted, which frees Martin to be mildly self-lacerating when alone with Kate again:

> 'So,' I say, sitting down beside her, 'we're in with the gentry. All our vaguely leftish prejudices down the drain. Instant corruption.'

And with that last attenuated and almost obligatory writhe, we leave conventional Frayn territory and are precipitated, or perhaps it would be more apt to say pitchforked, into a region of fantasy. Of course Churt has only asked this wet-behind-the-ears pair to dine because he wants something. He imagines that their citified and academic ways will permit a free valuation of some daubs in his possession, and some free advice about how to avoid taxes and commissions on the sale of same. One of the daubs he considers negligible. But at the very first view of it the mild-mannered and ironic Martin begins to vibrate and point like a well-trained setter on a shoot. He is convinced not just that the painting is a Bruegel, but that it is a Bruegel of Bruegels: the lost keystone to an arch of symbolic work. His abrupt farewell to reason and proportion is accompanied by a no less striking abandonment of any sense of self-preservation, and this descent into mania and obsession supplies the energy of the story thereafter.

Kierkegaard says that the whole problem with existence is that it has to be lived forwards and can only be reviewed or evaluated, so to say, backwards. How Martin the trained philosopher might have benefited from pondering this. To describe him as unreliable would be a kindness: he never actually gets another square look at the panel in question but when he is away from it he free-associates in the most torrential manner about its possible provenance. Auden in his 'Musée des Beaux

Arts' gives an unforgettable sketch of Bruegel's 'Icarus', with its painted ship and the white legs vanishing into the ocean, while the onlookers continue their quotidian round. Frayn's narrator almost skips the picture and instead gives us a frenzied tour, complete with much show of learning, of the whole Dutch school and indeed of the entire combat between Spain and the Netherlands. He consults, and cites at length, numerous authorities. He also succumbs to the lure of cupidity, quoting to himself from fabulous saleroom prices for comparable 'finds'.

An anonymous wit once rewrote an old admonition and gave it the heading 'A Word of Encouragement':

> O what a tangled web we weave
> When first we practice to deceive.
> But when we've practised quite a while
> How vastly we improve our style.

This doggerel recurred to me as I read through the torments visited by Frayn on his narrator. Martin has to deceive the ghastly Tony Churt about his real intentions, and pretend to be interested in selling and valuing another painting altogether. Having given Tony's ill-used wife, Laura, the mistaken impression that he is interested more in her than in the pictures (he is interested, but only sexually), he has to string her along, too. And he has to keep this stringing-along from his own wife, who has recently become a mother and has brought them all to the countryside so that he, Martin, can do some solid parenting and some serious work on his philosophy.

Frayn's gift for conveying embarrassment, especially sexual and matrimonial embarrassment, is considerable. In a moment of literal bedroom farce, Martin is about to be granted a view of his 'Bruegel', with Tony Churt absent in London and Laura as his guide. She gives him a drink and leads him upstairs, smoking:

> She suddenly darts toward the dressing table. The insane idea flashes into my head that she's going to stub the cigarette out on the picture. I hurl myself convulsively after her, with a kind of little groan, and fling out my arm to prevent her. My hand still has the glass of gin in it. It catches her on the elbow. She looks down at the silver splash of gin leaping out of the glass at her like a flying fish, then looks straight up into my eyes, startled.
> 'Wow!' she says, and laughs, amused and gratified. . . .

Extricating himself from this – not without difficulty – Martin returns home, again thwarted in his desire to study the picture, and decides it might be prudent not to mention that Tony Churt had been elsewhere. Without lying directly, he contrives to give Kate the impression of having seen both Tony and the painting. But with witchlike timing, as he is rummaging in a cupboard, Kate mentions that Churt telephoned from London while Martin was out:

> I don't attempt to explain anything. I simply ask, with passing curiosity in my voice, even if I have to keep my head in the cupboard under the sink to hide my face, 'What did he want?'

Martin's consciousness of the inadequacy of this return of serve is acutely registered. I should have liked more such episodes, and more flesh on some of the rather skeletal characters who are granted minor parts. Tony's braying South African brother is caught to perfection but then dismissed from the action. An obsequious rival art historian with the excellent name of John Quiss is likewise deployed rather perfunctorily. In part, this represents the obsessive narrowing of Martin's own field of vision, to the point where he can only concentrate on the next detail of his deception, or on a potentially confirming detail in the painting. He does not succeed in improving his style.

Working from the context to the picture instead of the other way about, Martin decides what it ought to represent. Denied access, and going only on his first startled glimpse, he concludes that Bruegel was employing his brush in order to convey certain arcane political and religious points; painterly dissents from the terrifying clerical and monarchical authorities of his day. After a while, and as a result of immersion in the subject, he reaches the stage – a working definition of fanaticism – where everything seems to confirm his hypothesis. Those who have read Motley or Simon Schama on the Netherlands will not need a reference map, those who have not read them may be encouraged to do so, because Frayn's educated interest and Martin's hysterical absorption are alike infectious.

Looming over the whole plot is the extraordinary milieu of today's frenetic art market, which makes terms like 'commodification' seem understated. Having – he thinks – persuaded Churt that his interest lies in another of his pictures, Martin finds himself having to act out the whole deception, and hauls Churt's suspected Giordano into the foyer of Christie's to see what if anything it will fetch. His own indifference to the decoy is not matched by the suave young valuer who greets him:

> He steps back and examines her. 'No, of course – it's Helen', he says at once, with the gracious ability of the really polite to place the names of people they hardly know, and to find the right things to say. 'Oh, yes! Yes, indeed! What a splendid piece! Such a bold, free treatment'.
>
> I wonder if I should tell him the name of the painter, before he embarrasses us both with a wrong guess. But he already knows. 'Absolutely off the cuff', he says thoughtfully, 'my feeling is that it may perhaps be the

best of all his Helens. How good of you to bring her in. She's been hiding away at Upwood for so long. Very exciting! Let me fetch Mr Carlyle'.

Here, in a few deft phrases, Frayn has caught the world of the late Bruce Chatwin, where clever young men conjure mighty sums from the mold-covered contents of rural fastnesses. (When a figure is casually mentioned, Martin at first doesn't realise that it's in thousands.) And, just as the protagonist of Chatwin's *Utz* is made a hostage and a martyr by his collection mania, so Martin finds that he has constructed a sort of prisoner's dilemma for himself:

> The only way I can fulfill my pledge is to study my picture until I find what I'm looking for. The only way I can study it is to acquire it. The only way I can acquire it is to break my pledge.
>   An antinomy, as we call it back in the department.

As if to confirm himself as antinomy man, Martin here means 'pledge' in two declensions: his pledge to himself to unlock the secret of Bruegel, and his pledge to his sinister business partner to be an honest intermediary. His self-wrought dilemma doesn't kill him, even though he is lucky to escape with his life, as he and we discover that Tony Churt is even nastier (and much less of a fool) than at first appeared. The closing passages are a sudden acceleration into shock, as the compounded illusions and deceits attain critical mass, and the ending is both more violent and more melancholy than anything in Frayn's work thus far. In one of the middle chapters, Martin the philosopher and Kate the art historian have a sharp domestic dispute, about the relative value of works of art and human lives. She seems to imply that the survival of art can in certain circumstances take precedence. He is all enraged moralism, with a dash of logic-chopping. The achievement of the novel is to show the narrator changing sides in this essential argument, and for him to show us how he has done so, without ever coming to realise it himself.

First published as 'The Real Thing' (a review of *Headlong* by Michael Frayn) in *New York Review of Books*, 2 December 1999

The Cosmopolitan Man

Here is a report from the *New York Times* of 12 September 1960, written from Poughkeepsie under the byline of Ira Henry Freeman:

> Gore Vidal, Democratic candidate for Representative in the twenty-ninth Congressional District, sprawled barefoot in a gilded fauteuil of his luxurious octagonal Empire study as he considered the question whether he could win the election.
>
> 'If this were not a Presidential year, I might have a chance', he said. 'As it is, every four years, about 20,000 extra people crawl out of their Hudson Gothic woodwork up here to vote for William McKinley.'
>
> Mr. Vidal is 34 years old, slender, smooth in dress and manner, bright, sharp, sophisticated. He looks like a juvenile lead and talks like Mort Sahl. 'I say 80 per cent of what I think, a hell of a lot more than any politician I know,' he said.

Take out the proper name in that story, and who could fail to guess the subject's identity? By then, he had written his first eight novels, two Broadway successes, and the screenplays for *Ben Hur* and *Suddenly Last Summer*. According to the *New York Times* reporter, he had also written some speeches for President Eisenhower. That detail – I'm unsure of its provenance – might have thrown some people off the trail. Yet it is essential, in the understanding of Vidal, to know how conservative as well as how radical he can be.

Having been defeated in Dutchess County while outpolling the presidential leader of that ticket, Vidal was pressed by the party managers to try again. He was offered backing if he would contest the same House district, or perhaps if he would run for the Senate against Jacob Javits. Having scored a critical and commercial hit with his play *The Best Man* (still, in its celluloid form, the only enlightening movie ever made about an American party convention) and having outperformed JFK as a man of the people, Vidal evidently felt that he had squeezed the political lemon dry for that season, and told the emissaries from New York that he was off to either Athens or Rome, to write a novel about Julian the Apostate.

This could, in ordinary times, have been a *reculer pour mieux sauter*.

There seemed to be space and leisure enough, for Julian and, perhaps, for a return to the fray on the part of Senator Gore's grandson. But 'Camelot', as he would never have dreamed of calling it, was to be as ephemeral as it was tawdry, and the Republicans were to surpass his most sardonic predictions by nominating Barry Goldwater, and every law of unintended consequence was to combine to make 1964 a landslide year in which even Dutchess County, New York, went for the Democrats.

From a number of hints, scattered through his texts and footnotes, it is possible to intuit that Vidal has never quite forgiven himself or the Fates for this turn of events. Even the dullest imagination might feast for a moment or two on the might-have-been: Congressman Vidal, or even Senator Vidal, his blade flashing from its scabbard at the Tonkin Gulf resolution, or at the Chicago convention. If there sometimes seems to be a law – artfully adumbrated in *The Best Man* – that keeps intelligent or original men out of politics, there is no law that says that once in they have to leave. 'I have a house in Italy and a house in the Hollywood Hills,' Vidal once told an interviewer, 'so you could say that I don't live in America at all.' Our most eminent literary émigré – or is it exile? – has, ever since Julian and Dutchess County, surveyed his native heath with a mixture of loyalty, resignation, anxiety, and satirical distance, in which mixture is compounded a small but crucial element of bitterness.

Vidal has another quarrel with the past, which lies deeper and even further from redress. In the storming of Iwo Jima in March 1945, his first love Jimmy Trimble was among the young men flung into the breach to die. The story was not told to Vidal's audience until the publication of his memoir *Palimpsest* half a century later, though its combination of stoicism and sentiment had been prefigured in an essay the preceding year, where Vidal made elegiac use of the old torch song 'Don't Get Around Much Any More'. This junction of Eros and Thanatos with male bonding had also been strongly present through his thrice-rewritten postwar novel *The City and the Pillar*, where in one version Jim rapes Bob and in another kills him, but there were restraints upon confessional realism in 1948 (the *New York Times* neglected to take serious notice of Vidal's work for a few years afterwards). Having matured in the cask, so to say, the story is partly and more relaxedly retold in *The Smithsonian Institution*, with the emphasis this time on salvage and survival; nearer to the heart's desire.

The hero and protagonist of the novel – its title almost pancake-flat, as if to disguise its ludic quality – is T. And T. (he always comes with this punctuation, as if to be twice capitalised) is a golden youth from St Albans school in Washington, DC, in the spring of 1939. Innocent within and without, he has the gift of understanding the quantum and of producing mental simulacra in the field of relativity. He is thus both Trimble and Time. Italo Calvino once wrote of Vidal's fantasy-fictions, which include *Kalki*, *Duluth*, and *Live from Golgotha*, that they were manifestations of 'the hyper-novel or the novel elevated to the square or to the cube'. Not the least achievement of this apparently unstrenuous book is the way that it mobilises several dimensions of space and time without losing its narrative thread, and contrives to deploy a historical sense in tandem with an awareness of physics and biology: recent revelations about Jeffersonian DNA and the practicability of cloning are anticipated in the pages, which are a cocktail of magical realism, science fiction, and historical revisionism.

Hard to encapsulate? Not necessarily. Held in a time warp within the Smithsonian, T. is able to visit the past, to interview the waxwork assemblage of ex-presidents and first ladies, and to preview the future. It soon becomes evident that war is on the way, that this war will take his life, and that it – and everything else – will end with a nuclear detonation. The only way to avert all these undesirable outcomes is to derail the locomotive of history well back on its track. This in turn necessitates a judgement of taste as well as of mass – which past president could we most do without? From a strong field of contestants – most entertainingly reviewed – T. does what I would have done and culls Woodrow Wilson. At one stroke, with some judicious blackmail, he removes the most sanctimonious and – high-mindedness notwithstanding – the most warmongering of the chief executives.

Contact with Princeton, New Jersey, furthermore, invites intercourse with Albert Einstein and allows Vidal full use of a wondrous and yet disturbing coincidence from his own biography – which is that, even as he was bidding farewell to Jimmy Trimble, he had left their old school St Albans and moved to another in Los Alamos, New Mexico. (This establishment was also Alma Mater, if the term can be employed in such a connection, to William Burroughs.) Over the historical romp and political *lèse-majesté* is therefore superimposed the shadow of what we now call, though usually only when possessed or developed by others, 'weapons of mass destruction'.

Connoisseurs will encounter some old Vidal favourites, distributed as markers in the labyrinth. Joseph Kennedy turns up, in the role of bootlegger to some American Indians ('Great Hyannis Hyena', they call him). Benito Mussolini is rumoured to be hiding out in 'the Englewood, New Jersey area', a frequent resort of Vidal's when he wishes to poke fun at innocent but hirsute Italian-Americans. Mr Lincoln is rescued from Ford's theatre and allowed to become a sort of resident Polonius. The Great Lingam of the Washington Monument receives its due propitiation. For the succulent whiteness of his skin, T. receives the nickname 'Veal' from the waxwork Indians who come to life outside visiting hours, and one remembers the metaphorical stress that Vidal has often laid on this controversial dish. Counterintuitively, all the sex is both joyous and hetero, a blend found also in *The Judgment of Paris* but infrequently attempted elsewhere.

Lighthearted though the treatment may be, the novel is a frontal attack on the retrospective fatalism which makes us say World War I and World War II, and forget that the First was once called Great because it had no ensuing partner. Vidal is serious about stopping the Second, and not just for T.'s sake. He determines – first things first – that this involves preventing Mr Wilson's War. As a consequence, the 'war clouds' still 'gather' in 1939, but there is no Adolf Hitler on the scene. This might be described as the progressive use of anachronism. Also as a consequence – because Vidal has other loyalties from that period aside from Trimble – Colonel Charles Lindbergh, for example, whose Spirit of St Louis is a centerpiece of the Smithsonian, resumes his place as an American patriot. While Franklin Delano Roosevelt, freed to fight only in the Pacific against the Emperor of Japan (and the Emperor's American adviser, Lieutenant General Douglas MacArthur), makes plain his global ambitions in an address to all the ex-presidents. Roosevelt proposes a 90 percent corporate tax to fund the arsenal of democracy, not to say empire:

> 'Socialism,' said Coolidge. 'Confiscation!'
>
> 'Don't worry, Calvin. The corporations will get the money back – with interest – in government orders for more and more arms. Then there is the personal income tax. Never exactly popular. Mr. Lincoln got away with it in an emergency. But later the Supreme Court said it was unconstitutional. Of course, we got it back again, but, as of last year, only ten percent of the workforce paid income tax, some four million returns. Drop in the bucket, my friends. Well, now, to finance the war, everyone will be paying . . .'
>
> 'How're you gonna make them?' Coolidge was sharp.
>
> 'No problem. We have devised something called the withholding tax. We take the money out of their paychecks before they get them.'

When President Taft breaks in to say that this really would be confiscation and that the courts will never uphold him, Roosevelt replies serenely that 'the courts I'm appointing will take a different view', and that anyway America has 'the whole world ahead of us to do, as Mr. Harding would say, business in'. President Grant proposes a vote to back the President from Hyde Park to the hilt.

In microcosm, then, *The Smithsonian Institution* revisits and refines several Vidalian tropes. There is, first, his long-held view that 'entangling alliances' are death to republican virtue, and that they become domestic entanglements as well. This belief, that a warfare state may evolve into a domestic tyranny, was first set out at length in an essay published in the month of the first Kennedy assassination, and took the form of a review of Edmund Wilson's polemic of that year, *The Cold War and the Income Tax*. Discussing the half-buried tradition of American tax-resistance (also present in his tribute to Daniel Shays and the whiskey rebels), Vidal noted:

> The line between Thoreau and Poujade is a delicate one. Yet it is perfectly clear that it must one day be drawn if the United States is not to drift into a rigid Byzantine society where the individual is the state's creature (yes, liberals worry about this, too), his life the property of a permanent self-perpetuating bureaucracy . . .

Vidal claims that it was he, and not Milton Friedman, who first coined the satirical line about the symbiosis between state planning and corporate power: 'Socialism for the rich and free enterprise for the poor'. The line to note above, however, is about another kind of line – the one that separates Thoreau from Poujade. In his polemics against empire and interventionism and the overmighty state, Vidal has been careful to avoid the paranoid school: the old gang who used to cry that 'FDR knew' about the attack on Pearl Harbor, the ones who referred to the President as 'Frankie Rosenfeld' and who now cluster sadly around the memory of Harry Elmer Barnes and other occult practitioners of the nation's 'hidden' history. (He has never, to my knowledge, written anything about the more respectable and even less fashionable Charles and Mary Beard, whose work fell under a different sort of intellectual ban because they were out of step with the American Century; this is an omission one would love to see him someday repair.) In the same essay, though, he referred approvingly to Edmund Wilson as 'something of a cultural America Firster'. This is an early sounding of a note that was to get him repeatedly into trouble, and that continues to do so. In *The Smithsonian Institution*, this note is defiantly resumed in the affectionate portrait of Lindbergh, to which I want to recur later.

The other essential and familiar elements in the novel are Vidal's heterodox view of Abraham Lincoln; his tendency to overestimate the Japanese; his contempt for stay-at-home patriots; his interest in the historical role of first lady; and his belief – derived as much as anything from Lucretius and *De Rerum Naturum* – that nature and philosophy, and the relation between atoms and infinity, are much fitter studies, and greatly more awe-inspiring and respect-deserving, than any religion.

In selecting for his Vidal 'reader', which serves as part prelude to his forthcoming authorised biography, Professor Fred Kaplan has enforced a distinction between Vidal the fabulist, Vidal the novelist and screenwriter, Vidal the historian, and Vidal the essayist. His choices are excellently made, and are partitioned by well-wrought passages of introduction from both editor and author. The interest and pleasure, though, derive largely from the blending effect, from what Vidal (who never attended any university) would certainly scorn to call the multi-cultural or the interdisciplinary. As he puts it here in a dismissive review of some overlong and overrespectful biography of Truman, there was a time when historians knew they were also composing literature. The corollary – why should not a litterateur be writing history? – would have been obvious before the age of specialisation overtook us. Even as it was, Vidal was able in his *Lincoln* to offer a portrait with background of 'The Ancient', to speculate with profit (and with evidence) about his racial and sexual attitudes, and to provoke a *Historikerstreit* among the academics of the post-Sandburg school, from which he emerged with distinction.

Here is the closing stave of Kaplan's selection from the novel. Lincoln has survived an attempt to impeach him – for violating the law and the Constitution in the matter of habeas corpus – but not an attempt to assassinate him:

> 'I have been writing, lately, about the German first minister.' Mr. Schuyler was thoughtful. 'In fact, I met him at Biarritz last summer when he came to see the emperor. Curiously enough, he has now done the same thing to Germany that you tell us Mr. Lincoln did to our country. Bismarck has made a single, centralised nation out of all the other German states.'
>
> Hay nodded; he, too, had noted the resemblance. 'Bismarck would also give the vote to people who have never had it before.'
>
> 'I think', said Mr. Schuyler to the princess, 'we have here a subject – Lincoln and Bismarck, and new countries for old.'
>
> 'It will be interesting to see how Herr Bismarck ends his career,' said Hay, who was now more than ever convinced that Lincoln, in some mysterious fashion, had willed his own murder as a form of atonement for the great and terrible thing that he had done by giving so bloody and absolute a rebirth to his nation.

The implication could not be plainer – the *unum* comes at the expense of the *pluribus*, and war is the health of the state, and the cost is often not counted. In *Lincoln* John Hay is the secretary to 'The Ancient' and the constant companion of John Nicolay. By the time of *Empire*, published only three years later, in 1987, he is teamed up with Henry Adams and the 'wounds' of the War Between the States are being heartily bound up by a joint all-American expedition against Cuba and the Philippines.

> He was Colonel Hay just as the President was always Major McKinley. But the President had actually seen action under his mentor, Ohio's politician-general Rutherford B. Hayes, whose own mentor had been yet another politician-general, James Garfield, and Hay's dear friend, as well. . . . Now, of

course, all the political generals from Grant to Garfield were dead; the
colonels were on the shelf; and the majors had come into their own. After
them, no more military-titled politicians. Yet every American war had bred at
least one president. Who, Hay wondered, would the splendid little war – oh,
fatuous phrase! – bring forth? Adams favored General Miles, the brother-in-
law of his beloved Lizzie Cameron. Lodge had already declared that Admiral
Dewey's victory at Manila was equal to Nelson's at Aboukir. But of course
Lodge would support McKinley, who would be reelected; and so there would
be no splendid little war-hero president in the foreseeable future.

Thus does Vidal slyly prepare the entrance of his least favourite
character, the prancing figure of 'Teddy' Roosevelt. His evocation of
political culture in Washington, sustained now through seven novels,
depends upon a high skill in depicting two sorts of personage – the
sinuous and flattering courtier and the military-imperial braggart, the
latter often being more of a secret sissy than the former. Note that
in his recommendation of Edmund Wilson Vidal characterised the
military-commercial nexus of state power as 'Byzantine': he was in the
midst of composing *Julian* when he wrote that.

Julian, which is his literary masterpiece in my opinion, takes place in
the world of fourth-century Romanism, when the capital has been
moved by the Christian convert Constantine to Constantinople. Julian's
cousin Constantius has succeeded Constantine. As pictured by Vidal,
the vicious court oscillates between intriguing eunuchs and boastful
tyrants who believe in the domino theory of empire:

> 'The empire is big. Distances are great. Our enemies many. . . . I mean to
> hold the state together. I shall not sacrifice one city to the barbarians, one
> town, one field!' The high-pitched voice almost cracked.

And here, for comparison purposes, is Brooks Adams trumpeting the
murder of McKinley and the ascension of 'TR' in *Empire*:

> 'Teddy's got it all now! Do you realise that he occupies a place greater than
> Trajan's at the high noon of the Roman empire?' Brooks, like his brother,
> never spoke when he could lecture. 'There has never been so much power
> given a man at so propitious a time in history! He will have the opportunity
> – and the means – to subjugate all Asia, and so give America the hegemony
> of the earth, which is our destiny, written in stars! Also', Brooks came to
> earth with a crash, 'today is a day of great importance to Daisy and me. It is
> our wedding anniversary.'
> 'History does seem to have us by the throat,' said Lizzie mildly.

Brooks Adams really did speak – and write – like that: the near-Wildean
bathos is, however, furnished by the author.

The occluded hero of *Julian* is the Greek philosopher Libanius, who
rejects the regimentation and superstition of Christianity (Julian refers

to Christian churches as 'charnel-houses' for their disgusting practice of keeping moldering remains as objects of veneration) and who wants to keep open the schools of disputation. He helps narrate the story of what emerges as the last battle to preserve the sunlit ancient world.

Vidal's nostalgia for the polytheistic or pagan Mediterranean has been a constant since his boyhood reading, and rivals that of Mary Renault in its fidelity to period and texture. But it usually avoids the vulgarity of romanticism; does not repeat the Christian error of imagining an ideal state before the fall. In *Creation* he takes a very detached and sometimes caustic view of fifth-century Athens – the golden age itself – by adopting the perspective of a sightless envoy named Cyrus, giving what Robert Graves in another connection called 'the Persian version'. Cyrus is a descendant of Zoroaster and has voyaged to India and Cathay and seen the roots of Tao, Confucius, and Buddha. There is, to him, something provincial and coarse about Athens:

> It is my view that despite the basic conservatism of Athenian people when it comes to maintaining the forms of old things, the essential spirit of these people is atheistic – or as a Greek cousin of mine pointed out not long ago, with dangerous pride, man is the measure of all things. I think that in their hearts the Athenians truly believe this to be true. As a result, paradoxically, they are uncommonly superstitious and strictly punish those who are thought to have committed impiety.

Iconoclast as he may be, Vidal does not imagine that the breaking of idols is a sufficient or necessary condition of emancipation. There is much to be feared from zeal of all kinds, especially the puritan variety. Interestingly enough, he does not follow Mary Renault and other writers in making the ancient world a location for the polymorphous perverse. He merely takes note of the fact that sexual love between men and men or women and women was not, in that formative period of 'Western' civilisation, considered either abnormal or profane.

The proselytizing for – maybe I should say his justification of – intersexuality is reserved for his modern entertainments and his essays. In *Myra Breckenridge* (I still feel for poor, straight, violated Rusty sometimes) he introduces a phrase which often recurs and which he employs as an all-purpose satire on monogamy and on same-sex discipline: 'I'll tell you who I was thinking of if you'll tell me who you were thinking of.' As Myra thoughtfully puts it, exploring the implications of this offer:

> It is curious how often the male (and sometimes the female) needs to think of those not present in the act. Even with Myron, I was always imagining someone else, a boy glimpsed at Jones Beach or a man observed briefly at the wheel of a truck or sometimes (yes, I may as well confess it) a slender blonde girl that used to live in the brownstone next door.

In his 1966 essay 'Pornography' (not reprinted here) Vidal opened one of the most polished of his reflections on masturbation – a topic on which he's been out front and done the hard thinking for all of us – by writing:

> The man and the woman make love; attain climax; fall separate. Then she whispers, 'I'll tell you who I was thinking of if you'll tell me who you were thinking of.' . . . For those who find the classic positions of 'mature' love-making unsatisfactory yet dare not distress the beloved with odd requests, sexual fantasy becomes inevitable and the shy lover soon finds himself imposing mentally all sorts of wild images upon his unsuspecting partner, who may also be relying on an inner theater of the mind to keep things going; in which case those popular writers who deplore 'our lack of communication today' may have a point.

And in 1991, in a piece of sparkling pedagogy which is collected by Kaplan ('The Birds and the Bees'), Vidal reviewed the current literature on sexual fantasy and concluded, in an image of indelible and electrifying gruesomeness:

> Actually, the percentage of the population that is deeply enthusiastic about other-sex is probably not much larger than those exclusively devoted to same-sex – something like 10 percent in either case.
>
> The remaining 80 percent does this, does that, does nothing; settles into an acceptable if dull social role where the husband dreams of Barbara Bush while pounding the old wife, who lies there, eyes shut, dreaming of Barbara too.

And here is another topic on which our author has done some hard thinking: the tricky concept of First Lady. He was a confidante of Eleanor Roosevelt. He was stepbrother to Jacqueline Bouvier Kennedy Onassis. Lady Bird Johnson and Pat Nixon and Rosalynn Carter were, in sooth, not his type, though I like to think he might have hit it off with game old Betty Ford. But, picking up the thread, about Nancy Reagan he was always deft and perceptive. From observing her, and from an understanding of her Hollywood background, he guessed early what few observers – and almost no intellectuals – ever allowed themselves to believe, namely that this devoted couple was White House-bound. ('The Late Show', September 1968, his report on the Republican National Convention). And now – having advised Jerry Brown during the 1992 primaries – he has emerged as a defender of Hillary Clinton. Some may prefer to see, in this alliance, an attempt to thwart any premature accession by the distant cousin Al Gore, whose warm connection to the editor of *The New Republic* is seen as fetid and ominous from the Ravello standpoint. Or it may be, as Vidal put it in a recollection of Eleanor Roosevelt in 1971, that:

It is a curious fact of American political life that the right wing is enamored of the sexual smear. Eleanor to me: 'There are actually people in Hyde Park who knew Franklin all his life and said that he did not have polio but the sort of disease you get from not living the right sort of life.'

The left wing plays dirty pool, too, but I have no recollection of their having organised whispering campaigns of a sexual nature against Nixon, say, the way the right wing so often does against liberal figures.

Or – to be scrupulously fair – the way that Vidal himself made a guess about Nixon in *The Best Man* ('When I based the character of the wicked candidate in the play on Richard Nixon, I thought it would be amusing if liberal partisans were to smear unjustly that uxorious man as a homosexual'). Later in the same very moving essay – Mrs Roosevelt had been among his champions in the Dutchess County campaign in 1960, and shared his own reservations about what he calls the Holy Family from Hyannisport – he recounts:

> She was also indifferent to her own death. 'I remember Queen Wilhelmina when she came to visit during the war' (good democrat that she was, nothing royal was alien to Eleanor) 'and she would sit under a tree on the lawn and commune with the dead. She would even try to get me interested in spiritualism but I always said: Since we're going to be dead such a long time anyway it's rather a waste of time chatting with all of them before we get there'.

This of course was written before the current First Lady confided to a therapist friend that she sometimes 'channeled' Eleanor Roosevelt from the private quarters. And before Vidal himself wrote, of that same Eleanor's husband:

> Certainly, he hurt her mortally in their private relationship; worse, he often let her down in their public partnership. Yet she respected his cunning even when she deplored his tactics.

Vidal shows the same gallant curiosity in his historical fictions, making rather a subject out of the distraught Mrs Lincoln for example, and even showing President McKinley in a more human light for his indulgence toward Clara, whose face had to be covered with a napkin during spasms of *petit mal* in mixed company, and whose unscripted irruptions into conversation are rendered drily in *Empire* as familiar signs that 'her unconscious had joined the party'.

Professor Kaplan's careful selection avoids repetition, and it is in any case one of Vidal's achievements as a writer that he can recur to a favoured subject many times without repeating himself. Three Vidalian commitments seem to undergird what he writes on any topic. The first is the curse of monotheism: enemy of pleasure and foe of rational inquiry. The second is the blight of sexual stereotyping. (He insists that acts, not persons, are homo- or heterosexual.) The third is the awful temptation of America to meddling and blundering overseas: imperialism, to give it the right name.

This Trinity sometimes becomes One in his polemics, and is the reason why Vidal has often been pelted with dead dogs by certain critics. In two major public combats with the spousal team of Norman Podhoretz and Midge Decter, Vidal has asserted that an uncritical pro-Israeli allegiance supplies some of the advocacy for US interventionism, and also that ancient moral creeds from primitive Palestinian sects are at the root of much of our libidinous discontent. This version of the Trinity has exposed him to his own private screening of *Live from Golgotha*. Not to mince words, he has been accused of the unpardonable offence of anti-Semitism: a charge of which no decent or serious person can even be suspected.

This accusation is, in my opinion, malicious as well as nonsensical. (One might try a brief thought-experiment: Vidal has written for years about an unelected and secretive 'permanent government' in Washington. Almost all those he cites – many of them from personal acquaintance or experience – are from what used to be termed the WASP establishment.) Vidal knows as well as anybody else, better than most in fact, that most American Jews are liberal on foreign policy matters and moreover opposed to theocracy in both Israel and the United States. When literal Mosaic precepts are thundered today, they come carefully packaged as Judeo-Christian.

No true admirer should press caution or restraint on Mr Vidal (it would be to miss the point, somehow), but for this admirer that leaves only one quarrel unresolved It concerns some aspects of isolationism. And this returns us to the ambivalent figure – featured positively in both the fiction and the nonfiction – of Charles Lindbergh.

Vidal's fealty here is not in the first instance a political one: his adored father was an inaugurator of American civil aviation (the essay to consult in this collection is entitled 'On Flying', and remains one of his best-observed glimpses of Americana, as well as a rather fine and unembarrassing evocation of filial love). In the pioneer winged cohort of the interwar years (that grey area again), 'Lindy' was someone to tip your hat to. However, successor generations have learned to think of Lindbergh and 'America First' as protofascist. And here is how Vidal approached the question when reviewing Scott Berg's excellent biography of Lindbergh in the *Times Literary Supplement* last October:

> In a notorious speech at Des Moines in 1941, he identified America's three interventionist groups: the Roosevelt administration, the Jews and the British. Although the country was deeply isolationist, the interventionists were very resourceful, and Lindbergh was promptly attacked as a pro-Nazi anti-Semite

when he was no more than a classic Midwestern isolationist, reflective of a majority of the country. But along with such noble isolationists as Norman Thomas and Burton K. Wheeler, not to mention Lindbergh's friend Harry Guggenheim's foundation, the 'America First' movement, as it was called, did attract some genuine home-grown fascists who would have been amazed to learn that there was never a 'Jewish plot' to get the United States into the Second World War. Quite the contrary. Before Pearl Harbor, as Berg notes, 'though most of the American motion-picture studios were owned by Jews, most were virtually paranoid about keeping pro-Jewish sentiment off the screen'. Also, Arthur Hayes Sulzberger, publisher of the *New York Times*, confided as late as September 1941 to the British Special Operations Executive agent Valentine Williams 'that for the first time in his life he regretted being a Jew because, with the tide of anti-Semitism rising, he was unable to champion the anti-Hitler policy of the administration as vigorously as he would like, as his sponsorship would be attributed to Jewish influence by isolationists and thus lose something of its force'.

Everything stated above is uncontroversial, and could probably have been put with even more emphasis. But there is an elision of which Vidal seems unaware. If Hollywood studios and New York publishers, neither of them exactly divorced from the pulses of public opinion, were so impressed by the anti-Semitic element in isolationism as to fall into a defensive or reticent posture, then one must ask: At whose expense is this supposed irony? Where did 'the tide' come from? When Vidal says 'quite the contrary', he is saying correctly that there was no Jewish plot. But his supporting evidence is that there was no Jewish plot because even the most Establishment Jews were in real dread of anti-Semitic populism. This won't do as an acquittal of 'America First'.

But nor will it do as an insinuation of prejudice on the part of Vidal. I once came almost to tears in an argument with him about Bosnia. He lives much nearer Sarajevo than most Americans, and can also tell the difference between Dacia and Dalmatia, yet nothing would persuade him that such a crisis was any business of the United States, or had not somehow been overstated by the pundits of the Committee for the Free World, or On the Present Danger. It would have been otiose to accuse him of anti-Muslim bigotry, just as (to take up the missing term in Lindbergh's triad of 'enemies within') it would have been absurd to accuse Vidal of harbouring anti-English feeling in 1941.

The ironic mode is Vidal's metier, and for all I know he has felt ironic nudges from history ever since graduating from short to long pants at Los Alamos, and then becoming a sailor on the Arctic front of an imperialist war that was nonetheless fought for freedom. Certainly he knows the least tinge of irony when he sees it. Richard Nixon, when asked to what use he would put the auditorium in his dreadful presidential 'library', said that it should be employed to re-enact 'great debates like – oh, Vidal and Buckley'. This of course delights our author. But here, too, the irony is reciprocal. When Vidal and Buckley almost grappled in Chicago, and exchanged views on appeasement, fascism, faggotry, anti-Semitism, they were at least momentarily obliged to overlook, even to forget, the main thing they had in common, which was their families' feeling for the 'America First' tradition.

It is perhaps some unresolved confusion on this score, even now, that causes Vidal to reprint his least prescient essay ('The Day the American Empire Ran Out of Gas', 1986), in which the flag of the Rising Sun is again hoist, this time in the sign of the triumphant yen, not merely over Mount Suribachi and the hecatombs of Iwo Jima but over the Federal Reserve. Could it be that émigré/exile status sometimes prompts a slight, overcompensating twinge of the provincial?

But Gore Vidal's real debt is not to any nativist counterpart like William Jennings Bryan or even – specialised affinities to one side – Charles Lindbergh. If he were 'only' an American, he could have imbibed from the wells of Mark Twain and H. L. Mencken, commingling and contradicting both at once. Like Twain and Mencken, hostile to empire and especially sulphurous about the missionary element. Like Twain but unlike Mencken, warm towards the Southern states and their odd, durable patrimony. Like Mencken and unlike Twain, a protector and patron of neglected or fragile reputations (Dawn Powell, Thornton Wilder). Like both Twain and Mencken, contemptuous of both Old and New Testaments.

Yet Vidal is inescapably cosmopolitan. A cosmopolitan within America – early Southern exposure, at home in Washington, DC, likewise on the Hudson, in Hollywood, on Broadway, even briefly at Hyannisport – and also a cosmopolitan in the customary sense of assimilation and ease in London, Rome, Paris. (There is even, in *Palimpsest*, the merest suggestion of a Sephardic and Venetian trace in his line.) Dutchess County, even when a rising tide was lifting all Democrats, would have been too small a compass for this versatility. So indeed might Washington have been. These losses are our gain: a writer standing at an acute angle to his subject, and making imperishable sentences as well as – no less a pleasure, one suspects – passing and pronouncing them.

First published as 'The Cosmopolitan Man' (a review of *The Essential Gore Vidal* edited by Fred Kaplan and *The Smithsonian Institution: A Novel* by Gore Vidal) in *New York Review of Books*, 22 April 1999

After-Time

I recently paid a solemn and respectful visit to Gore Vidal's grave. It is to be found in Rock Creek Cemetery in Washington. You take a few paces down the slope from the graveyard's centrepiece, which is the lachrymose and androgynous *Mourning Figure* sculpted by August St Gaudens for Henry Adams's unhappy wife Clover (whose name always puts me in mind of an overworked pit pony). And there in the grass is a stone slab, bearing the names and dates of birth of Vidal and his lifelong companion Howard Auster. The hyphens that come after the years (1925 and 1928 respectively) lie like little marble asps waiting to keep their dates. Who knows what decided the cemetery authorities to advertise their prospective clients in this way? Elsewhere among the crosses and headstones one may find Upton Sinclair, Nobel Laureate and defeated Socialist candidate for the governorship of California, Alice Warfield Allen (mother of Wallis Simpson) and Alice Roosevelt Longworth, *grande dame* of Washington dynastic bitchery. (She had a motto emblazoned on her sofa-cushion in Georgetown. 'If you can't think of anything nice to say about anybody come and sit by me.') A clutch of Supreme Court Justices, political bosses and Civil War generals completes the roll. And all this seems fitting for Vidal: radical candidate in a California Senate race, collector and generator of gossip from the exile Windsors and the Georgetown ladies, and master in novel form of the Washington of Henry Adams, John Hay and Teddy Roosevelt.

Or is it so fitting? On second thoughts, is not Vidal a natural for the Protestant Cemetery in Rome, hard by Keats and Shelley and Gramsci and Labriola, and sheltered, in serene pagan and Mediterranean style, by the pyramid of Sestius? What is an exile cosmopolitan doing in this WASP rockery in the District of Columbia? Even before *Palimpsest*, it was possible for close readers of Vidal's fiction to make a shrewd guess. The following passage in the confessedly autobiographical *Two Sisters*, published a quarter of a century ago, supplies one clue. The narrator is set off by a recollection of Henry James, who, after fifty years remembered 'a boy cousin being sketched in the nude at Newport before his life was "cut short, in a cavalry clash, by one of the Confederate bullets of 1863"'.

Death, summer, youth – this triad contrives to haunt me every day of my life for it was in summer that my generation left school for war, and several dozen that one knew (but strictly speaking, did not love, except perhaps for one) were killed, and so never lived to know what I have known – the Beatles, black power, the Administration of Richard Nixon – all this has taken place in a trivial after-time and has nothing to do with anything that really mattered, with summer and someone hardly remembered, a youth so abruptly translated from vivid, well-loved (if briefly) flesh to a few scraps of bone and cartilage scattered among the volcanic rocks of Iwo Jima. So much was cruelly lost and one still mourns the past, particularly in darkened movie houses, weeping at bad films, or getting drunk alone while watching the *Late Show* on television as our summer's war is again refought and one sees something that seems to be a familiar face in the battle scenes – is it Jimmie?

A couple of years ago, Vidal dropped another hint in an article looking back on the Pacific war. He said that he gave way to emotion on hearing, even now, the song that goes:

> Missed the Saturday dance
> Heard they crowded the floor
> Couldn't face it without you
> Don't get around much any more.

And then, going back almost to the beginning, there was the matter of those initials on the dedication page of *The City and the Pillar*. This homoerotic drama, Vidal's second novel, won him attention and execration in about equal measure. The dedicatee was one 'J.T.' Just a few feet away from that marble slab in Rock Creek, one can discover a small grey stone with the inscription 'James Trimble III. 1925–1945 Iwo Jima'. And here the quest is over. Vidal intends to be buried as near as he can be to his first and only love, who played the saxophone and shone on the playing-fields and whose anthem for doomed youth is in the refrain of 'Don't Get Around Much Any More': a combination of *Whitman's Leaves of Grass* and the more candid letters of Wilfred Owen. *Palimpsest* fills in the blanks. For half a century, Gore Vidal has been living selfishly and hedonistically, because all this time he has been living for two. It is via the Jimmy Trimble romance that the madeleine of these memoirs is unwrapped, and it is with that incomplete or uncompleted love that it closes. Along the way, it is the thread of Ariadne in the narrative. Vidal has written often and well about himself and others. In fact, he has written better. The chief enchantment of this book has not to do with the celebrated dustups between himself and Mailer, himself and Capote, himself and Tennessee Williams, or himself and William Buckley. Rather, we learn, not without preceding markers but in many ways for the first time, about Vidal's family and about the Kennedy branch of it. We come to understand how divided a self he is; not just as between love and death but as between literature and politics, America and the world, the ancient and the modern, the sacred and the profane. And we get the goods not just about his sex life, but about his sexual nature.

To get the beastliness out of the way first, then. In his rather sere and melancholy condition, Vidal tells some old stories rather less well than he recounted them the first time. Of a disastrous visit to Cambridge, provoked by an invitation from E. M. Forster that had been meant for Tennessee Williams:

> Forster's look of disappointment was disheartening. But, dutifully, he took me on a tour. We crossed the river to the chapel, which I coldly termed 'pretty', thus disheartening *him*.

Now from an essay ('On Prettiness', written for the *New Statesman* in 1978):

> As we approached the celebrated chapel (magnificent, superb, a bit much) I said, 'Pretty'. Forster thought that I meant the chapel when, actually, I was referring to a youthful couple in the middle distance. A ruthless moralist, Forster publicised my use of the dread word. Told in Fitzrovia and published in the streets of Dacca, the daughters of the Philistines rejoiced; the daughters of the uncircumcised triumphed.

Of these two versions, the second and earlier is the more spirited and (frightful dangler in the last sentence notwithstanding) the better-written. But in *Palimpsest*, much of which is set down in a terse, almost shorthand style, we learn that Forster had been cruel as a cat to Christopher Isherwood the night before, that he had sucked up to Williams in a queenly manner and that, in the opinion of 'The Bird' (Vidal's usual term for Tennessee's person of plumage and flutter), he was an old gentleman 'with urine-stained flies'. Thus the newer version is more instructive and nearer to the nitty, if not indeed the actual gritty. In a letter to Jack Kerouac in April 1952, William Burroughs demanded to know: 'Is Gore Vidal queer or not?' Burroughs, who had once been at the same boys' boarding-school as Vidal, can now slake his curiosity. Or he could have pressed Kerouac himself, as Vidal certainly did almost a year later:

> At what might be nicely called loose ends, we rubbed bellies for a while; later he would publish a poem dedicated to me: 'Didn't know I was a pat come-onner, did you? (come-on-er).' I was not particularly touched by this belated Valentine, considering that I finally flipped him over on his stomach. Jack raised his head from the pillow to look at me over his shoulder.

Come, now, this is more like it. And it also supplies part of the answer to Burroughs's question. Vidal is not a pillow-biter or a mattress-

muncher. Nor does he suck. I once heard him declaim: 'I don't want
penises near me. I have *no* plans for them.' It should by now be
unnecessary to draw the reader a picture. Is he queer? Or is he on to
something in saying that there are no homosexual people, only homosexual acts? The memoir also details many encounters with women,
usually of the theatre like Diana Lynn, but also of the bar and the café
and, in the case of Anaïs Nin, of the world of heterosexual narcissism.
None of these matches is rekindled in order to prove any defensive
point. Since Jimmie's death, sex and love have been blissfully de-
coupled. What might have arrested the development of some has
emancipated it in our author. Though, as he commissions researchers
to inspect the minutest reminiscence of Jimmie's short life and hard
death, and as he discovers breakdowns and traumas among the boys
and girls and even schoolmasters who knew the golden lad in real time,
one wonders. In a last letter home from the Pacific, Jimmie asked his
mother to send him some Walt Whitman poems. And Vidal wants very
much, still, to know who it was that recommended this front-line
reading to the hoplite. Is that a proof of an unsentimental carapace?

At various other points in the story, also, he makes himself out to be
slightly more emotion-proof than I would guess he really is. The
depiction of family life is amusing, often sideholdingly so, but must
have been extremely gruelling at the time. To *fear* one's mother, a
drink-sodden bag of malice and conspiracy, may have accelerated the
growing-up process and been useful in the dispelling of illusion, but
still ... Here is an account of mama's supposed *mariage blanc* to the
rich footler Hugh ('Hughdie') Auchincloss:

> I should note that the only advantage for a child in having an alcoholic
> parent is that you acquire, prematurely, quite a bit of valuable data. Appar-
> ently, there was going to be Sex whether Nina liked it or not. She did not
> like it. But then no woman could have liked Hughdie's importunate fum-
> blings. He ejaculated normally but without that precedent erection which
> women require as, if nothing else, totemic symbol of a man's true love not
> to mention a homely source of hedonistic friction. Since Hughdie wanted
> children, Nina was obliged in some fashion that she, on several occasions in
> her admittedly never-long-empty cups, vividly described to me and I would
> promptly erase from memory. I *think* she inserted – with a spoon? – what she
> called 'the bugs', in order to create my demi-siblings.

Here is Hamlet contemplating 'the nasty sty' but without an ounce of
feeling for either mother or stepfather. (His unaffected liking for his
father, an innovator in the age of aerospace and an ornament of FDR's
Government, is one of the charms of the book.) But who would not
have preferred to flee the home of fetid sex, booze and old money and
embrace the clean limbs of Jimmie? The memoir is partly diaristic and

at intervals loops back to the writing-desk at Ravello and to the present day. As often as not, this is to update us on a recent lunch with Jimmie's mother, with a letter from a long-lost trench mate on Iwo Jima, or with further bulletins from research into Jimmie's girlfriends and boy-friends. The love supplies a refuge from the everyday now, as indeed it must have done then.

From his grandfather, the sightless Senator Thomas Gore of Oklahoma (common ancestor with the current Vice-President, whom Vidal refuses to meet because of his connection to Martin Peretz's plaything, the *New Republic*), the boy became steeped in American political lore and in the unending battle between 'We the People' and the robber barons and malefactors of great wealth. Engaged as a reader to the blind old man, he also became an omnivorous consumer of books and lover of libraries. Here again, there is a sentimental ambiva-lence which is registered rather than resolved. Vidal knows that much American populist talk, with its loud affectation about the common man, is bullshit. He even back-chatted the old senator about it: ' "When I was young, cheese and crackers was one word to me," he used to say, emphasising his poverty. Bored with this repetition, I am said to have responded, at the age of six or so: "Well, ice cream and cake are one word to me." ' Not only is this a precociously Wildean remark and just the sort of thing that one writes a mcmoir in order to record, but it was a perfectly apt rejoinder to a wearisome pose. Yet not much later, Vidal writes approvingly that 'for Gore and the other populists, the imperialism of the two Roosevelts and Woodrow Wilson–Polk, too, earlier – was a terrible distraction from our destiny, which was the perfection of our own unusual if not, in the end, particularly "excep-tional" society'. The let-down at the end of that sentence is one that I wish he would pursue. He expounds at length his view of the war and foreign entanglement as a racket run by the Morgans and Rockefellers, and recounts with some relish his student campaigns for 'America First' in the run-up to the Second World War. Yet when he writes about his years in Guatemala in the Fifties (setting for *Dark Green, Bright Red*), he admits to great shock at the discovery of what American intervention in the southern hemisphere had really been like. Now, Williams Jennings Bryan and Colonel Lindbergh had not been opposed to the Monroe Doctrine or to the American empire: they had been opposed to American engagement in Europe. Moreover, the sort of 'America First' isolationists who managed to be for war in China and Nicaragua but not in defence of the Spanish Republic or Czechoslovakia were exactly the kind of people who would have had *The City and the Pillar* burned by the public hangman. Vidal, most cosmopolitan and interna-tionalist of American novelists, is in bizarre company when he views Europe as the polluter of American native innocence.

It is more honest to say, as he does, that the whole Second World War was not worth Jimmie's life. This is oddly reminiscent of his friend Isherwood's view that one could not risk harming a lover (admittedly a lover who would have been serving in the Wehrmacht) for any grand strategic consideration. But *Williwaw* is actually a rather fine novel of the American wartime and, though one agrees with Vidal's retrospective opinion that it is written in somewhat carpentered prose, it remains a source of pride to him to this day, and was at the time a healthy source of rivalry between himself, Norman Mailer and James Jones. There is no reason for him not to try and have this both ways, like so much else. But that would mean noticing that he was trying to do so. In a way that is not perhaps quite dissimilar, Vidal returns again and again to his contempt for the life of the American professional politician. He saw it up close when young. He saw it up close in the Kennedy era. He has the lugubrious example of young cousin Al always before him. Yet he knows he could have been a player, and he still likes to tell of the advice he gave to Jerry Brown as late as the 1992 Democratic primaries. It could of course be a luxury to be in his position. How wonderful to have been able to compose this paragraph, for example, about that hideous Palace of Culture that still squats – appropriately next to the Watergate building – on the banks of the Potomac: 'The Kennedy Centre, a real-estate metaphor for the arts in America'.

> As a member of the Advisory Council on the Arts (my advice had been, Don't built the centre), I was in the groundbreaking. The Kennedys were all on display. Hughdie and Janet, too. President Johnson wore a white camel's hair coat and a suit of rich green never before seen on a first magistrate, or perhaps anywhere else on earth. He shovelled the dirt with casual contempt, more Kennedy grave digger than keeper of the flame.

Vidal ran, not on the Kennedy ticket but with the somewhat sluggish Kennedy tide, for Congress in a reactionary district of upstate New York in 1960. With some rather feline help from Eleanor Roosevelt – who never trusted JFK – he came marvellously close to winning. Pressed to try again, or even to try for the Senate, he declined. In 1964, the year of the donkey *par excellence*, his mediocre Democrat successor was lifted into the seat by the LBJ surge. Can Vidal really say with complete composure that he is delighted not to have been that man? Clues in the text, and in other texts, suggest not. He could have been the perfect inside/outside Washington Congressman, who was needed by his own party managers more than he needed them. (Not for nothing was he a friend of Tom Driberg, whose own non-political needs also made him the perfect division-of-labour cruising companion.) Vidal has spoken elsewhere of never missing a sexual trick, and of not having to decline in years while brooding over the lost chance of this one and that one. I suspect that he still wishes he had given the rough trade of Congress a fair shake.

But in general, what a blessed life. Right places at right times. Sound bets made on the writing possibilities offered by Broadway and Hollywood, in both of which he shone while shining was still possible in those dark mills. Then, having succumbed to boredom but having proved that he could make his own way, off to Rome to write *Julian*. And a good companion, Howard Austen, of whom he says (twice) that the secret of their domestic felicity is – and has ever been – a strict 'No Sex' rule. (On the gravestone in Rock Creek Cemetery, Howard is incised as 'Howard Auster', the New York Jewish name that stopped him getting a job in advertising until Vidal proposed a one-letter amendment. How nice that such a deft piece of editing should have made such a difference, and how nice also that it is restored to the original when the lapidary question comes up. 'They say I'm anti-Semitic,' Vidal once intoned with sweet mockery in Howard's presence. 'Every morning I breakfast with someone who looks more every day like – *like Golda Meir!*')

There are some excellent phrases, though Vidal prefers to think of himself as 'making sentences'. He says that he tortured his mother 'with heartless kindness'. Seeing Henry Kissinger in the Sistine Chapel at an American Academy soirée, and noticing his gaping at the Hell section of *The Last Judgment,* he observes: 'Look, he's apartment-hunting.' Campaigning in 1960, he comes up against the titanic subsidies paid to the farm interest and quips about 'socialism for the rich and free enterprise for the poor', which I think pre-empts Milton Friedman as author of that essential line about the way we live now. There is also a pregnant observation borrowed by Vidal from his post-war visits to the monkish cell of George Santayana. He judges the author of *Egotism in German Philosophy* to have been an opponent of fanaticism rather than an anti-Semite, and cites his critique of Fichte's and Hegel's propaganda (about German destiny) as 'the heir of Judaism'. In the continuing quarrel between Vidal and the Podhoretz school of New York neo-conservative Zionism, I have heard Vidal defended as someone who doesn't dislike organised Jewry *an sich* but who a. blames the Zionists for keeping the militarist and interventionist home fires burning and b. blames Judaism for leading to monotheism: and the militant Pauline theology of heterosexual and repressive 'family values'. So here is a new take, which by no means invalidates the earlier ones (especially when you reflect on what family did to, and for, Vidal). Podhoretz, I always thought, made his fatal mistake when he accused Vidal not of being anti-Semitic but of being anti-American. The blood of the clan was thereby aroused. Vidal, chronicler of the Civil War and the birth of America, was just not going to take this from someone who once said that the battlefields of Gettysburg and Bull Run were as remote to him 'as the War of the Roses'. If you don't want tribalism, in other words, don't incite it. Rather in the way that he doesn't care about his bad reviews while remembering every last one of them, Vidal maintains indifference to the charge of anti-Semitism and includes a learned piece of genealogy which strongly suggests that he is, by virtue of his ancient surname, not unconnected with *converso* or *marrano* lineage. Could be. The fact is that Vidal is and was one of the few 'gentiles' – ghastly term – to have written for *Partisan Review, Commentary* and the *Nation* in their heroic periods (when he also made his most surprising friend – Saul Bellow) and would be better off protesting not at all about such a cheap and politicised slander.

The finest and most revealing passages in *Palimpsest*, those which best synthesise the public and the personal, are the ones which treat of the Kennedy court. It's a test of character whether one repudiates Camelot or not, and Vidal passes this test with all pennons flying. (He even admits, with a moue of distaste, having helped deceive Richard Rovere as early as 1960 about Kennedy suffering, as he obviously did, from the disabling ravages of Addisons disease.) For this and other services to power and family and deceit, the triptych under review, he is properly contrite. His description of a vacation spent in the Kennedy compound at Hyannis, at the time of the bogus crisis over Berlin, is a real document of tawdriness and vulgarity and opportunism. Jack and Bobby argue about which of them first hilariously called James Baldwin 'Martin Luther Queen'. Portentous and shallow power-worship pervades the scene, and it becomes appallingly clear that JFK himself can only be interested or excited by risky and violent and gamey solutions to the boredom and impotence which he is already feeling. Young 'Bobby' appears in the character of an envious thug, anxious to please and eager to show that he is no faggot (an impression which Rudolf Nureyev elsewhere slyly revises). Written from notes made at the time, this is a seriously revealing chapter. As for the hugely overrated 'Jackie' (step-sister of Vidal's half-sister), she appears as a spoiled and mercenary minx:

> I have often wondered what would have become of Jackie had Nina stayed with Hughdie. Jackie would certainly have married money. That is to be taken for granted. But she would never have got Jack. One shudders to think that there would never have been a Jacqueline Kennedy Onassis if Hughdie could have had a satisfactory erection.

The business of 'making sentences', as Vidal likes to put it, is intimately connected to the *pronouncing* of sentences. Both faculties get their outing here. Vidal's sentence on himself is that he will only be whole when he is in some way reunited with Jimmie. His sentence on the culture is that it has mistaken showbiz for diversion, and has abandoned literature and the novel for the vacuously meretricious. He fears that he himself has been forgotten, dismissed even from TV and exiled from an academy that rewards only the arid practice of 'theory'. (He should make more of not having gone to university, an unusual distinction in the now totally 'credentialled' America. For one thing, he has always followed the practice of I. A. Richards in reading literature without any canonical crib.) A faint self-pity disfigures the closing passages of the book, which are much preoccupied with the possibility of a last career in 'the films': 'I arrive back in Ravello. Three offers to act, but the agent is firm: "The parts are too small."' Experience might have taught him that there are no small parts, only small players. This palimpsest, however much scored out and scribbled over, and however much a keening for the golden gone to dust, is nonetheless a record of the transmutation, of the base into the gold, that is the raw stuff of literature – and our slight and sardonic hope.

First published as 'After-Time' (a review of *Palimpsest: A Memoir* by Gore Vidal) in *London Review of Books*, 19 October 1995

Ireland

I can remember very distinctly the last time I was in Belfast. It was during the crucial general election which brought Margaret Thatcher to power. I was writing an article for the old *New Statesman* about the neglected Ulster dimension of this conjuncture – it having been Northern Ireland more than any other matter which had brought an end to the period of what we would now have to call 'Old Labour' rule. My essay, when it was published, recommended above all things that the question of the Six Counties, and indeed the Six Counties themselves, be internationalised. Only by placing the issue in a context at once Atlantic and European, I argued, could the petrifying grip of antiquity be broken, and the fetishes of sovereignty be deposed by the revived notion of self-government. (I hope you notice that I have already referred to this historic part of this extremely historic province by each of its three loaded colloquial names. People who say that terminology isn't worth fighting over are saying in effect that language doesn't matter. The latter proposition is much more dangerous than the former.)

I don't particularly care for numinous dates, except that everybody cares for numinous dates and that, as I walked around in the steady rain, it was 13 April; in that hinge year of Thatcherism also both Easter and my thirtieth birthday. April 13 is as well the birthday of Seamus Heaney, and I rounded off my piece with a stave from 'Linen Town':

> It's twenty to four
> On one of the last afternoons
> Of reasonable light.
> Smell the tidal Lagan:
> Take a last turn
> In the tang of possibility.

(People sometimes complain about Heaney, and certainly since 1979 far too many journalists have tried to wrap up a short piece by raiding him for an encapsulating couplet or so, but I ask you to look again. Who else, even suggesting that time might be running out, would put it so mildly and genially as to say that it was 'twenty to four, on one of the last afternoons of reasonable light'? The usual game here is to say, 'five minutes to midnight' or 'the eleventh hour' or some such. It's like the old joke about the relationship between Gaelic and the sense of urgency.) Compare, for example, Louis MacNeice's 1931 poem, 'Belfast':

> The hard cold fire of the northerner,
> Frozen into his blood from the fire in his basalt
> Glares from behind the mica of his eyes
> And the salt carrion water brings him wealth.
> Down there at the end of the melancholy lough
> Against the lurid sky over the stained water
> Where hammers clang murderously on the girders
> Like crucifixes the gantries stand.

Not at all the benign 'Giant's Causeway' account. Even in the Ulster passages of Anthony Powell and Philip Larkin, indeed, neither of them conditioned to subversive or anti-national accounts, one can find in their sojourn the explicit sense of being, as English or Welsh people in this province, somehow definitively expatriated if not in fact 'abroad'.

Anyway, on the very same day exactly ninety years before I was revolving these reflections, on 13 April 1889 to be precise, Oscar Wilde published a review article in the *Pall Mall Gazette*. The book under discussion was J. A. Froude's novel *The Two Chiefs of Dunboy*. In an effort to capture the annihilating dullness of this work of fiction, composed as it was by a noted historian of the Anglo-Irish relationship, Wilde compared it to a government 'Blue Book', or policy report. Let me quote from his review:

> The last of these Blue Books, Mr Froude's heavy novel, has appeared, however, somewhat too late. The society that he describes has long since passed away. An entirely new factor has appeared in the social development of the country, and this factor is the Irish-American, and his influence. To mature its powers, to concentrate its action, to learn the secret of its own strength and of England's weakness, the Celtic intellect has had to cross the Atlantic. At home it had but learned the pathetic weakness of nationality; in a strange land it realized what indomitable forces nationality possesses. What captivity was to the Jews, exile has been to the Irish. America and American influence has educated them. Their first practical leader is an Irish American.

Wilde's peroration was:

> There are some who will welcome with delight the idea of solving the Irish question by doing away with the Irish people. There are others who will remember that Ireland has extended her boundaries, and that we have now to reckon with her not merely in the Old World but also in the New.

Allowance made for Wilde's slightly diva-like Fenian style, this must count as one of his more prescient and incisive judgements. He was raising the curtain on the future Americanisation of the entire Irish and Ulster question. Parnell did indeed have an American mother. It's generally thought that de Valera's American connection may have saved his life at the time of the Rising, since England needed not to offend American sensibility while seeking Washington's entry into the Great War. Men like O'Donovan Rossa had led effectively American-Irish (rather than Irish-American) lives, giving rise to the unshakeable belief on the British mainland – still extremely often met with – that the entire source and arsenal of mischief in Ireland is the great Republic across the Atlantic.

Now I'm back in Belfast and I find that the stewardship of Northern Irish affairs is substantially in American hands. An ex-senator of Lebanese-American background, George Mitchell, chairs important discussions on politics and economics, and on political economy, while reporting back regularly to a president who has sponsored most of the public elements of political or, if you prefer, of national dialogue and mediation. American money, American prestige, American spirit if you will, are slowly but unmistakably beginning to assert themselves. I don't mean to down-grade the importance of economic and community initiatives from the European Union, because I also believe that the co-membership of the two Irelands in one customs and political union was a necessary if not a sufficient precondition for the present stage, but Americanisation is becoming so much the world's pattern and mould that it's here we must look for the waves of the future, in point of character and tone and the other unquantifiable things that go to make up a nation, and a culture.

In the course of a stay in Belfast a matter of a year or two ago, President Clinton bit his lip with that special insincerity that he believes to be at least a *version* or simulacrum of sincerity, and announced that 'Blessed Are The Peacemakers, for they shall inherit the earth'. He had made exactly the same observation at a signing agreement between Israel and the Kingdom of Jordan a short time before. I call it an 'observation' because of course, in the Beatitudes that form the culmination of the Sermon on the Mount, it is the meek who inherit the earth. The peacemakers are called the children of God. Either the President – who sometimes ostentatiously claims to be a Bible student – had confused his Beatitudes or, no less probably, he had balked at referring to his immediate political and diplomatic partners – Mr Trimble, Mr Adams, Mr Peres and King Hussein – as 'children of God'. On one interpretation of course, since we are all, often, referred to in scripture as God's children, we can all be counted peacemakers. But that seems to me too trite and uplifting a piece of hermeneutics. More likely, perhaps, that the President was much influenced when young by screenings of *The Life of Brian*.

Accidentally perhaps, Mr Clinton still performed a service by neatly encapsulating the three crucial moral elements of an American future: If this part of this province, like the three tigers of Munster, Leinster and Connacht and the three frisky cubs of Monaghan, Cavan and Donegal, is going to develop henceforth as part of the American universe, it may as well do some reflecting in advance on the American way. And the Clinton slip reminded us of the three most salient and distinctive features of the American public sphere. America is the special country: one might almost say the Promised Land, first of the multi-ethnic and the multi-cultural, second of the secular and third of the amnesiac. None of these, I believe it is safe to say, has been the distinguishing mark of Ulster life in this century.

It's a good question as to how far plural citizenship and nationhood – those two elusively compatible entities – need to depend upon the friendship of amnesia. In *One Hundred Years of Solitude*, Gabriel García Márquez has a population in Macondo which suffers from an epidemic of insomnia, leading to eventual amnesia. The absurd results of total forgetting are eventually tragic. Yet many are those who have resorted to Ernest Renan's justly celebrated essay *'Qu'est-ce qu'une nation?'* (What is a nation?) and posed his dangerously paradoxical definition:

> Or l'essence d'une nation est que tous les individus aient beaucoup de choses en commun, et aussi que tous aient oublié bien des choses.

Simple translation: Those who wish to make up a nation must possess much in common and also be willing to forget many things.

I actually used this as a chapter-heading in a book I wrote about Cyprus – Britain's other large European island colony – and was fully conscious that, only a few chapters earlier, I had quoted Milan Kundera, in his wonderful *Book of Laughter and Forgetting*, as saying that: 'The struggle of man against power is the struggle of memory against forgetting.' Does this only appear to us as a contradiction? We must bear in mind that, in demotic speech, forgetting is a close ally of forgiving. The best epigram here is Arthur Balfour's remark – 'I can never forgive, but I always forget.' That is a mnemonic by most definitions. Some say that only the work of educated memory can begin the work of intelligent forgiveness; that only by making a moral decision to remember can one make a distinction, among one's former antagonists, between guilt and responsibility or between the collectivis-ation of these in the figures not of other people, but of whole other peoples. A theory not unlike this supplies the animating principle of the National Holocaust Museum, in my home town of Washington. But if the theory was as effective as it is advertised to be, surely there should have been a National Museum of Slavery, on the very ground of the market and the auction block, well before now? The responsibility of the memory you assume, like the guilt you accept, must be your own. Note, again, that there is a modern proposed connection between memory and our theme of this evening, which is that of reconciliation or I suppose you could say – not a term I propose to employ – 'the healing process'. But in that case, why is that other modern phenomenon of retrieved or recovered memory – a sudden and perhaps conditioned access of the blessed mnemonic – such an ally of revenge and of renewed bitterness? Finally, let us bear in mind that one of the prime functions of the human memory is precisely to forget and to discard, and that a person who is unable to flush and void his or her memory can only be one kind of savant, and an idiotic one at that. To say that memory is selective is not in principle a condemnation – because the forgetting faculty must know how to discriminate, just as the aware and conscious faculties must know how to discriminate also. Incidentally, by what awful ironic betrayal of our language do we find ourselves accusing bigots and tribalists of the sin of 'discrimination'? They are the ones who judge severely by category, and yet can't tell anyone apart. 'Discrimination' is only one of the moral and intellectual exercises that they are quite unable to perform.

These old selection processes have a way of reiterating and reinserting themselves. I was recently reading the splendid new account of the repressed woes of modern Germany, another country with a memory and identity and unification problem of the sort to put most to shame, *The File*, by my friend Timothy Garton Ash. Not at all to my surprise, he also and early reprinted the quotation from Ernest Renan on the business of common things here being combined with forgotten things there. But, in a quite separate section, he tried to imagine an English history and English present that would not compromise him or make him feel awkward:

> Personal memory is such a slippery customer. Nietzsche catches it brilliantly in one of his epigrams: '"I did that," says my memory. "I can't have done that," says my pride and remains adamant. In the end – memory gives way.' The temptation is always to pick and choose your past, just as it is for nations: to remember Shakespeare and Churchill but forget Northern Ireland. But we must take it all or leave it all; and I must say 'I'.

I nearly dropped the book when I read Tim's blunt and brutal candour there. Incidentally, Garton Ash's excellent narrative carries a blurb from John Le Carré, as most books about Berlin do if they can contrive it. Le Carré's most recent novel, *The Tailor of Panama*, depicts one secret and diplomatic Englishman abroad as a survival of a more noble and plain-speaking and ethical era, now hopelessly overborne by the meretricious and the mercenary and the wised-up. The youngish innocent's name is Nigel Stormont. So don't assume that everybody deals purely in stereotype.

And I am forced to remember, in my own disquisition on memory, that the great Victorian historian G. M. Young once wrote that: 'What the English can never remember, the Irish can never forget.' The English in this, are, you might think the ones easy to identify. But who then are the Irish? Are they the ones with the longer memories, or the less selective ones? What if Young had written that 'what the *British* can never remember . . .'? Would this suggest that loyalists had shorter memories? Not much of an aphorism or epigram, if so.

When I first visited Belfast as an Englishman, as I would much prefer to describe myself, in the early days of the present phase of the 'troubles', I was struck not so much by the fact that I seemed to be in a foreign country (the past, as we know, has always been another country) as by how *multiply* foreign it was. In the nationalist areas, the telephone boxes could be as red as you liked but one was, inescapably, in Ireland. In the Brown Bear on Shankill Road, where I came the closest I have ever come to being roughed up on account of my accent alone, Englishness was also at something of a discount. Certainly, any Englishman who had been brought up to think that the saving flavour of irony had something English about it would have been in a similar quandary. (Was it 'Go back to Britain' or 'Go back to England' that certain loyalist banshees yelled at Prime Minister Blair on his last visit?) One seemed to have wandered into an irony-free zone where, in a way that might have been reassuring but was somehow not, everyone honestly meant exactly what they said. My original interest in Oscar Wilde, and in his imperishable confrontation with Sir Edward Carson, was not solely in the ways that it prefigured the later confrontation over Home Rule and the right to raise rebellion. Colour does matter: I have for example always thought of Conor Cruise O'Brien as not orange or green but *purple*. Wilde's carnation was by no means the only green thing about him, and Carson's orange was to develop red hands in Ulster and in Flanders before his political career was over, but one of them – I submit – was a votary of irony and would have seen irony in the other's dilemma, while the other was not and could not. If Oscar Wilde had been allowed to live, do I think that he would have wept – fully and genuinely – for what happened to the Ulster Regiment and the Ulster Volunteers on the Somme in June 1916? Of course I do. Of course he would have. My other interest in that court case is that I believe it to be one of the clearest written records, since the indictment of Socrates, of the confrontation between the ironic and the literal mentality.

This helps me to introduce two further elements in the contemporary American style that may be helpful. First, America is still refreshingly – not to say devastatingly – an irony-free zone of its own. Second, the search for alternative history or, better say, alternative histories, is a permanent feature of the American discourse. Every day brings news of a revisionist account, whether it be of the Columbus narrative or the Amistad slave ship or the original intent of the framers of the Constitution. America, furthermore, is 'so large, so friendly and so rich', as Wystan Auden put it, that by an admixture of wealth and capacity and spaciousness and ecological concern it can even undo the irrevocable past. Recently, the Nez Percé Indians of Oregon were contacted by the state authorities and offered their old ancestral valley back. We don't need it any more, said the descendants of the settlers and conquerors, and the only people who seem to know how its water and agriculture and animals really work are you guys. Won't you take it back? The Nez Percé, who had astonished Lewis and Clark and the other explorers and mappers and claim-stakers sent out into a supposed wilderness by Thomas Jefferson, had to be gathered in from internal exile and years of dismal expulsion and contumely, and convinced that this was no trap. America does not just pledge to its true believers a better future. If they really play their hand well, it can promise them a better past. Its narrative, read aright, was not progress from an age of innocence to a time of bitterness and bigotry and ethnic cleansing, but *through* a time of bigotry and bitterness and ethnic cleansing towards a time of relative innocence. If there is a moral here, it had better not be lost upon any adopted children of the American experiment, or any candidates for such an adoption.

I don't at all mean to sound Utopian about this, because America is still gravely disfigured by many awful cuts and slashes and abscesses. But, as the millions of Ulster Presbyterian and Celtic Catholic emigrants can tell you, a larger sky can yet work marvels as a solvent of parochial or ghetto-like differences. Because of the great roof of the Constitution, which stubbornly refuses to make any mention of any god of any kind whatsoever, and which was rightly denounced as 'godless' by its enemies and critics at the time of its promulgation, America is the most religious country in the world and the one that is furthest from any official denomination of national faith. There have been, in one estimate that is put about by jovial Hibernian sources in the Irish-American Cultural Institute, fourteen presidents of Scots-Irish Ulster Presbyterian provenance, the greater number originating in Antrim though I've no intention of appealing to any local enthusiasm, and the most famous surviving political dynasty is a Catholic Irish one, and you know the rest of the story. 'No religious test' for any form of public office, pronounced the Founders. This will one day mean, not just a Catholic but even a Jewish or 'Mohammedan' president, said the detractors. As a result, quite literally any stripe of faith in the Oval Office can be visualised or imagined except, to my sorrow, a secular or agnostic one of the sort who wrote the Constitutional safeguards in the first place. Still, if one has to have ironies of history, this is by no means the cruellest one. The secular State is the guarantee of religious pluralism. This apparent paradox, again, is the simplest and most elegant of political truths. It has been educational to watch the British Crown and the Irish Free State, as they have wrestled in their different ways with this problem transmitted from a narrow and superstitious past. The great old three-masted rigger of Crown/Parliamentary prerogative, United Kingdom, and Established Church has become un-moored and rudderless, becalmed between Europe and the stormy seas. 'Ukania', as my old comrade Tom Nairn dubs it, has a monarchy that is now neither dignified nor efficient, a Church which cannot fill its pews or find a reputable or willing crowned head, and a 'kingdom' structure that reflects none of the centripetal aspirations on the peripheries – especially the Scottish and Irish ones. Meanwhile, the Irish Republic has been compelled, partly for reasons of public relations and partly for reasons of pressure and partly – this last being the crucial element – by reason of the demand of its own citizens for self-government, to accept the idea that Church and State must be separate in their own interests. Some of the early moves to adjust the constitutional order in Dublin may have been conditioned by the requirements of the 'peace process', and even created resentment against it. But more recent ones, such as the arduous lifting of the constitutional prohibition upon divorce, were undertaken so to speak for their own sake. From Ukania to ukase: the petrified dogmatic walls that used to enclose these Six Counties from both directions have melted into air. And a partitioned province in a partitioned country, which used to be the orphan of Ukania by being part of the United Kingdom yet not of Great Britain (or was it the other way about?) and the orphan of Cathleen ni Houlihan by being only the rump of once-proud Ulster, can now peer about itself as a potential international platform and site of post-modern, post-national, multi-continental experiments. Has the scope and wonder of this Big Chance, I ask you, quite sunk in yet?

A word of admonition, before any celebration can begin. The excitements of MacWorld can also be the prelude to the intoxications of homogenisation. There may even be sudden nostalgia for the passions of a more antique and primitive time. Louis MacNeice, literary orphan and still neglected child of the Auden/Day-Lewis/Spender school, saw this coming, in a way. I love his poetry, for its combination of sly and subtle effects and bold, open strokes. His autobiography is told in the poem 'Carrickfergus':

> I was the rector's son, born to the Anglican order,
> banned for ever from the candles of the Irish poor;
> The Chichesters knelt in marble at the end of a transept
> With ruffs about their necks, their portion sure.

In prose he tells us, in *The Strings Are False: An Unfinished Autobiography*:

> The Cook Annie, who was a buxom rosy girl from a farm in County Tyrone, was the only Catholic I knew and therefore my only proof that Catholics were human . . .
>
> The mill-girls – rude, bold creatures, Miss Craig said – all with black shawls over their heads and the older ones haggard, dark under the eyes, their voices hard and embittered and jeering. . . .
>
> When we went through the town there were always men standing at the corners – standing there at least till the pubs opened – in shiny blue suits and dirty collarless shirts fastened with a collar-stud, and cloth caps pulled down over narrow-leering eyes, and sour mouths which did not open when they spoke but which twisted sideways as they spat. The pavement around them was constellated with spittle and on the drab cement walls at their back there was chalked up 'To Hell With The Pope'.

One day, to revert to verse again, young MacNeice was taken away from this and sent off to boarding school in England:

> I went to school in Dorset, the world of parents
> Contracted into a puppet world of sons
> Far from the mill-girls, the smell of porter, the salt mines
> And the soldiers with their guns.

And yet here, in this subordinate universe, MacNeice recorded an interesting self-discovery. It must be plain from the extracts that I cited above that he had no liking for the raw essences of Ulster; the grit and bone and harshness of it, and the fierce sectarianism. (A *love* perhaps, but I repeat, no *liking*.) He yearned for a little taste, a little elevation and refinement. Not only did he not like the bang of the Lambeg drum, he had discovered that at least one side of his family were recent converts from Catholicism. Yet the cock will crow in the most awkward way, at the most inopportune times.

Just after the Armistice in 1918, his father put him on a boat-train to England 'in charge of a dear old man':

> The dear old man had rosy cheeks and a watch-chain tight on his paunch. We sat opposite a tipsy American soldier, large and raw and angry, who insisted on talking politics. 'England: he said to the dear old man, a Unionist, 'England's no better than Germany. Kings and dukes the lot of them . . . And as for the dear old man, what did he think of Carson? The dear old man drew himself in, his watch-chain sagged on his belly, he said he admired Carson. The American soldier turned to me; 'You're only a kid,' he said, 'but

you look like an American kid. What do you think of Carson?' Feeling shockingly disloyal to the dear old man but remembering my father and Home Rule, I said I thought Carson was a pity. The American soldier was delighted, asked the old man if he was not ashamed, a white-haired old man like himself and a little boy like me had more sense . . .

Again one sees and feels, even if only in its most vulgar form, the prefiguration of the American century and the American solution. The United States doughboys have just 'turned the tide' and plucked the British Empire's chestnuts from the flame: there is no question of being rude to them in railway carriages. On the other hand, their President Wilson is about to proclaim an era of self-determination in which Irish nationalists hope to have a share. Later at Sherborne in Dorset, as MacNeice is growing to adolescence he finds that he really does have to serve two masters – Mr Cameron, a fellow Ulsterman, and Mr Powys, a more flamboyant nature-loving type:

> On the Twelfth of July Powys came into my dormitory and said: 'What is all this they do in your country today? Isn't it all mumbo-jumbo?' Remembering my father and Home Rule and the bony elbows of Miss Craig and the black file of mill-girls and the wickedness of Carson and the dull dank days between sodden haycocks and foghorns, I said Yes it was. And I felt uplifted. To be speaking man to man to Powys and giving the lie to the Red Hand of Ulster was power, was freedom, meant I was nearly grown up. King William is dead and his white horse with him, and Miss Craig will never put her knuckles in my ears again. But Powys went out of the dormitory and Mr Cameron came in, his underlip jutting and his eyes enraged. 'What were you saying to Mr Powys?' Oh this division of allegiance! That the Twelfth of July was mumbo-jumbo was true, and my father thought so too, but the moment Mr Cameron appeared I felt rather guilty and cheap. Because I had been showing off to Powys and because Mr Cameron being after all Irish I felt I had betrayed him.

Here is a good instance of elementary human solidarity and decency, shot in negative if you like, and developed in reverse. In his beautiful long later poem 'Autumn Journal', when MacNeice was to curse repeatedly the false loyalties and strange oaths of Ulster, and call down a plague on the Romans and the Orangemen and the bombast and the sentimentality (a lethal and toxic combination, by the by, as of the drunken and impotent wife-smasher, or the sobbing and self-pitying hostage-taker, or the slobber and glare of a weak king), he still gave it the common name of Irish and asked, parodying I think another author's sarcastic question:

> Such was my country and I thought I was well
> Out of it, educated and domiciled in England,
> Though yet her name keeps ringing like a bell

In an under-water belfry.
Why do we like being Irish? Partly because
It gives us a hold on the sentimental English . . .

So that, to loop back to where I was a moment or so ago, the desire for authenticity – for the genuine and unfeigned – can at least sometimes be the equal of the lust for modernity, for prosperity, for unbearable lightness and emancipation from guilt. Thus much will depend on the sort of Americanism, or perhaps I had better say cosmopolitanism, that Ireland or Northern Ireland now decides upon, or learns to discriminate between.

In other words, I don't mean at all to stand before you and recommend the uncritical or the wholesale adoption of the American mass culture. As those coming perhaps a little later to it, you have a better chance to pick and choose. May I give a single instance or example of what I mean?

In early August of this year, in the beautiful city of Stanford, California, I was honoured by an invitation to the Obon Festival. Obon is the celebration of the Japanese people, in particular those Japanese people who follow the Buddhist path. Over time, it has become the annual cultural festival of a large community. I strolled through the stalls that showed Japanese writing, painting, food, music and calligraphy to greatest advantage. I watched as Japanese dancers and players enchanted a large audience. Stanford and Palo Alto are a short drive from Silicon Valley, and the Japanese talent for miniaturisation – whether grounded in the aesthetic of Japanese art or the ingenuity of Japanese privatisation – is, if you will forgive my feebleness, no small thing. In this area of California, it has also been a potent source of resentment.

Not that alone, but my mother-in-law, who accompanied me with the rest of my family and who was able to greet some ladies and gentlemen by name, has a clear and ghastly memory of turning up to school one morning in 1942 and finding that her best friend, a little Japanese-American girl, had been taken away to an internment camp along with all of those of Japanese ancestry, whether citizens or not, who could be rounded up. My father-in-law, who was the actual invited guest of our family through business and social contacts, had as an American sailor put in at Hiroshima only a few days after the terrible blast that gave us the obscene and laconic term 'Ground Zero'. He had later become a theoretical nuclear physicist in one of the California labs, before quitting for what I might call Einsteinian reasons. Einstein, you may recall, addressed the scientific community and said: 'Remember Your Humanity – and forget the rest'. It would, I propose, be wrong to interpret this as another invitation to simple amnesia. Those who are being enjoined to remember their humanity are being urged to remember Quite A Lot.

Nor was the numinous or ominous date aspect absent from our Obon Festival, conducted as it was under sunny California skies. The weekend was that of the 2–3 August, nearest to the Hiroshima anniversary. It was not just the Japanese hosts who were aware of this. Let me recapitulate then. In the most modern bit of the world's most modern country, at a time of considerable suspicion and competition between two 'motherlands', and in a context where language (Japanese and English), history (Pearl Harbor and internment; Hiroshima and Nagasaki) and religion (Buddhism versus Christianity) could not easily be more in contrast and where physical features underlined or delineated the fact of profound difference, many thousands of people put their day in the safekeeping of friendship, solidarity, mutual curiosity and good taste. As the great Yogi Berra contentedly said, on being told that a Jew had been elected Mayor of Dublin, 'Only in America'.

I prefer not to think of this event, which had no official sponsorship and which reaped no headlines, as a mere exercise in good manners or nervous 'community relations'. Nobody had to be there; nobody would have been missed if they hadn't turned up. But I can't offhand think of a more relaxed and cross-fertilised cultural festival, given the recent past and the high stakes, than this wee event. For it to happen, much that can't be too crassly emphasised must happen too. There must be an unspoken agreement that the future is common property, and that it belongs above all to those who haven't been born yet, or those who've just arrived. There must be a Renan-like understanding that the past is most useful as a source of interest and instruction. There must be a sense of awe – here's where modernity comes in – at the latest discoveries in physics and genetics, which have uncovered and mapped an amazingly complex and intricate common humanity, just beneath our skins, at the very moment when an external world is presented that reminds us again to be modest in the extreme about being the paragon of animals. So let me use the word 'America' as our metaphysical poets used to use it, as Marvell might say 'My America, My New Found Land'; a generic America with no bounds and no proscriptions, where the past is respected – so much so that it is kept in bounds. Perhaps tomorrow, after Mahler's *Resurrection*, we might ask the combined forces of RTE and The Belfast Symphony to tune up informally and give us the New World Overture.

In Seamus Deane's amazing four-volume anthology of the writing and saying and poetising and singing of Ireland (where 'speeches from the dock' form part of his taxonomy of letters), there is a wonderfully strict correction of Louis MacNeice. In 'Autumn Journal' he commits the solecism of translating the Gaelic words *Sinn Fein* as 'Ourselves

Alone'. This is how every English schoolboy has been taught to render those words since before the Black and Tans.[2] No, say the editors – Messrs Heaney and Friel and Deane and Paulin and Carpenter and William and the rest. This is too common a mistake. The words mean 'We Ourselves'. I cannot think how such an important literal translation, with all its ironic implications, took so long to be made. Still, what correction could be accepted with more grace? Who will not be sad to think of what was perhaps lost in translation?

'We Ourselves' did not get here from nowhere, and we did not arrive without baggage, and would be boring and banal if we had. 'We Ourselves' cannot be expected to be ashamed of having taken seriously certain ideas of nationality and religion and community. Some imperishable writing and some unforgettable history has emerged from this crucible, and become common property even in an age where Faith is the most overestimated of the virtues, and physics more awe-inspiring than religion. Peacemaking may not need to be termed a blessed or sanctified activity, suffering may be an experience to be recalled with sobriety rather than banished or obliterated in mind, and redemption will begin when the life of all free citizens is enhanced in common by music and letters and philosophy, and the qualities of eloquence and irony, and when it may be fairly said, in no mean city, that when we hear the word 'gun' we reach for our culture.

First published as 'Ireland. "We Ourselves": Suffering, Faith and Redemption' in *Critical Quarterly*, vol. 40, no. 1, Spring 1998

Notes

1. Lecture to precede Mahler's *Resurrection* Symphony at the Belfast Literature Festival, 15 November 1997.
2. It was Arthur Griffith who proclaimed *Sinn Fein* and who also supplied the more common and more strenuous translation. A Gaelic Leaguer, he was also an extreme nationalist and Anglophobe – the deadly foe of Erskine Childers – and one remembers the description of his portrait given by the (monoglot) Yeats in 'The Municipal Gallery Revisited', where Griffith is 'staring in hysterical pride'. The recovery of spoken demotic and literary Irish was largely the achievement of German philologists, and it would be interesting to know what variant renditions were available to Griffith's contemporaries.

Stuck in Neutral

In *Poetic Justice*, her extended essay, Martha Nussbaum seeks to marry the tough and the tender-minded, chiefly through an exploration of one poem (Walt Whitman's 'Song of Myself') and one novel (Charles Dickens's *Hard Times*). She sets herself to focus on the way in which novels embody and generate to Mr Gradgrind's chagrin the activity that he calls 'fancy', that ability to imagine nonexistent possibilities, to see one thing as another and one thing in another, to endow a perceived form with a complex life. She is strongly of the opinion that such activity is not luxurious or frivolous and that it is, rather, an essential element in the rounded or completed human picture. Children like Sissy Jupe are wiser in this respect than their elders and betters; the great achievement of Dickens is to have retained the sense of wonder (and of injustice) that he acquired as a child. Nothing can be worse than the soul-murder inflicted on infants by Coketown utilitarians.

Nussbaum is an eminent member of the American 'public intellectual' race-and-gender-and-sexuality professoriat. She has also co-operated with Amartya Sen on a project to enrich development economics with a 'quality of life' dimension. It is the balance between 'heart' and 'head', whether in law or philosophy or social policy, that preoccupies her. Indeed, much of her introductory chapter is more concerned with establishing that balance than with actually weighing it:

> The literary imagination is a part of public rationality, and not the whole. I believe that it would be extremely dangerous to suggest substituting empathetic imagining for rule-governed moral reasoning, and I am not making that suggestion. In fact, I defend the literary imagination precisely because it seems to me an essential ingredient of an ethical stance that asks us to concern ourselves with the good of other people whose lives are distant from our own.

Yet, however distant the narrative of the presumed 'other': *de te fabula narratur*. It is because *Hard Times* concludes by addressing the 'dear reader' and saying that 'it rests with you and me whether, in our two fields of action, similar things shall be or not' that Nussbaum makes it the centrepiece of her consideration. She spends rather a lot of time in nerving herself to do it. Not only are there many academic throat-clearings ('My question, then, will be'; 'And I shall ask as well'), but there are also some interdisciplinary demarcations to be made. For example, history is held to be inferior to literature because historical works are not literary works. Except, that is, when they are, in which case, 'to the extent that they promote identification and sympathy in the reader, they resemble literary works'.

Where the danger is not tautology, it is the corollary or correspond-ing one of a false antithesis. Nussbaum feelingly cites Bitzer in his pitiless address to a Gradgrind, now in need of mercy, who hears his own arid precept played back to him:

> I am sure you know that the whole social system is a question of self-interest. What you must always appeal to, is a person's self-interest. It's your only hold. We are so constituted. I was brought up in that catechism when I was very young, sir, as you are aware.

This seems to Nussbaum to be mechanistic and to abolish 'even those residual notions of love and altruism' to which Gradgrind has become suddenly vulnerable. But take away the automaton style and see the alternative residue. Both Oscar Wilde and Bernard Shaw wrote with great wit and intelligence about self-interest and its utility. Workers should have baths for my sake as well as theirs. Socialist ethics would free us from 'that sordid necessity of living for others which, in the present condition of things, presses so hardly upon almost everybody'. Self interest is wholesome and defensible and (a consideration that never enters these pages) always open to ironic attack. Now put the case of John Stuart Mill. Reared to think only of the general good and of universal improvement, even as he 'endeavoured to pick up as many flowers as I could by the way', he found his entire life stale, weary, flat and unprofitable at the age of twenty:

> In this frame of mind it occurred to me to put the question directly to myself, 'Suppose that all your objects in life were realised; that all the changes in institutions and opinions which you are looking forward to, could be completely effected at this very instant: would this be a great joy and happiness to you?' And an irrepressible self-consciousness distinctly answered, 'No'!

There are three reasons for finding it odd that Nussbaum doesn't bother with this famous episode of melancholy. First, Mill was an unintended victim of the utilitarian calculus, and that in its most pure, exalted and altruistic form. Second, his 'irrepressible self-conscious-ness' might be held to have some kinship with Adam Smith's celebrated inner 'spectator' (who does receive some Nussbaumian attention along with the *Theory of Moral Sentiments*). Third, Mill found his principal relief in poetry. Having made the sad discovery that he was not a machine and that 'the habit of analysis has a tendency to wear away the feelings: as indeed it has when no other mental habit is cultivated, and the analysing spirit remains without its natural complements and correctives', Mill turned to Coleridge and to Wordsworth and Byron and found that, while Byron's condition was too much like his own, the *Lyrical Ballads* possessed powers of reflection and consolation. (Being Mill, he did not forget to add that they contained 'two passages of grand imagery but bad philosophy'.) Finally, by his reading of Marmontel he was induced to see that living for others can be a pleasure as well as a dire duty; he doesn't employ the word 'solidarity' or coin the phrase 'gift relationship', but he helps us towards such an understanding. He accomplishes all this in a very few pages.

Well before Milton made allusion to 'A poet soaring in the high reason of his fancies', we have had the idea that poetry is more than a felicitous arrangement of words and rhythms. We have also understood that the heart and the head may have surprising appositions. Dylan Thomas, talking to a Member of Parliament just returned from the investigation of Buchenwald, said: 'They should send poets there' and thus made (without realizing it) a direct challenge to Adorno. The late Joseph Brodsky claimed rather extravagantly that a whole new religion could be founded on the tiny, joky couplet of Auden's about unequal affections. The examples of Akhmatova and Miloscz and others have made Shelley's idea of the 'unacknowledged legislator' into a near-cliché. Yet Nussbaum only really considers one stanza, and that because (as near as may be judged) its author radiates worthy sentiment. For Whitman, the poet is 'the arbiter of the diverse' and 'the equalizer of his age and land'. It is the apparently unexceptionable aim of this book to show that we must see the whole man, or the whole woman, and that law and criticism must become more capacious and subtle in consequence. Only as the author proceeds does this ambition reveal its difficulties.

'The point, then', she avers, 'is that the "fact" school, which denies subjective experience to cows and horses, humanity to workers, engages in fiction-making as much as do novel-readers and fanciers.' True enough as far as it goes – are we not familiar with the extreme sentimentality of the supposedly hard-boiled? – but burdened with a subjectivity of its own. On the almost preceding page, Nussbaum has committed herself to the view that the 'moral operations' of *Hard Times* 'are not independent of its aesthetic excellence'. On the page immediately following, she tells us about a student of hers who loved nursery jingles, and who in consequence had come to love his dog, and says: 'The birth of fancy is non-neutral and does, as Dickens indicates, nourish a generous construction of the seen.' But would we rather have had young Mill forego his fearsome education? What about the child in Nabokov's short story, who is mysteriously afraid of a single picture in a storybook? Or the lost boys in Kenzaburo Oe? For them, fancy is non-neutral (difficult to see how it could be neutral) but is far from generous or benign. Emotions and fantasies are capable of doing just as much harm as cold and unfeeling calculations. Sometimes the unacknowledged legislator is D'Annunzio.

A judge who sees a close friend appear in the dock is supposed, in the old distinction, to be disinterested but not uninterested. As she moves towards a consideration of the 'law and economics' school, and the principle of rational interest-maximisation, Nussbaum tries to separate the untaught promptings of emotion from the acquired temper of the *homme moyen sensuel*:

> On the first view, emotions are neither taught nor embodied in beliefs; on the second, they are taught along with evaluative beliefs. On the first, they can be neither educated nor entirely removed; on the second, both are possible. On the first, emotions are unstable because of their unthinking external structure; on the second, because they are thoughts that attach importance to unstable external things.

In support of the second interpretation, Nussbaum mentions Plato's proposed ban on literature in the ideal city, and what she thinks of as Marxist hostility to the project of the 'bourgeois' novel (She might be on target here with Lukács, but not with the Marx who asserted that one Balzac was worth a hundred Zolas.) Selecting an example of the sorts of emotion that may need to be contained or subjected, she chooses anger and observes that:

> Being angry seems to require the belief that I, or something or someone important to me, have been wronged or harmed by another person's intentional action. If any significant aspect of that complex belief should cease to seem true to me – if I change my view about who has done the harm, or about whether it was intentional, or about whether what happened was in fact a harm – my anger can be expected to abate or to change its course accordingly. Much the same is true of other major emotions.

This conforms more or less to what Aristotle said about anger in his *Rhetoric*. But might it not profitably be remembered that Aristotle added an earthy and almost voluptuous rider, saying of anger that:

> It must always be attended by a certain pleasure: that which arises from the expectation of revenge. For since nobody aims at what he thinks he cannot attain, the angry man is aiming at what he can attain, and the belief that you will attain your aim is pleasant. Hence it has been well said about wrath:

'Sweeter it is by far than the honeycomb dripping with sweetness, / And spreads through the hearts of men'.

Since the latter quotation comes from the *Iliad*, it could be said to deserve a place in any treatment of poetry and justice. Dickens himself was said, by George Orwell, to be 'generously angry'. But in support of her rather restricted definition of the emotions, and of the role of rhetoric in swaying them, Nussbaum cites something rather more modern:

> When George Bush wanted to make the American public fear the prospect of a Dukakis presidency, he did not need to inject ice water into their veins. All he needed to do was to make them believe that a Dukakis presidency would mean significant dangers for them that they would be powerless to ward off – namely, Willie Hortons running free in the streets of every city, ready to prey on innocent women and children. This position is compatible with the view that emotions have other noncognitive components (such as feelings or bodily states) in addition to beliefs, but it insists that the relevant beliefs are sufficient causes of these further components.

You might not guess from this that the Willie Horton case (a case of a paroled black rapist who struck again) was first employed against Dukakis in the Democratic primaries, by then-Senator Al Gore. It did not 'resonate' with the public then, partly because Gore was thought of as a wooden and expressionless politician. It did resonate later, again because Dukakis himself was widely seen as a man suffering from some sort of weird emotional neutrality. Nussbaum briefly recommends the Stoic Chrysippus for his belief that emotions are merely identical with certain types of belief or judgement, requiring no specific feeling or bodily state, before (wisely in my view) dropping that line of speculation.

It's a strange observation to have to make, but Nussbaum seems almost unaware that there is any element of caricature in Dickens. When the utilitarian teacher M'Choakumchild – perhaps a clue there? – tells Sissy Jupe that in a town of a million inhabitants only twenty-five are starved to death in the streets, Sissy responds that 'it must be just as hard upon those who were starved'. Nussbaum wholly approves of the letter and spirit of this reply. 'What a fine low percentage, says M'Choakumchild, and no action, clearly, need to be taken about that.' Really? Is not M'Choakumchild applauding the actions and policies that have made such a low measurement possible, and is there not some humanity in that? Passing over this consideration, Nussbaum adds what she calls 'a genetic thesis', stressing the importance of family values over social ones and restating Aristotle's belief that removing the family will ensure that nobody cares strongly about anything. She says that intimate family bonds, formed in infancy, are 'indispensable for

an adult's ability to do good in the wider social world'. But are there
not many pathetic waifs, orphans and victims of brutal childhoods who
have gone on to do precisely that? (Where would Dickens have been
without this thought?) Proudhon may have expressed a certain truth
when he said that if all men were brothers then he had no brothers,
but if I say that I am bound indissolubly, by ties of self-interest as well
as fellow-feeling, to people in the Brazilian rain-forest I have never met
(I yearn for them to thrive, in other words, so that I can breathe their
habitat's oxygen), I do not axiomatically utter something that is either
intellectually vacuous or emotionally null.

In her closing chapters, Nussbaum turns to the law and makes an
eloquent case for reaching verdicts, and making judgements, that have
considered every aspect of the plaintiff and defendant. She instances
precedents, among them *California vs Brown*, which instruct juries to
disregard 'extraneous emotion', while permitting them to consider
'relevant facets of the character and record of the individual offender
or the circumstances of the particular offense'. Her two classic citations
here are some remarks by Justice Stephen Breyer at his recent confirmation hearings, and some lines from Richard Wright's *Native Son*.
Justice Breyer quoted 'one of the Brontës' as saying that 'each one of
those persons in each one of those houses and each one of those
families is different, and they each have a story to tell'. Wright, of
course, portrayed his Bigger Thomas as a murderer but also as a man
whose predicament was beyond society's comprehension. These two
observations are not quite the same. No legal system has time for every
potential Ancient Mariner narrative, and to judge is by definition to be
'arbitrary'; if we attend closely, we may hear the still, sad music of
humanity, but it will be found beyond our powers to listen to every
human story. Wright understood this about Bigger: 'He knew as he
stood there that he could never tell why he had killed. It was not that
he did not really want to tell, but the telling of it would have involved
an explanation of his entire life.'

Nussbaum's most finely rendered passage is her last. Through the
prism of a written opinion by her colleague Richard Posner, a seminal
member of the 'Law and Economics' school, she reconstructs the true
background of a sexual-harassment suit brought by a female tinsmith
against the General Motors Corporation. By the time you have finished
reading the story of Mary Carr, you are trembling with righteous
indignation. (Anybody wanting to expose themselves to the serious
ugliness that lies behind the latest cliché of 'white male rage' should
digest these few pages.) To the catalogue of menace and foulness and
humiliation – rendered in marvellously cool prose by Posner – Nussbaum adds a telling gloss about 'fancy' and asks us, in effect, to put
ourselves in this person's place. For dialectical purposes, she also

reviews the excuses made for this mistreatment and asks us scornfully if we can imagine ourselves making them. It is an exercise both of passion and reason, and persuaded me at any rate that Nussbaum could spend less time in attempting to distinguish these two faculties and more time in combining them.

First published as 'Stuck in Neutral' (a review of *Poetic Justice: The Literary Imagination and Public Life* by Martha C. Nussbaum) in *Times Literary Supplement*, 15 March 1996

A Regular Bull

I once had the luck to meet the great Saul Bellow, who in the course of the evening told me the following story. In 1945 he had been engaged as a book reviewer for Henry Luce's *Time* magazine. Or he thought he had been so engaged. When he turned up for work, he was informed that Whittaker Chambers, chief Pooh-Bah of the 'back of the book', wished to see him. He entered the sanctum and found the stout, surly presence waiting behind a desk. 'Sit down Mr Bellow. Tell me, what did you study at university?' Bellow replied that his study had been English literature. He was asked to give his opinion of William Wordsworth as a poet. He responded that he had always thought of William Wordsworth as one of the Romantics. 'There is no place for you,' said Chambers on hearing this, 'in this organisation.' The future Nobel Laureate was fired before he had been hired. Reflecting on this in 1989, he said he still had two questions about it. The first and unanswerable one was: what if he'd kept the job? He might be a book critic for *Time* to this very day. The second question was: what answer could possibly have saved him? I thought then, and I think now, that the books editor wanted the junior scribe to look him in the eye and say that William Wordsworth, a one-time revolutionary poet, had seen the error of his ways and – braving the scorn and contumely of his one-time comrades – become a reconciled conservative.

Bellow's novel *The Victim*, published in 1947, has a strong scene in which the protagonist Asa Leventhal is given the mother of all horrendous job interviews by the fat, bullying editor Rudiger. Leventhal strives not to be cowed:

> Too many people looking for work were ready to allow anything. The habit of agreement was strong, terribly strong. Say anything you like to them, call them fools and they smiled, turn their beliefs inside out and they smiled, despise them and they might grow red, but they went on smiling because they could not let themselves disagree. And that was what Rudiger was used to.

Having defied Rudiger and been shown the door, he finds while relating the incident to a friend that his euphoria is abruptly dissipated:

'You said that to Rudiger? Oh golly, that must have been something. Really something, Asa my boy. He's a bull, that man. I've heard stories about him. A regular bull!'

'Yes. Well, you've got to remember one thing, Dan,' Leventhal's spirits dropped suddenly. 'Someone like that can make trouble for me. He can have me blacklisted. You've got to realise . . . Eh, can he?'

Incidental as it is to the main plot, this episode demonstrates again Bellow's uncanny facility for encapsulating an atmosphere. Here was the America of the immediate post-war: the most powerful and proud and strong nation in the history of the world. It had just demonstrated thermonuclear supremacy and – at what was literally a knock-down price – acquired an empire. It had no serious adversary, foreign or domestic. Yet at this precise moment ('There were blacklists; that was well-known. After all, Rudiger was influential, powerful. And who knew how these things were done, through what channels?') the whole suffocating business of loyalty oaths and heresy hunts began to disfigure an entire culture. The obvious and immediate answer to this conundrum – that there was nothing imaginary about the ghastliness of Stalinism – is insufficient. The Cold War was fought just as hard in France or Germany or England, but without the same grotesque paranoia or the chilling readiness to surrender liberty and believe the absurd. The enduring interest of this period is the light it throws, or fails to throw, on the matter of American insecurity.

Whittaker Chambers is the essential symptomatic miniature here. And, when we consider how he unwittingly saved Saul Bellow for American letters, we are guided in the right direction. Much of the Chambers story has to do with unintended consequences. And it can be viewed as a quasi-literary narrative. Chambers himself appears as a fiercely dedicated and principled character – a penitent ex-Soviet agent named Gifford Maxim – in Lionel Trilling's novel *The Middle of the Journey* (also published in 1947). He is the precipitating agent, in another sense of that term, in Alistair Cooke's great account of the time, *Generation on Trial.* He was the man who made Richard Nixon's self-serving book *Six Crises* (a 'campaign book' for an entire career) possible in the first place. *Witness,* his own work, had a marked influence on Arthur Koestler and on Czeslaw Miloscz and is, indeed, the nativist American equivalent of *Darkness at Noon* or *The Captive Mind.* With its ostentatious religiosity and its relentless emphasis on redemption and conversion – and its subplot concerning the triumph of the plain man over the devious intellectuals and sinister pointy-heads – it was one of the building-blocks for McCarthyism, for the Goldwater campaign and for what eventually became the 'Reagan revolution'.

Yet the man at the centre of it was anything but the simple, honest all-American type. Chambers was an intellectual of a sort, and a poet and writer of some gifts. To an extent probably greater than his more 'educated' antagonist Alger Hiss, he was in thrall to the potency of ideas. And he never doubted his own centrality; his sometimes subjective and at other times objective importance as an instrument of history. He had, in every declension of the word, a rich and vivid imagination. In consequence, melodrama and bathos were always close at hand.

Born into a family of astonishing dysfunction (a gay father, a brittle and over-protective mother, the deplorable and never-to-be-forgiven birth-name Vivian, alcoholic and suicidal siblings) Chambers could well have become a drifter if he had not signed on at Columbia University and been noticed by Mark Van Doren. Even though he dropped out of Columbia, and joined the Communist Party in the unpropitious year of 1925 (excited typically into this decision by one gripping Lenin pamphlet discovered in a secondhand bookshop), he was always to be able to win a living by his pen. He was a fine translator as well as a writer, and brought some works of Thomas Mann and Franz Werfel into English. Only a paltry nickel-and-dime dispute lost him the commission to complete Scott Moncrieff's version of *A la recherche du temps perdu*. (As you reel from this thought, reflect that instead he attained immortality by his translation of the Austrian folk tale *Bambi*, which carried a moist Foreword from John Galsworthy.)

This was the literary bridge that bore Chambers from relative hackdom on the *Daily Worker* to pre-eminence at the Stalinist flagship of letters, *The New Masses*. Indeed it was his usefulness and ability in this department that got him rehabilitated by the Party apparat. He had been briefly unpersoned by Stalin's purge of the generally pro-Bukharin leadership of the American Communist Party – known to history and to aficionados as the Lovestone faction – but his talent as a 'proletarian writer' gained his re-admission. Some of his short stories were at least as good as the early Steinbeck. He also took a Party wife, a devoted Russian-born loyalist named Esther Shemitz. She seems to have supplied him with two sorts of cover, since his recruitment for 'special work' by the newly Sovietised Party overlapped in time with his discovery, or perhaps better say 'self-admission', that he was a homosexual. Opportunities for anonymous meetings, rapid switches of identity and habituation to the world of the covert signal and the shared code were to increase as the crisis of the Thirties became deeper. From his shabby rural retreat in Maryland, he made various theatrical forays into New Deal Washington, where sympathisers with the Great Soviet Experiment were not wanting. Tanenhaus calculates that between about 1931 and 1937, when he toiled for the Fourth Department of Russian military intelligence, he had been 'without a fixed identity, lived at a total of 21 different addresses, had signed false names to leases, passports and cheques, had invented aliases for his wife and children, had paid no income tax'. His main triumph in Washington was his penetration of the Department of Agriculture and its New Deal farm plans, though, as a comrade of mine points out, contemporary Soviet agricultural policy does not seem to have profited much by the penetration.

It's not absolutely clear whether, when he read a transcript of the Moscow trials in 1937, Chambers was more affected by fear than revulsion. At any rate, he underwent an excruciating self-examination. He had not failed to notice that other members of his subterranean fraternity, when recalled to Moscow, had a marked tendency to check out. (One such 'disappeared' member, Donald Robinson, falsely accused of contact with Trotsky in Mexico, later turned up in Hiss's handwritten notes of the period and is the reason some on the Left have always doubted Hiss's word.) Chambers contrived to separate himself from the clandestine Communist world and, after a short period of indigence, find a roost at *Time* magazine in 1939. There, he quickly won golden opinions by executing what must have been a very delicate commission – a cover story on James Joyce and *Finnegans Wake*.

So by the time that Chambers fired Bellow in 1945, he was himself in the very middle of his journey. He had led a shadowy life in which he dreaded two varieties of exposure. He had been badly frightened, both physically and morally. He had moved in circles where a heterodox opinion on the Wordsworth question could be a deadly serious matter. He was still liable, under American law, to charges as a spy for Stalin. And he was still ostensibly scared of his former employers. A colleague in the *Times* books department named Sam Welles offered him lunch and met with repeated rebuffs. Finally agreeing to the date, Chambers took Welles through a nightmarish mid-town routine, getting on and off subways, ducking through crowded shops to shake off tails and eventually eating lunch in silence at the Empire State Building. He later opened his jacket to show Welles the gun he was carrying, and said that he thought the lunch proposal might have been a set-up for a Soviet ambush. But at this stage, mark well, Chambers was still unknown outside literary circles and had made no charges against anyone.

This excellent book is intended as a biography and not as a study of the Hiss–Chambers case (which has generated a vast secondary litera-ture of its own). Tanenhaus simply makes the assumption, increasingly common among American intellectuals, that Hiss was lying and Chambers was telling the truth. But his narration makes it perfectly easy to understand why so many people at the time took the opposing view. Let's see now. An unstable fantasy-merchant signs up as an agent of Joseph Stalin. He lives a series of lies for almost a decade, and cultivates the habits and practices of deception. He then tries to go straight, and denounces his former comrades. But he steadfastly denies that Communists and fellow-travellers were involved in spy work. Then, as the Cold War pressure-cooker heats up, he remembers that there was some espionage after all. He lends himself to the most depraved right-wing circles, whose real objective is the undoing of the New Deal and the imposition of a politically conformist America. He amends and updates his story. Eventually, under what amounts to a threat to make good on his allegations – a threat issuing from the ambitious and neurotic Richard Nixon – he finds evidence against Alger Hiss hidden inside a hollowed-out pumpkin on his Maryland farm. Has there ever been a more discreditable or less probable tale?

Add to this two further elements: the elements of class and sex. Alger Hiss was not exactly a patrician but he had been a law clerk for Justice Oliver Wendell Holmes; he had been one of the bright boys of the Roosevelt New Deal and he had been energetic and instrumental in setting up two of the pillars of the postwar liberal American imperial order – the United Nations and the Carnegie Endowment for International Peace. He was handsome and lively and charming withal. Was it bearable that such a man should be brought down and trampled, on the word of a bulbous, paranoid deadbeat? I met Alger Hiss a few times and was impressed, as it seems most people were, by his manners and bearing and address. On the last occasion on which I saw him, the dinner-table was a convention of all that is noblest in the New York left-wing tradition. (I do not name names.) As coffee-time drew near, I whispered sarcastically to the hostess: 'Why don't we secure the doors and say: 'Look, Alger, it's just us. Come on. You're among friends. Tell us why you really did it.'' She gave me a look, and a pinch, which eloquently conveyed the words Don't Even Think About It. And it's true that this has long been, for many people, a loyalty oath of its own. If Hiss was wrong, then Nixon and McCarthy were right. And that could not be.

The element of sex is supplied by the fascination which Hiss evidently possessed for Chambers. He repeatedly cried out that he admired him and didn't wish to injure him – only his Communist masters. He was suspected by some of harbouring a passion for the more lithe, easy, boyish rival. It was in the course of his depositions to the FBI in the matter that he came clean about his own homosexual life: a disclosure that in another context could have meant that it was he and not a former comrade who was in the dock. Hiss's partisans pointed meaningly to one of the Franz Werfel books translated by Chambers: a story entitled *Class Reunion*, in which a charming and successful boy is ruined by the false witness of a jealous schoolmate. In the circumstances, the most wounding thing that Hiss could conceivably have said was the thing that he actually did say – that he had never even met anyone 'named' Whittaker Chambers. This lofty claim is believed by some to have been a legal technicality on which the hitherto unimpeachable Hiss got himself impeached by his own arrogance. He had indeed not met anyone so 'named', because Chambers had gone under pseudonyms all his life and most especially during his years as a spy. He was going under the moniker of George Crosley when Hiss knew him. Not since Oscar Wilde regretted the ugliness of his serving boy while under oath has any cleverly crafted reply exacted such a stiff price.

One of these days I'm going to write a book called 'Guilty as Hell: A Short History of the American Left'. Revisionism has cut great roads through the *causes célèbres* of the *bien pensants*. Where are we now? Joe Hill probably guilty as charged, according to Wallace Stegner. Sacco and Vanzetti darker horses than we thought. The Rosenbergs at least half-guilty. Most of the Black Panthers (always excepting those murdered by the FBI) amazingly guilty. The Macnamara brothers certainly guilty. The Haymarket martyrs probably innocent, and the later Chicago conspiracy defendants also, even if they tried their best to be guilty. Mitigation is supplied by the fact that many of these former heroes and heroines were framed whether they were guilty or not – even J. Edgar Hoover was disgusted by the court's treatment of the Rosenbergs – and by the fact that many anonymous Wobblies and civil rights workers were brutally railroaded without a murmur. There is also my companion volume to bear in mind. (It's to be called 'Soft on Crime: The American Right from Nixon to North'.) What you learn is that an honourable fealty is easily corruptible into base utilitarianism: the injunction becomes one of 'not giving ammunition to the enemy'. In some cases, though not in the present one, this is a rough translation from 'not in front of the goyim'. Of course, a really determined denial of ammunition to the enemy could have licensed the abandonment of Hiss, in order to thwart Richard Nixon and Joseph McCarthy and thus accomplish a great good. But this historically justifiable tactic did not recommend itself even to people who had swallowed the Moscow trials without gagging, and who had explained away the Hitler–Stalin Pact (which Chambers opposed, while predicting that Hitler would break it before Stalin would) in easy phrases. As ever, one discovers that those who boast of taking the long view of history are hopelessly wedded to the short-term.

The McCarthy period is doubly ridiculous from this perspective, because it involved apparently intelligent people in contending, as a matter of principle, either that American liberals were really Communists or that American Communists were really liberals. Not everybody matches this brainless Cold War identikit. I. F. Stone never believed that the Rosenbergs were pathetic innocents, and the late and dearly mourned Murray Kempton always thought that Hiss must have been in touch with Moscow Centre, and both of these men were tougher opponents of McCarthy than the Communist Party, with its evasions and euphemisms, ever was. Nor does this exhaust the ironies. Whittaker Chambers earnestly counselled William Buckley and the fledgling *National Review* to steer clear of Joe McCarthy and his thuggish tactics. Buckley and his supporters flatly ignored this advice from the man they acclaimed as their Founding Father. So that the chief lesson learned and inculcated on the Right – the supposed superiority of the American populist Volk over the untrustworthy and even treasonable intellectuals – is easily shown to be silly, and nasty, and void.

It must be said for Tanenhaus, who on intuitive and other evidence is a neo-conservative of some stripe, that he makes the demented sequence and evolution of Chambers's actions into something intelligible. Why did he deny that there had been 'treason' in Washington for such a suspiciously long time? Because he had been a part of what he later alleged, and because the statute of limitations had not expired. Why did he hold back his clinching evidence? Because he thought he needed an insurance policy or ace-in-the-hole. Why did he stuff the material into a pumpkin? Because he was a paranoid solipsist. Why did he fear assassination? Because he knew of other defectors who had fallen victim to 'wet-jobs'. Why did he act as if he was Jesus of Nazareth when he was only being used as a launching-pad by the unscrupulous Nixon? Because he still thought that the Communists were on the winning side of history. This crazy salad of moves and motives, alternately loopy and rational, is somehow more believeable for being absurd. And always there is the clumsy gallantry towards Hiss himself: the slightly creepy element of more in sorrow than in anger. Having given the decisive evidence of Hiss's handwriting to Nixon, Chambers made a determined attempt to kill himself. When Hiss was released from Lewisburg Penitentiary, after serving forty-four months for perjury, Chambers refused to write a lucrative article on the event and quoted Marvell: 'He nothing common did or mean/Upon that memorable scene.' The ode, remember, was to Cromwell but the bow was to King Charles I. With Chambers and Hiss, it can be hard to determine which was the Roundhead and which the Cavalier.

As soon as possible after the collapse of Communism, Hiss asked the Russian authorities to look in their files and clear his name which, under the stewardship of the late General Dmitri Volkogonov, they briefly did. This impressed a good number of people: why would Hiss take the risk of asking for a search in the first place? However, subsequent disclosures from the Hungarian archives, chiefly concerning the bewildering quadruple agent Noel Field, and from the Venona NKVD traffic don't look so hot from the defence point of view.

Devotees of the case may want to fault Tanenhaus for repeating what earlier witnesses told Allen Weinstein for his book *Perjury*, and for taking the Hungarian papers at their face value, while excluding some second thoughts in both cases. There is no reason this argument should not continue until the last person who remembers it has expired.

Of William Wordsworth's desertion, Browning wrote that he did it 'just for a handful of silver' and 'just for a ribbon to stick in his coat'. That was probably unfair to Wordsworth and would be quite inadequate as a condemnation or explanation of Chambers. Of his own renunciation, Chambers said: 'I am a man who is very reluctantly and grudgingly, step by step, destroying myself so that this nation and the faith by which it lives may continue to exist.' This was the atrocious style the Cold War had taught him. He was capable of much better stuff. In 1951, he was commissioned to write a long essay on Graham Greene, but after a month's work told his editor he couldn't do it because he was too immersed in *Witness*. The review was to have been of *The End of the Affair*. What a shame that he never turned it in.

First published as 'A Regular Bull' (a review of *Whittaker Chambers: A Biography* by Sam Tanenhaus) in *London Review of Books*, 31 July 1997

Not Dead Yet

The Feast of St Valentine, 1989; a day of hearts and flowers and (since there can be no love without pain) a day for the depiction of arrows fired into the most sensitive viscera by cherubs and seraphs.

On this day I receive the news of a black arrow, launched from the heart of a supposedly holy city of ancient Persia, and aimed not at the heart but at the mind. The senile theocratic head of Iran's Islamic revolution, Ayatollah Ruhollah Khomeini, has announced a *fatwa*, a large bounty as an additional incitement to the murder of an author of fiction.

President's Day, 1989; timed in the national calendar to coincide as nearly as possible with the birthday of George Washington. Members of PEN (a union of sorts for poets, playwrights, essayists, and novelists) gather in a hall in rainy downtown Manhattan, and are endlessly frisked by uniformed police so that they can attend their own meeting in favour of free expression. A crowd waits in line in the drizzle and around the block so as to undergo the same experience. The meeting might not have taken place without the fortitude of Susan Sontag, this year's PEN Board Member at Large, who shames many backsliders into showing up, or at least sending messages. (One day, perhaps, the names of those who asked to be excused will become known.) There is fear everywhere. The big bookstore chains have announced that they will not stock *The Satanic Verses*, by Salman Rushdie, for 'security' reasons. Cardinal O'Connor of New York becomes the first of many religious leaders to say – in less time than it can possibly have taken him to read it – that the novel is 'blasphemous' and offensive.

This fear – of 'giving offence' – begins to spread through the respectable classes. The right of the author must, of course, be defended, but need the right have been exerted so ... well, *promiscuously*? At the rally, where the usual protest petition is circulated, I try and point out that this situation is different – in fact it is without precedent; a direct and open threat of murder against a prominent writer who is a citizen of another country, and against 'all those involved in its publication'. This is somewhat more than censorship, or even arbitrary imprisonment. To inscribe one's name to yet another protest disagreement or demurral seems insipid. I propose instead that all present sign their names as 'co-responsible for publication'. Come and get us: the mythical Spartacus reply and also – according to another old legend that also doesn't check out – the response of the King of Denmark to the Nazi order that his Jewish subjects wear a yellow star. Nonetheless, and despite these discouraging precedents, perhaps good for morale. To my surprise, the petition is drawn up in this way, and circulated and signed and reprinted. When first reprinted in London's *Times Literary Supplement*, however, the words 'while we regret any offence caused to believers' have been anonymously inserted by nervous hands. For the first time I have really noticed – maybe I should have seen it coming – how the terms of multicultural 'sensitivity' can be used to impose uniformity, and to create a cringe.

Salman Rushdie – who was forced to disappear into an extremely harrowing isolation during the week I have just recalled – is a friend of mine, and was a friend of mine then. I like to think that, in common with the many who came to the meetings in New York and Berkeley and elsewhere that I spoke (and in common with the terrific staffs of those craven bookstore chains, who rebelled and insisted on stocking and selling the book), my reaction would have been the same without this personal connection. However, it did help to know a bit about the subject or to put it another way, to know the subject himself.

For example, a few months earlier I had been at Edward Said's house for dinner when the manuscript of *The Satanic Verses* had been delivered. An accompanying note from the author asked for Edward's learned opinion and said something like: 'I anticipate some cries from the faithful.' In other words, Rushdie had known perfectly well all along that the fundamentalists and fanatics would not welcome his novel, which was an attempt to use holy writ for experimental and literary purposes. And he was seeking expert advice. In other words, 'he knew what he was doing'. Yet those very words, muttered darkly by cynics and conspiracy-theorists, were to be endlessly used against him, as if he had been the author not of a courageous novel, but of his own predicament as someone uniquely subject to a life sentence and a death sentence.

In the ensuing months, Rushdie's Japanese translator was to be murdered (and his body foully mutilated), and his Italian translator very badly injured by gangsters with direct connections to the Iranian secret services. Later, his Norwegian publisher was to be shot three times in the back and left for dead in the snow by elements of the same network. These three, too, 'knew what they were doing', and were willing to defy serious and believable threats in order to keep free thought and free expression alive. Not so Salman's publishers, who make a fortune every day out of the First Amendment and associated liberties, but who reneged on their contractual obligation to bring out a paperback. Not so British Airways, which runs a lucrative route to Tehran and which announced that it would not carry him as a passenger on any trip. (Air France, I might add for those booking tickets to Europe, said that it was a signatory of the International Declaration of the Rights of Man, and would fly him as a matter of principle.) And not so then-President George Bush, who declined to comment on the Ayatollah's lethal edict because 'American interests' were not involved. As Susan Sontag witheringly pointed out, the United States usually at least claims to have an interest in the defence of human rights and the repudiation of 'terrorism'. But Mr Bush was perhaps too fresh from his under-the-counter arms deals with Tehran to think clearly on this question.

Most bizarre of all, though, was the noise emitted by a number of eminent writers and authors. John Le Carré, John Berger, Roald Dahl, Hugh Trevor-Roper, and others began a sort of auction of defamation in which they accused Rushdie variously of insulting Islam, practising Western-style cultural colonialism and condescension, and damaging race relations. (They also accused him, most amazingly of all, of writing for money. What next?) Another school, chiefly composed of vulgar neo-conservatives in New York like Norman Podhoretz and A. M. Rosenthal, accused him of being a friend of Third World terrorism, and of thus having been hoist on his own petard. It's easy to notice that the first lot of allegations and innuendos completely contradicts the second, and also – and therefore – that there's something about the Rushdie case, and perhaps about Rushdie himself, that causes irrational irritation in certain people. It's not perhaps surprising that this should extend to the professionally religious. Cardinal O'Connor's denunciation was followed by the Archbishop of Canterbury, the Chief Rabbi of Israel, and the Vatican newspaper *L'Osservatore Romano*, ecumenicism in reverse, but acting in the spirit of the Counter-Enlightenment. But the annoyance of some secular figures – even those who expect to get paid for their work – has different roots. I suspect that one such root is the deep-seated need, among certain people, to say something raw and different. A ghoulish ayatollah issues a call for murder for pay; the bleeding hearts all set up a cry of protest: why not pull a pseudo-intellectual face and say: 'Well, it's more *complicated* than that'?

Actually, it *is* more complicated than that. For a long time now, a major fissure has been opening in the Muslim world. Tracing it is complex all right, but one need not despair at the task. To speak very roughly and approximately, Muslim societies are undergoing a general crisis of adaptation to modernity and to the 'West'. Some states, like Turkey and Egypt and Algeria, are faced with violent internal challenges to secularism, because secularism has been the guise either of corruption or of arbitrary rule. Others, like the Gulf States and Pakistan and Indonesia, have seen Islamic rhetoric used as the excuses for corruption and arbitrary rule, and have still faced rebellions from those who claim to be more truly Islamic. Among the most secular and pluralist Muslim populations, which are probably the Bosnians and the Palestinians, maltreatment at the hands of non-Muslims has caused some to value secularism more, and some to draw the opposite conclusion and value Muslim principles more dearly.

Rushdie's origins are Muslim and Indian – which by one definition, incidentally including the British colonial one, would make him a Pakistani. However, his heart belongs (as any reader of *The Moor's Last Sigh* will know) to the cosmopolitan city of Bombay, and to the long mixture of creed and culture in the Indian subcontinent. *The Moor's Last Sigh*, for example, deals at some length with the almost-forgotten topic of South Indian Jewry, and to the filiations which connect this idea to the old Moorish–Christian–Jewish synthesis that once flourished in Andalusia. In *Midnight's Children* and – even better in my opinion – in *Shame*, he satirized the ways in which Islam is used for purposes of national pomposity and illusion, and also for short-term propaganda. This however did not make him, as the ultra-orthodox claimed, into an apostate. Not long before the Iranian *fatwa* of 1989, he made a documentary in India about the little-understood threat of Hindu chauvinism, and predicted the grim confrontation that later took place over the destruction of the Babri mosque at Ayodhya. For this, interestingly enough, he was denounced in the Hindu extremist press as a tool of Islam. The only evidence for this preposterous idea was that he had won – as the Ayatollah's defenders often forget – the main Iranian fiction prize for his novels about partition and hypocrisy and postcolonialism in the Indian subcontinent.

Without exactly electing himself to the task, in other words, Rushdie had become one of the threads in the labyrinth, as well as one of those tracing it. Disaffected intellectuals in Iran, who had hated the Shah as a despot and a Western puppet, saw him overthrown by people who hated *everything* about the West, including the concept of the disaffected intellectual. (Think of Professor Benjamin Barber's book-length formulation *Jihad vs MacWorld*). After the Iranian revolution, there was a kaleidoscopic separation between those who were against both Jihad and MacWorld (the Left in Pakistan and Palestine, for example); those who were for MacWorld and against Jihad (the élites in Egypt and Turkey, yearning for integration into the global economy); those who were for Jihad and against MacWorld (the Taliban in Afghanistan come to mind, with their destruction of all the television sets in Kabul); and – perhaps most forbidding of all – those who favoured combining

MacWorld and Jihad. The Iranian rulers, with their arms deals and technological aspirations and medieval rhetoric, were perhaps the purest instance of the last hybrid, though I would bet that they will have their emulators in some of the Caucasian republics and perhaps in Malaysia and Indonesia too, as they have had their forerunners in Pakistan, the first Muslim state to develop a thermonuclear weapon.

One thing that obviously couldn't go unchallenged, in this boiling-up of contradictions, was the simplistic acceptance of the Koran as the only assembly-manual any society could ever need. Yet the amazing thing is that, until *The Satanic Verses*, no one had come right out and said as much. There were ostensibly Muslim societies that had gone ahead as if leaving the question behind or to one side, but without quite resolving it; just as there are states of the American Union that rely on e-mail and oil revenues, but elect snake-handling Biblical literalists to local, and even national, prominence. Try making this occluded question explicit – even in the form of a play or a novel in lower Tennessee – and see what you get. Then multiply by various factors and picture the impact in Anatolia or upper Egypt. Or in America or Britain for that matter – crowds of Pakistani immigrants demonstrated in favour of Rushdie's execution in the early days of the crisis, perhaps over-compensating for the feeling that they had left their 'roots' behind; and in the United States, I was told by Fouad Ajami, an apparently suave academic and frequent TV 'consultant' on Shi'a Muslim affairs, that he would never agree to speak with Rushdie or to debate his vile book.

By accident or merit of timing, the novel and the controversy fell right athwart the fault line. One of the most absorbing books on my shelf is a collection, first published in France under the title *Pour Rushdie*, of comments by leading writers and intellectuals in the Arab and Persian and Kurdish worlds. Generally more forthright and more courageous than their Western cousins, these authors – from the Egyptian Nobel Laureate Naguib Mahfouz to the Palestinian poet Mahmoud Darwish – stipulated not just their fellow feeling for good old Salman, but their sense of *identification* with the personal and social dilemma he had exposed. Many Iranian writers contributed under their own names, which took nerve unavailable to most petition-signers. It wasn't, in other words, a question of adopting Western values, but of attaining to a freedom that predates the concept of the West – the freedom to experiment with ideas and with language, and to defy the proscriptions of stone tablets or holy writ or unalterable codes. Anyway, many writers from the 'Muslim' world got the point more clearly, and more swiftly, than some of their 'free world' counterparts.

Even in the early days of the *fatwa* crisis, when all seemed bleak and there was actually more 'Western' sympathy for official Islamic self-pity than many people care to remember, there were some interesting things that did not happen. No other Muslim state, for example, joined the Iranian call to impose the death penalty for money. This may have been partly an aversion to needless unpleasantness – the Saudis, for example, claim to be more fundamentalist than anybody, but Saudi banks in the United States do not follow the Koranic prohibition against charging interest – and it may also have reflected the lack of love between Sunni and Shi'a Islam. But there was a reticence. Translations of the book, many of them pirated, soon became available in countries like Turkey and Egypt and even Iran. It became possible for readers to discover for themselves that Rushdie had not defamed the Prophet Mohammed or lampooned his wives as whores, as the Ayatollah, who most definitely had not scanned the book, had said. The 'offending' phrases occur in the course of a nightmare dream experienced by an obvious madman. (I should add Rushdie would have had every right to insult religion in this way, even if he didn't choose to exert it.) All the excitements of a prohibited book had their usual effect, one of which, as always, is to expose the fact that the censors don't know what they are talking about. If 'globalisation' means anything, it means that this sort of discovery is easier to make, even in the poorest society, than it was in the days when *Ulysses* had to be purchased under the counter.

Things went on in a somewhat routine way for much of the intervening time between 1989 and today. Each year it became a little harder to know what to do to mark the anniversary. Rushdie's case became one among many, without losing its distinctiveness. He involved himself vocally on the side of the Muslims of Bosnia, while those who had shouted loudest about his profaning of the Koran – not excluding many Muslim fundamentalists – greeted the awful bulletins from Sarajevo and Srebrenica with a yawn. The Bosnians were too cosmopolitan and sophisticated (quite a different concept from feel-good 'multiculturalism', incidentally) to attract much attention from the fanatics. Hindu fascists seized positions of power in India – as he had warned they might – and were much satirised in Rushdie's novel *The Moor's Last Sigh*, but didn't quite succeed in banning his new novel and didn't issue any blood-curdling threat, so didn't get as much attention. Every now and then, there were rumours of a deal between Iran and the European Union, which had defined the case as an obstacle to 'normalisation', but these tended to be false alarms. Starting with Vaclav Havel, and Mary Robinson of Ireland, some heads of state agreed to receive Rushdie and to make his case a test not of trade or sanctions, but of a common international standard for the defence of free speech. Even Bill Clinton, after some persuasion, consented not to follow the precedent of indifference set by Bush.

Then, on 24 September last, everything changed. The Iranian Foreign Minister, Kamal Kharrazi, met the British Foreign Minister, Robin Cook, and announced that the Iranian government would never attempt anything to threaten Rushdie's life, and would dissociate itself from the bounty, and would discourage any who looked like acting upon it. This statement was held up to the light and examined from all angles for reservations and small print, and other symptoms of the false alarm. It could have been more beautifully phrased, I must say. But it was adjudged believable, by Rushdie and by the relevant diplomatic and security analysts, because it seemed authentic for other reasons. In a long-delayed presidential election, held under relatively democratic rules, Mohammed Khatami had easily defeated the clerical extremists and assumed at least the titular leadership of the country. As a former hard-liner (he'd been of the fearsome 'Ministry for Islamic Guidance' during the hot days of the anti-Rushdie campaign), Khatami had every reason to understand that hysterical threats of this sort brought diminishing returns. He had also guessed that there was a deep desire among ordinary Iranians to be done with the time when bearded inquisitors told everyone what to do. Furthermore, he was faced on one border by appalling challenges from the Taliban in Afghanistan, who had executed Iranian envoys and put the Shi'a minority in their country to the sword. In the mirror, he could read the consequences of unchecked medievalism, and actually moved large forces to the frontier in order to ensure against them.

As anyone who has ever attended a film festival or been to a decent college can attest, the world is full of intelligent and cultivated Iranians, compelled to live in diaspora by a dismal and boring and vicious regime. Khatami wants some of this talent back. He also wants the good relations with other countries that go along with it. The symbol of the old and failed and now corrupted system is the *fatwa*. But of course, there were people who knew better than him. One was Daniel Pipes, the cynical and ignorant Middle East polemicist for *Commentary* magazine, and the others were the death-squad die-hards in Iran itself.

Writing in *Commentary* last December, Pipes described Rushdie and his friends as 'deluded' in accepting Khatami's assurances. He pointed to the following reactions inside Iran:

One newspaper editorialised that 'the issue of Rushdie will end only with killing him and all the elements associated with the publishing of the book'. A leading ayatollah declared that executing Rushdie remains a duty incumbent on all Muslims 'until the day of resurrection'. In Parliament, 150 of the 270 members signed an open letter stressing the edict's utter irrevocability. The Association of Hezbollah University Students announced it would add a billion riyals ($333,000) to the reward for Rushdie's assassin; theological students in the holy city of Qom pledged a month's salary as an additional bounty; and a small village in northern Iran sweetened the pot by offering his executioner ten carpets, 5,400 square yards of agricultural land, and a house with a garden.

Be afraid . . . be very afraid. The academic experts on 'terrorism' insist upon it. But look back over that list of bat-winged menaces. The unsourced editorial from 'one newspaper' is pure wind. They've been publishing bluster like that for a decade and nobody has donned a shroud and suicide-bombed any of the publishers in any language en route to paradise. The unnamed ayatollah (all ayatollahs are 'leading' by definition; it's a title of leadership) seems to be taking an almost metaphysically long view of the matter, perhaps to avoid disappointment in this vale of actually existing tears. One hundred and twenty members of parliament, we learn, did *not* sign a statement that described an empty edict as 'irrevocable' – surely a sign of progress. If the 'Association of Hezbollah University Students' has so much spare cash, which I take leave to doubt, then I hope they have put their deposit in an escrow rather than an interest-bearing and usurious account. What is the monthly salary of a theological student in the unholy dump of Qom anyway? Does Pipes know that they all kicked in? The last rustic detail is truly touching. In the same way as those scabies-ridden hamlets in the time of George III, which offered to burn Thomas Paine in effigy and had no literate citizen to read *The Rights of Man*, but who hoped by a pathetic demonstration of zeal to attract favourable notice from the squire.

Unwilling to admit or even consider that the scenery of Oz had collapsed, Pipes was particularly upset by what he called Rushdie's 'gratuitous' retraction of his 1990 statement affirming Islamic belief. This retraction, on the day of last September's victory press conference, he sniffily described as an 'insult'. I have news for Pipes – two bits of news, as a matter of fact. Rushdie, who was brought up as a Muslim, first retracted that statement in public in 1992; it had been extorted from him in bad faith by clerical negotiators who did not keep their word. Second, he did not so much retract it as describe it as the moment he most regretted in the affair. And here is where I part company with him: I like that moment of hesitation and trepidation. I didn't like it at the time (we had a narrow but deep, and friendly but absolute difference about it) but I like it now. I see it in retrospect as the moment when a novelist, a lone producer working in imperilled isolation, saw that he'd become enmeshed in something global and lethal and irrational, and apparently unending; and sought, if possible, to preserve himself and his privacy. Galileo did the same, and the planets went on moving around the sun whatever the Church said. For Salman to crook the knee, however, would have been to disown – or, at any rate, to cheapen – his earlier statement that free expression was more important than his book or even his life and so, with a heavy shrug, he disowned his disowning. Having then accepted the implied burden of responsibility, he lived up to it with great gaiety and determination. He has helped set up an international network for the rescue and protection of persecuted writers. He has set aside his own work to help authors on the run, from the distinguished Wole Soyinka to the rather sad Taslima Nasrin. Meanwhile, it will become steadily more embarrassing for him to be passed over for the Nobel Prize for Literature, because he is continuing to raise an edifice of fiction about the one world in which we're all condemned to live, which the late inconvenience has been powerless to destroy.

The true refutation of Pipes came in January 1999. A series of filthy and cowardly attacks on Iranian writers took place at the close of 1998, with several killed at home with their families and others assaulted or threatened. It became obvious that the assailants were trying to create a 'strategy of tension', aimed at the reformist and open-minded initiatives of the fledging Khatami government. But in a much more astonishing development, the Iranian Ministry of Information announced that some of the gangsters had been apprehended, and were 'irresponsible, misguided, and unruly' members of that same ministry's own personnel. No matter whether or not the guilty are eventually punished, or even identified; this has now become an argument not between Iran and the world, but with Iran and itself. The Iranians are forced to have the internal dispute, not to please some theoretical Western opinion, but in order to clarify and make whole their own society and its principles.

This, in my view, crowns the victory. Although some deadly and dangerous thrusts were made at my friend (and it's still not possible to give details, except that the efforts were made by state agents and not demented freelancers from obscure northern Iranian villages), the *fatwa* did not kill him. It did not stop him from writing. It did not silence the debate on first principles in the Muslim intellectual world. It did not stop publishers in all countries and tongues from putting his work into circulation. I sometimes can't believe my own good fortune: to have had the chance to defend civilisation's essential principle (no more than payback time, really, for someone who makes a living from free speech), and to have done so in the company of one of the world's greatest novelists. How odd it is that such a cultural triumph has occurred right before our eyes, and that we are so grudging and cramped and envious and suspicious as hardly to have noticed or appreciated it.

First published as 'Not Dead Yet' in *Black Book*, Spring 1999

II

'In Spite of Themselves . . .'

Old Man Kipling

In *Regeneration*, the opening book of Pat Barker's 'Ghost Road' trilogy about the First World War, one of the characters summons the waking nightmare of the trenches: 'I was going up with the rations one night and I saw the limbers against the skyline, and the flares going up. What you see every night. Only I seemed to be seeing it from the future. A hundred years from now they'll still be ploughing up skulls. And I seemed to be in that time and looking back. I think I saw our ghosts.'

A ghost is something that is dead but won't lie down. Those who were slaughtered between 1914 and 1918 are still in our midst to an astonishing degree. On the first day of the Battle of the Somme, in July 1916, the British alone posted more killed and wounded than appear on the whole of the Vietnam memorial. In the Battle of Verdun, which began the preceding February, 675,000 lives were lost. Between them, Britain, France, the United States, Germany, Turkey, and Russia sacrificed at least *10 million* soldiers. And this is to say nothing of civilian losses. Out of the resulting chaos and misery came the avenging forces of fascism and Stalinism.

One reason for the enduring and persistent influence of the Great War (as they had to call it at the time, not knowing that it would lead to a second and even worse one) is that it shaped the literature of the Anglo-American world. Think of the titles that remain on the shelves: *Good-Bye to All That*, by Robert Graves, 'Anthem for Doomed Youth', by Wilfred Owen. The poetry of Rupert Brooke and Siegfried Sassoon. Translations from German and French, such as Erich Maria Remarque's *All Quiet on the Western Front* and *Under Fire*, by Henri Barbusse. By enlisting in the Great War, a whole generation of Americans, including William Faulkner, Ernest Hemingway, e. e. cummings, and John Dos Passos, made the leap from small-town USA to twentieth-century modernism. Loss of moral virginity and innocence is the burden of Sebastian Faulks's elegiac novel, *Birdsong*, written in this decade, but as full of pain and poetry as if composed in his grandfather's time. We owe the term 'shell shock' to this period, and it sometimes feels as if the shock has never worn off.

I've been passing much of my time, over the past year or so, in trying to raise just one of these ghosts. On September 27 1915, during the Battle of Loos, a young lieutenant of the Irish Guards was posted 'wounded and missing'. His name was John Kipling, and he was the only son of the great Bard of Empire, Rudyard Kipling. Kipling never goes out of print, because he not only captured the spirit of imperialism and the white man's burden but also wrote imperishable stories and poems – many of them to the boy John – about the magic and lore of childhood. And on that shell-shocked September day, the creator of Mowgli and Kim had to face the fact that he had sacrificed one of his great loves – his son, whom he called his 'man-child' – to another of his great loves: the British Empire. You can trace the influence of this tragedy through almost every line that he subsequently wrote.

Go to the small towns of northern France today if you want to discover that the words 'haunted landscape' are no cliché. Around the city of Arras, scattered along any road that you may take, are cemeteries. Kipling called them 'silent cities'. (I came across an article in a French tourist magazine that recommended Arras to those who wished to pursue '*le tourisme de nécropole*' – mass-grave tourism. Indeed, there isn't much else to see.) This used to be the coal-bearing region of France, and great slag heaps and abandoned mine works add an additional layer of melancholy to the scenery. But otherwise it's graveyards, graveyards all the way. Some of them are huge and orderly, with seemingly endless ranks and files of white markers stretching away in regimental patterns. But many are small and isolated, off in the middle of fields where French farmers have learned to plough around them. These represent heaps of bodies that simply couldn't be moved and were interred where they lay. Huge land grants have been made by the government and people of France, in perpetuity, to Britain and Canada and India and the United States, just to consecrate the fallen.

This is one of the few parts of France where the locals are patient with Anglo-Saxon visitors trying to ask directions in French. And those French ploughmen know what to do when, as so often happens, they turn up a mass of barbed wire or a batch of shells and mortars or a skeleton. ('A hundred years from now they'll still be ploughing up skulls.') They call the police, who alert the Commonwealth War Graves Commission. And then the guesswork can begin. There's a good deal of latitude. Of the 531,000 or so British Empire dead whose remains have been fertilizing the region for most of the century, about 212,000 are still unidentified.

'Every now and then we have a bit of luck', I was told by Peter Rolland of the commission, which runs a large and quiet office just outside Arras and which is charged with keeping all the graves clean. 'Last year we dug up twelve corpses. Most of their dog tags and uniforms were eroded or decayed hopelessly. But we did manage to identify one Australian chap called Sergeant J. J. White. We even found his daughter, who was two years old when he was killed, and she came over for the funeral.'

And a few years ago, almost eight decades after he went missing, they found Kipling's son, John. His body had lain in no-man's-land for three years and then been hastily shovelled into an unmarked grave. Kipling and his wife made several desperate visits to the area in the hope of identifying him, touring battlefield after battlefield. But this was in the days before proper dental records and DNA, and they gradually gave up. In 1992, thanks to painstaking record-keeping and the amateur interest taken by a member of the commission staff, one anonymous grave in one small cemetery was finally commemorated as John's.

This means that a new marker has been erected. The old one read, A LIEUTENANT OF THE GREAT WAR. KNOWN UNTO GOD. The wording is actually that of Kipling Sr, who in order to atone for John's disappearance became a founding member of what was then called the Imperial War Graves Commission, and helped design its monuments and rituals. As another atonement, he took on the unpaid job of writing the wartime history of the Irish Guards. In that work, he coldly summed up the regiment's toll of 324 casualties in a single battle and noted that 'of their officers, 2nd Lieutenant Pakenham-Law had died of wounds; 2nd Lieutenants Clifford and Kipling were missing . . . It was a fair average for the day of a debut.'

Kipling's autobiography, *Something of Myself,* is even more eerily detached. 'My son John arrived on a warm August night of '97, under what seemed every good omen.' That's the only mention of the boy in the entire book. Kipling had already lost a beloved daughter to influenza. He seems to have felt that if he wrote any more he wouldn't be able to trust himself.

For a father to mourn or to bury his son is an offence to the natural order of things. Yet another reason for the endless fascination of the Great War is the reverse-Oedipal fashion in which, for several lunatic years, the sight of old men burying young men was the natural order. And this in a civilised Europe bred to the expansive optimism of the late nineteenth century.

John Kipling was only sixteen when the war broke out. Pressed by his father to volunteer, he was rejected on the grounds of poor eyesight. (Those who have read 'Baa Baa, Black Sheep', Rudyard's chilling story derived from his own childhood at the mercy of sadistic guardians, will remember the horror of the small boy being punished for clumsiness and poor scholarship when actually he has an undiagnosed myopia.) The proud and jingoistic father used his influence with the high command to get young John commissioned anyway. His mother's diary recorded that 'John leaves at noon . . . He looks very straight and smart and young, as he turned [*sic*] at the top of the stairs to say: "Send my love to Dad-o." '

He didn't last more than a few weeks. The village of Loos, where he disappeared, was also where the British found out about modern warfare; it was at Loos that they first tried to use poison gas as a weapon of combat. (It blew back into their own trenches, with unimaginable results.) In a neighbouring sector a short while later, the British became the first to deploy a tank. But in late 1915, war was mainly blood, mud, bayonets, and high explosives.

Accounts of the boy's last moments differ, but Kipling's friend H. Rider Haggard (creator of *King Solomon's Mines* and *She*) took a lot of trouble interviewing witnesses. He recorded in his diary that one of them, a man named Bowe, 'saw an officer who *he could swear* was Mr Kipling leaving the wood on his way to the rear and trying to fasten a field dressing round his mouth which was badly shattered by a piece of shell. Bowe would have helped him but for the fact that the officer was crying with the pain of the wound and he did not want to humiliate him by offering assistance. I shall not send this on to Rudyard Kipling – it is too painful.'

Indeed it would have been: a half-blind kid making his retreat under fire and in tears, with a devastating wound. No definition of stiff upper lip would have covered it. And almost the last of John's letters home had said, 'By the way, the next time would you get me an Identification Disc as I have gone and lost mine . . . Just an aluminum Disc with a string through it.' Probably it's a good thing that the poet of the Raj never knew his boy died weeping. At one point he wrote, in a cynical attempt to brace himself, 'My son was killed while laughing at some jest. I would I knew / What it was, and it might serve me in a time when jests are few.'

To a friend he wrote, 'I don't suppose there is much hope for my boy and the little that is left doesn't bear thinking of. However, I hear that he finished well . . . It was a short life. I'm sorry that all the years' work ended in one afternoon, but lots of people are in our position, and it's something to have bred a man.' His wife, Caroline, wrote more feelingly to her mother, 'If one could but know he was dead . . .'

Haggard may have wished to spare Kipling pain, but one has to say that Kipling did not try to spare himself. His whole personality as an author underwent a deep change. At different stages, one can see the influence of parental anguish, of patriotic rage, of chauvinistic hatred, and of personal guilt. A single couplet almost contrives to compress all four emotions into one: 'If any question why we died, / Tell them, because our fathers lied.'

These Spartan lines are anti-war and pro-war to almost the same extent. The fathers had lied, not just by encouraging their sons to take lethal risks, but by not preparing enough for war and therefore letting the young people pay for their complacency. Kipling's longer poem 'The Children' possesses the same ambiguity:

> These were our children who died for our
>   lands: they were dear in our sight.
> We have only the memory left of their
>   home-treasured sayings and laughter.
> The price of our loss shall be paid to our
>   hands, not another's hereafter.
> Neither the Alien nor Priest shall decide
>   on it. That is our right.
>   *But who shall return us the children?*

After a few lines of expressive loathing about the German foe, Kipling returns to the idea that the massacre of the innocents has an element of domestic responsibility to it:

> . . . Our statecraft, our learning
> Delivered them bound to the Pit and
>   alive to the burning
> Whither they mirthfully hastened as
>   jostling for honour –
> Not since her birth has our Earth seen
>   such worth loosed upon her.

(Chalk Pit Wood was the last place his son was seen alive.) And then, giving vent to all the ghastly rumours he and his wife had heard about what happened to bodies caught in no-man's-land, he continues:

> The flesh we had nursed from the first in
>   all cleanness was given
> To corruption unveiled and assailed by
>   the malice of Heaven –
> By the heart-shaking jests of Decay where
>   it lolled on the wires –
> To be blanched or gay-painted by fumes –
>   to be cindered by fires –
> To be senselessly tossed and retossed in
>   stale mutilation
> From crater to crater. For this we shall
>   take expiation.
>   *But who shall return us our children?*

Uncertainty was torturing Kipling here into imagining the worst and most obscene fate for his son. At other times he was more resigned and more wistful, as in the short poem 'My Boy Jack':

'Have you news of my boy Jack?'
Not this tide.
'When d'you think that he'll come back?'
Not with this wind blowing, and this tide.
'Has any one else had word of him?'
Not this tide.
For what is sunk will hardly swim,
Not with this wind blowing, and this tide.

The inquiring voice asks for a crumb of hope or comfort, and receives the reply:

Then hold your head up all the more,
This tide,
And every tide;
Because he was the son you bore,
And gave to that wind blowing and that tide!

The penultimate line reinforces the impression that the seeker in the poem is a woman. Odd to think of Kipling as having a feminine aspect, but perhaps the verse is meant as a tribute to his American wife, who was driven almost out of her mind with grief. On the other hand, one might throw sentiment to one side and remember that Kipling famously wrote (in a poem designed to tease a daughter who favoured women's suffrage) that 'the female of the species is more deadly than the male'. And this is most certainly true of the main character in a subsequent short story of Kipling's entitled 'Mary Postgate'. Angus Wilson once described it as evil; at all events it is a paean of hatred and cruelty and shows Kipling banishing all his doubts and guilts in favour of one cathartic burst of sickening revenge.

Mary Postgate is a wartime spinster who looks after an elderly lady in an English village. One day, a German airman crashes in her garden and lies crippled in the laurel bushes. Mary Postgate decides to see how long it will take him to die. She tells nobody about the intruder and makes no effort to summon help. She waits and watches 'while an increasing rapture laid hold on her'. As the young man finally expires, she 'drew her breath short between her teeth and shivered from head to foot'. Then she takes a 'luxurious hot bath before tea' and, 'lying all relaxed on the other sofa', startles her employer by looking, for once, 'quite handsome!'

It's really seriously creepy to find Kipling – normally rather reticent in such matters – writing a caricature of a female orgasm and wallowing in the voluptuousness of sadism. The justification for it all is that a child has been killed by a bomb in the village. 'I have seen the dead child', says Mary Postgate to the dying airman. So the link is unmistakable. And the story – published in 1917 – is closed by one of the worst sets of verses that this splendid poet ever composed. Its refrain is the line 'When the English began to hate.' Omitted from most anthologies, it is a vulgar and bullying rant, which promises that 'Time shall count from the date / That the English began to hate.'

I first became aware of the poem when it was dished out as a leaflet by a British Nazi organisation in the 1970s. (David Edgar makes use of it in *Destiny*, his incisive play about the mentality of fascism.) I have often thought it very fortunate that Kipling died in 1936. He had already begun to praise Mussolini by then, and God knows what he might have said about the manly new Germany – even though his visceral dislike of all Germans would perhaps have kept him in check. He certainly disliked Germans (whom he habitually called 'Huns') even more than he did Jews (whom he generally called 'Hebrews').

His letters are fiercer than his poems and short stories, and like them they took a turn for the worse after John's disappearance. To his old friend L. C. Dunsterville he wrote, at the height of the bloodletting in September 1916, that things seemed to be going jolly well on the Western Front. 'It's a scientific-cum-sporting murder proposition with enough guns at last to account for the birds, and the Hun is having a very sickly time of it. He has the erroneous idea that he is being hurt, whereas he won't know what real pain means for a long time. I almost begin to hope that when we have done with him there will be very little Hun left.'

The word for this, in or out of context, is 'unseemly'.

Most interesting, though, was his extensive wartime correspondence with Theodore Roosevelt. One has to remember that Kipling at that time was the best-known living writer in the English language. His following in the United States was immense. His famous poem 'The White Man's Burden', more often quoted than read, had actually been written for Roosevelt in 1898 and was addressed to the US Congress. It urged that body (successfully) to 'take up the white man's burden' by annexing the newly conquered Philippines. Such was Kipling's ability to sway public opinion on both sides of the Atlantic that in 1914, when the Liberal British foreign secretary Sir Edward Grey heard that Kipling was planning a trip to America, Grey told the Cabinet that unless he was assured that this dangerous Tory poet was going in an unofficial capacity he would resign at once.

Teddy Roosevelt, of course, favoured American entry into the Great War, and Kipling made a point of supplying him with ammunition. The poet didn't hesitate to make very emotional appeals, and as a result gave a few hostages to fortune. In December 1914 he wrote to T. R. telling him encouragingly that the Germans 'have been sending up their younger men and boys lately on our front. This is valuable because these are prospective fathers, and they come up to the trenches with superb bravery. Then they are removed.'

The letter goes on, 'Suppose my only son dies, I for one should not "view with equanimity" Mr Wilson (however unswayed by martial prejudice) advising or recommending my country how to behave at the end of this War.' Kipling really despised Woodrow Wilson and his hypocritical neutrality, and after John's death he gave his contempt free rein, describing Wilson as equivalent to an ape looking down from a tree. 'My grief', he wrote, 'is that the head of the country is a man unconnected by knowledge or experience with the facts of the world in which we live. All of which must be paid for in the lives of good men.'

This relentless drumbeat, which also urged T. R. in menacing tones to beware of the millions of potentially disloyal German-Americans, helped breed a pro-war atmosphere in the United States. Many of the Americans who went to fight in Europe did so as volunteers, preparing the ground for later, full-scale intervention. And when the American Expeditionary Force got going, it took heavy casualties. Among these was Quentin Roosevelt, son of Teddy, who was killed while serving as a pilot. T. R.'s reponse was almost Kiplingesque in its gruffness. 'My only regret is that I could not give myself', he said. But of course he could not have given himself, any more than Kipling could. This was an opportunity open strictly to sons.

The current tenant of Headstone Two in Row D of Plot Seven in St Mary's Advanced Dressing Station Cemetery never had any idea of what a titanic conflict had snuffed out his life. Nor had he any notion of the role his death would play in his father's poetry or his father's propaganda. His is just one of 1,768 British and 19 Canadian graves in St Mary's ADS, 1,592 of which are unidentified and likely to remain so forever.

The gardener, Ian Nelson, met me at the gate and took me around. He was a working-class type from my hometown in Hampshire, just one of the many hundreds of people who live and work in northern France, stranded in time, preserving a moment and observing the decencies. He wasn't the garrulous type, preferring to roll his own cigarettes and to say briefly that he was 'old-fashioned' and 'felt we owed something' to the fallen. His main enemies were the moles, which spoil the flower beds and lawns. He explained to me how certain alpine and herbaceous plantings protect the headstones from mud splashes in the winter and mowing machines in the summer. Floribunda roses were in profusion, and baby maple trees, and there was the odd Flanders poppy.

The register and the visitors' book were kept in a metal-and-stone safe in a corner of the cemetery, and as we got there we found an old metal button in the dirt. It was a standard-issue Great War soldier's button, with a faded lion-and-unicorn motif, and Mr Nelson let me keep it with a look that said, Plenty more where that came from. Most of the names in the register are printed and have been for decades, and it is reprinted every few years. But a hand-written addition had just been made, showing that John, only son of Mr and Mrs Rudyard Kipling of Bateman's, Burwash, Sussex, England, had made the supreme sacrifice while serving as a lieutenant in the Irish Guards. The visitors' book had a space for remarks, and many visitors had done their best to say something. I didn't want to let down the side, so I put in the last few lines of Wilfred Owen's 'The Parable of the Old Man and the Young'.

Owen was killed in a futile canal-crossing skirmish just a few days before the end of the war, in November 1918 (his mother got the telegram just as the church bells were pealing for victory and a general rejoicing was getting under way), but before he died he composed the most wrenching and lyrical poetry of the entire conflict. Nearly fifty years later, it furnished the libretto for Benjamin Britten's *War Requiem*. In Owen's rewriting of the story of Abraham and Isaac, the old man is about to press the knife to the throat of his firstborn:

> When lo! an angel called him out of heaven,
> Saying, Lay not thy hand upon the lad,
> Neither do anything to him. Behold,
> A ram, caught in a thicket by its horns;
> Offer the Ram of Pride instead of him.
> But the old man would not so,
>   but slew his son,
> And half the seed of Europe, one by one.

First published as 'Young Men and War' in *Vanity Fair*, February 1997

Critic of the Booboisie

In my spare time I collect significant encounters that never took place. Karl Marx and Charles Darwin were intended by a mutual friend to meet but the rendezvous did not occur. George Orwell waited for Albert Camus to keep an appointment in a café in St Germain but gave up and slouched away. Almost as soon as he was exiled to Switzerland, Alexander Solzhenitsyn made a date to have lunch with Vladimir Nabokov, but apparently lost his nerve and failed the feast. On the day of the terrible stroke that pulled down his mental shutters for good, H. L. Mencken was due to break bread with Evelyn Waugh.

It would have been good to have (even from Alistair Cooke, who had proposed the introduction) an account of this aborted conversation between two Tories, two snobs, two racists, two masters of prose and humour and invective, two literary products of the vulgar industry of journalism. One was a self-caricaturing English type with a disdain for America and the other a snarling Anglophobe who believed that American English was a distinct language; one was a preposterously dogmatic Roman Catholic and the other a man who described himself as 'a materialist's materialist'. Both men had a surreptitious fancy for fascism, but fascists are by definition hard to internationalise, and it might be that their antagonisms would have outweighed their sympathies. Between those who are hardily cynical about human nature and those who profess a belief in original sin, there is no necessary agreement.

Mencken, though, survives as much more of a conundrum for enlightened and 'progressive' Americans than does Waugh for their English counterparts. While Waugh was a self-proclaimed and classic reactionary, once famously excoriating the Conservative party for failing to turn back the clock by as much as a minute, Mencken comes down to us as an advocate of literary and scientific modernism. He was the first American editor to publish James Joyce. He admired Joseph Conrad almost as much as he did Mark Twain, and won Conrad's respectful acknowledgement as a critic. He did much to convince American readers to throw off nativism and 'uplift' in their choice of fiction. In one of the great confrontations between Reason and Reaction – the Scopes trial in Tennessee – Mencken was the impresario to Clarence Darrow and became, for all succeeding generations, the official historian and quote-meister of the episode. Yet he was a bigot. Indeed, not so much a bigot as an actual 'scientific' or quasi-anthropological racist. And he was not so much an opponent of the New Deal, or of reformist and optimistic enterprises and utopias, as he was a foe to democracy itself.

But, as has been shown by writers as diverse as Murray Kempton and Gore Vidal, it is sometimes necessary for a radical critic to be contemptuous of 'public opinion'. Cynicism, which is most often the affectation of conservatives, can also be part of the armour of those who are prepared to go through life as a minority of one. Populism, which is in the last instance always an illiberal style, may come tricked out as folkish emancipation. That is when it most needs to be satirised. In his wonderful novel *The Child in Time*, Ian McEwan describes the experience of watching daytime television audiences as 'the democrat's pornography'. I thought of Mencken when I read that. He had very many grievous moral and intellectual shortcomings and even deformities. But the itch to be at one with the wisdom of the majority was not one of them. *Vox populi, vox dei* – a treacherous saying that has often been used to cement alliances between the plutocracy and the mob. It helps, of course, in resisting the *populi* bit, if you are convinced that the *dei* part is nonsense also. Thus we have Mencken, in his heroic period, defending Eugene Debs and Robert LaFollette not because they were tribunes of the plebs but because they were individuals of integrity who stood out against the yelling crowd as well as against the oligarchy. If only all of his ironies had been so pleasing.

The best attack on Mencken has been written in our own time by Garry Wills, who so to speak re-opened the Scopes trial in his *Under God*. Far from being 'the idol of all Morondom', in Mencken's lapidary phrase, William Jennings Bryan was a serious exponent of the 'social gospel'. He actually had a sincere concern with the political implications of Darwinism: 'this doctrine of the strongest'. Having spent an admittedly rather bellowing career as a defender of the downtrodden, an advocate of female suffrage, and an opponent of capital punishment, he feared that 'Social Darwinism' – a term not actually coined until later in the century – would resurrect ancient cruelties and unfairness and guise them as scientific findings or necessities. One can overstate Bryan's decency and compassion (even Wills concedes that he was feeble about segregation because 'few populists could afford to oppose their poor white constituents') but there is no question that Mencken did take the viewpoint of 'natural selection' precisely because it validated his own views of Nietzsche and the pitiless battle for mastery:

There must be complete surrender to the law of natural selection – that invariable natural law which ordains that the fit shall survive and the unfit shall perish. All growth must occur at the top. The strong must grow stronger, and that they may do so, they must waste no strength in the vain task of trying to lift up the weak.

Mencken wrote this in his first serious book, a study of Nietzsche published in 1908. It is thus possible to derive all of his finest and most memorable polemics – against the First World War, against Christian fundamentalism, against the Anglophile WASP aristocracy, and against the backwardness and misery of the Dixie states – from an essentially vile and infirm premise that he adopted from the outset. He opposed the First World War because he thought Wilhelmine Germany to be the embodiment of Nietzschan strength and virtue. He opposed the Christian fundamentalists because they made it easier for him to attack religion itself – the source of all sickly and irrelevant feelings of charity. Dislike for the Anglophiles and WASPs was a natural corollary for a man who believed in Teutonism, while contempt for the states of the old Confederacy was a merely pleasurable corollary of that, because it offered up the Anglo-Saxon white trash at their trashiest and their Christianity in its most maudlin and twisted form. No wonder, then, that in his ill-tempered and misanthropic shape, he has been adopted as a premature foe of 'PC' by the rancorous crowd of minor swells who put out the *American Spectator*, and who imagine themselves quite bold as they gulp down subsidies from Olin, Scaife, and the think tanks of post-Darwinist plutocracy.

But any reductionist analysis of Mencken runs the risk of ignoring a fine mind that engaged itself in some high duties. Whatever the foulness of some of his private and public thoughts (and the newly released Baltimore papers, in which he freely employs such low terms as 'nigger' and 'kike', add nothing essential to our existing stock of understanding), Mencken is fascinating because he often transcended what he freely called his 'prejudices'. Take the following extract from his *Holy Writ*, where he argues that the English translation of the Bible is imperishable:

To this day it has enchanted the English-speaking peoples so effectively that, in the main, they remain Christian, at least sentimentally. Paine has assaulted them, Darwin and Huxley have assaulted them, and a multitude of other merchants of fact have assaulted them, but they still remember the Twenty – Third Psalm when the doctor begins to shake his head, they are still moved beyond compare (though not, alas, to acts) by the Sermon on the Mount, and they still turn once a year from their sordid and degrading labours to immerse themselves unashamed in the story of the manger. It is not much, but it is something. I do not admire the general run of American Biblesearchers – Methodists, United Brethren, Baptists and such vermin. But try to imagine what the average low-browed Methodist would be if he were not a Methodist but an atheist!

I submit that, despite a few infelicities like 'main' and 'remain', this is very finely written. It shows something of the feeling for the religious pulse that Marx evinced in his critique of Hegel, and it does so without making any concessions to illusion. It also, and curiously, echoes a favourite observation of Evelyn Waugh, who used to ask his outraged friends to imagine how much nastier he would be if he were not a Catholic.

In his polemics against Woodrow Wilson and the First World War (clearly the root of his animus against Bryan, who had been bamboozled into serving as Wilson's Secretary of State) Mencken may have been actuated by Nietzchean contempt for that 'anaemic offspring of the slave-morality of the post-Exodus Jews' as against 'the sturdy reassertion of the master morality of the Periclean Greeks ... Germany is strong, and fearless, and ruthless, and resolute. Ergo, Germany must, shall and will prevail'. But this bombast (ill-written, aside from any other consideration) was to give way to clearer and sweeter notes. Mencken took his anti-war positions seriously, and ended up making common cause with despised underdogs: bullied German waiters and socialist agitators, to say nothing of contemptible bleeding-heart outfits like the infant American Civil Liberties Union, Some of his best prose dates from this period, when, as we like to forget, the American academy and the preponderance of the intelligentsia were consumed by the dingiest chauvinism and conformity, and when the Constitution was simply heaved overboard. The caustic review that he wrote concerning the power-worshipping jurisprudence of that old coward and fraud Oliver Wendell Holmes is, among other things, a masterpiece of forensic legal analysis and would not disgrace the most meticulous civil libertarian.

In the decades between the wars, Mencken kept up his loathing of populist intolerance and small-time tyranny, and was always ready to empty the vials of his wrathful contempt over the KKK, over the provincial censors, and over all varieties of the Babbitt and the Rotarian. The special signifier of his independence was an unslackening scorn of the religious; then as now America's most salient taboo. He knew that we do not 'have' bodies but that we *are* bodies, and that the realm of illusion begins at the door of the Sabbath school, and if he over-used certain metaphors ('Chautauqua', 'Bible Searcher') it was partly because he would return to the fray again and again:

The *boobus Americanus* is a bird that knows no closed season – and if he won't come down to Texas oil stock, or one-night cancer cures, or building lots in

Swampshurst, he will always come down to inspiration and optimism, whether political, theological, pedagogical, literary or economic.

The unpleasant realisation that this is true (I read it last on the day President Clinton beat his chest at the National Prayer Breakfast) is an aspect of that 'democrat's pornography' that I cited earlier, the indecent thrill that you can get when you see the credulous filling the hat at rallies commanded by Oliver North and Pat Robertson and Louis Farrakhan.

With Mencken, the lucid interval is the thing to look for. He could write for page upon page about how the 'feminine' principle was one of feebleness and unreason, based on weakness and deceit. And he would regularly refuse to meet any man whom he suspected of being homosexual. Yet he wrote beautifully and with insight about the trials of American womanhood at the hands of the brutish male (said male's efforts in *amour* memorably likened to a gorilla's essays upon the violin). And he composed an extremely well-wrought essay in defence of Oscar Wilde, perhaps in part because he recognised another victim of the jeering, taunting mob. Bertrand Russell, an élitist radical of a very much different provenance, once said that his life changed when his grandmother taught him the biblical injunction: 'Thou shalt not follow a multitude to do evil'. This very much materialises Mencken's point about the scriptures as a chiefly literary influence. If it had been said by a respectable German philosopher he could have adopted it entire as his own motto.

Fred Hobson's biography allows one to take a longer look at Mencken, and to savour his more obvious contradictions. He seems to have been 'imprinted' early on, by a family of slightly oppressive respectability, which, while warm and nurturing in its way, also sought to indenture the young Henry to the equivalent of a Dickens blacking factory. Steeped as a youth in the English declension of literature, he was avid for Kipling as soon as he could discriminate. Interested in bloodlines – perhaps too much interested – this later foe of Anglo-Saxondom was pleased to find that his roots were in Saxony. He was even more delighted to discover a noble ancestor, Johann Burkhard Mencke (sic), who had in 1715 authored a satirical compendium entitled *De Charlataneria Eruditorum* (On the Charlatanry of the Learned), which one would pay a good price to see updated for this year's market. 'The tracking down of quacks of all sorts', as Mencken was to put it, had become so much his own *raison d'être* that the discovery of the book had an almost superstitious effect upon him: 'All my stock in trade was there – loud assertions, heavy buffooneries, slashing attacks on the professors. It really was uncanny'.

Hobson also shows another attractive side to Mencken, which was his unstinting attitude to work. He could not bear to be unproductive, and looked with disdain upon those who did not labour, or those who wasted their talent (Scott Fitzgerald conspicuous here) or those who were slothful. He was interested in what people made, and how much they made for it, and did not despise the meat-and-potatoes aspect of existence. ('Henry James,' he wrote in *The Smart Set*, 'would have been vastly improved as a novelist by a few whiffs from the Chicago stock-yards'.) He was, in general, a friend to the working stiff, and this sympathy, again, allowed him to take holidays from his other obsessions. As he once wrote to Theodore Dreiser, with whom he had a lifelong if rather fraught comradeship:

> It seems plain to me that the most valuable baggage that you carry is your capacity for seeing the world from a proletarian standpoint. It is responsible for all your talent for evoking feeling. Imagine *Sister Carrie* written by a man without that capacity, say Nietzsche. It would have been a mess.

That anyone should be preferred to Nietzsche is, as we have seen, quite a concession for Mencken to have made. Nor was this a singular instance conditioned by friendship, Mencken also became an adoptive editorial parent to James T. Farrell, whose *Studs Lonigan* trilogy possessed the same proletarian integrity and whose Trotskyism Mencken affected not to mind about.

No sooner has one observed this than one looks for its contradiction or negation, and finds it without overmuch difficulty. Later in life, Mencken became the representative of the Baltimore *Sun* group in its labour negotiations, and proved a tough nut as a boss's man. Indeed, Hobson suggests that encounters with Jewish union leaders helped to fuel his animus. He became fond of adding the prefix 'Jewish' to the words 'radical' or 'Communist', just like any Roosevelt-baiting Rotarian. This is especially melancholy when one recalls that in 1917, in the course of his great philippic against the wretchedness of Georgia in *The Sahara of the Bozart*. Mencken had ridiculed the morality of segregation and concluded:

> But if you marvel at the absurdity, keep it dark! A casual word and the united press of the South will be upon your trail, denouncing you bitterly as a scoundrelly damnyankee, a Bolshevik Jew.

Everybody has now heard of the tranche of Mencken papers released to researchers in 1989. The disclosures – reliably misogynistic in tone, as well as surreptitiously nasty about former friends and openly mean about blacks and Jews – have ignited one of 'those' rows, not dissimilar to the convulsion over Philip Larkin's letters in England. The great disadvantage of such disputes is that they are (a) posthumous and (b) require no intellectual equipment of the participants. Without a personal knowledge of Mencken, I should not care to say for sure whether he was a bigot or just bigoted. We can at least identify a contradiction between the defender of Richard Wright and lifelong friend of Alfred Knopf, and the man who gave way to racist vulgarity in private. He was scrupulous and mannerly in his dealings with individual Jews and African Americans, while apparently harbouring crass suspicions of them in the mass, so to speak. Among some hypocrites of today, the paradox is more commonly met with the other way about. I know this is progress.

In the final reckoning, however, Mencken's politico-philosophical ambivalences do not cancel one another out. What I have said about his brilliance and verve can only be said of the period between about 1910 and the end of Prohibition – the years when he could be *contra mundum*, and the heroic decades of American hysteria and prudery. One may re-read much of this output today, skipping over or even forgiving the rough bits out of sheer relish. The false note is usually the heavily affected Germanophilia. And this is not the Germany of Goethe, Heine, or Marx; it is unashamedly *Junkerish*, beery, and chauvinistic, laced with the sort of sentimentality that Mencken generally despised. (It never seems to strike him, when he writes about warfare and the manly German virtues in 1914, that his first literary hero, Rudyard Kipling, was doing precisely the same thing on 'the other side'.)

By the mid-1930s, this strain in Mencken had ceased to be a mere quirk and was becoming a problem. In 1922, reporting from Munich, he wrote with alarming prescience about German resentment of Versailles and said that 'Every intelligent man looks for a catastrophe. If it comes, there will be a colossal massacre of Jews,' Is there, or is there not, a hint of vicarious satisfaction in that phrasing? We know at any rate that in 1933, reviewing *Mein Kampf* for the *American Mercury*, he was so even-handed as to draw a pained howl from Knopf himself. About the rise of fascism in general, Mencken was sanguine: more sanguine, let us say, than he was about FDR. That might be condemnation enough. Yet it is not. Think of the incredible *literary* failure that is involved in Mencken's refusal to write a serious polemic against Hitler. Here aside from the grotesque embodiment of all hatred and superstition, was the quack, charlatan, and crank to end all quacks, charlatans, and cranks. Such a target! And from the pen that had flayed and punctured the 'booboisie', there came little or nothing. Hobson tries his best to be fair, quoting Mencken on Hitler's 'obscene monkeyshines' and a number of other disobliging asides, but the overall effect is of somebody going on record, covering a flank, cutting short an argument. On the great confrontation of his time, the sage of Baltimore funked it. His wartime stuff is not really worth re-reading, and he became more and more interested in family folklore and the amassing of large clippings-files and anthologies concerning his own person and papers. In 1948, the last four-party election in American history, he managed some fairly spirited abuse of the Henry Wallace ticket but ended up casting his own ballot for Strom Thurmond – whose 'American Party' condensed all the Southern crackerdom, religiosity, and bellicose patriotism that he had spent a lifetime defaming. And that, more or less, was that.

The great thing about biographies, and about great troves of personal papers, is that they remind us how few years, in a real human life, are well spent. Napoleon Bonaparte, according to George Orwell, once remarked that, had he been hit by musketry on entering Moscow, he would have gone down to history as its greatest general. We could have been well spared the decline of many other authors and statesmen who only rose briefly above their frailties. As it turns out, Mencken's own obsequy for Ambrose Bierce will do duty here:

> I have a suspicion, indeed, that Bierce did a serious disservice to himself when he put those twelve volumes together. Already an old man at the time, he permitted his nostalgia for his lost youth to get the better of his critical faculty . . . the result was a depressing assemblage of worn-out and fly-blown stuff, much of it quite unreadable. His good work is lost in a morass of bad and indifferent work . . . filled with epigrams against frauds long dead and forgotten, and echoes of old and puerile newspaper controversies.

With Mencken, the face grew to fit the mask, and the playful *Prejudices* became the drone of authentic prejudice. Those who flirt with race theory should learn to beware their own dominant gene.

First published as 'Critic of the Booboisie' (a review of *Mencken: A Biography* by Fred Hobson) in *Dissent*, no. 415, Summer 1994

Goodbye to Berlin

In *The Color of Truth*, the American scholar Kai Bird presents his study of McGeorge ('Mac') and William Bundy. These were the two dynastic technocrats who organised and justified the hideous war in Vietnam. Cold War liberals themselves, with the kept conservative journalist Joseph Alsop they formed a Three of Hearts in the less fastidious quarters of Washington DC. Another player made up an occasional fourth man. Isaiah Berlin was happy, at least when Charles (Chip) Bohlen was unavailable to furnish an urbane ditto to their ruthlessness. Almost as if to show that academics and intellectual may be tough guys, too – the most lethal temptation to which the contemplative can fall victim – Berlin's correspondence with this little cabal breathes with that abject eagerness that was so much a part of the one-time Anglo-American 'special relationship'. To Alsop he wrote, on 20 April 1966, an account of a dinner with McGeorge Bundy:

> I have never admired anyone so much, so intensely, for so long as I did him during those four hours . . . his character emerged in such exquisite form that I am now his devoted and dedicated slave. I like him very much indeed, and I think he likes me, now, which was not always the case.

Looking back on the fantastic blood-letting in Indonesia in 1965 – an event which Alsop and the Bundys later decided was confirmation of their own sapience in Indochina – Mac Bundy returned the compliment, writing to Alsop in 1967 that he wished he had Berlin's stout resolution:

> I think more and more the truth of Vietnam is in the nearby countries . . . I don't have the wonderful self-confidence of Isaiah – 'I'm a terrific domino man' – but I share the feeling that's where we have done best.

There were fainthearts, of course, as there always are when great enterprises of the will are afoot. As an ever-increasing number even of Establishment types began to sicken of the war, Alsop reflected bitterly that he might no longer be able to claim the standing of stern prophet and moral tutor to the military-industrial (and military-intellectual) complex. Berlin responded in the same tones of seasoned statesmanship:

> I can see the thin red line, formed by you and Mac and me, and Chip Bohlen – four old blimps, the last defenders of a dry, and disagreeably pessimistic, tough and hopelessly outmoded position – one will perish at least with one's eyes open.

'Take my arm, old toad. Help me down Cemetery Road.' Except that it was actually many thousands of conscripted Americans, and uncountable numbers of Vietnamese, and not the intellectuals at the elbow of power, who were marched down that road before their time. Almost everything is wrong with the tone and address of the above extracts: the combined ingratiation and self-piety no less than the assumed and bogus Late Roman stoicism. A 'terrific domino man' indeed! What price 'negative liberty' now? And what of the sceptical humanist who warned incessantly about the sacrifice of living people to abstract ends, or totemic dogmas?

As against all that, the pleadings of Alsop to Mac Bundy did succeed in getting the latter to release a huge tranche of Ford Foundation money to endow Wolfson College, Oxford, the foundation of which was Berlin's noblest enterprise. So perhaps he was on to something when he expatiated about ethical 'trade-offs' between contrasting or alternative positions: the one transaction that he really did believe was historically inevitable. (The 'Colour of Truth', you will not be astonished to learn, was 'grey' in the opinion of the Bundys.)

Now I know that Michael Ignatieff was aware of the existence of the above correspondence at least a year ago. And I also urged Bird to send it to him. But the Vietnam drama takes up less than a page of his biography, and mentions Berlin's real positions not at all. We are given, instead, a familiar impressionist sketch of an honest and troubled man – the word 'detachment' makes its appearance – unable to ally himself with the extremists of either camp. There is scarcely a hint of his actual influence in post-Camelot Washington, or of the way in which it was actually employed. We hear that he 'joked' in Oxford about being 'an old mastodon of liberalism . . . a last feeble echo of J. S. Mill to be treated gently as a harmless, respectable old relic', which is certainly stylistically congruent with the more embarrassing letters to Alsop and the Bundys. (Please keep in mind, also, Berlin's choice of forebear in that last instance.) Typical is Ignatieff's sentence: 'Berlin congratulated himself on remaining on good terms with friends who could barely stand to be in the same room.' Ah yes, by all means: to be remote from both sides is a tremendous reinforcement of one's own rectitude and a tribute in its way to one's own lonely and yet somehow – yes – brave and upright objectivity. 'Congratulated himself', however: isn't that slightly to give the game away? This congratulation was not, after all, being bestowed for the first time. Look up Berlin's essays on Turgenev in *Russian Thinkers*, and you will find yourself enlisted on the side of

> the small, hesitant, self-critical, not always very brave, band of men who occupy a position somewhere to the left of centre, and are morally repelled both by the hard faces to their right and the hysteria and mindless violence and demagoguery on their left . . . This is the notoriously unsatisfactory, at times agonising, position of the modern heirs of the liberal tradition.

Whether being rueful about Mill in some sheltered quadrangle, or vicariously biting Turgenev's bullet in the pages of any number of respectable quarterlies or, indeed, while seconding the efforts of unscrupulous power-brokers in Washington, Berlin could not discard the affectation of the embattled, the lonely and even the agonised. Of liberalism and its quandaries and dilemmas it deserves to be asked, in this century in particular, and no less than of other ideologies: agonising for whom?

Woe is me and lack a day. There is a sense in which if you chafe at the present complacently 'liberal' consensus, the reputation of Isaiah Berlin stands like a lion in your path. But the task of confronting said lion is not at all easy or simple: by no means as much as the preceding paragraphs may have made it appear. True, he was simultaneously pompous and dishonest in the face of a long moral crisis where his views and his connections could have made a difference. True, this is the kind of story that never, ever, gets told about Berlin by his legion of memorialists and admirers. I admit that I turned first to Ignatieff's scanty passage on Vietnam and, having some private knowledge, became incensed and thought for a while that his whole sodding book was going to bleed on in the same, so to speak, vein. But then I flipped back to the beginning and settled in. It swiftly broke in upon me that the lion was still there, in all his mingled splendours, part mangy, part magnificent. Isaiah Berlin may have been designed, by origin and by temperament and by life experience, to become one of those witty and accomplished *valets du pouvoir* who adorn, and even raise the tone of, the better class of court. But there was something in him that recognised this as an ignoble and insufficient aspiration, and impelled him to resist it where he dared.

The anecdotal is inescapable here, and I see no reason to be deprived of my portion. I first met Berlin in 1967, around the time of his Bundy/Alsop pact, when I was a fairly tremulous secretary of the Oxford University Labour Club. He'd agreed to talk on Marx, and to be given dinner at the Union beforehand, and he was the very picture of patient, non-condescending charm. Uncomplainingly eating the terrible food we offered him he awarded imaginary Marx marks to the old Russophobe, making the assumption that he would have been a PPE student. ('A beta-alpha for economics – no, I rather think a beta – but an alpha, definitely an alpha for politics.') He gave his personal reasons for opposing Marxism ('I saw the revolution in St Petersburg, and it quite cured me for life. Cured me for life') and I remember thinking that I'd never before met anyone who had a real-time memory of 1917. Ignatieff slightly harshly says that Berlin was 'no wit, and no epigrams have attached themselves to his name', but when he said, 'Kerensky, yes, Kerensky – I think we have to say one of the great *wets* of history,' our laughter was unforced. The subsequent talk to the club was a bit medium-pace and up-and-down the wicket, because you can only really maintain that Marx was a determinist or inevitabililist if you do a lot of eliding between sufficient and necessary conditions. But I was thrilled to think that he'd made himself vulnerable to such unlicked cubs. A term or two later, at a cocktail party given by my tutor, he remembered our dinner, remembered my name without making a patronising show of it, and stayed to tell a good story about Christopher Hill and John Sparrow, and of how he'd been the unwitting agent of a quarrel between them, while ignoring an ambitious and possessive American professor who kept yelling 'Eye-zay-ah! Eye-zay-ah!' from across the room. ('Yes,' he murmured at the conclusion of the story. 'After that I'm afraid Christopher rather gave me up. Gave me up for the Party.')

Many years later, reviewing *Personal Impressions* for the *New Statesman*, I mentioned the old story of Berlin acting as an academic gatekeeper, and barring the appointment of Isaac Deutscher to a chair at Sussex University. This denial had the sad effect of forcing Deutscher – who had once given Berlin a highly scornful review in the *Observer* – to churn out Kremlinology for a living: as a result of which he never finished his triad or troika of Stalin, Trotsky and Lenin biographies. In the next post came a letter from Berlin, stating with some anguish that while he didn't much approve of Deutscher, his opinion had not been the deciding one. I telephoned Tamara Deutscher and others, asking if they had definite proof that Berlin had administered the bare bodkin, and was told, well, no, not definite proof. So I published a retraction. Then came a post card from Berlin, thanking me handsomely, saying that the allegation had always worried and upset him, and asking if he wasn't correct in thinking that he had once succeeded more in attracting me to Marxism than in repelling me from it. I was – I admit it – impressed. And now I read, in Ignatieff's book, that it was an annihilatingly hostile letter from Berlin to the Vice-Chancellor of Sussex University which 'put paid to Deutscher's chances'. The fox is crafty, we know, and the hedgehog is a spiky customer, and Ignatieff proposes that the foxy Berlin always harboured the wish to metamorphose into a hedgehog. All I know is that I was once told – even assured of – one small thing.

Close reading is necessary with a customer like this. The First World War was, like the abattoir in Vietnam, quite describable as a liberals' war. Any medium-run view of history will show that it did more damage to 'Western civilisation' than any form of ideology, not least in clearing the very path, through the ruins and cadavers, along which totalitarians could later instate and militarise themselves. (In that sense, and by his insistence that a gutted and humiliated Russia should stay in the war and meet its obligations to imperialism, Kerensky can be described as a little more bloody than merely 'wet'.) As a small Jewish boy, and only child with a defective left arm, tenderly raised in Riga and removed to St Petersburg because of the exigencies of combat and of disruptions in the timber trade, Isaiah Berlin saw a terrified tsarist cop being dragged away by a mob. The sight – it recurs in numerous interviews and reminiscences, including those recorded here – powerfully coloured his view of disorder and insurrection; the more so, perhaps, because his infant imagination furnished the subsequent scene of lynching or drowning that he did not in fact witness. In only one interview ('Recollections of a Historian of Ideas', uncited by Ignatieff) did he remember to say that these cops were fond of firing on civilians.

One could argue that if he had been exposed to another contemporary scene of cruelty – the mass slaughter of peasant conscripts at Tannenberg, for example, or the Cossacks dealing with a demonstration, or perhaps the Black Hundreds falling to work in a shtetl – the formative effect would have or might have been different. Yet I think it's clear, from his own recurrence to the story, and from other evidence, that it was the disturbance to the natural order that made the young Isaiah tremble and flinch. Other members of his family, including a much-loved uncle and aunt, were quite active supporters of the SR (Socialist Revolutionary) movement. Neither then nor in retrospect did he register any allegiance of that sort. Ignatieff is surely right to say that the episode with the arrested policeman 'continued to work within Berlin, strengthening his horror of physical violence and his suspicion of political experiment'. But it would have been more precise to say: only for certain sorts of physical violence and political experiment. Policemen are supposed to control crowds, not crowds policemen. Vietnam, for example, was not just an instance of horrific premeditated violence. It was a laboratory experiment run by technician-intellectuals and academic consultants, who furnished us with terms like 'interdict', 'relocate', body count' and 'strategic hamlet'. To cope with the ensuing calamity, the Bundys and McNamaras later evolved the view that, while the war might have been a blunder, the error could, for reasons of State and for reasons of face, not be admitted. In this, too, they were seconded by Berlin. No doubt his reassuring 'blimp' line came in handy here, as well. It's astonishing how often the men of power need, and appreciate, and also get, a bit of solid senior common-room emollience.

The lifelong strength that Berlin drew from his 1917 baptism was, however, often applied in less obvious ways. I was fascinated to learn, from Ignatieff, that his Latvian family had a direct kinship with the Schneerson clan who ran, and still run, the fanatical sect known as Lubavitch or Chabad. (This family tree also includes Yehudi Menuhin, who might in other circumstances have become a rare fiddler on the roof.) So the charismatic loony rebbe from Brooklyn Heights, the late Menachem Schneerson – he who opposed blood transfusions because they compromised unique Jewish DNA – was Berlin's cousin. Any mention of these Hasidic fanatics, according to Ignatieff, would cause Berlin's face 'to tighten into a rare and uncharacteristic expression of dislike'. That's good, and good to know, (Leon Wieseltier, in his gushing goodbye to Berlin last year in the *New Republic*, could not have been more wrong than in depicting him as a medieval Jewish sage.) There are probably two additional and reinforcing reasons for Berlin's disdain. One is that the Russian rabbinate had historically supported the anti-Semitic Tsar against Bonaparte, viewing the French as bearers of secularism and enlightenment. The other is that he saw, in the attachment of many Jewish intellectuals to Marxism, a sort of displaced messianic impulse. This certainly aided his persistent misreading of Marx and of what he thought of as Marx's teleology. But it also, by way of an internal mutation, made him distrust the zealotry of Zionism whether this was offered in political nationalist or black-coated Orthodox form, let alone in the nasty synthesis of the two that now defines the Israeli Right.

'Synthesis' was Berlin's special gift, while an educated wariness of any 'tyranny of concept' larger than the human was his essential admonition: indeed constitutes his chief bequest. Yet, in his work and in his life, syntheses were often eclectic agglomerations and his allegiances – transferred not so much to England as to the Anglo-American supranational 'understanding' – frequently bore the stamp of realpolitik and, well, calculation. He, did however, understand this part of himself and I was surprised at how often Ignatieff made a puzzle where none exists:

> He liked to say that his success – professorship, a knighthood, the Order of Merit – depended upon a systematic over-estimation of his abilities. 'Long may this continue,' he always said. Self-denigration came naturally, but it was also a pre-emptive strike against criticism. 'I am an intellectual taxi; people flag me down and give me destinations and off I go' was all he would ever offer, when pressed to say what his intellectual agenda had been.

Ignatieff, himself a Russo-Canadian exile or émigré, never seems quite able to make up his mind whether this was a joke, and (if it was) whether it was one of those jokes that are revealing and confessional. His confusion is expressed in the choice of the term 'self-denigration'. To deprecate self is one thing, while to denigrate self is masochistic. Without self-deprecation much English literary and academic conversation would become difficult to carry on. 'Pre-emptive' comes closer to the mark: you say this sort of thing about yourself before anyone else can. But that's public, and a recognised 'act'. In 1978, Berlin wrote a private letter to the psychiatrist Anthony Storr, wondering why he, a beloved only child, should still be visited with the feeling that his many attainments were 'of very little or of no value'. This takes us some way beyond the pose of false modesty, but nowhere near as far as self-hatred.

I propose that Berlin was somewhat haunted, all of his life, by the need to please and conciliate others; a need which in some people is base but which also happened to engage his most attractive and ebullient talents. I further propose that he sometimes felt or saw the need to be courageous, but usually – oh dear – at just the same moment that he remembered an urgent appointment elsewhere. That this was imbricated with both his Jewish and his Russian identities seems probable. He may also have felt that luck played too large a part in his success – a rare but human concession to superstition. The difficulty with Berlin's views on political matters is that they are vulnerable to the charge not so much of contradiction as of tautology. (And perhaps of want of originality: Berlin's favourite, Benjamin Constant, proposed a distinction between the 'liberty of the ancients' and the 'liberty of the moderns'; T. H. Green spoke of liberty in the 'positive' and 'negative', and the same antithesis is strongly present in Hayek's *Road to Serfdom* – the title page of which quoted Lord Acton saying that 'few discoveries are more irritating than those which expose the pedigree of ideas'.) The greatest hardship experienced by a person trying to apprehend Berlin's presentation of 'two concepts' of liberty is in remembering which is supposed to be which. I know of no serviceable mnemonic here. When Berlin delivered his original lectures on the subject, at Bryn Mawr College in Pennsylvania in 1952, he divided ideas about liberty between the 'liberal' and the 'romantic'. Positive and negative were the successor distinctions. To be let alone – the most desirable consummation in his own terms – is the negative. To be uplifted by others, or modernised or forcibly emancipated, is, somewhat counter-intuitively, the positive. Yet it is readily agreed, even asserted, that *laissez-faire* can lead to the most awful invasions and depredations of the private sphere, while an interventionist project like the New Deal can be a welcome aid to individual freedom. In a long interview, originally published in Italy, which has just appeared in full in the excellent *Salmagundi*, Berlin says that he liked the 'positive' examples of Lloyd George and Franklin Roosevelt, not least because they insulated their respective societies from socialism *tout court*. One assumes that, with his sense of history, he means the Lloyd George who was the patron of Field Marshal Douglas Haig, and the guarded admirer of Hitler, just as much as he means the Lloyd George who was the father of Welsh Disestablishment. And one must suppose that he comprehends FDR the originator of the war economy, and FDR the prime mover of American acquisition of European empires, in the avuncular figure who proposed the Tennessee Valley Authority. At any rate, keen endorsement of either statesman is a distinctly bizarre way of registering any kind of objection to social engineering. Thus, there are contradictions in his view, but they languish from being untreated by their author. At least Lloyd George and Roosevelt, when they ordered up slaughters and conquests, or when they used authoritarian tactics, did not do so in obedience to any fancy theory. Once again, I think we may see the ghostly figure of that mobbed policeman – much more unsettling than a policed mob.

As it happens, Rosa Luxemburg in her great disagreement with Lenin said roundly that there was a real peril of practice hardening into theory, and vice versa. And, if you care, I agree with her. Dogma in power does have a unique chilling ingredient not exhibited by power, however ghastly, wielded for its own traditional sake. But the 'two concepts' don't bridge the gap between the divine right of kings, overthrown by the Enlightenment, and the age of ideology. It's especially unhelpful, in this regard, that Berlin should have assumed that all Marxists were mechanists and determinists, and that there could be no quarrel in principle among them. (I don't recall him being so harsh on the fatuous and also tautological slogan about the 'Inevitability of Gradualness' with which the Fabians advanced their own version of a managed and graded society. But then the Fabians were quintessentially English, and their quiet authoritarianism was not threatening to power so much as envious of, and ancillary to, its customary exercise in these islands.)

In 1971, in an episode not explored by Ignatieff, Anthony Arblaster published a review of *Four Essays on Liberty* in the journal *Political Studies*. 'Vision and Revision: A Note on the Text of Isaiah Berlin's *Four Essays on Liberty*' was in some ways a minor-key achievement; it took the form of a meticulous study of the alterations made between the different editions of Berlin's best-known works. But it resulted in a major-chord huff, with Berlin making no effort to be urbane about his annoyance. It is easy to see what gave rise to his irritation. Arblaster instanced the following textual emendation:

From Zeno to Spinoza, from the Gnostics to Leibniz, from Thomas Hobbes to Lenin and Freud, the battle-cry has been essentially the same; the object of knowledge and the methods of discovery have often been violently opposed, but that reality is knowable, and that knowledge and only knowledge liberates, and absolute knowledge liberates absolutely – that is common to many doctrines which are so large and valuable a part of Western civilisation.

The earlier printed version had begun the list 'From Plato to Lucretius', had stuck with the Gnostics and Leibniz, but had had Thomas Aquinas instead of Thomas Hobbes, almost, as Arblaster woundingly put it, 'as if it had to be Thomas somebody'. He went on, detailing other reworkings of the same passage, 'Reality was "wholly knowable" not just "knowable", and this alteration, while typical of the general toning down, almost destroys the point of the sentence, for what is distinctive, let alone sinister, about the belief that reality is knowable?' Rather than taking Berlin up on the slothful prose that had led him to use clichés like 'battle-cry', and to recycle the most worn and familiar Actonian trope, Arblaster inquired, mildly for him: 'Where in the works of Hobbes is there anything which suggests that he believed that knowledge and only knowledge liberates, and absolute knowledge liberates absolutely?' It was Whitman, I think – I really must check this when I get the time – who said:

> Do I contradict myself?
> Very well then I contradict myself,
> (I am large, I contain
> multitudes).

Berlin, it seems, had a huge capacity for internal multitudes and for torrents of reference but, whoever he lit on or deployed, they turned out happily to confirm, in the first place one another and in the second place whatever he was going to say anyway. Have you ever read an article on Berlin which did not mention his extraordinary facility with cross-fertilised 'thinkers' – the conjuring names usually beginning with H rather than T? A biographer might have examined his subject more closely on the question: did an English society, and indeed academy, deeply wedded to compromise and to consensus, overvalue a polyglot chap who could mention a lot of Continental theorists and still come out with sound and no-nonsense views? I can't call to mind anybody in the native empiricist tradition who ever challenged Berlin on his high-wire juggling, or on his role as official greeter, waving the new arrivals through a normally rather suspicious customs. Ernest Gellner, however, always said he was a fraud. Berlin returned the lack of cordiality, perhaps feeling that it was uncomfortable having too many Central European polymaths about the place. (His distaste for George Steiner took something of the same form.) Incidentally, Perry Anderson's general matrix of the 'White' intellectual emigration, which suggested that the radical exiles went to America while the conservative ones – with Gellner exempted – settled in England, understates the manner in which Berlin's Washington period was the making of him.

Berlin's promiscuous capaciousness also shows itself in his rather shifty attitude to Mill. In 'John Stuart Mill and the Ends of Life', one of his essays on liberty, he could not lay enough stress on Mill's opposition to 'some kind of hegemony of right-minded intellectuals'. Again, it's not as if Mill's defenders continually and stupidly insist on this one point. Nor, on the other hand, is it the case that there is no evidence for his intellectual 'élitism'. Berlin merely fails to cite any of it. And Mill possessed in common with Marx and in bold contrast to Berlin, a consciousness of class. He clearly thought that the ends, of female suffrage, freedom for the Jamaicans, and other such utopian objectives, might require somewhat more discipline than could be summoned by mere appeals to reason or good will. It's quite possible to imagine him regarding the positive/negative duet as a distinction somewhat lacking in a difference. In the *Salmagundi* interview Berlin was asked his opinion about Mill:

> I took Mill almost for granted.
> But you wrote about him and gave a rather existentialist reading of him.
> Well, I didn't think he was the utilitarian he thought he was. I didn't enjoy Mill. Save for the essay on Liberty. I didn't read Bentham properly I read who were the important names? – Carlyle, Emerson; who else was there in England?
> T. H. Green?
> I was not deeply impressed by him, nor by Hobhouse, admirable as they are. You see, it's the enemy who interests me; brilliant opponents who so to speak put their swords, their rapiers into one and find the weak spot.
> Do you think that description applies to Marx?
> Yes, up to a point it does. The point is that his particular criticism of the liberals he wrote about did not seem to me to be particularly effective. His positive ideas were of great importance but the idea that liberty is a bourgeois concept and all that sort of thing, or that it was a capitalist concept – no. But I did read Lassalle and I was impressed by his concept of profit and marginal utility. I want to retract what I said about J. S. Mill. I admire him immensely. He is a major, great, positive British thinker.

Whew! Not a moment too soon. Hobhouse and Green admirable in their way, even Marx quite impressive apart from some things he never said, and Mill not merely plucked from the burning, but hurriedly garlanded with the multiple encomia of being major, British and positive. Or should it be negative? The question is not merely sarcastic. Berlin supplied many admonitions that were strictly in the negative, most of them warning liberals against the hazard and fallacy of monism. But who can remember anything he suggested about what liberalism, or liberals, might actually accomplish? Rawls, Dworkin and Galbraith have all laid out avenues of potential meliorism. Berlin's design omits these spacious features.

The Oxford debating tradition does possess one great strength, drawn indirectly from the Symposium. You are supposed to be able to give an honest account of an opposing or different worldview, and even as an exercise to be able to present it as if you believed it yourself. It is a striking fact about Isaiah Berlin that, in his first and most serious and only full-length book, he is unable to meet this condition, even in the exegetical sense. The essay 'Isaiah's Marx, and Mine', written by his pupil, and successor in the Chichele Professorship, Gerry Cohen, is full of love and admiration for the man. But it cannot acquit Berlin of the charge of elementary misrepresentation, or at best misunderstanding. The fact that all the mistakes and omissions (alienation did not feature in the first edition, and is sketchily discussed in the second) are hostile is unlikely to be accidental. Berlin himself told *Salmagundi*:

> In 1933 Mr [H. A. L.] Fisher, the Warden of New College, asked me to write a book on Karl Marx for the Home University Library. I said: 'What is the audience for the book?' He said: 'Squash professionals.' I had never read a line of Marx . . .

One sees the famous charm at work. But not even a line, by 1933, even after St Petersburg? Anyway, it shows. And it's of interest that Berlin repeatedly describes his subject, admiringly for once, as a synthesiser. 'A thinker of genius. I don't deny that. But it was the synthesis that was important. He never acknowledged a single debt.'

Coming from the fabled synthesiser who acknowledged all debts and none, and could change his indebtedness from Hobbes to Aquinas at the drop of a hat, this is of interest also. Without checking, I can think of Marx's open indebtedness to Hegel, to Adam Smith, to the 'Blue Books' of the Victorian factory inspectorate, to Balzac and to Charles Darwin. In other words, Berlin was being vulgar when it must decently be presumed that he know better. Of his other subjects, not even Joseph de Maistre receives such offhand treatment.

Oddest of all, Berlin presents Marx and other 'utopians' as apostles or prophets of ultimate harmony, while offering his agreeable and consensual self as the realistic man who recognises the inevitability of conflict and contradiction. It is only the radicals who allegedly believe in the following prospectus:

> A society lives in a state of pure harmony, in which all its members live in peace, love one another, are free from physical danger, from want of any

kind, from insecurity, from degrading work, from envy, from frustration, experience no injustice or violence, live in perpetual, even light, in a temperate climate, in the midst of infinitely fruitful, generous nature.

It is not possible to cite any authority for this florid caricature. Nobody, except the Christian Church (by law established in his adored and adopted England), has ever proposed such an idiotic stasis as desirable, let alone attainable. But Berlin's facility for citation again chooses this moment to desert him. In the presentation of himself as the guardian of complexity and of unintended consequence, and of the inescapable clash of interests and desires, there may even be some element of displacement or transference. It was the despised Hegel who told us that tragedy consisted of a conflict of rights. It was Berlin, whenever faced with a conflict of rights, who sought to emulsify it. In other words, his emphasis on complexity had a strong element of . . . simplification.

I said earlier that Berlin was lucky. He did not actually consider himself fortunate, when posted as a diplomat to wartime Moscow on Guy Burgess's initiative, to find himself stranded and unwanted in New York instead. But, when told to make the best of his American contacts, he found himself in the perfect milieu. Ignatieff's passages on this period are excellent. Berlin's networking skills and, it's not unfair to say, his ability to be all things to all men, were ideally suited to address an American pluralism which exhibited multiple ambiguities about the war, and about the British. Once transferred to Washington, he could rotate – we would now say 'spin' – between tough but stupid isolationists, between the old guard at the British Embassy and the new Churchillian bosses in London, between the Anglophile hostesses of Georgetown and the anti-Nazi émigrés from Central Europe. In what must have been at the time a dizzying subplot, he also involved himself intimately in the quarrel between Chaim Weizmann and David Ben-Gurion over the project of a Jewish National Home, and in the attempts by both to play off the British against the Americans. And, though he showed himself willing to take risks in leaking classified material that favoured the Zionist cause, he also found himself acutely sensitive to any suspicion, even on his own part, of a dual loyalty. (In a memo to Churchill on some Berlin cables from Washington that were thought to be too clever by more than half, Anthony Eden minuted his view that there was too much of the 'Oriental' about this subordinate.) The resolution of this internal conflict took the form of backing Weizmann's moderation against Ben-Gurion's pugnacity, and also of repressing or postponing too much thought about the Final Solution. There was a small battle to be won in Palestine, and a larger one to be won in Europe, and the first had to wait, morally and tactically, upon the latter. There was much to be brilliantly sublimated meanwhile.

This talent for compromise, and also for diplomatic and drawing-room manoeuvre, was to equip Berlin superbly for this later career in academic and intellectual politics. His slogan might well have been '*surtout, pas de zèle*', but muttered rather zealously. He had an instinct for multiplicity, and a liking for intrigue, but a need for conciliation. No wonder he was to write so contemptuously of those who saw a problem-free society, while so freely depicting himself as a proponent of hard choices. A foot in both camps of the Atlantic alliance, further-more, was the ideal postwar 'positioning' for a cosmopolitan, who had been a fluent and persuasive Greek at the initial moment of the new Rome. In the Cold War years, indeed, Berlin often found himself quite close to the throne. There are several accounts of an evening of electrifying embarrassment, when he was questioned about Russia in a close but philistine way by the young President Kennedy. Ignatieff puts the most lenient construction on these engagements with power. Describing an exchange between Berlin and the old mandarin George Kennan, he writes that 'it was a fixed principle of his that so-called élites – intellectual or otherwise – had no business presuming that they knew better than the man or woman in the street'. A recently unearthed interview between Berlin and Arthur Schlesinger shows that he omitted to clarify this fixed principle to the intellectuals of Camelot. When asked by Phillip Toynbee and others to take a position on nuclear disarmament, as Ignatieff describes it,

> Berlin replied – with rather uncharacteristic bravado – that liberal principles were of little meaning unless one was prepared to risk one's very survival in their defence:
> 'Unless there is some point at which you are prepared to fight against whatever odds, and whatever the threat may be, not merely to yourself, but to anybody, all principles become flexible, all codes melt, and all ends in themselves for which we live disappear.'

This is bluster, not bravado. With its loud talk of 'survival', also, it is casuistry of a low order. The whole case against nuclear weapons is that *they* threaten to melt everything and make everything disappear, and thus that their use in geopolitical contests is or would be unpardonable. There was always another essential element to the critique: namely, that 'nuclearism' creates an unaccountable and secret priesthood or élite which doesn't just think it 'knows better' than the man and woman in the streets, but is prepared to annihilate all of them, including all non-combatants in all other countries and indeed all people who have been born or might be born. The positive-negative poles as you might say, are highly charged here. Rather feebly, Ignatieff attributes this vaporous reply to Berlin's hatred of the Soviet system. A non-sequitur. Apart from anything else, it was Andrei Sakharov who educated millions of people to see the obviousness of the points I've just made.

(Incidentally, and on a point that often gives rise to gossip, Ignatieff asserts that Berlin was as shocked as anybody by the surreptitious CIA funding of *Encounter*, to which he often contributed, and further asserts that 'he certainly had no official or unofficial relationship with either British Intelligence or the CIA'. He doesn't give an authority for this flat (and unprovoked) denial, but if we presume that its source was Berlin himself, the following inductive exercise might be permitted. It is improbable in the highest degree that Berlin was never even approached by either Smiley's people or The Cousins. So, if he turned them down, would that not have made a fine anecdote for his biographer? The *Encounter* disavowal, if taken literally, would mean that Berlin was abnormally incurious, or duller that we have been led to suppose, or had wasted his time in Washington. If you look up Peter Wright's *Spycatcher*, though, you will find a record of some affable chin-wags with Berlin, tending to confirm Auden and MacNeice's award, in *Letters from Iceland*, of a 'dish of milk' to the feline Isaiah. And some other living cloak-and-gown experts can tell a tale or two. Ignatieff's own respectful credulity on this minor point is a microcosm of the shortcomings of his approach.)

In every instance given by Ignatieff, or known to me, from the Cold War through Algeria to Suez to Vietnam, Berlin strove to find a high 'liberal' justification either for the status quo or for the immediate needs of the conservative authorities. (I'm reserving the Israel–Palestine question for the moment.) There is a definite correlation between these positions and his scholarly praise for what he disarmingly termed the 'banal': his general view that the main enemy was activism. At a State Department reception I once met a gloomy Argentine banker, a certain Señor della Porta, who discoursed about his country's greatest failure. With a good climate and much natural wealth, Argentina had failed to evolve a liberal and stable party of the middle class. 'One day, however,' he said, 'we will indeed succeed in having such a party and such a leadership. And our slogan will be' – here he brightened up a bit – '"Moderation or Death!"'

A lapidary phrase from Immanuel Kant – 'Out of the crooked timber of humanity no straight thing was ever made' – served Berlin almost as a mantra. It appeared once in *Russian Thinkers*, twice in *Against the Current*, three times in *Four Essays on Liberty* and even more frequently in a 1990 volume entitled *The Crooked Timber of Humanity*. It features three times in Ignatieff's biography, in circumstances that are severally illuminating.

In November 1933, writing to Elizabeth Bowen, he advanced in capsule form his two chief propositions or preoccupations: I quote Ignatieff's summary:

> The Philosopher Malebranche had observed that since the moral ends which human beings commonly pursued were in conflict with each other, the very idea of creating a perfect society was incoherent. This seminal idea had also cropped up elsewhere. Hadn't Kant said, he wrote to Bowen, that 'out of the crooked timber of humanity no straight thing was ever made'? These were the chance encounters with ideas – not the fevered discussions with Ayer and Austin – that generated his later thought.

In 1950, Arthur Koestler gave an interview to the *Jewish Chronicle* in which he said that every diaspora Jew had a choice, but that it was only one choice, and a hard one at that. One could either assimilate fully into the non-Jewish world, and abandon Jewishness altogether. Or one could emigrate to Israel and there lead a fully Jewish life. In between, there was no room. Berlin wrote a reply to this, entitled 'Jewish Slavery and Emancipation'. He described Koestler's counterposing of the issue as coercive. Surely, if there was a point to Israel, it was that it increased freedom of decision for Jews. 'There are too many individuals in the world who do not choose to see life in the form of radical choices between one course and another and whom we do not condemn for this reason. "Out of the crooked timber of humanity," said a great philosopher, "no straight thing was ever made."'

In 1969, he came upon a piece of moral idiocy from Herbert Marcuse – or at any rate a piece of moral idiocy from Marcuse quoted in *Encounter* – and went into a towering rage, writing that people like Marcuse and indeed Hannah Arendt were products of:

> The terrible twisted Mitteleuropa in which nothing is straight, simple, truthful, all human relations and all political attitudes are twisted into ghastly shapes by these awful casualties who, because they are crippled, recognise nothing pure and firm in the world!

It may be relevant that Berlin detested the assimilated German Jews, like Hannah Arendt, while pressing his hardest for assimilation in England. It may also be relevant that he always refused to reprint 'Jewish Slavery and Emancipation', partly because his All Souls colleague Keith Joseph had been upset by an anti-assimilationist joke it contained. (Steinmetz the hunchback and Kahn the 'accepted' converso are walking past the synagogue on Fifth Avenue. Kahn says, 'I used to attend services there,' and Steinmetz retorts: 'And I used to be a hunchback.' Every Jew, said Berlin, has his or her own hump: some deny it, some flaunt it and some – 'timid and respectful cripples' – wear voluminous cloaks.)

In 1933, the date of the first known reference, Berlin was only twenty-four, but he has obviously found and seized on his essential dictum. It is of course a thoughtful and provocative one, and full of implication. By the November of that particular year, however, it must have occurred to many people that politics and policy could indeed succeed in making humans more crooked, not to say more twisted. And, this being true, is it worth considering whether the converse might ever apply?

In the second extract, Berlin is making a perfectly intelligible attack on the Procrustean faction and the either/or tendency, as he would have been bound to do on general principles but as he felt additionally moved to do when faced with Jewish absolutism. The Kantian allusion is near-superfluous, however. Koestler is not trying to make people grow straight at all. He is telling them that they must warp in one pronounced and final manner, from their current pattern of growth, or in another manner that is no less strenuous.

In the third case Berlin is suddenly willing to grant that there is purity and firmness to be attained, though not by people who are twisted and misshapen partly by environment. The specific location of this in Mitteleuropa is odd.

I shall not be able to improve on Perry Anderson's review of *The Crooked Timber of Humanity*, which appeared in these pages eight years ago, except perhaps to broaden his point with help from these later gleanings. Briefly, in his 'Idea for a Universal History in a Cosmopolitan Perspective' – one sees how the very title might have magnetised Berlin's omnivorous attention – Kant stated that humanity was indeed capable of overcoming its tribal and backward heritage, and of realising a latent common interest. However, the need for leadership in this great task is a problem in itself, because the innate brutishness that 'we' need to overcome is also manifestly present in each one of us, and therefore poses a practically insuperable contradiction. '*Das höchste Oberhaupt soll aber gerecht für sich selbst und doch ein Mensch sein*' – 'The highest magistrate should be just in himself and yet be a man.' (I note, at the risk of attracting a raised eyebrow from Anderson, that the concept of an individual, no less than a class, needing to be *für sich* rather than *an sich*, seems in this rendering to invert Marx's later usage.) There is but one way to assuage this need for a double positive that must still be derived from a double negative. As Kant phrases it, in Anderson's translation:

> Only in such an enclosure as civil unification offers can our inclinations achieve their best effects; as trees in a wood which seek to deprive each other of air and sunlight are forced to strive upwards and so achieve a beautiful straight growth; while those that spread their branches at will in isolated freedom grow stunted, tilted and crooked.

There may be a slightly dank and collectivist timbre to the above, and the German forests may not have been greenhouses either of generous solidarity or of robust free thought, but that irony would seem to count at Berlin's expense. Kant is explicitly saying the opposite to what he supposes. At different points, indeed, in the *Four Essays on Liberty* Berlin returned the 'compliment' by describing Kant both as an advocate of 'severe individualism' and of 'pure totalitarian doctrine'. Then again, having found the rationalism of the Enlightenment to be forbidding and authoritarian, he invested his hopes in a Romantic movement that could hardly claim to be immune from visionary and unsettling temptations. But the wonder, even in a career as intellectually eclectic as Berlin's, is that he should have cut so many crutches (and so many cudgels) from such a frail – not to say, distorted – trunk as this.

Anderson amusingly, and I trust intentionally, describes the repetitive woodcutter and carpenter image that Berlin took from Kant as 'a saw'. It is an old saw of the English Tories, and their empiricist and pragmatist allies, that 'you can't change human nature'. Rightly or wrongly, it was confirmation of this stout and hearty assertion that they took from the anti-prophet Isaiah. The ur-Tory, Samuel Johnson, phrased it most prettily in the lines he added to Goldsmith's poem 'The Travellers':

> How small, of all that human hearts endure,
> That part which laws or kings can cause or cure!
> Still to ourselves in every place consigned
> Our own felicity we make or find.

(Of course, if the human timber can only grow crooked, then there's no need for the exertion of the conservative interest to maintain the situation.)

A word that rises naturally to the mind, in considering the foregoing, is 'insecurity'. Despite his great and confident presence on the podium – which we know always put him into an anticipatory state of nerves until the end of his days – and despite his legendary performances in the salon and at table, Berlin was uncertain of his welcome, unsure of himself and, possibly, uneasy about the uncritical admiration he received from some acolytes. Ignatieff makes it abundantly plain that Jewishness lay at the bottom of this unease. Using great new material this time, he also demonstrates that Berlin suffered much private anxiety over Zionism. Though he felt that his adopted England was uniquely tolerant of the Jewish presence, he never allowed himself quite to relax. And though he thought that a Jewish national home in Palestine was a necessary and even a good thing, he was acutely aware that it was as much a project of the positive – the interventionist – as of the negative, or the right to be let alone.

Two instances illustrate this to perfection, and both involve his friend and ally Lewis Namier. In the *Salmagundi* interview, Berlin said of the problem of assimilation:

> Sir Lewis Namier explained this extremely clearly. He said that Eastern European Judaism was a frozen mass until the rays of the Western Enlightenment began to beat on it. Then some of it remained frozen, some evaporated – that meant assimilation and drifting – and some melted into powerful streams: one was socialism and the other Zionism. That's exactly right.

Score one for the poor old Enlightenment, at least: it emancipated Jews not just from legally imposed disabilities but from the control of their own stasis-oriented clerical authorities. (It wasn't the anti-Semites or Christians, after all, who persecuted Spinoza.) Then there is the single story which Berlin was most fond of relating. In the Thirties, a number of supposedly suave Germans were sent over to England to work on élite opinion. There was one academic setting in which they were always sure of a hearing. In the Ignatieff version of this much-repeated anecdote:

> He remembered one particularly clumsy member of the German aristocracy who, in the common room of All Souls, happened to say that he thought German territorial demands in Europe were as reasonable as British imperial claims overseas. This remark, delivered into the stillness of the common room, was suddenly interrupted by a guttural growl from a man whom Isaiah had never seen before, seated in one of window recesses. '*Wir Juden und die andere Farbigen denken anders*' ('We Jews and the other coloured peoples think otherwise'), the stranger growled, and stalked out. This was Isaiah's first encounter with the Polish-born historian and devoted Zionist, Lewis Namier.

One sees at once the utility as well as the beauty of such a piece of raconteurship. It puts the British, the Jews and the 'coloured peoples' all on one side, in a pleasingly multinational manner. It leaves the fish-faced outsider gasping for air. It is an instance of a good return of serve, delivered across a celebrated common room. And it shows how even Galicians can become, if you like, Englishman. It's the *echt* Berlin tale; arousing the same warm emotions as *Chariots of Fire* while illustrating grand matters.

This is of course the same Namier who not only become *plus anglais que les anglais* – no shame in that one naturally hopes – but who wrote that 'the future of the white race lies with Empires, that is, those nations which hold vast expanses of land outside Europe'. If he ever advocated Zionism as a movement for the emancipation of coloured peoples, I think I would have read of it.

An ambivalence on this score is palpable in Berlin's own attitudes

to Palestine, and to the British Empire of which it was for a long time
a province. Benjamin Disraeli, proposed by Berlin in a famous essay
as the Jew who overcame outsiderdom by identifying with the British
upper class (a far more agreeable choice than Marx's rancorous allegiances in the opposite directions), was a stern racial nationalist as
well as a mustard-keen promoter of imperialism. And Arthur Balfour,
author of a famous Declaration on the subject of Palestine, had been
the British politician most opposed to Jewish immigration from Eastern Europe. (Berlin never alludes to this as far as I know, but he must
have been aware of it.) Furthermore, whether or not the establishment
of a Jewish state in Palestine was to be mainly dependent on British
imperial goodwill, what were its founding principles to be? To his
credit, Berlin never lied about Palestine being 'a land without a people'. But, if Jews were to demand, in that same land, not the equal
rights that they demanded in America or Europe, but special and
transcendent proprietorial rights, how could this claim be founded? It
could only be founded on (a) the claims of revealed and prophetic
religion or (b) the claims of an unbreakable tie of blood, and of that
blood to that soil. Yet what could be less agreeable, to Berlin, than
language or argument that originated from those ancient and superstitious sources?

An immediate answer to this conundrum of atavism was supplied, for
Berlin and for many others, by the homicidal atavism of Christian and
conservative Europe, which became infected with the madness of
fascism and thus made Palestine a question of safety for Jews. Yet
Berlin, again to his credit, did not allow this consideration to silence
all of his misgivings. Visiting Mandate Palestine in 1932, he found the
perfect English assimilationist metaphor to describe the conflict of
rights. The place was an English public school, with the British High
Commissioner as headmaster, and two 'houses'. Most of the masters
preferred the Arab house, whose boys were 'gay, affectionate, high-
spirited and tough, occasionally liable to break out and have a rag and
break the skulls of a few Jews or an Englishman perhaps', while the
Jewish house was full of clever rich boys, 'allowed too much pocket
money by their parents, rude, conceited, ugly, ostentatious, suspected
of swapping stamps unfairly with the other boys, always saying they
know better, liable to work too hard and not play games with the rest'.
Golly. In one way, this illustrates a talent for stereotype. In another, it
shows his gift for imagining the workings of other, opposed minds.
Leaving Palestine by sea:

> He met a handsome, poetic young man named Abraham Stern, travelling to
> Italy to take up a scholarship in classics at the University of Florence, offered
> by Mussolini's government. When they got talking, Isaiah asked him what

Stern thought of the recent British move to create a legislative council in Palestine. We shall fight that, Stern said. Why? Because it would give the Arabs representation in proportion to their demographic superiority. But, Isaiah countered, the council was merely advisory. It does not matter, Stern replied. We shall fight and fight, and if blood has to be shed . . .

Stern, and his distinctly less aesthetic deputy Yitzhak Shamir, went on to offer military and political collaboration to Hitler in the battle to expel the British and to make a manly, even skull-breaking, nation out of the Jews. And Berlin, normally so eager to please, was later to refuse to shake Menachem Begin's hand when he met him in the lift of the King David Hotel. For as long as seemed feasible, he took the part of those Jews who favoured a bi-national state. It could be argued that he adopted this 'moderate' line to try and defuse any quarrel between his new English home and a putative Jewish national one, but – though such a conflict was indeed an agony to him, especially during the war years in Washington – it would be paltry to reduce his dilemma to this proportion. He clearly saw it in the light of an issue of conscience, and also of a serious challenge to his own 'philosophy', personal and political.

I was, however, quite surprised to read Ignatieff's disclosures under this heading. In public, Berlin always seemed to take the same 'damage control' positions on the issue as he adopted on so many others. For example, in *Personal Impressions* he says of Chaim Weizmann that he 'committed none of those enormities for which men of action, and later their biographers, claim justification on the ground of what is called *raison d'état*'. Well, that's true only if you compare Weizmann to the usual suspects of this and other centuries. By the standard of mild and tolerant Jewish idealists, though, he justified a fair bit of ethnic cleansing on precisely that ground. (In 1944, he complained to FDR that 'we could not rest our case on the consent of the Arabs'. That consent was specified in the Balfour Declaration.) I know that Berlin once complained earnestly to the editor of the *TLS* about a fairly neutral review of a collection on Palestine edited by Edward Said and myself. I remember the huge row he forced, at the offices of *Index on Censorship* of all places, concerning an essay by Noam Chomsky which happened to mention in passing that Israel, under Weizmann's presidency, was only admitted to the UN on condition that Palestinian refugees would either be compensated or permitted to reclaim their homes. And there were many comparable instances. He even once told Susan Sontag that he had caught himself thinking of Israel as the old fellow-travellers thought of the Soviet Union. (In the context, or any context, a more than startling admission.) He kept his admonitions, and his reservations, extremely private until the very last possible moment, when, on the verge of death, he dictated a statement critical of Netanyahu and in favour of a utilitarian two-state partition. The letter, I was recently told by its Israeli recipient Avishai Margalit, contained, as he drily put it, 'nothing to write home about'. Coming well after the Oslo Agreement, and stressing Muslim holy places in Jerusalem rather than the actual Arab inhabitants of many denominations, it was little more than a coda to the loveless Arafat-Netanyahu embrace. But Margalit told me also that, before releasing it to the press, he decided to solicit Berlin's express permission. The request arrived as the old man was being taken to hospital in his final crisis. So his signal to go ahead and publish was his very last act on earth. Gerry Cohen tells me that at about the same time, Berlin was trying to evolve a petition calling on the British Government to institute a major 'New Deal' programme of public works, in order to eradicate unemployment. Neither appeal was very muscular or particularly bold. However, the making or signing of public appeals had never been his practice. (A friend speculates that he avoided signing letters to *The Times* because his name began with B.) So at the very end, Berlin seemed to believe that he had an unredeemed debt to the friends on the Left whom he had so often disappointed.

There's another instance of that same impulse, in a story told on tape to Ignatieff. Berlin claims that in 1968, while lecturing at Columbia during the campus rebellion:

> He gave a lecture so close to the police lines that his friends told him to wet a handkerchief to place over his mouth and eyes in case teargas canisters were fired in his vicinity. His Marxist graduate students Bert Ollmann and Marshall Berman attended the lecture, ready to defend him against hecklers and if necessary against physical attack. It was not an auspicious time to be a liberal philosopher.

Well, I know Bertell Ollmann and Marshall Berman, both of them members of that strange and interesting sub-set, Berlin's Marxisant diaspora, and I've asked them about this episode. They both love 'Isaiah', and they would both gladly have done that for him, and more. But they say they can't recall the event, and Ignatieff has certainly not checked it with them, and my own view is that – vertiginous though the times undoubtedly were – they are unlikely to have forgotten it . Had Berlin been menaced with martyrdom in the manner that he fondly invents, and Ignatieff fondly sets down, it would not, really, have been for his liberalism. (I don't know how to break it to the comrades about the Bundys.) One begins to see how myths are made.

Avishai Margalit was giving a lecture when I met him, at a New York conference on 'Post-Zionism' organised for the centennial of Herzl's romantic Viennese project. He spoke with great brio about the startling proposition that European Jews – the *Luftmensch* – could only be made healthy and whole by becoming farmers and peasants in the Levant. This, he said, both detached the Jews from their historic occupations and made it inevitable (because the land to be tilled had to come from somewhere, or rather from somebody) that there would be a confrontation with dispossessed Arabs. 'If this is not the original sin,' he remarked, 'it is certainly the immaculate misconception.' I close my eyes and think of Berlin's character and upbringing and preferences. To take educated and musical Latvian Jews and put hoes in their hands? Never mind the dire fate of the indigenous Palestinians, as Berlin's friend J. L. Talmon always painstakingly emphasised that he didn't. Does this not mean that the shtetl and the ghetto, and sooner or later the magical rabbi, will be back? And isn't there a class question involved?

Many people's attitude to Zionism is conditioned by their exposure to anti-Semitism and here, too, Berlin registered certain insecurities and uncertainties. He maintained two positions about Britain: first that it was the most 'tolerant' country in which to be a Jew and, second, that you never knew when you might not get an old-fashioned reminder of your outsider status. In 1950, he was refused membership by the St James's Club, even though 'put up' by Oliver Lyttelton, and had to settle for Brooks's. The St James's committee was blunt enough to leave Berlin in no doubt as to the reasons for his rejection. The following year, he became involved in a difficult correspondence with T. S. Eliot, to whose prose work he alluded in the same article on 'Jewish Slavery and Emancipation' that had served as a rejoinder to Koestler. Eliot protested in a letter that, for him at least, 'the Jewish problem is not a racial problem at all, but a religious problem'. In that case, returned Berlin, why did his notorious lecture 'After Strange Gods', delivered at the University of Virginia in the year after Hitler's accession to power, insist that 'reasons of race and religion make any large number of free-thinking Jews undesirable'? Other considerations apart, how did this observe a distinction between race and religion?

Eliot's reply mumbled some words of contrition for the odious sentence, asserted that Judaism had been made redundant by the marvellous advent of the foretold Christ, and warned that assimilated secularisation would be death to both Christians and Jews. To this sectarian arrogance Berlin did not respond, at least not in public. (He wrote to Eliot in 1952, effusively complimenting him on 'your most effective and fascinating letters about the Jews'.) I said earlier that Berlin suppressed republication of 'Jewish Slavery and Emancipation', which in English at any rate he did. But in the essay's one Israeli republication, he removed all the offending references to Eliot. 'Much later in life,' Ignatieff observes rather briefly, 'he felt that his politeness had shaded into obsequiousness.' I admire the choice of 'shaded'.

Anglomane that he was, Berlin may have unconsciously felt that Eliot was a native squire. He certainly did not suffer from Jewish self-loathing. (That is, if one exempts the strictly physical dislike which, Ignatieff reveals, he felt for his soft and, as he thought, sexless and effeminate appearance.) It is more that he wished to be English than that he yearned to be other than what he was. In the essay contrasting Disraeli and Marx, where every allowance is granted to Disraeli and nary a one to the old incendiary, and where incidentally Berlin refers unaffectedly to the 'colonisation of Palestine', there appear the following lines, in praise of the 'Jew d'esprit' who stole the Suez Canal and proclaimed the Empress of India:

> He wanted recognition by those on the inside, as one of them, at least as an equal if not as a superior. Hence the psychological need to establish an identity for himself, for which he would secure recognition, an identity that would enable him to develop his gifts freely, to their utmost extent. And in due course he did create a personality for himself, at least in his own imagination. He saw before him a society of aristocrats, free, arrogant and powerful, which, however sharply he may have seen through it, he neverthe- less viewed with bemused eyes as a rich and marvellous world.

The only inept word there is 'bemused', which applies neither to the brilliant and amoral Tory statesman nor to the man who wrote of him with such vicarious, almost voluptuous admiration.

A crucial element of good form, in the case of those fortunate enough to have become 'securely recognised', is the ability to be light- hearted and lenient about some controversies over Jewishness, while reserving the right to be heavy-handed, even juridical, in others. (In case I'm being too elliptical, I mean to say how to avoid being thought of as 'chippy', while knowing when to call in your chips.) Berlin made himself master of the nuances of this code. I know of a pointed example. In 1960, Professor Norman Birnbaum, then at Oxford and a friend of Berlin's, wrote an article for *Commentary* about the English scene. In it – I possess the original typescript – he proposed to make the following observation for his readers in New York:

> It is philosophical feat of no small order to celebrate, simultaneously, the essential Britishness of British politics and to derive from it prescriptions applicable to all of mankind's ideological ills. Not surprisingly, this feat has been accomplished by a very cosmopolitan group of philosophers long resident in the British Isles. The writings of Professor Isaiah Berlin, Michael Polanyi and Karl Popper are adduced wherever British self-congratulation seeks intellectually reputable credentials. Foreign voices have also been heard. Professor Jacob Talmon's writings have been praised by the *Times* itself, and Professor Raymond Aron has been honoured as if he were a jazz- age Montesquieu, looking admiringly across the Channel from Paris.

One pauses to note that *Commentary* was once a critical magazine. Anyway, Birnbaum sent the essay up to Headington House, in draft form, in a friendly manner, as one does. I also possess the excitedly annotated original reply:

> If you publish your piece as it stands I shall certainly find myself compelled to write to *Commentary* to point out the following things . . . You speak of us all as 'cosmopolitans' who have lived for various periods in England. The latter words are perfectly true. You do not add the adjective 'rootless'; but since all the persons mentioned by you are Jews, the expression too strongly reminds one of the fact that this is how it is used by the professional anti-Semites in the Soviet Union – and indeed everywhere else. This I shall certainly have to point out to *Commentary*, which is the very journal for such points. It would be better if instead of saying 'cosmopolitans' you openly said 'Jews of foreign origin'. Other Jews, 'ideologues' of equally foreign origin from Marx onwards: Namier, Laski, Deutscher, Shonfeld [sic], Hobsbawm – I need not go over the list – oppose 'us' and dominate the discussion and influence gentiles. It may be a sound point, but it is certainly anti-Semitic; and as *Commentary* enjoys lacerating itself, it will surely not decline to print my letter.

Where to begin? With the idea of a point being simultaneously 'sound' and anti-Semitic? With the objection to the word 'cosmopolitan' from the fan of Disraeli? Or with the bracketing of Namier and Deutscher? (Those lists of names, again.) The article, which must have made Norman Birnbaum wish that he had expended more fire on Michael Oakeshott, later appeared in a version only slightly toned down. Mark the sequel.

In the Seventies, when Hugh Trevor-Roper put up his frightful Christ Church friend Zulfikar ali-Bhutto for an honorary degree, there was a row. Richard Gombrich and Steven Lukes led a petition to deny Oxford's imprimatur to the man who had – among his many other crimes – displayed lethal chauvinism over Bangladesh. After the vote in the Sheldonian, which went heavily against Bhutto, I saw Trevor-Roper stalking away and asked him, in my journalist capacity, for a comment. 'We've been ambushed,' he yelled, 'by the Left. The Left and the Jews.' I invited him to repeat this, which he did, and which he did many times later on when the initial fury had abated. There was then another row. Lukes and others circulated a petition critical of the Egregious Regius, and of his . . . want of circumspection. It was Isaiah Berlin who spent many patient hours trying to persuade them that this did not constitute prejudice. There are times to wheel out the big moral gun, and there are times to be discreet. And there are those who can decide which time is which. And that's power, of a kind.

In the long *Salmagundi* interview by which I help keep count, there appears the following exchange:

Do you think that liberalism is, in this sense, essentially European, then? or Western?

It was certainly invented in Europe.

Historically, of course. But, I mean now – is it an essentially Western principle?

Yes. I suspect that there may not be much liberalism in Korea. I doubt if there is much liberalism even in Latin America. I think liberalism is essentially the belief of people who have lived on the same soil for a long time in comparative peace with each other. An English invention. The English have not been invaded for a very very long time. That's why they can afford to praise these virtues. I see that if you were exposed to constant pogroms you might be a little more suspicious of the possibility of liberalism.

Here is the rich man's John Rawls. Liberalism is for those who don't need it; free to those who can afford it and very expensive – if even conceivable – to those who cannot. But the clash of ideas here is more chaotic than confused. Should one deduce that liberalism can't be derived from the experience of pogroms? In that case, why did Berlin argue that liberalism was the answer to the experience of this uniquely grim – as he thought – century? Meanwhile, if liberalism is geographically and even ethnically limited, where is its universality? (And what became of Namier's 'Jews and other coloured peoples'?) Should one be an English invader in order to be a carrier of liberal ideals? Finally, what's the point of a tumultuous and volatile and above all 'cosmopolitan' society, like that of America, if high liberalism can only be established with common blood and on common soil?

Again, one gets the queasy impression that Berlin's opinions were a farrago: an unsorted box raided for lucky dips. Incidentally, 'people who have lived on the same soil for a long time in comparative peace with one another' must be close kin to 'the same people living in the same place' – Eliot's *sine qua non* for a stable and organic (and static) society in 'After Strange Gods'.

I've kept for last Isaiah Berlin's most luminous moment: his encounter with Anna Akhmatova in St Petersburg, as it was called when Berlin first saw it and as it is again called today. When he made his visit in November 1945, as First Secretary at the British Embassy, it was called Leningrad and had, under that name, resisted, and thrown back the Nazis. During the unspeakable siege, Stalin and Zhdanov, in that mad way they had, took personal steps to rescue Anna Akhmatova and evacuate her to Tashkent, where she shared quarters with Nadezhda Mandelstam. But they did this insincerely and pedantically (and in Stalin's own case perhaps superstitiously), regarding her as part 'asset' and part witch. Many people were not sure that she had survived. Berlin himself only discovered her whereabouts by accident, while visiting a rugged and bohemian bookstore. Wherever he travelled,

Berlin carried a certain idea of Oxford. He had not yet read any of Akhmatova's poems, but he knew that they had been kept in print by his friend Maurice Bowra. (Score one, then, for the Wadham man so often described as having squandered his gifts.)

When he set off to call at N.44 Fontanka, therefore, Berlin stepped out of his usual cocoon. He was taking a risk, leaving everything to chance, acting on human instinct. The resulting meetings are much better rendered by Ignatieff than by György Dalos. Not only was Berlin, in a later phrase of an Akhmatova poem, 'the guest from the future', he was also a revenant from the past and a catalyst for the fusion of the Russian intellectual diaspora with those like Akhmatova, who had decided to stay on, no matter what. He brought her some Kafka. They disagreed vividly about Turgenev. In a freezing flat with nothing to eat but cold spuds, the emotional thermostat was set very high. Dalos doesn't mind pruriently canvassing the possibility of a tryst, but it's very clear that this was one of those few occasions where that really would have spoiled everything. Ignatieff, who gives us the impression that Berlin was a virgin until middle age, is emphatic and on good authority. Berlin, he writes,

> remained on one side of the room, she on the other. Far from being a Don Juan, he was a sexual neophyte alone in the apartment of a fabled seductress, who had enjoyed deep romantic entanglements with half a dozen supremely talented man ... Besides, he was also aware of more quotidian needs. He had already been there six hours and he wanted to go to the lavatory. But it would have broken the mood to do so, and in any case, the communal toilet was down the dark hallway.

At last, a Boswellian moment, Berlin's subsequent report to the Foreign Office, instead of processing political intelligence in the conventional way, was a learned and spirited brief on the artists and writers of the Soviet Union, and on the thuggish nullity of those who tried to break them. And this was prescient, as well as fine. (The only really stupid critique of Isaiah Berlin that I have ever read was by that recreational vulpicide Roger Scruton, who accused him of being soft on Communism.) If Akhmatova was persecuted afresh as a result of the rendezvous, she had no illusions, and had not been trapped into anything. Berlin's Uncle Leo was later treated barbarously during the Jew-baiting that surrounded the Doctors' Plot, but Soviet anti-Semitism was *sui generis*. The only subsequent meeting between Berlin and Akhmatova was an anti-climax as, given her queenly manners, it more or less had to be. But without her vanity, an aspect of her irreducible courage and confidence after all, she would not have proved that an individual may outlast both a state and an ideology.

There was one moment of bathos during the Leningrad meeting, which was the fault of neither participant. As Berlin and Akhmatova talked, there came disconcerting bellows of 'Isaiah' from the courtyard below. This was Randolph Churchill, puce and solipsistic, demanding that his friend come without loss of time to the Hotel Astoria, there to explain to the domestics of the famine-stricken city that Mr Churchill's newly purchased caviar should be placed on ice. Berlin actually broke off conversation with Akhmatova to go and see to the matter. But then, poor dear Randolph was very much a part of that same 'package' of Englishness which he had already bought.

If it is fair to say, as Ignatieff does, that Berlin never coined an epigram or aphorism, it is also fair to add that he never broke any really original ground in the field of ideas. He was a skilled ventriloquist for other thinkers. Still, even in proposing wobbly antitheses ('positive v. negative', 'liberal v. romantic', 'Enlightenment v. Counter-Enlightenment', incomparable goals as distinct from incompatible or incommensurable ones) he turned over some mental baggage. The letters, too, promise to be magnificent trove, even if they contain some rude shocks to his liberal fan club. Perhaps, then, to paraphrase Wilde, the real genius was in the life and not the work: 'a real 20th century life', as Avishai Margalit puts it. Fearing that English liberalism on its own was too diffuse and benign and insipid, he tried to inject it with a dose of passionate intensity, much of it necessarily borrowed from some rather illiberal sources. Convinced also that pluralism of values was inescapable – a 'relative' commonplace – he helped to refresh the sometimes arid usage of irony which the English regard as their particular discourse. In our native terms, the ironic style is often compounded with the sardonic and the hard-boiled; even the effortlessly superior. But irony originates in the glance and the shrug of the loser, the outsider, the despised minority. It is a nuance that comes most effortlessly to the oppressed. Czeslaw Miloscz, Isaiah Berlin's non-Jewish Baltic contemporary, went so far in his poem 'Not like This' as to term irony 'the glory of slaves'. He did not, I am certain, intend to say that it was a servile quality. But Berlin's aptitude in this most subtle of idioms was conditioned in part by his long service to a multiplicity of masters.

First published as 'Moderation or Death' (a review of *Isaiah Berlin: A Life* by Michael Ignatieff and *The Guest from the Future: Anna Akhmatova and Isaiah Berlin* by György Dalos) in *London Review of Books*, 26 November 1998

The Grimmest Tales

A thing that you have to read, if you desire to know what's cooking in the culture, is the *Newsletter on Intellectual Freedom* of the American Library Association. It carries reports from innumerable fronts in the long guerrilla war for the hearts and minds of children. Here, for example, is a parent named Mary Arnold from Amana, Iowa, who can know no peace until Roald Dahl is removed from the curriculum. She doesn't care for his best-selling efforts *The BFG* (Big Friendly Giant) and *The Witches*:

> Arnold charged that the books were too sophisticated and did not teach moral values. She read passages to the committee that included a witch plotting to kill children, a reference to 'dog droppings' and people's 'bottoms' being poked or skewered.

Fat chance, lady. The word is out about bottoms and dog doo doo, and while you may want less of it, the kids are unanimous. They want more. They also wish for more and better revolting rhymes, sinister animals, and episodes where fat children get theirs.

And the buying spree this Christmas won't be any different. As it got under way, I went and stationed myself in the children's book section of Doubleday in New York, where I kept a loitering vigil until I attracted too many glances. Young purchasers – the ideal Dahl age-group is between seven and eleven, though books such as *The Enormous Crocodile* and *Fantastic Mr Fox* are for first-graders – made straight for the Dahl shelf. It was pointless, for the most part, to try to interest them in anything else. And this was not just because of the dismal worthy competition, which did include (I swear to God) prominent display of an exciting volume called *Carl Goes to Daycare*.

It was a few Christmases ago that I gave a Roald Dahl to the bright nine-year-old daughter of some friends. She actually got up and left the heaped Christmas lunch table to lie down and – this really is the *mot juste* – devour the book. I was impressed enough to start reading the stuff myself. Apart from anything else, why did this appetite so upset her parents?

Dahl, I discovered, is more than a Pied Piper. He is a genuine subversive. In his world, kids are fit to rule. They understand cruelty and unfairness and, I'm very sorry to say, are capable of relishing it. They also have a rather raunchy idea of what's funny:

> And then, a little further down
> A mass of others gather round:
> A bacon rind, some rancid lard,
> A loaf of bread gone stale and hard,
> A steak that nobody could chew,
> An oyster from an oyster stew,
> Some Liverwurst so old and gray,
> One smelled it from a mile away,
> A rotten nut, a reeky pear,
> A thing the cat left on the stair.

Ah, the joys of the gross and yucky! The above is the fate of little Veruca Salt on her way down the garbage chute at Willy Wonka's chocolate factory.

Children need their own world, with secret rooms and eerie happenings. That Dahl furnishes these rooms cannot be doubted. It was well put by Teresa Root of Altoona, Wisconsin, who tried to pull *James and the Giant Peach* from a local reading list. To quote the ALA report:

> The book is about a boy's adventures when he spills magic crystals onto a peach tree and is taken into another world. Root objected to the use of the word 'ass' and to parts of the book that dealt with wine, tobacco, snuff and certain other words, including a reference to a female spider that she said can be taken two ways.

You couldn't put it much better than that if you were Dahl's own publicist.

The same proof is offered in a different form by Bruno Bettelheim in his classic *The Uses of Enchantment*. Anyway, he phrased it well, if rather doggedly:

> There is a widespread refusal to let children know that the source of much that goes wrong in life is due to our very own natures – the propensity of all men for acting aggressively, asocially, selfishly, out of anger or anxiety. Instead, we want our children to believe that, inherently, all men are good. But children know that they are not always good: *and often, even when they are, they would prefer not to be.* [Italics mine.]

In his pedantic way, Bettelheim went on to make several other good points about children's relative closeness to nature and animals, and about the guilty thrill that accompanies the loss of a parent or parents. But expert as he was, he could no more have written *Danny the Champion of the World* than he could have flown to the moon. In Danny,

Dahl introduces us to a seven-year-old boy whose mother is dead and whose father illegally keeps him out of school so that he can help in the auto-mechanic business. No wonder the child is devoted to Dad, who also shows him around some scary woodland in order to teach him how to poach pheasants. A fine example to our budding youth! By the way, when the boy does get to school he finds that the headmaster has been driven to the gin bottle by his wife, and that the most prominent of the teachers is a twitching and irrepressible sadist.

Charles Dickens, who understood something about children and who, what is more, understood something about the durability of an unhappy childhood, once wrote: 'Little Red Riding Hood was my first love. I felt that if I could have married Little Red Riding Hood, I should have known perfect bliss.' Not after the wolf had finished with her, he wouldn't. But one sees the potency of a good yucky tale nonetheless. Roald Dahl also grasped the point of Charles Dickens, who is often thought by children to be an adult's idea of a good read, and it's suggestive that in *The BFG* the child is advised to get hold of *Nicholas Nickleby*, by an author named 'Dahl's Chickens'.

Roald Dahl's life, which has been read by millions of children, in his two memoirs, *Boy* and *Going Solo*, was full of ripe stuff. His father and an older sister both died when he was three. At school he was bullied and thrashed in fairly spectacular ways, and quite obviously never forgot the fact. (The vile teacher in *Danny* is a straight lift from *Boy*.) Having been sent to the colonies to earn a living, and having been badly injured as a wartime flier, he married and had several children of his own, with the actress Patricia Neal, to whom he famously wasn't very nice. One of these, his daughter Olivia, died of measles when she was seven. Another, her younger brother, Theo, suffered brain damage when his stroller was hit by a taxi. So Dahl knew from the outset that God and nature are not just, that parents and teachers are not to be counted on to stick by you, that Providence doesn't protect the innocent, and that not all animals are furry friends. Perfect.

I'm only guessing, but I believe that Dahl must have read the stories of 'Saki' in his youth. H. H. Munro, who took this pen name from the cup-bearer in *The Rubáiyát of Omar Khayám*, was a natural genius at making up absurd and sinister names. He was a snob and a bit of a Jew-hater and died heroically on the Western Front in 1916. His best-known short story, 'Sredni Vashtar', is still read with shudders by parents and guardians with bad consciences. It concerns a beautiful and vicious polecat of that name, kept as a pet by an affection-starved boy named Conradin, who is only ten years old:

Mrs De Ropp was Conradin's cousin and guardian, and in his eyes she represented those three-fifths of the world that are necessary and disagreeable and real: the other two-fifths, in perpetual antagonism to the forgoing, *were summed up in himself and his imagination.* [Italics mine.]

In the end, after various propitiations and incantations, 'Sredni Vashtar the Beautiful' tears out the bad woman's throat and runs off to freedom. It's one of the most moral stories I have ever read.

There's nothing very mysterious about Roald Dahl's formula. It consisted, as he proudly confessed in one of the last interviews before his death in 1990, of 'conspiring with children against adults'. He described it with some satisfaction as 'the path to their affections'. One of the reasons for adult dislike of Dahl's work is undoubtedly that of jealousy. In the mega-selling *Matilda,* for example, the parents and siblings of this precocious and put-upon pint-sized heroine are coldly set down as 'the father', 'the mother' and 'the brother'. An enchanted privacy is woven by Matilda to escape these horrors, and the stuff of enchantment is great literature.

And then, of course, because it had to happen, come the forces of PC. Having spent years decrying and deconstructing the very idea of authorship, and saying that as an individual exercise it hardly counts at all, the same forces are now concentrating entirely on the private life of the writer. Dahl, it appears, was mean to his wife. He was explicitly anti-Semitic. He's been accused of giving dope and booze to his own kids to keep them quiet. So, is it true? *Of course* it's bloody well true. How else could Dahl have kept children enthralled and agreeably disgusted and pleasurably afraid? By being Enid Blyton?

In his memoirs Kingsley Amis, who must be rated as having a high tolerance for the politically incorrect, describes Roald Dahl as one of the most repellent people he ever met. For one thing, he arrived at a lunch party by helicopter (something, of course, that no child would ever be interested in doing). For another, he scorned Amis's own, relatively low income from fiction, and urged him to try children's books because 'that's where the money is today, believe me'. When Amis doubted that he had the requisite sensitivity, Dahl cut him off by saying, 'Never mind, the little bastards'd swallow it.' Shocked? Amis was almost struck dumb. But I was charmed, as I was by Dahl's breezy dispatch of another Establishment fiction writer:

> The one thing I hate more than anything else in anyone who is success-ful is pomposity. It's a very easy thing to acquire – especially for men. You don't very often see pompous women. What happens to women is something else – somebody like Iris Murdoch. What would you call her? Not pompous. But there's definitively something irritating there. I saw her about six months ago on television saying it was very important children should read books and I thought: 'Well, you silly old hag, why don't you write some for them?'

Having once met Dame Iris, I hugged myself when I read that. But I can't say that I exactly hugged myself when I heard Dahl on Salman Rushdie, whom he blamed for his own misfortunes, or on the Jews, of whom he said, 'I am certainly anti-Israel, and I have become anti-Semitic.'

The best defence here has probably been mounted by Michael Dirda, the children's book critic, who won a Pulitzer for his efforts: Roald Dahl 'remains the Evelyn Waugh of children's books – compellingly readable, deeply disturbing, outrageous, manipulative and witty'. Not to mention a racist, sexist colonialist.

A torrent of gunk is about to break over the scene with the publication of Jeremy Treglown's *Roald Dahl: A Life*. Here indeed we learn about the scuzzy bits of the author, Jew-hating and all. And never fear, there is lots of gruesome stuff about the Dahl family circle. In the press, early warnings are starting to appear, as if the grown-ups were saying, with some satisfaction, '*See, I told* you so. I told you not to take sweets from that nasty Mr Dahl', before going back to the routine sweep of the metal detector over the Halloween and Christmas candy.

'As a matter of fact', Treglown told me, 'though Dahl loved to be shocking and nasty in his private conversation, he's actually a very intriguing figure. He started writing for children when he was in his twenties, which is an odd age to start. Then he dropped it all in favour of a rather sour adult fiction. And then in the Sixties he began to write for kids again because he had some of his own'.

Treglown describes Dahl as someone who was misanthropic and slightly sentimental – a near-ideal natural combination. 'He was himself always in search of father figures, having lost his own father. He was also in pursuit of mother and child figures. His ideal plot involves small children making friends with middle-aged or elderly people; people above the age of the ordinary parent.'

As usual, the political-correctness accusation turns out to be a snare and a delusion. 'It was pointed out to Dahl that teachers were reluctant to read *Charlie and the Chocolate Factory* aloud in, say, downtown LA, because the Oompa-Loompas seemed too much like pickaninnies. So he rewrote and reissued that chapter to make them pink-faced hippies with long hair', said Treglown.

'The overwhelming bulk of the rest of so-called "children's literature",' wrote Bruno Bettelheim in *The Uses of Enchantment*, 'attempts to entertain or to inform, or both. But most of these books are so shallow in substance that little of significance can be gained from them.' He recommended the primeval drama of the folk fairy tale, with all its random seductions, imprisonments, executions, cannibalisms, and monstrosities. There is a reason Twain and Kipling and Saki go on succeeding generation after generation, even more than the ghastly

Brothers Grimm, and it is the same reason that motivates the bores and schoolmarms to try to repress them. Much to the discombobulation of respectable and tedious parents, their children quite like the idea of a mysterious uncle and, given the choice, they will always pick the wicked one.

First published as 'The Grimmest Tales' in *Vanity Fair*, January 1994

The Importance of Being Andy

In Graham Greene's novel *Travels With My Aunt*, which was written in 1969, the narrator is Henry Pulling, a grey, inoffensive and reclusive former bank manager. Thanks to an aunt who will brook no disagreement, perhaps because she is really his mother, he finds himself on the Orient Express between Venice and Belgrade. Through no fault of his own, he has become the confidante of a dangerously innocent young American girl named Tooley. Thrown together in a couchette, they improve the shining hour with an interlude of mutual incomprehension:

'Julian did a fabulous picture of a Coke bottle once,' Tooley said.

'Who's Julian?' I asked absent-mindedly.

'The boy-friend, of course. I told you. He painted the Coke bright yellow. *Fauve*,' she added in a defiant way.

'He paints, does he?'

'That's why he thinks the East's very important to him. You know, like Tahiti was for Gauguin. He wants to experience the East before he starts on his big project. Let me take the Coke.'

There was less than an hour's wait at Venice, but the dark was falling when we pulled out and I saw nothing at all – I might have been leaving Clapham for Victoria. Tooley sat with me and drank one of her Cokes. I asked her what her boy-friend's project was.

'He wants to do a series of *enormous* pictures of Heinz soups in fabulous colours, so a rich man could have a different soup in each room in his apartment – say fish soup in the bedroom, potato soup in the dining room, leek soup in the drawing room, like they used to have family portraits. There would be these fabulous colours, all *fauve*. And the cans would give a sort of unity – do you see what I mean? It would be kind of intimate – you wouldn't break the mood every time you changed rooms. Like you do now if you have de Staël in one room and a Rouault in another.'

The memory of something I had seen in a Sunday supplement came back to me. I said, 'Surely somebody once *did* paint a Heinz soup tin?'

'Not Heinz, Campbell's,' Tooley said. 'That was Andy Warhol. I said the same thing to Julian when he first told me of the project.'

'Of course,' I said, 'Heinz and Campbell are not a bit the same shape. Heinz is sort of squat and Campbell's are long like English pillar-boxes. I love your pillar-boxes. They are fabulous. But Julian said that wasn't the point. He said that there are certain subjects which belong to a certain period and culture. Like the Annunciation did. Botticelli wasn't put off because Piero della Francesca had done the same thing. He wasn't an *imitator*. And think of all the Nativities. Well, Julian says, we sort of belong to the soup age – only he didn't call it that. He said it was the Art of the Techno-Structure. In a way, you see, the more people who paint soups the better. It *creates* a culture. One Nativity wouldn't have been any use at all. It wouldn't have been noticed.'[1]

Graham Greene was a passionate if unorthodox Roman Catholic. That is the only resemblance that I can unearth between him and Pittsburgh's most famous son. Yet this extended piece of aesthetic bafflement, with its brilliantly Warholian aperçu that '*One* Nativity wouldn't have been any use at all. It wouldn't have been noticed,' is testimony to the way in which Andy Warhol permeates our culture. Writing of Thomas Carlyle in 1931, George Orwell described him as enjoying a 'large, vague renown'.[2] I thought of annexing this phrase for my title this evening, but I decided instead on 'The Importance of Being Andy' because, if dear Oscar's admirers will not find the comparison to be blasphemous, it can be argued that Warhol only put his talent into his works, while reserving his genius for his life.

 There was a time when I would have laughed pityingly at anybody who attempted such a comparison. I may have been jaundiced by the fact that I came to live in the United States at the beginning of the Reagan era; that period of what Robert Hughes scornfully termed 'supply-side aesthetics'.[3] Not only had Warhol been to dinner at Ron and Nancy's infamous table – at a banquet for Ferdinand and Imelda Marcos, which must have made it the most intense shoe-fetishist soirée in recorded history – but *Interview* magazine had published a conversation of excruciating falsity and embarrassment between Andy, Bob Colacello, and the brittle First Lady herself. Following as this did so hard on the heels of *Interview*'s Peacock period, when it was too breathlessly impressed by that supreme patron of the arts the Shah of Iran, this was too much for friends of mine like Robert Hughes and Alexander Cockburn. In fact, Alexander published a spoof *Interview* conversation, in which Andy and Bob took Adolf Hitler for a sustaining lunch at Mortimer's restaurant on the upper East Side. Since I used later on to write a book column for *Interview* myself, I know for a fact that this parody had the effect of seriously upsetting its targets. And you can see why from this extract:

> *Bob:* Don't you wish you'd been able to spend Christmas in Berchtesgaden?
> *Hitler:* Yes, it would have been fun to go along there and see them light up

the tree and all that sort of thing. Do you spend a lot of time in Europe, Andy?

Andy: Gee. Maybe we should get a waiter and order.

Hitler: Just a salad for me, thanks. What about you?'

Andy: I'd like a medium cheeseburger and french fries and a lot of ketchup. Tom Enders was saying the other day that the Polish thing shows what a lot of trouble the Russians are in.

Hitler: Here fate seems desirous of giving us a sign. By handing Russia to Bolshevism it robbed the Russian nation of that intelligentsia which previously brought about and guaranteed its existence as a state. It was replaced by the Jew. And the end of Jewish rule in Russia means also the end of Russia as a state.

Bob: Did you enjoy being Führer?

The conversation winds through swathes of *Mein Kampf* which neither interviewer recognises, until the desultory finish:

Bob: Is there still pressure on you to think of your image and act a certain way?

Hitler: I don't think of image so much anymore. I really don't, Bob.

Bob: Well.

Hitler: Have I stopped you cold?

Andy: Well, no. It's just that it's interesting to be here, that's all. This is very exciting for us.[4]

That parody of atonal fascist chic summarised for many people the amoral, spaced-out, affectless and cynical chill that seemed to emanate from the Warhol world and was caught so crisply by Warhol's self-description of his own 'blank, autistic stare'. In a recent conversation, Bob Colacello – Andy's Boswell in both senses of the term – made to me a point which may be helpful in explaining my own reconsideration. Warhol, he stressed, was never verbal. Indeed, much of the time he was almost monosyllabic. Gee. Great. Really up there. These were his superlatives. Really, really, really great might describe a transcendent experience, such as meeting Jackie Kennedy at Studio 54. Warhol's mother never broke out of the linguistic ghetto of her Ruthenian background. We may thank her for ensuring that Andy spent so many hours of his boyhood gazing at the vivid colours of the Catholic iconostasis, and we may thank her also for helping give him the idea of borrowing someone else's signature. But it is salutary to bear in mind that Warhol was semi-articulate and also partly dyslexic. Essentially nonverbal and quasi-literate, he had to realise from the first that he would communicate through images. This makes the durability of some of his cryptic sentences the more remarkable for their brevity and pith. Not just '. . . I want to be a machine',[5] or 'when I have to think about it, I know the picture is wrong',[6] or even the imperishable remark, usually misquoted, that 'In the future, everybody will be world famous for fifteen minutes'.[7] This appeared in the catalogue of his first retrospective, which was shown at the Museum of Modern Art in Stockholm in February 1968. Just a few weeks later, Andy was pronounced clinically dead at Columbus-Cabrini Hospital in New York, after taking three bullets from Valeria Solanas. Her list of non-negotiable demands, it may be recalled, ran as follows: she wanted an appearance on the Johnny Carson show, publication of the SCUM manifesto in the *Daily News*, $25,000 in cash and a promise that Andy would make her a star. She might have had better luck if she hadn't made her *démarche* on the day that Bobby Kennedy was blown away in Los Angeles. When Warhol came to and saw the Kennedy funeral on the TV, he thought he was watching his own obsequies. Robbed of that particular fifteen minutes by the coincidence, he nonetheless contrived another terse one-liner. When Ultra Violet asked him why he'd been the one to get shot, he observed that he'd been in the wrong place at the right time.[8] Today, Los Angeles, the city of which Andy said in that same Stockholm catalogue that 'I love Los Angeles. I love Hollywood. They're beautiful. Everybody's plastic, but I love plastic. I want to *be* plastic',[9] is the setting for a national Warholian Kabuki drama. Bridget Berlin, Andy's collaborator in early reel-to-reel tapings, evolved with him the postmodern pastime of watching TV on the telephone. The brilliant nullity of this was somewhat in advance of the nullity of either medium; soporific separately and narcotic together. Recently she was talking to Colacello about the old days and said that the O. J. Simpson affair had made her miss Andy more than ever. 'He would have thought it was just so really, really, really great.'[10] Pity the luckless network or Hollywood underling who draws the job of making a mini-series or a drama out of the black man in the white bronco. It has all, from the very night of the crime, been on screen already. And so, all unconscious, an ungrateful nation honours Andy Warhol in its daily devotions.

But this is to keep us in the area of the large, vague renown. In 1987, the American artists David McDermott and Peter McGough, who operate as a daubing duo, painted a tribute to Warhol in an atrium. In what might be termed a post-Raphaelite or neo-Victorian manner, they mimic the passing of a nineteenth-century polymath and omnivore. The muses are all represented, or almost all. Art. Music. Journalism. Theatre. Society. Photography. Philosophy. Literature. In strict conformity with their anti-anachronistic project they omit Film.

Film

But the medium of film meant more than most to Warhol. Though his films never had the success he yearned for in America, being confined mainly to cult houses in New York and Los Angeles and San Francisco, in Europe they often did fantastically well and could also be said to have exerted a wide influence. In 1971, in Germany, *Trash* very nearly outgrossed *Easy Rider*, and we might not have heard as much from Rainer Werner Fassbinder in later years if this had not been so. Godard's practice of having people orate directly into the camera is a tribute of a kind and, if you ask me, one that could have been made more sparingly. Bernardo Bertolucci freely admitted that he took the idea for the climactic scene of *Last Tango in Paris* from Warhol's *Blue Movie*, where Viva and Louis Walden divide their time between coupling and discussing the war in Vietnam. *Blue Movie*, of course, was banned in the United States. It also tempted Warhol out of his usual costive or cryptic syntax. Generally, when quoted on matters filmic he would be himself, saying for example that, 'The best atmosphere I can think of is film, because it's three-dimensional physically and two-dimensional emotionally',[11] or, 'All my films are artificial, but then everything is sort of artificial. I don't know where the artificial stops and the real starts'[12] (as if anybody does, by the way). On *Blue Movie* he came dangerously close to actual enthusiasm, 'I think movies should appeal to prurient interests. I mean, the way things are going now – people are alienated from one another. Movies should – uh – arouse you. Hollywood films are just planned-out commercials. *Blue Movie* was real. But it wasn't done as pornography – it was an exercise, an experiment. But I really do think movies *should* arouse you, should get you excited about people, should be prurient.' Wow. (That's me talking.) Gee. Warhol on engagement and authenticity can be infectious. How wise he was to make sure that such moments were rare, and collector's items. I specially like the bit where Warhol attacks Hollywood for its commercialism.

Art

To take the other muses in order, then. In January I went to the gala opening of the new San Francisco Museum of Modern Art. Mario Botta's edifice is so arranged that one can start at the top, at an atrium lit mostly by natural means, and work one's way down. On the top floor, in an airy wasteland of Koons and Kiefer, you are suddenly arrested by 'National Velvet', Warhol's 1963 homage to Elizabeth

Taylor. The references are all filmic. For a start, the painting is a silver screen. The use of different pressures and consistencies gives the effect of separate and partial exposures to the forty-two separate frames, which includes some very worn ones and some blank ones too. As a sort of grace note at the end, the frames betray a slight but unmistakable flicker.

On a lower level, we find 'Lavender Disaster 1964', the 'Electric Chair' and the red and black 'Atomic Bomb', where the bottom line of the multi-exposure chessboard is almost black. Foucault wrote of this period of Warhol's painting in the following terms:

> the oral and rich equality of these half-opened lips, these teeth, this tomato sauce, these hygienic cleaning products, equality of a death inside a ripped-open car, high up on a telephone pole, between the blue-sparking arms of an electric chair. If we study this unmitigated monotony more closely we are suddenly aware of the diversity that has no middle, no up, no beyond.

Though he does not cite it, this was the sort of encomium that irritated Robert Hughes in his batteries against Warhol in the famous *New York Review of Books* polemic in 1982. Read with care, this essay is actually an attack not on Warhol as a painter but on *Warholism* as a cultural influence.

> To the extent that his work was subversive at all (and in the sixties it was, slightly) it became so through its harsh, cold parody of ad-mass appeal – the repetition of brand images such as Campbell's soup or Brillo or Marilyn Monroe – a star being a human brand-image – to the point that a void is seen to yawn beneath the discourse of promotion.[13]

Yes, yes, I said to Hughes a few days ago, but what about the *pictures?* Not altogether grudgingly, he conceded that much of the work between 1961 and 1964 was very impressive. He specifically cited the 'Electric Chair'. Let's build on this moment of consensus for a second. Look at the electric chair, or call it to mind. It sits untenanted, with the restraining straps dangling suggestively in an almost sado-masochistic fashion. But what remains on the retina the longest? To speak for myself, I would say that it is the word that appears on the wall of the cell. The word is SILENCE. That single injunction or admonition has a tremendous latent power. It expresses simultaneously the absolutism of the process, and also its futility and limitation. (Who cares about the noise?) It also anticipates the banalisation of capital punishment as we have come to know it. I have made a number of visits to Death Row, and on each of them have had Andy Warhol strongly in mind; another testimony to his potency. 'He was in our minds at all times,' says Ralph Ellison of a character in *Invisible Man,* 'and that was power of a kind.'[14]

Music

On music I am less qualified to pronounce than many who will come after me, but I know that Warhol's encouragement of Lou Reed and the Velvet Underground, apart from its well-known consequence of sponsoring a genre of later punk, had the effect of preserving the lyrical aspects of Delmore Schwarz for a generation that might not otherwise have bothered with him as a poet. And I agree with Mick Jagger that Warhol's album cover for *Sticky Fingers* is one of the best such things ever done. Blondie and The Cars perhaps owe more to Warhol, being ahead of the game on video, while Madonna the Material Girl is a Warhol kid in more ways than one.

Journalism

Journalism, in a way, speaks for itself. Some people believe that the resolution of contemporary journalism into celebrity coverage, gossip and ahistorical amnesiac media events is 'Warholian'. By this common attribution, they cannot presumably mean that the networks and the news magazines have actually modelled themselves on *Interview*. The question, rather, is whether Warhol had a finer instinct for the idea of celebrity narcissism than the omnivorous media do today. Bear in mind that when he decided to focus on Elvis Presley and Marilyn Monroe he had no way of knowing that they would have become iconographic figures a full generation later on. (It might, for all we knew, said one of his friends to me once, have been the Everly Brothers.) Bear in mind also, in an age when journalism is dominated by fact-checking and the literal mind, so that the press conference and the interview are means whereby frauds and murderers may seize the megaphone, that the idea of the tape-recorder anticipates the practice of the edited or unedited transcript, the gross raw material of today's coverage.

Today's coverage is only self-satirising by accident. Warhol's reporters occasionally knew what they were doing. When Warhol took Jackie Kennedy Onassis to the Brooklyn Museum with Lee Radziwill, the following exchange occurred as narrated by Bob Colacello:

> After the usual greetings, Mrs Onassis's first words were, 'So tell me, Andy, what was Liz Taylor like?' I couldn't believe it. Here was the only person in the world more famous than Elizabeth Taylor and she wanted to know what Elizabeth Taylor was like. Her first question was right out of an *Interview* interview. And what's more, it was asked in the voice of Marilyn Monroe![15]

Some like to sneer at Warhol's pathetic attachment to stardom and celebrity. Seeing Greta Garbo at a party when he was young, he drew a paper flower and wordlessly pressed it on her. When she left it behind, all crumpled up, he signed it and entitled it 'Flower Crumpled by Greta Garbo'. Here we have the boy who wrote from the Ruthenian quarter of Pittsburgh to 1930s screen goddesses. And of course he was much too thrilled to be included in a 1957 volume entitled *One Thousand New York Names and Where to Drop Them*. But remember that at this stage one of his body and soul jobs involved having just his hands made up so as to draw clouds on the weather map of a local TV station. After that, it might seem more justifiable for him to say, as he did to one of his amanuenses, 'You should write less, and tape record more. It's more modern.' And so, in a way, it is.

Theatre

Here one can be brief but perhaps, with luck, also pungent. In 1953, Warhol fell in with a reading and writing experimental theatre group – Brechtian in its initial character – which paged through everything from Dylan Thomas to Kafka to the Elizabethans and Jacobeans. The chronicler of this period, a rather lugubrious German named Rainer Crone, records in a mirthless manner that 'some of the plays written by members of the group were actually performed'. Set designs and illustrations were supplied by Warhol, whose collages and Japanese screens embodied a consistent admiration for Bertolt Brecht. If this had been a strong motive, we would have known more about it.

Society

Here Warhol knew what he wanted. He wanted to be 'right up there' or 'way up there' in his favourite vernacular, and he also wanted to have a *nostalgie de la boue*. He got his way both ways because, as a close comrade once told me, he knew that everybody was secretly corrupt. The anomic space debris of the imploded Sixties went on a whirl with the spoiled kids and rich Eurotrash of the catch-up generations. Any fool can become master of this subject in a few hours. Someone had to be responsible for the sub-Weimar impression given by that period, and Warhol was chosen by the media to be the exemplar. But we still postpone the question of who was laughing at whom. Suicide and drugs and despair played their part, but they had been cast in it already. This was not known as being non-judgemental.

Photography

Warhol restored the idea of portraiture, and this achievement ought not to be denied him. He grasped the idea of the Polaroid and the rehearsal shot, and encouraged newcomers like Robert Mapplethorpe. He knew that the cheapest and most instant techniques could set a pose or capture a moment of character. It didn't always work. Andy and Mapplethorpe together, both with Polaroids and one with a tape-recorder, were almost defeated by Rudolf Nureyev. To quote the opening of the interview:

Andy: What color are your eyes?
Nureyev: The interview is cancelled.

In the end, Nureyev executed major dance steps while Warhol and Mapplethorpe competed with Polaroid flashes to catch the scissoring of his limbs.[16]

Or you could say that every painter who has incorporated the negative into their own work – Jeff Koons, Keith Haring, Jean-Michel Basquiat – is a linear descendent. The completion of Ed Ruscha's long meditated project – a three-dimensional unspooling of the entire length of both sides of Sunset Boulevard at all times of day through video, photography and film – will, in fact, mark the culmination of a Warholian venture.

Was Warhol just lucky? His earlier remark about being in the wrong place at the right time was actually a satire on his ability to know which people would be said to matter, whose fame was going to last, and when to show up or be seen where. For example, in *Couch* there exists the only known image depicting Jack Kerouac, Gregory Corso, Peter Orlovsky and Allen Ginsberg within the same frame. I don't think that this really is just luck.

Philosophy

I think we've done philosophy, if not from A to B and back again. The philosophy is connected on the surface to the idea that nothing strenuous or arduous is worth the anxiety or the excitement or the naiveté. It is so laid back that it almost falls out of the shot. It is, in an inverted and perverse way, also connected to a religion of abjection and fatalism and surrender. John Richardson says mistakenly that only when Andy died did people understand what an intense and devout Catholic he had been.[17] I *dis*agree. Twenty years ago, I was mentally scanning the title Pop-ism and inwardly translating it as Pope-ism. A friend of mine was hired onto *Interview* because he had reviewed *Trash* as a Catholic reworking of Jean Genet's version of *Our Lady of the Flowers*. Cultish Catholicism, with its hints of camp and guilt, were of the essence. Walter Benjamin once defined surrealist art as a series of 'profane illuminations'. 'Profane Illuminations' was another title that I considered for this evening, until I realised that the subliminal trope was the sacred and not the profane.

Literature

The above makes it the more interesting that William Burroughs never guessed the truth about Andy's religiosity. But in his own 'cut-up' style of composition, he clearly acknowledged a prosaic debt, not to mention an attitudinal one. Perhaps they both owed it to Jean Genet; at all events one can trace a lineage of obligation here. Here we also find Warhol's greatest disappointment. He admired Truman Capote with an almost adoring consistency. He designed a shoe for him, in gold. He tried to catch his attention. He understood at once the idea of the non-fiction novel, because it comprised one of his own definitions of film. But he was repeatedly snubbed by Capote, who once said that Andy was 'a sphinx without a riddle'. Warhol's own later comment, that Capote said he could have anybody he wanted while Andy didn't want anybody he could get,[18] is one of the best definitions of homosexual thwartedness that has ever been compressed into a phrase.

Uneven as this all is, it manifests an amazing touching of bases. If it is undervalued – at least aesthetically if not commercially – it may be because Warhol always spoke with a flat, defiant economism about the subject:

> Business Art is a much better thing to be making than Art Art, because Art Art doesn't support the space it takes up, whereas Business Art does. (If Business Art doesn't support its own space, it goes out-of-business.)[19]

He made the same unhypocritical and down-to-earth point in a different tone of voice when he said, 'rich people can't see a sillier version of *Truth or Consequences* or a scarier version of *The Exorcist*. The idea of America is so wonderful because the more equal something is, the more American it is.'[20] I think he must have thought about this paean to conformity and sameness a lot, because it appears several times in interviews throughout his life, often with tiny variations (such as the President having to relish the same cheeseburger as the rest of us) but always making the same celebratory point.

Here is a style that is often held against him, like his obsessive parsimony and his preoccupation with accountancy and his anal-retentive attitude towards savings and collections and even time capsules and souvenirs. But of what does it remind you? The answer should not, in a city of industrialism and abundance like Pittsburgh, seem very surprising. The voice that is speaking is the voice of that great artist and innovator Henry Ford. The Henry Ford who said that history was bunk. The same Henry Ford who announced, this time really anticipating Andy, that any colour was fine as long as it was black. Warhol's achievement was to define the aesthetics of mass production, not to be a business artist. Business artists are more common than we want to think or like to believe. Michael Fitzgerald's new book on Pablo Picasso, *Making Modernism: Picasso and the Creation of the Market for Twentieth Century Art*, has more tales of painterly stock manipulation and artistic insider trading than Warhol had cans of soup. The thing is that Warhol cheerfully and in a way challengingly affirmed what the 'community' of painters and dealers was at some pains to muffle.

Don't knock business art unless you are very sure of yourself. Anthony Powell once wrote that he never did his insurance policy without imagining it landing on the desk of Aubrey Beardsley before being passed to that of Wallace Stevens and eventually landing up in the in-tray of Franz Kafka.[21] And if you think these insurance men are scary, think of the ad-business. Public relations as an American science was pioneered by Edward Bernays, the nephew of Sigmund Freud. Salman Rushdie began his career as a writer of enticing ads and jingles. Jasper Johns and Robert Rauschenberg also worked in what was politely termed 'commercial art', but (of course) only to support themselves while they did the real stuff. Only Andy Warhol proclaimed that there was no difference between the two things, except in the way you did them, and thus opened the question of whether there was or is an artistic way of making or finding art. Partly, this was his settling of accounts with Picasso, of whom he said, 'When Picasso died I read in a magazine that he had made four thousand masterpieces in his lifetime and I thought, "Gee, I could do that in a day." You see, the way I do them, with my technique, I really thought I could do four thousand in a day. And they'd all be masterpieces because they'd all be the same painting.'[22] More insulting still, Warhol used to say that the same faculty would have made him into an ideal Abstract Expressionist. More is involved here than being a fool for God.

Having been pronounced clinically dead twenty years too soon, Warhol was pronounced actually dead several years too early. He survives in our references, in our imagination, and in the relationship of his own sense of timing to ours. Just because he knew the price of everything doesn't mean he didn't know the value of some things.

First published as 'The Importance of Being Andy' in *Critical Quarterly*, vol. 38, no. 1, 1996

Notes

1. Graham Greene, *Travels with My Aunt* (Viking Press, 1969), pp. 99–100.
2. George Orwell, *The Collected Essays, Journalism and Letters of George Orwell: An Age Like This*, ed. Sonia Orwell and Ian Angus (Harcourt, Brace & World, 1968), p. 33.
3. Robert Hughes, 'The Rise of Andy Warhol', *The First Anthology: 30 Years of The New York Review of Books* (The New York Review of Books, 1993), p. 216. (First published in 1982 in *The New York Review of Books*.)
4. Alexander Cockburn, *Corruptions of Empire* (Verso, 1987), pp. 278–81.
5. G. R. Swenson, 'What is Pop Art?: Answers from 8 Painters, Part I', *Artnews*, 62 (November 1963), p. 26.
6. Andy Warhol, *The Philosophy of Andy Warhol: From A to B and Back Again* (Harcourt Brace Jovanovich, 1975), p. 149.
7. Andy Warhol, Kasper König, Pontus Hultén, and Olle Granath (eds), *Andy Warhol* (Moderna Museet, 1968), n.p.
8. Ultra Violet, *Famous for 15 Minutes: My Years with Andy Warhol* (Harcourt Brace Jovanovich, 1988), p. 178.
9. Warhol, König, et al., *Andy Warhol*, n.p.
10. Conversation with Bob Colacello.
11. Warhol, *The Philosophy of Andy Warhol: From A to B and Back Again*, p. 160.
12. Read by Nicholas Love at Warhol's memorial service (1 April 1987).
13. Robert Hughes, 'The Rise of Andy Warhol', p. 216.
14. Ralph Ellison, *The Invisible Man* (Random House, 1952).
15. Bob Colacello, *Holy Terror: Andy Warhol Close Up* (HarperCollins, 1990), p. 160.
16. Colacello, *Holy Terror: Andy Warhol Close Up*, pp. 107–8.
17. John Richardson, 'Eulogy for Andy Warhol', published in *Andy Warhol: A Retrospective* (The Museum of Modern Art, 1989), p. 454.
18. *Andy Warhol's Exposures* (Andy Warhol Books/Grosset & Dunlap, 1979), p. 176.
19. Warhol, *The Philosophy of Andy Warhol: From A to B and Back Again*, p. 144.
20. Ibid., p. 101.

21. Anthony Powell, *A Dance to the Music of Time: A Question of Upbringing. A Buyer's Market. The Acceptance World* (Little, Brown, 1962).
22. Warhol, *The Philosophy of Andy Warhol: From A to B and Back Again,* p. 148.

How Unpleasant to Meet Mr Eliot

Was T. S. Eliot an anti-Semite? What a question! Of course he was an anti-Semite, if the term retains any of its meaning. He was a public supporter of two political movements – the Action Française of Charles Maurras and the Social Credit party of Major Douglas – that identified Jews as the enemy of civilisation. His magazine of high culture, the *Criterion*, was at best loftily indifferent to the rise of fascism. And in a famous 1933 lecture at the University of Virginia, published as *After Strange Gods*, he sought to identify the elements of a good society and stipulated that 'any large number of free-thinking Jews' was precisely what such a society did not need. It's no good saying, as some of his defenders still do, that he only reflected the genteel anti-Semitism of his day. There were many contemporary writers, such as E. M. Forster, who took public stands against prejudice. W. H. Auden issued a memorable rebuke to G. K. Chesterton, who had argued that 'criticism of any other nation on the planet' should be allowed, and that people should not be immune 'merely because they happen to be members of a race persecuted for other reasons'. In his reply, Auden pointed to Chesterton's 'quiet shift from the term *nation* to the term *race*. It is always permissible to criticise a nation (including Israel), a religion (including Orthodox Judaism), or a culture, because these are the creations of human thought and will . . . A man's ethnic heritage, on the other hand, is not in his power to alter.' By this standard, incidentally, the key word in *After Strange Gods* is 'free-thinking'. Eliot's objection was not to Zionism, let alone Judaism, but to Jewishness and its triumphs in the secular world. (It's true that he later repudiated the lecture, but it may be doubted whether he made what Catholics smugly call a firm purpose of amendment.)

But are Eliot's poetry and prose hopelessly infected? A new book by Anthony Julius, titled *T. S. Eliot, Anti-Semitism and Literary Form*, argues for the affirmative. Mr Julius is the divorce attorney for Princess Diana, and it's amusing to surmise what Eliot might have thought of such a man – the shyster lawyer for a gold-digging airhead. He and his allies advance the novel theory that anti-Semitism was 'Eliot's muse', that it 'animated' his poetry and that he, in effect, made art out of it. This argument is different from that of earlier critics, such as Christopher Ricks, in that it stresses one couplet, one anonymous book review and one phrase. The couplet is from 'Sweeney Among the Nightingales':

> Rachel *née* Rabinovich
> Tears at the grapes with murderous paws

The anonymous book review appeared in the *Criterion* in 1936. It concerned 'The Yellow Spot', an early document about Nazi atrocities. The reviewer took a rather languid position, saying disdainfully that even if the allegations were true they were of no special concern to the British. And the phrase is 'the blood kinship of the same people living in the same place'. This appeared in *After Strange Gods*, and was part of Eliot's definition of the wholesome, organic, traditional way of life.

Let us take these in order. Of the couplet, Julius asserts that it repeats the medieval practice of comparing Jews to beasts. But everyone in 'Sweeney' is an animal of some kind:

> Apeneck Sweeney spreads his knees
> Letting his arms hang down to laugh,
> The zebra stripes about his jaw
> Swelling to maculate giraffe.

The mysterious 'silent man in mocha brown' is later described as a 'vertebrate'. If the entire poem is a bestiary, then Julius's point is a weak one. And his insistence that the lines 'Branches of wisteria/ Circumscribe a golden grin' are redolent of bigotry (because they evoke Jewish *teeth*, for heaven's sake) is pure silliness. One might as well say that 'Mr Eugenides, the Smyrna merchant/Unshaven, with a pocket full of currants' is a foul libel on all Levantine Greeks.

Of the *Criterion* review, Julius argues that internal evidence suggests it was written by Eliot, and that it reflects his style. An annihilating letter has since appeared in the *Times Literary Supplement*. Written by Eliot's grim official widow, Valerie, it points out coldly that the review was authored by Montgomery Belgion, the magazine's regular contributor on such matters, and that this fact is readily established from the *Criterion's* records. A low score, here, for Julius's forensic skills.

More fascinating still is the question 'the same people living in the same place'. Linked as it was by Eliot to the words 'blood kinship', the expression can be made to seem redolent of race theory and eugenics. But where does it come from? The poet Craig Raine reminds us that it is taken directly from the 'Cyclops' episode in James Joyce's *Ulysses*. Moreover, it happens to be the definition of a nation put forward by Leopold Bloom. He offers it to a Jew-baiting bigmouth who wants to purify Ireland. And Bloom, it might be added, is a 'free-thinking Jew', who is upholding his right to remain in Dublin. Yet here is Eliot proposing, in Bloom's own words, a standard for society.

We do not know why he chose to do so. We cannot always be sure, even of the foul remarks made about Jews in 'Gerontion', whether Eliot is speaking in his own voice or the voice of his narrator and character. Make the worst assumption that you like, given Eliot's fascist sympathies. But the Julius book reminds one, yet again, to hesitate once, hesitate twice, hesitate a hundred times before employing political standards as a device for the analysis and appreciation of poetry.

First published as 'How Unpleasant to Meet Mr Eliot' in *The Nation*,
12 August 1996

Powell's Way

Suppose yourself to be netted in some elaborate dream, where the examination topic for tomorrow involves the invention of a fictional conversation. The characters must be Englishmen, located at some midpoint in the recent age of ideology, who are part upper-crust and part bohemian, yet who are earnestly discussing the supernatural:

'My own occult interests are so sketchy. I've just thumbed over *Dogme et Rituel de la Haute Magie*. Never participated in a Black Mass in my life, or so much as received an invitation to a witches' Sabbath.'

'But I thought Dr Trelawney was more for the Simple Life, with a touch of yoga thrown in. I did not realise that he was committed to all this sorcery.'

'After you knew him he must have moved further to the Left – or would it be to the Right? Extremes of policy have such a tendency to merge.'

'Trelawney must be getting on in age now – Cagliostro in his latter days, though he has avoided incarceration up to date.'

'What will happen to people like him as the world plods on to standardisation? Will they cease to be born, or find jobs in other professions? I suppose there will always be a position for a man with first-class magical qualifications.'

This is taken from *The Kindly Ones*, the sixth novel of Anthony Powell's twelve-volume cycle collectively entitled *A Dance to the Music of Time*. The sequence may be said to 'cover' the span of years that lay between the Great War and the Sixties. And Mr Powell himself, now enjoying his ninety-second year, is and was very much a part of the social and literary history of England (and, he would wish to have it noted, of Wales too) over that protracted period of crisis and decline. He is one of the few living authors who was on easy and familiar terms with George Orwell, Cyril Connolly, Graham Greene, and Malcolm Muggeridge, and his collection of criticism, *Miscellaneous Verdicts*, together with four volumes of memoirs and three books of journals, provides an imperishable trove of first-hand acquaintance and reminiscence. A seven-hour dramatisation of *Dance*, made and transmitted on British television in late 1997 after almost two decades of aborted schemes and rehearsals, may or may not have enlisted a wider audience for his work.

It is a certainty, however, that the novels have gradually won for themselves a consecrated readership which is impervious to changes in fashion.

This is true in spite of a number of objections or perhaps reservations that have hindered the cycle's acceptance thus far, perhaps especially (though there does exist an Anthony Powell Society in Kalamazoo, Michigan) in these United States. It is sometimes said that Powell works on too small a canvas, and depends for his effects on too much coincidence occurring within a too-limited circle. The response to this among some of his fans, as he would emphatically not wish to call them even if they do hail from Kalamazoo, has been to announce him as 'the English Proust'. Whether or not this helps matters it may be too early to say.

Certainly, *Dance* is a work, and an exercise, of memory. Anthony Powell, who pronounces his name to rhyme with 'pole' rather than 'towel',[1] is a Welshman who was born into a solid family, was educated at Eton and Oxford, worked in London publishing and literary journalism, became a novelist and the biographer of John Aubrey, served in the British army in Northern Ireland during the Second World War, married the daughter of a noble line – Lady Violet Pakenham, of the celebrated Anglo-Irish Longford-Fraser writing dynasty – and holds High Tory opinions.

His narrator in *Dance*, Nicholas Jenkins, is the relatively 'straight' man in the conversation above. He has a Welsh name with no pitfalls of pronunciation, is born of a solid family, and follows all the steps just traced for Powell except that his biographical subject is Robert Burton, author of *The Anatomy of Melancholy*. His Tory instincts are so automatic as to be, for many readers, practically impalpable.

Both author and character are guarded admirers of the elliptical Marcel: Powell going so far as to make a stout comparison between Proust and the Galsworthy of *The Forsyte Saga*, and to define his own oeuvre as occupying a place equidistant from both. (The most obvious and frequently made contrast, which is with the work of Evelyn Waugh, is one that Powell finds himself resenting in his own diaries. For one thing, as he says, 'everything "serious" in Waugh is confronted with the Roman Church; less serious matters, as often as not reduced to farce'. For another, Waugh, the striver and arriviste, really is open to the charge of snobbery.) Powell's novels are unusual in that they leave the religious conscience and experience entirely untreated, and replace it by an emphasis on the numinous and the occult.

'Nick' Jenkins does not give us his long life story, or the story of his contemporaries in, so to speak, first gear. In the opening volume, *A Question of Upbringing*, for example, he is a boy at Eton and the time is just after the First World War. At the start of the sixth volume, *The*

Kindly Ones, he is a smaller boy living at home in the pregnant summer of 1914. The general title of the sequence is taken from a painting done by Nicholas Poussin in 1639, and hanging at present in the Wallace Collection. It represents Time as rather gloatingly savouring his advantage over those who gyrate to his lute. Musical and painterly allusions recur throughout the novels, providing many of the binding references that are necessary in a work of a million words and almost five hundred characters, and several of the crucial subordinate figures are either painters or musicians by profession.

What Powell is aiming for is the harnessing of counterpoint. Characters appear and disappear and then reappear, as do certain events and objects (a practical joke here, a painting there). People die in one book and are encountered afresh in a later one. But as the sequence takes hold of the reader, the separate melodies become slowly subordinate to the basic one, and strive for a harmonic whole. A strong minor figure, the war-invalid Ted Jeavons, is described not by accident as 'seething with forgotten melodies' and does exert a bonding force on numerous large changes of scene. By a happy chance, the dictionary definition of 'counterpoint' also has an application to heraldry. It denotes the meeting of two chevrons at their 'points', or apexes, in the centre of an escutcheon, or shield. This has a real analogue in Powell's method, which relies to an unusual degree on kinship and lineage. (In life as in fiction, his most consistent interest is in genealogy. The best-known cartoon drawing of him, executed by the late Mark Boxer, shows him standing before a well-bookmarked volume of *Burke's Landed Gentry*, the British version of the *Almanach de Gotha*, to the revised edition of which Powell himself contributed a very feeling and expert preface.)

As composer and as orchestrator, and indeed as herald and genealogist, Powell chiefly means to control. He attains this objective by striking certain chords which, echoing in the mind even of an inattentive reader, will firmly but gently recall him to an earlier one. Let me give a single illustration. In the first volume, *A Question of Upbringing*, we are introduced to the school friends who will feature in the life of Nick Jenkins. Among these are Kenneth Widmerpool, the most dogged and fearsome solipsist in modern fiction, and Charles Stringham, the languid and epicene loser, who, at once fatally charming and fatally languid, succumbs to a combination of alcohol and inanition. (Stringham, I have found, is one of the few of the dramatis personae to hold the attention of female readers in a story that some but not all complain of finding excessively masculine.)

Widmerpool is insufferable from the start, but more as someone prematurely pompous and absurd than, as he later proves, someone decidedly sinister. The charming Stringham makes game of him, imitates him to perfection, and treats him as a figure of fun. 'That boy,' he asserts in a commonplace phrase, 'will be the death of me.' Eight volumes and two decades later, in *The Soldier's Art*, Widmerpool does deliberately and cynically, by the exercise of bureaucratic fiat in sending the unresisting young man to a front-line wartime posting, cause Stringham's death. Widmerpool's callousness is also the oblique cause of his own ensuing ruin and disgrace, these being precipitated when (in another coincidence mediated by about four degrees of separation) he contracts an ambitious but calamitous marriage to Stringham's unstable niece. And yet there is nothing of the morality tale in the way that this complex evolution is set down. Nor does Jenkins make any effort to assist the reader to judgements or conclusions.

The events and developments are so widely spaced in time, yet so intimately filiated by the social class and background of the participants, as to make any complaint about the over-strenuous exertions of coincidence seem almost ill-natured. Powell is so much at his ease here that he describes Eton and Oxford without ever going to the bother of identifying them by name. We thus learn a great deal about Widmerpool – about Powell, too, perhaps – by discovering that he is a meritocratic child of a rural manure supplier, and that he does not go 'on' from school to university. The strings are slowly drawn together with extreme deftness. And Jenkins himself often gets small details 'wrong'. just as a real narrator would. In *Temporary Kings*, for example, he sees a character named Odo Stevens colliding with Pamela Widmerpool at a conference in Venice. 'Pamela had hit him in the face the last time I had seen them together,' he recalls of a memorable evening in the London Blitz that is set down in *A Soldier's Art*. He has forgotten that the volatile pair also ran into each other just after the war, at a party to launch the radical *Fission* magazine in *Books Do Furnish a Room*.

But more than this, it is very far from improbable that a small and highly stratified island society should find its more educated and leisured members running into one another at successive conjunctures. (The disruptions of wartime, so well evoked by Powell in the third of what are really four trilogies, often makes this more likely rather than less. Malcolm Muggeridge and Arthur Koestler actually did discover themselves in the same latrine-digging platoon on the outbreak of hostilities in 1939, and nobody will say that this coincidence lacks either aptness or verisimilitude.)

That defence entered, it is no less true that Powell keeps his pages well-peopled with new arrivals, that he maintains the familiar ones in plausible yet unpredictable circulation, and that he steps well outside the immediate social milieu of his chief characters. The aforementioned Odo Stevens, a self-made jeweler from Birmingham, doesn't

come on stage until the third trilogy, in *The Valley of Bones*. He has
changed his name from Bert, and flourishes in wartime and combat
conditions. By the close of the cycle, he has bedded half the 'society'
women Jenkins knows. Jenkins is observant and active, he is curious
about others, and he has a strong sexual drive. As the tempo of the
dance increases, what more natural than that he should find himself
meeting a former partner or dreaded rival? It is while he is waiting for
an especially ubiquitous and mobile young critic named Mark Members
– who I should surmise is modelled on the figure of the late Sir
Stephen Spender – that we discover an early 1930s Jenkins in the third
novel, *The Acceptance World*:

> I began to brood on the complexity of writing a novel about English life, a
> subject difficult enough to handle with authenticity even of a crudely
> naturalistic sort, even more to convey the inner truth of the things
> observed. . . . Intricacies of social life make English habits unyielding to
> simplification, while understatement and irony – in which all classes of this
> island converse – upset the normal emphasis of reported speech.

It is this 'inner truth' or 'inscape' that more than anything has
foredoomed the television dramatisation. Fidelity to period and costume and accent are one thing, and the producers expended a too-
literal effort in this regard while carelessly rendering the crucial
Kenneth Widmerpool as a hapless rather than a hateful figure. Irony
and understatement are not easily relayed to the screen, and still less
are Jenkins's long inward monologues, encapsulated conclusions, or
aperçus, of the sort that punctuate *Dance*. In *At Lady Molly's*, for example,
when Jenkins finds himself a witness to a quarrel between strangers:

> His hostess was determined to let him off nothing. I had the impression that
> she was teasing him, not precisely for my especial benefit, but, at the same
> time, that my presence as a newcomer to the house afforded a particularly
> favourable opportunity for the application of torments of this sort. I found
> later that she was indeed what is called 'a tease', perhaps the only outward
> indication that her life was not altogether happy; since there is no greater
> sign of innate misery than a love of teasing.

In *Casanova's Chinese Restaurant*, Jenkins shows himself equally quick at
detecting a nuance:

> 'Charles uses gouache now', said Mrs Foxe, speaking with that bright firmness
> of manner people apply especially to close relations attempting to recover
> from more or less disastrous mismanagement of their own lives.

Or at pointing out to us something that perhaps, subconsciously, we
knew already:

He also lacked that subjective, ruthless love of presiding over other people's affairs which often makes basically heartless people adept at offering effective consolation.

Sometimes, too, these maxims or aphorisms are put into the mouths of Jenkins's circle of friends:

'What is wrong with Widmerpool?'

'Feeling low generally,' said Templer. 'Mildred had to drag him out tonight. But never mind that. It is extraordinary those two should be engaged. Women may show some discrimination about whom they sleep with, but they'll marry anybody.'

('I was careful and logical about affairs,' says a key female character in Don DeLillo's *Underworld*, 'really sort of scrupulous about who and where and when, and completely reckless when it came to marriage.') Then there is Bernard Shernmaker. 'One of his goals was to establish that the Critic, not the Author, was paramount. He tended to offer guarded encouragement, tempered with veiled threats, to young writers.' Or an Indian school contemporary in *The Acceptance World*, named Ghika, who 'fixed his huge black eyes on Widmerpool, concentrating absolutely on his words, but whether with interest, or boredom of an intensity that might lead even to physical assault, it was impossible to say.' And of two Members of Parliament, Labour and Tory, meeting at a funeral: 'The two had gravitated together in response to that law of nature which rules that the whole confraternity of politicians prefers to operate within the closed circle of its own initiates, rather than waste time with outsiders; differences of party and opinion having little or no bearing on the preference.'

These are all Jenkins supplying his own chorus. The almost chilly detachment can strike closer to home, as in the glimpse we get of his own pre-1914 military parent in *The Kindly Ones*:

Certainly the tense nerves of men of action – less notorious than those of imaginative men – are not to be minimised. This was true of my father, who, like many persons who believe primarily in the will – although his own will was in no way remarkable – hid in his heart a hatred of constituted authority. He did his best to conceal this antipathy, because the one thing he hated, more than constituted authority itself, was to hear constituted authority questioned by anyone but himself. This is perhaps an endemic trait in all who love power, and my father had an absolute passion for power, although he was never in a position to wield it on a notable scale.

This annihilating filial verdict, and the other less solemn ones, demonstrate Jenkins's practice of stopping the music, often for several beats, and standing back. It might be said that he gives himself time. Not for him the pell-mell of Dickens, who went into a shop to buy writing paper and heard a woman customer inquiring after the serial chapter he was going to write on it. Jenkins/Powell's dry and laconic style is particularly evident in exchanges, such as the one in *A Buyer's Market* with the sluttish radical Gypsy Jones ('Why are you so stuck up?' she asked, truculently. 'I'm just made that way.' 'You ought to fight it.' 'I can't see why.'), as is an occasional slapdashery in the prose. In the paternal reminiscence cited above, the word would be 'underestimated' 'rather than 'minimised'. Also, any sentence by Powell that begins with the word 'Although' is fated to end in a dangle. 'Although a Saturday evening, the place was crowded,' in *The Acceptance World*, is typical. Interestingly, Powell does not commit this *bêtise* in any of his nonfictional writing. But, although generally hostile to postmodern readings, he is fond of saying that his readers and his narrator are the coauthors of the novels, just as 'Galsworthy is essentially a Forsyte novelist.'

Aside, then, from its many well-cut sapiences about the unchanging elements in human nature, the series is kept moving forward by two energies – humour and history. English radical and liberal critics have generally been leery of Powell. Raymond Williams's retrospective *The English Novel*, for instance, makes no mention of him at all. The late Sir Victor Pritchett, who reviewed several novels in the cycle as they came out, was somewhat more generous in saying; 'In the Fifties Mr Anthony Powell was the first to revive the masculine traditions of English social comedy. He retrieved it on behalf of the upper classes. The joke that he is a Proust Englished by Wodehouse has something in it'. Only the Marxist Perry Anderson has thought to connect the history in the novels to their humour:

> There is no other work in the annals of European fiction that attempts meticulously to recreate half a century of history, decade by decade, with anything like the emotional precision or details of Powell's twelve volumes. Neither Balzac's panorama of the Restoration, nor Zola's chronicles of the Second Empire, nor Proust's reveries in the Belle Epoque can match a comparable span of time, an attention to variations within it, or a compositional intricacy capable of uniting them into a single narrative.... The elegance of this artifice was only compatible with comedy.

Although this is not to say that Balzac and Proust, to say nothing of Chekhov, are lacking in humour, such a synthesis goes a long way towards explaining the tremendous impact of Powell's grotesque antihero and Everyman, Kenneth Widmerpool. The shortest way of capturing the essence of this grotesquely fascinating and repellent figure might be to say that he is a monster of arrogance and conceit, but entirely wanting in pride. Bullying to those below him, servile and fawning to those set in authority, entirely without wit or introspection, he is that type of tirelessly ambitious, sexless, and charmless mediocrity that poisons institutional life, family life, and political life. He is the perfected utilitarian and philistine:

> Widmerpool remained totally unimpressed by the arts. He was even accustomed to show an open contempt for them in tête-à-tête conversation. In public, for social reasons, he had acquired the merest working knowledge to carry him through a dinner party, content with St John Clarke as a writer, Isbister as a painter.
>
> 'I don't know about those things', he had once said to me. 'If I don't know about things, they do not interest me. Even if artistic matters attracted me – which they do not – I should not allow myself to dissipate my energies on them.'

Widmerpool haunts the series from the first page to the last, making both his entrance and his exit as a dogged and uninspiring runner rather than as a dancer of any kind. But it is at a dance that he experiences the moment of humiliation that some regard as the climactic point of the novels, and to which Jenkins recurs again and again as the story progresses. The unwilling object of his affections, a girl named Barbara Goring, decides that Widmerpool is sour and requires 'sweetening'. She intends to sprinkle a little sugar over him. But the top of the large sugar shaker is poorly secured and:

> More from surprise than because she wished additionally to torment him, Barbara did not remove her hand before the whole contents of the vessel – which voided itself in an instant of time – had descended upon his head and shoulders, covering him with sugar more completely than might have been thought possible in so brief a space. Widmerpool's rather sparse hair had been liberally greased with a dressing – the sweetish smell of which I remembered as somewhat disagreeable when applied in France – this lubricant retaining the grains of sugar, which, as they adhered thickly to his skull, gave him the appearance of having turned white with shock at a single stroke, which judging by what could be seen of his expression, he might very well in reality have done underneath the glimmering incrustations that enveloped his head and shoulders. He had writhed sideways to avoid the downpour, and a cataract of sugar had entered the space between neck and collar; yet another jet streaming between eyes and spectacles.

That final placing of the word 'writhe' completes the abjectness of the picture, while also conveying the almost masochistic humility with which Widmerpool receives this and other buffets from life and fate. Powell's detachment here is extraordinary, as his gift for halting the frame and capturing an instant of time is displayed to full effect. Perhaps, too, there is something Proustian in the vague redolence of Widmerpool's pomade. It might also be mentioned here that Powell wrote several short, brittle novels during the Jazz Age, of which the first and arguably the most important, his *Afternoon Men,* was published in 1931. In that novel appear the sentences, not at all untypical, 'They ate. The food was good.'

In the decades of silence that intervened before the inaugural volume of *Dance,* Powell did something more than mature in the cask as a stylist. He metamorphosed both himself and his writing. The result is anything but Wodehousian: the creator of Jeeves and Bertie would not have written the sugar scene that way and famously shunned the least suggestion of the sexual motive. One of Powell's achievements is an unusual down-to-earthness about what used to be called the facts of life. When Jenkins has a crudely carnal interlude with the taunting and disliked Gypsy Jones in *A Buyer's Market,* Powell not only expends almost three pages on the encounter – which he would never have done in *Afternoon Men* – but also contrives to summon the exact thrill of disgust which men are liable to experience on such occasions. 'Any wish to remain any longer present in those surroundings had suddenly and violently decreased, if not disappeared entirely.'

But the chief attainment of the long fallow period before this volume of *Dance* was Powell's evolution from amoral, even prim, spectator to fully engaged social and political raconteur. The world in which Nick Jenkins grows to manhood is the interwar world, and most of his intellectual and aesthetic seniors or contemporaries are moving to the 'left.' Powell makes as plain as he possibly can his distaste and contempt for this herd phenomenon. The old Oxford tutor Sillery, whom Jenkins revisits as he would a zoo animal in order to study and record his peculiarities, is portrayed as a posturing nincompoop, wedded to fashion and with his sails trimmed to power. So, in their varying forms, are half a dozen or more of Powell's signature characters, from the critic J. G. Quiggin to the guilt-ridden aristocrat Erridge, and from the vain old belle-lettriste St John Clarke to the ambitious publisher Howard Craggs. The term 'fellow traveller' was not in common currency in England before the cold war, but in a passage of unusual zest in *The Kindly Ones* Powell sums up what might be called his encapsulating view of matters:

> Simple lifers, utopian socialists, spiritualists, occultists, theosophists, quietists, pacifists, futurists, cubists, zealots of all sorts in their approach to life and art, later to be relentlessly classified into their respective religious, political, aesthetic or psychological categories. . . .

This tirade is of interest, because it echoes so well a similar piece of liverish invective by George Orwell, in *The Road to Wigan Pier.*

> One sometimes gets the impression that the mere words 'Socialism' and 'Communism' draw towards them with magnetic force every fruit-juice

drinker, nudist, sandal-wearer, sex maniac, Quaker, 'Nature Cure' quack, pacifist and feminist in England.

Powell knew Orwell, shared his interest in Bohemia and Fitzrovia (and his contempt for Bloomsbury), and often discussed arcane ideological and sectarian matters with him. In his *Journals*, Powell, a supporter of Franco, claims to have elicited from Orwell the admission that even the victory of the Generalissimo would have been preferable to a triumph of the Spanish Communists. Yet there is no character remotely corresponding to Orwell in the twelve novels, unless we make a slight guess about the chaotic but attractive Bagshaw in *Books Do Furnish a Room*: the burned-out radical who preserves an interest in doctrinal schism, literary low life, and the pamphleteering style. Virtually every other political radical is represented throughout as either a knave or a fraud or a crook. And Widmerpool, here, is the Proteus. Though averse to all risk and a stranger to all principle except that of advancement, he still throws in his lot with 'the Left', as when, working in the City of London as a broker in the 1930s, he expresses approval of the Moscow show trials and becomes an especially nasty specimen of the apologist type.

The simplest means of delineating Powell's extreme and splenetic conservatism, then, is probably to contrast it with the manners of his famous contemporary. Orwell would not, I think, have straightforwardly described a character as resembling 'a thoroughly ill-conditioned errand-boy', as Powell's narrator does, as naturally as breathing itself, in *The Acceptance World*. He would not have done so because he would not have assumed that all his readers used or shared the social reference; he would not have done so because he would have had occasion to wince at hearing others employ similar braying tones and judgements; and he would not have done so, I surmise, because of the implication of the word 'conditioned'. Moreover, if Orwell had served in a regiment made up chiefly of Welsh coal miners, and fictionalised it as carefully as Powell did in *The Valley of Bones*, he would not have dreamed of saying, after an encounter with a faintly bibliophile fellow officer (Roland Gwatkin, the luckless but honest bank manager turned honest but luckless soldier who is one of Powell's most finely realised minor characters): 'This was the first evidence come to light that anyone in the unit had ever read a book for pleasure.' The Welsh miners were rightly famed for their literacy, their workingmen's institutes, and their splendid union-endowed lending libraries: Powell degrades the speech of the 'other ranks' and the lower echelons to the low-comedy status of semi-disaffected plebeian singing and babbling, of the sort that might be loftily overheard by a junior officer eavesdropping in the pub.

Finally, I do not believe that Orwell would ever have made use of the expression 'to work like a black', as Powell does in *Casanova's Chinese Restaurant*. I do not mean, here, to deploy retrospectively what Powell's admirers would take pleasure in apostrophising as 'correctness'. The fact is that these attitudes seem instinctive, and that they are revealing. Powell knows perfectly well how to 'signal' a commonplace phrase, and to detach himself from any lazy attitude to its implications. Indeed, I have never read an author so fond of the ironic quotation mark. Widmerpool the schoolboy is described as going not for a run but for a 'run' and the same technique is used to mark off terms as quotidian as 'backstage', and as loaded as 'Munich'. The decision not to use inverted commas in this case, then, is a decision.

The number of political and historical references is astonishingly high, and occurs with a minimum of concession to the uninstructed reader. If you don't recall Count Karolyi, or Sforza, you will miss some important allusions in the table talk of the windbag diplomat Sir Gavin Walpole-Wilson, whose paralysingly stuffy dinner parties are an essential part of young Jenkins's initiation into London life. (This man's awkward sister is made by Powell to summon a world of silly high-minded do-goodery by stating her intention of spending an evening at home. 'I can make a start on my article about the Bosnian Moslems for the news-sheet of the Minority Problems League.')

Elsewhere, Powell shows himself highly alert to the difficulty of being an anti-modernist modernist, and also acutely desirous that Nick Jenkins should not be 'out of touch', by making a series of well-timed references to Marx, to Jung, and to Virginia Woolf. A single aside in *A Buyer's Market*, set in the 1920s, does duty for the whole by describing 'that wayward and melancholy, perhaps even rather spurious, content of the self-consciously disillusioned art of that epoch'. His only complete failure in this line is a protracted satire on a minor outbreak of Trotskyism in the artistic classes: he must have relied upon a cruel practical joker as his source for a running joke that does not 'work' in the least. (While the society novelist St John Clarke, author of such literary atrocities as *Fields of Amaranth*, *Match Me Such Marvel*, and *Dust Thou Art*, is represented as being seduced to Trotskyism by a nasty German male secretary, and thus as having upset his more hard-boiled Stalinist spongers, he continues to speak only in the same sheepishly 'progressive' tones that any fellow traveller might have employed at that epoch.)

Powell's politics also betray him into the one great absence, or perhaps better say refusal, that mars his fiction as an echo or mirror or madeleine of the period. The television dramatisation of *Dance*, though feeble enough for some of the inescapable reasons I have tried to suggest, was at least pedantically faithful to the text. It inserted only one incident that occurs nowhere in the work. As Jenkins watches a

Socialist/Communist parade of unemployed 'Hunger Marchers' into Hyde Park, and notes with amused contempt the number of modish and fashionable dons and scribblers who have attached themselves to the procession, a gang of Blackshirts rushes forward with knuckle-dusters and truncheons and falls upon the subversives. It isn't simply that the Mosley element makes no appearance at this point in *Dance*. It is more that the fascist and crypto-fascist element in upper-class British society makes no appearance at all. The only actual Blackshirt who is mentioned even *en passant* is the unnamed daughter of a Soho Italian restaurateur.

Think of it – a lovingly etched social portrait, with background, of the British upper classes in the 1930s, and there isn't a Unity Mitford or a 'Chips' Channon or a Lord Halifax among the lot of them. It is, given Powell's enormous acuity and fidelity, quite out of the question that this should be a mistake or an omission. Pro-Hitler opinions are indeed voiced, as are naïve estimates of the German threat (the first volume of *Dance* was not published until well after the war). But these are put into the mouth of Kenneth Widmerpool, who is otherwise represented as a Stalin-worshiper, and of Jenkins's Uncle Giles, else-where always referred to as 'a bit of a radical' and as the family's black sheep.

Yet Powell clearly has the capacity to summon history to his aid. The schoolboy Nicholas, for example, is visited by a military friend of his father's on the day that the archduke and duchess are assassinated in Sarajevo. General Aylmer Conyers, an excellent and deceptively buffer-ish 'friend of the family' figure, subjects him to a gruff senior-junior interrogation about the neighbours in the district, and their children:

> 'Fenwick in the Gloucesters?'
> 'Yes, I think so – the regiment that wears a badge at the back of their cap.'
> 'And Mary Barber's father?'
> 'He's in the Queen's. Richard Vaughan's is in the "Twenty-Fourth" – the South Wales Borderers.'
> 'What about the father of the Westmacott twins?'
> 'A Gunner.'
> 'What sort of a Gunner?'
> 'Field, but Thomas and Henry Westmacott say their father is going to get his "jacket" soon, so he may be Royal Horse Artillery by now.'
> 'An exceedingly well-informed report', said the General. 'You have given yourself the trouble to go into matters thoroughly, I see.'

A few pages later, Jenkins is looking back on the war and reports, almost as tersely as a Powell Jazz Age character: 'The Fenwicks' father was killed; Mary Barber's father was killed; Richard Vaughan's father was killed; the Westmacott twins' father was killed.' In other equally brusque asides, we learn that Jenkins's uncle was also killed on the Western Front, and his father wounded in Mesopotamia. The master of the longueur knows, in other words, how to be curt when the need arises. A similarly potent sentence occurs five novels later, in *Temporary Kings*, when Jenkins leaves the bedside of Hugh Moreland – after Stringham, his most endearing friend – and records: 'That morning was the last time I saw Moreland. It was also the last time I had, with anyone, the sort of talk we used to have together.' This is the melancholy of change and decay but it is derived, very substantially, from the associated decline in the fortunes and indeed the values of England.

Some of these effects, though, take their shape as quasi-mystical. Another way in which Powell differs from his friend Orwell is in his approach to the paranormal. Powell may have appeared to share Orwell's disdain for superstition and quackery but, in *Dance* itself, if a shaman or prestidigitator makes a prediction, it invariably comes true. A Tarot card reader accurately divines a future romance for Jenkins in *The Acceptance World*, and in *Hearing Secret Harmonies* the saturnine Scorpio Murtlock astonishes a rural Jenkins neighbour by telling him with mystic precision where to locate a lost dog. Even that most pathetic of 'psychic' contrivances, the Ouija board, is granted the power to foresee an immediate crisis by spelling out some key phrases from *The Communist Manifesto* and thereby to embarrass the dogmatic Marxist materialist J. G. Quiggin.

The lack of paradox here – Powell seeming as credulous as his own characters – somewhat upsets the otherwise well-kept balance between the historical and the comical. It also calls attention to an underremarked element in his cast: the large number of witches that it contains. *Dance* is positively hag-ridden. Charles Stringham is unmanned by a selfish mother and later gelded entirely by Miss Weedon, a cold-blooded and ambitious governess with a saving mission. Her working-class counterpart, the harridan-cum-slut and Communistic *petroleuse* by the name of Jones, is as previously noted given the sobriquet 'Gypsy'. Jenkins's Uncle Giles is only one of the characters to be severely put out by the Tarot-wielding lady, who is named Myra Erdleigh. A serving girl goes mad and disrobes before the assembled Jenkins family. Albert, the family's faithful retainer, is haunted by a fear of terrorism from the early suffragettes. 'The Kindly Ones' themselves, or the Eumenides of Greek drama, are none other than the fatally empowered female Furies. Lady Warminster, Jenkins's stepmother-in-law, is described as a 'witch' on her first introduction, possessing 'a calm, autumnal beauty that did not at all mask the amused, malicious, almost insane light that glinted all the time in her infinitely pale blue eyes'.

Most deadly of all her species, though, is the frigid nymphomaniac Pamela Flitton, who subsequently becomes the second wife of Kenneth

Widmerpool and is rivaled only by Widmerpool's own mother as a study in hysterical malice. Her end, which takes the gruesome form of a necrophiliac tryst in the penultimate novel *Temporary Kings*, completes the moral and emotional ruin of a number of men, including the brilliantly named pseudo-intellectual Leon-Joseph Ferrand-Seneschal. This, with its echo of the then notorious romance between Sonia Orwell and Maurice Merleau-Ponty, may be partly taken from life and if so would sharpen my proposed outline of the difference between Orwell and Powell.

V. S. Pritchett wrote that 'Mr Powell's English are punishing and punished. Their comedy has no silken threads; the threads are tweed.' He said this while considering only the first trilogy, but I think even at that stage it was evident that much more than merely tweedy materials were involved. The highest pitch attained by *Dance* is in the long stretch (*The Valley of Bones*, *The Soldier's Art*, *The Military Philosophers*) comprising the years of the Second World War. After a frustrating period of service in Ulster, Jenkins finds himself attached as a liaison officer to those governments-in-exile that have stationed themselves in London. His portrayal of the gallantry of the forgotten combatants – the Belgians and Dutch and Poles – is a series of beautifully executed miniatures. (It also calls subliminally on the natural sympathies of a Welsh writer and soldier for the predicament of small nations.) He witnesses the liberation of the Low Countries, revealing the strong painterly qualities in his makeup:

> On the whole, a march-past of Belgian troops summoned up the Middle Ages or the Renaissance; emaciated, Memling-like men-at-arms on their way to supervise the Crucifixion or some lesser martyrdom, while beside them tramped the clowns of Teniers or Brouwer, round rubicund countenances, haled away from carousing to be mustered in the ranks.

This somewhat recalls the figure of Rowland Gwatkin, Jenkins's commander in the Welsh battalion:

> He had draped a rubber groundsheet round him like a cloak, which, with his flattish-brimmed steel helmet, transferred him into a figure from the later Middle Ages, a captain-of-arms of the Hundred Years War, or the guerrilla campaigning of Owen Glendower. I suddenly saw that was where Gwatkin belonged, rather than to the soldiery of modern times, the period which captured his own fancy. Rain had wetted his moustache, causing it to droop over the corners of the mouth, like those belonging to effigies on tombs or church brasses. Persons at odds with their surroundings not infrequently suggest an earlier historic epoch. . . .

This is chivalric, perhaps, but by no means tweedy. It is chivalry, too (as well as anti-Communism), that motivates the disgust of Jenkins at the pusillanimity of the British Government in helping to suppress the news of the massacre of Polish officers at Katyn: an ignoble moment in which Widmerpool, by now a military intelligence officer, plays an especially ignoble part, denouncing the Polish exiles for their 'lack of circumspection' in choosing to embarrass Great Britain's gallant Soviet allies. Other off-scene occurrences, most notably Hiroshima and the Final Solution, play no part at all, though Jenkins may surprise some readers when, on learning of Hitler's invasion of the Soviet Union, he experiences the instantaneous sense that now, at last, everything will be all right. Only when the war is won, and Jenkins finds himself in Normandy and posted without warning to Cabourg – the Balbec of Proust, Albertine, Charlus, and the Swanns – does an air of anti-climax supervene:

> Proustian musings still hung in the air when we came down to the edge of the water. It had been a notable adventure. . . . At the same time, a faint sense of disappointment superimposed on an otherwise absorbing inner experience was in its way suitably Proustian too: a reminder of the eternal failure of human life to respond a hundred per cent; to rise to the greatest heights without allowing at the same time some suggestion, however slight, to take shape in indication that things could have been even better.

That is very fine. 'Anti-climax', however, is an inadequate word for the extreme disappointment that awaits in *Hearing Secret Harmonies*, the closing volume of *Dance*. Here, the shortcomings of the preceding novels appear condensed and intensified. Confronted by what he would doubtless call 'the Sixties', Powell sounds less and less like a stoical and skeptical observer and instead takes on the lineaments of a vapouring old bore. The book supposedly concerns the cult of youth and the traps that this cult will set for the trend-crazed older person who needs or desires to appear contemporary. But it is no longer informed by experience and curiosity, well-recollected and hard-won and wrought over in reflection. Rather, it resembles the plaintive tone of a beached colonial retiree, convinced that all around him is going to the dogs. There's a distinctly elderly quaver in the way that Jenkins alludes to a current 'pop star', and also his cringe-making effort at the capturing of 'youth culture' usages. (Things are 'a drag'. People 'freak out'.)

Worst of all, an ill-carpentered and strenuous scenario almost enlists our sympathy for the dread Widmerpool. It becomes plain at last that, having recruited Widmerpool to the roles of conceited schoolboy, arrogant businessman, overbearing staff officer, intolerable Labour politician, crypto-fascist, crypto-Communist, and potential model for the Fifth Man (to name only the most salient ones), Powell has run out of things to do with him, has exhausted the capacity of his most vivid creation. Widmerpool's Nemesis – as a ludicrous cult-slave to a boy young enough to be his son – does not come close to matching his earlier hubris. Nor is it consistent with his grossly well-nurtured sense of self-interest and self-preservation. Some of the country house scenes, of the sort in which Powell elsewhere excels, are more farce than comedy and often read like a rough draft for *Four Weddings and a Funeral.*

In the preceding novels, the dubious thaumaturges and mystic adepts are, so to speak, kept under restraint. Even at their most irritating, they sometimes succeed in supplying some salt and leaven to the narrative. Here, they take over entirely. Powell loses his way in a sort of pallid drizzle of New Age babble, picked up at third hand along with his other impressions of 'the Sixties', and allows even his most robust characters to succumb to runes, horoscopes, and the sickly blandishments of Aleister Crowley. To invert, in fact, what has been so often and unfairly said against Powell, the verdict here must be that events are random and unstrung rather than intricately coincidental. The series does not end or conclude, still less achieve a resolution. It just stops.

The later entries in Powell's *Journals* often rise to similar self-parody: that of the disaffected country squire. He pens devotional entries to Mrs Thatcher ('The answer'), complains about modern education, loves cats, reiterates his glee at the death of the traitorous bumboy W. H. Auden, watches the press to see who has been knighted or ennobled, quarrels intermittently with Philip Larkin and Kingsley Amis, misses the firm hand of the Shah of Iran, admires his sound rural neighbour Vidia Naipaul, and expresses strong distaste for Salman Rushdie unless the latter is physically menaced by Muslims ('If they live here, they must obey the laws of this country like everyone else. If they don't, they must get out'). When invited to a literary prize event in Jerusalem, he revolts at the prospect of having to be civil to 'the terrorist Menachem Begin'. (It would be a great mistake to construe such an entry as being, in any sense, pro-Palestinian.) This is all intensely enjoyable but it diminishes that very distance – between the Waugh style and the Powell style – which was once thought, and felt, to be important to his readership, and to himself.

The success and failure of *Dance* are both of epic dimensions. And it is Time – an element that Powell himself sometimes capitalises – that has the final victory. An undertaking that set out to be, and was, an updating of the English novel manages to sustain itself with grace and wit over several long movements before being overtaken and outpaced by history and events. 'Time,' as Powell's despised Auden famously wrote, will forgive many things. It will certainly 'pardon Kipling and his views' and will even pardon Paul Claudel: 'Pardon him for writing well.' But the strains die away, the syncopation begins to falter, the band wants to go home, and the characters lose definition as they begin to droop. As in Poussin's framing, only Time calls the tune and distinguishes the dancers from the dance. I first began to read *Dance* when it was incomplete and there was something to look forward to. The pleasure then afforded was rather greater than that which is offered by a long look back.

First published as 'Powell's' Way' (a review of *Journals 1989–1992* by Anthony Powell and *Miscellaneous Verdicts: Writings on Writers 1949–1989* by Anthony Powell) in *New York Review of Books*, 28 May 1998

Notes

1. Sir Charles Powell, former chief political advisor to Margaret Thatcher, pronounces his name Pole-style. Jonathan Powell, chief of staff to Prime Minister Tony Blair, is a staunch Towellist. The fact that the two men are brothers makes Anthony Powell seem more of an English social realist than he is sometimes credited with being.

Something about the Poems

To Julian Barnes, on 27 September 1985, Philip Larkin wrote concerning an encounter with almost the only woman he ever admitted to 'adoring':

> Your anecdote reminds me of a brief exchange I once had with Mrs T., who told me she liked my wonderful poem about a girl. My face must have expressed incomprehension. 'You know', she said. 'Her mind was full of knives.' I took *that* as a great compliment – I thought that if it weren't spontaneous she'd have got it right – but I am a child in these things. I also thought that she might think a mind full of knives rather along her own lines, not that I don't kiss the ground she treads.
>
> Anyway, there must be something about the poem.

The poem in Mrs Thatcher's subconscious can only have been 'Deceptions', a line from which also furnishes the title of Larkin's anthology *The Less Deceived.* It has the longest superscription of any of his poems, and one which may be worth giving in full:

> Of course I was drugged, and so heavily that I did not regain my consciousness till the next morning. I was horrified to discover that I had been ruined, and for some days I was inconsolable, and cried like a child to be killed or sent back to my aunt.
> Mayhew: *London Labour and the London Poor*

Prompted by this miniature *trouvaille* of helpless misery and exploitation, the poem takes up the story transmitted across the past:

> Even so distant, I can taste the grief,
> Bitter and sharp with stalks, he made you gulp.
> The sun's occasional print, the brisk brief
> Worry of wheels along the street outside
> Where bridal London bows the other way,
> And light, unanswerable and tall and wide,
> Forbids the sun to heal, and drives
> Shame out of hiding. All the unhurried day,
> Your mind lay open like a drawer of knives.
> Slums, years, have buried you. I would not dare

Console you if I could. What can be said,
Except that suffering is exact, but where
Desire takes charge, readings will grow erratic?
For you would hardly care
That you were less deceived, out on that bed,
Than he was, stumbling up the breathless stair,
To burst into fulfilment's desolate attic.

This exchange then, between Britain's most reactionary postwar prime minister and Britain's most conservative literary icon, seems almost but not quite to deserve the name of irony. On the face of it, Mrs Thatcher's appreciation of poetry comes off as both rather slack and slightly didactic, while Philip Larkin's feeling for the woes of womanhood and the hidden injuries of class emerges, even if bathed in a slightly sentimental melancholy, in a stronger light than has recently been emphasised. Most of all, by an accident of correspondence we have the charming and durable picture of the Tory Boadicea, and the curmudgeonly provincial she so admired, as they exchange confusions over an image appropriated from Mayhew's anatomy of the lower social depths.

This is a microcosm, not of the hidden reserves of humanity within Philip Larkin, but of the zone of ambiguity in which the argument over his artistic contribution must take place. Without wishing to seem even-handed about it, I have found perilously little in the current controversy – a controversy which has imported 'Larkinesque' into our vernacular as a synonym for crass or brash callousness – which evinces the least respect for the crucial and delicate task of discrimination. The Communist Party of Great Britain used to be associated with a journal of opinion entitled *World News & Views*. One contribution to that journal was an essay entitled 'T. S. Eliot – Enemy of the People'. Polemics like these, apart from being bovine and obscurantist in their own right, are a free gift to the cause of reaction, which ever seeks to disguise itself as aesthetic detachment. The reception accorded to the publication of Larkin's *Selected Letters* and to the biography by Andrew Motion[1] was aptly summarised in a letter I received from Tom Paulin after the first wave of astonishment, disgust and rationalisation had begun to recede. Paulin had opened a spirited exchange in the *Times Literary Supplement*, hoping to ignite a debate over the relationship between literary and political ideas; between Larkin's standing as 'national monument' in poetry and the 'open sewer' of scabrous loathing over which that monument had been raised. His reach had exceeded his grasp – you could not get from the monument to the sewer, or back again, in time. A dialogue of dunces was the outcome:

Impossible to get an argument going – politically correct fools pushed in on the act, others flew the transcendental kite. The level of racist abuse in England is constant – my kids experience it daily at school – but in literary London the values of Edwardian England still pertain.

Paulin, of course, is an Ulster Protestant Republican with an Indian wife. He can scarcely be expected to find the funny side of a rhyme like the one which Larkin sent, variously, to Robert Conquest and to Charles Monteith, friend of Auden and Eliot at Faber and Faber:

> Prison for strikers
> Bring back the cat
> Kick out the niggers
> How about that?

(This ditty, incidentally, was composed to be set to the tune of *Lilliburlero*, the Orangeman's jingle that sang King James II out of Ireland and his other dominions, and which was then the signature tune of the BBC World Service. So the flatulent term 'quintessentially English', which is so routinely and clumsily attached to both Larkin's life *and* work, may have a special unintended aptness in this instance.)[2]

It is, indeed, the totemic standing of Larkin as quasi-official national bard: 'unacknowledged legislator', almost, of the Ukanian ideal, that lends polemical energy to his critics. Terry Eagleton, in a broadcast entitled *J'accuse*, and John Newsinger in the pages of *Race and Class*, both saw their quarry – the national tradition, the literary canon, the myths of patriotism – in plain view. Quoting Janice Rossen's book *Philip Larkin*, John Newsinger, cited her to the effect that: 'there is a well-known photograph of Larkin sitting next to a roadside sign bearing the word "England" and the pose seems to exactly typify him'. To which he at once added: 'Now of course the game is up and Larkin is revealed in his *Selected Letters* to have been a reactionary bigot; racist, sexist and gripped by class hatred.'[3]

However, Newsinger's brief philippic, which actually opens by conceding that only with the publication of the *Letters* is any 'game' actually 'up', manages to conclude by saying that Larkin's 'own bigotry was such that it could no longer be rendered into verse' and adding that 'for this much we should be grateful'. Any sarcasm here, however, can only be at Newsinger's expense since, apart from 'Homage to a Government', published in 1969 and expressing resigned contempt for Harold Wilson's 'cost-cutting' rationale for withdrawing from Aden, he can point to no published poem that illustrates Larkin's resentful conservatism. And 'Homage to a Government' contains no element of vulgar intolerance. It is, rather, a mournful and sardonic 'End of Empire' elegy, which succeeds rather well in recalling the mediocre

Wilsonian argument for withdrawing from East of Suez, the better to defend the sterling area.

Here, I should perhaps disclose my own interest. I have never had any difficulty in comprehending the appeal of Larkin to some part of the British (not so much the English) consciousness. This is because I recall, with very little trouble, the tone of my own father's table talk. (Readings of the old Peter Simple column in the *Daily Telegraph*, or of the Denis Thatcher epistolary parody in *Private Eye*, have the same effect upon me, and I simultaneously envy and mistrust those who fail to see the authentic seriousness of such jocularity.) What are the psychic and biographical ingredients here?

For the interwar petty-bourgeois and functionary generation, these would include a consciousness of life – indeed youth – passed in the exigencies of the Depression, the Second World War and the subsequent age of austerity. To this would have to be added the strain imposed by the 'scholarship or nothing' fork in the education system; itself very often an enforced choice between over-work and conformism on the one hand and relegation to menial or bureaucratic work on the other. With the privileged above and the forces of craft unionism below them, it is a mercy that more of this class did not turn to fascism than actually did. In the postwar period, though, their rancour was sublimated into a diffuse but persistent drizzle of complaint. End of Empire and Commonwealth immigration were disliked for their own sake, to be sure, but probably more formative was the sense that these momentous decisions had been taken without anyone's permission – without, as it were, a by-your-leave. Juvenile delinquents and wildcat strikers were a Poujadiste staple, as, briefly, were 'revolting students' in the 1960s. (Especially painful to comrades of this journal will be Larkin's August 1969 letter to Brian Cox, commenting on a contemporary piece of pedagogic repression by saying 'Isn't it splendid about that young swine Blackburn?') The nearest this mentality came to acquiring a leader was in the advent of Enoch Powell, and its most acute anatomist has been David Edgar, most particularly in his play *Destiny*.

Beneath the unstable political manifestations lay a profound, inchoate sense of loss about the erosion of the English countryside, the diminished prestige of the nation and the amoral amnesia of the Affluent Society. No doubt there were elements of vicarious envy behind the scorn and disapproval: my father never read Larkin's 'Annus Mirabilis', which locates the beginnings of sexual freedom 'Between the end of the *Chatterley* ban/And the Beatles first LP/(Which was rather late for me)', but I can recall him saying wistfully that he was sorry to have missed the Permissive Society. Actually, I don't think he read much poetry at all. But I could have given him '*Going, Going*' ('And that will be England gone') or a half-dozen other mournful laments, and seen them strike a chord. As with Larkin himself, there were moments of antic subversiveness, where it was suddenly doubted that a dutiful life spent on the pursuit of traditional obligations had been worthwhile, or had been appreciated by those superiors in whose service it had been passed. Andrew Motion's biography tells us, of that celebrated emblematic photograph, that it 'shows Larkin sitting demurely, ankles crossed, on the large sign which says "ENGLAND"; immediately before posing he had urinated copiously behind the word'.

There was one large difference between my father and Larkin, which was that my father spent most of his life wearing the King's uniform; an honour that Larkin steadfastly, not to say assiduously, declined. Very occasionally, though, and usually bearing some relationship to the state of the decanter and the lateness of the hour, one could hear them both taking leave to doubt that the Second World War – the 'Finest Hour', the 'Valiant Years', the special source of cross-class pride – had really been 'worth it', succeeded as it had been by an era of superpower triumph and money-worship. I want to return to this trope but for now it's enough to say that the proneness of English culture to this sort of pessimistic chauvinism is a subject insufficiently explored. That is why many on the Left have condemned themselves to experiencing major phenomena – the Falklands fever; Mrs Thatcher herself – as a surprise. The stubborn persistence of chauvinism in our life and letters is or ought to be the proper subject for critical study, not the occasion for displays of shock.

There isn't much room for paltry irony or contradiction in a short screed like Newsinger's. This partly because he's a very shockable person. When I worked at the *New Statesman*, and came to know ex-radicals like Kingsley Amis and Robert Conquest, who now wished to shock by saying allegedly 'unsayable' things, I was amazed by their mildness. What were a few cracks about Nkrumah or the Irish, to set against the literal-minded John Bullshit out of which I had spent years reading and arguing myself? True, the thing about the sustained *épater* style is that the face can grow to fit the mask. (It did that in the case of John Braine, who became a sort of Union Jackshirt.) But in my experience, when men like Conquest came across a real, one-dimensional, humourless bigotry they were bored by it. It all seemed so . . . pointless. My reservation here will no doubt strike John Newsinger as delinquent. He puts it like this, imagining Larkin's correspondents: 'How did these eminent men respond? Did they protest against his remarks, ignore them? How, for example, did Kingsley Amis respond when Larkin urged him to keep up his "cracks against niggers and wogs"? Presumably we shall have to wait for Amis to die (hopefully not too long) before we find out.'

Then let me inquire. How did the editor of *Race and Class* respond to that last sentence? He let stand the misuse of the world 'hopefully', so he may not have read it at all. But did he mean to print an apparent wish for the death of an author? Or would he rather claim that the metaphorical and satirical intention was – even though *not* couched in a private communication – abundantly clear to anyone with a sense of humour and proportion?

Terry Eagleton's labour in the same vineyard is, if anything, even more fruitless. He opens his *J'accuse* by saying of Larkin that 'few poets of his stature have been so remorselessly concerned to negate rather than affirm, diminish rather than enhance'. I had not before understood that Professor Eagleton believed in poetry as uplift. Nor did I gather, until I read that 'the Hull setting was symbolically apt for Larkin: as the twentieth century unfolded its wars and revolutions, he cowered behind the book stacks in this remote provincial outpost', that the ivory tower or the academy were to be hawked upon from the height of a dreaming spire. Nor would I, as a tutor even in Oxford, have given high marks to an undergraduate submission which said that: 'if Larkin hadn't existed then he would have to have been invented'.

After these mediocre jibes Eagleton enlists John Lucas to rescue him from insecurity. And John Lucas offers the following:

> For example in that poem *Going, Going* OK, good glum poem, in its way, about what's wrong with England, the concrete and tyres that are all that's left. But who put the concrete and tyres there? Why doesn't he talk, if he's going to write about going, going, about the England that is responsible for the concrete and tyres. Why? Because he can't talk about Mrs Thatcher whom he adores.

This testifies rather more to Larkin's strength as an impressionist poet than it does otherwise since (as Mr Lucas went on to concede without otherwise breaking stride) 'Going, Going' was written and published in 1972. In that admittedly pre-Thatcherite era, it was to furnish the frontispiece of a White Paper on the environment, and did in part do so. It was in 1973 that I and others learnt that the following lines had been struck out by members of the Heath regime:

> On the Business Page, a score
> Of spectacled grins approve
> Some takeover bid that entails
> Five percent profit (and ten)
> Percent more in the estuaries: move
> Your works to the unspoilt dales
> (Grey area grants)! . . .

Even had I forgotten this amputation of the poem by those who commissioned it, I would have been reminded by Larkin's letter to Robert Conquest on 31 May 1972, which is quite as easy to locate in the *Selected Letters* as any other of the much trumpeted entries: 'Have you seen this commissioned poem I did for the Countess of Dartmouth's report on the human habitat? It makes my flesh creep. She made me cut out a verse attacking big business – don't tell anyone. It was a pretty crappy verse anyway, not that she minded that.'

And this is the poem ('the shadows, the meadows, the lanes: the guild halls, the carved choirs') which is so often cited as 'quintessentially English'. Censored by Peter Walker and Robert Jackson because it captured the England of Heath and Slater–Walker too well (almost as well as the earlier poem had caught something of Wilsonism) the offending verse was defiantly restored by Larkin when the *High Windows* collection appeared in 1974. How about that?

Having missed and bungled all this, and much more besides, Eagleton closes by alleging, in another lapse into cliché, that: 'in Philip Larkin post-imperial Britain got the poetic talent it deserved. *The Less Deceived* (or, one might translate, No Flies on Philip) is the title of one of Larkin's early volumes. But few poets have been more deceptive.' A glance at the lines quoted in my opening should convince the most indifferent reader that Eagleton has never consulted, or does not remember, the poem whose title he annexes for his sophomoric play on words. Mysteriously, he concludes his hasty script by asserting that Larkin 'trapped his readers with him in a state of permanent casualty'. In another context, this accusation might be described by an analyst as 'projection'.

Let us take every Larkin incitement ('nigger', 'wog', 'foreigner' and the rest of the gang) and overlook the blustering claim that it all depends on your keen sense of humour, and merely take the last stanza of 'Sympathy in White Major' (1967).

> *A decent chap, a real good sort,*
> *Straight as a die, one of the best,*
> *A brick, a trump, a proper sport,*
> *Head and shoulders above the rest;*
> *How many lives would have been duller*
> *Had he not been here below?*
> *Here's to the whitest man I know –*
> Though white is not my favourite colour

First, this is taken from Théophile Gautier's *Symphonie en Blanc Majeur*, which shows that Larkin didn't mean absolutely everything he said in various postscripts about 'bloody abroad'. Second, it demonstrates beyond contest that he knew the uses of satire and irony, and knew when these came in at his own expense. So the question becomes one of when? And also of why? When is Larkin being intelligibly literal and when is he otherwise?

His defenders here are often his feeblest friends. Did John Bayley really mean to say, in *Philip Larkin's Inner World* in 1989, that he was: 'more free of cant – political, social or literary' than any of his peers? (Apparently he did, because he recently wrote as if the publication of the *Letters* made no difference to our understanding.) Does Andrew Motion now regret saying that Larkin's work had the 'capacity to create a recognisable and democratic vision of contemporary society'? Other defences have been mounted since the recent disclosures of the *cloaca* that ran through Larkin's psyche. John Saville, one of the anchors of the British Left and one of the stalwarts of Hull, deposes that Larkin was uniformly helpful in his compilation of the magnificent *Dictionary of Labour Biography*, and that despite referring to the project as 'subversive' was professional and exemplary as a librarian. 'Motion has allowed himself to be overwhelmed by his discoveries of Larkin's private life,' wrote Saville, 'and much else has been missed. I suppose this is how Eng. Lit. approach their subject these days.'

This last response, which is proper in its way, ought to be forwarded direct to Terry Eagleton. But though with greater generosity and with more safeguards against vulgar politicisation, it misses the same mark. It is not unlike the frequently heard claim that Larkin was no racist because he so much loved and popularised jazz music.

Larkin was not just a bigot or a foul-mouth or a chauvinist, or any other modish personifier of 'insensitivity'. He was an artist and he was a thwarted fascist. His defenders, who would naturally prefer to take the high ground of literary licence, do not care to examine that last rather toxic and over-used term, which they have spent years in devaluing by describing it as 'indiscriminate'. And his pseudo-Leftist critics prefer the easy vernacular of deconstructed, race-and-gender-derived vagary. Nonetheless the point holds.

Marxists are often reluctant to employ the denomination 'fascist' because it has become suspect as propaganda and also, one sometimes fears, because fascism has a disconcerting populist element. Anti-plutocratic, often anti-clerical, contemptuous of the hereditary principle, possessed of certain utopian and idealist myths – it has been known to fool credulous customers who think they dislike the Establishment. In England, of course, it has been somewhat emulsified by various Chestertonian and indeed Eliotian tropes – preference for the countryside over the town, an instinct for history and the nation, reservations about the 'cosmopolitan', a dislike of capital and the City, a belief in the common sense of the folk. Some of these are strongly embedded in Larkinism but some – which is part of what makes him intriguing – are not. For instance, he detested the institution of the family, and though reverent about churches and liturgies had no use at all for religion. He also had at least some awareness of the potency of repressed homosexual yearnings, and little if any trust in popular sapience. On the Jewish question, he was muted even in private correspondence but there are hints of a prompting that he had drilled himself to keep under restraint. These exceptions to the pattern would have put him, in a slightly different time and place, on the more iconoclastic – even Romantic – wing of the European fascist tendency.

At the material time and place, however, there was little doubt of his fundamental instinctive allegiances. The *Selected Letters* and the biography both contain, if they do not choose to stress, clear evidence that Larkin chose the opposing side in the Second World War. One observation can therefore be made at once. However such a pose may be classified, it is highly difficult to describe it as 'essentially' or even 'quintessentially' English.

Larkin's father, who tyrannised over a weak mother and a vapid sister, was a staunch, open admirer of the Third Reich. He took the boy on two trips to see and to relish 'the new Germany'. Sydney Larkin, we learn, also started up an enthusiastic correspondence with Dr Hjalmar Schacht, Hitler's Minister for Economics, and kept a statuette of the Führer on his mantelpiece at home. The home was in Coventry, first target of the Luftwaffe in 1940, where Larkin père served as a martinet in the municipal bureaucracy.

Trained to sniff only for banal 'insensitivity' towards, say, blacks and women, the English and American reviewers of 1992 failed utterly to discover the traces of this infection in the *Selected Letters*. Yet here is Larkin, writing in December 1940 that: 'Germany will win this war like a dose of salts, and if (saying) that gets me into gaol a bloody good job too. Balls to the war. Balls to a good many things, events, people and institutions.' In 1942 he wrote to a friend: 'I agree we don't deserve to win.' Later in the same year, he made what is much the most suggestive of his many pro- or quasi-Nazi observations:

> If there is any new life in the world today, it is in Germany. True, it's a vicious and blood-brutal affair – the new shoots are rather like bayonets. It won't suit me. By 'new' life I don't mean better life but a change, a new direction. Germany has reverted back too far, into the other extremes. But I think they may have many valuable new habits. Otherwise, how could DHL be called Fascist?

This, taken with the generally Lawrentian violence and disdain of much of Larkin's wartime correspondence, is an assistance in 'situating' him politically and aesthetically. John Harrison's valuable 1968 study *The Reactionaries* (introduced by William Empson) tried to analyse the overt sympathy for fascism that was manifested by T. S. Eliot, Ezra Pound, W. B. Yeats, D. H. Lawrence and Wyndham Lewis. To revisit this book in the company of the Larkin 'revelations' is to experience a shock of recognition.

Harrison examined the Catholic anti-Semitism of Eliot, the blood theories of Lawrence, the sacrificial nationalism of Yeats, the currency obsessions of Pound and the contempt for the Enlightenment proclaimed by Lewis. Of this group, the one most congruent with Larkin is undoubtedly D. H. Lawrence – though it should be said that Larkin's admiration here must have been in great degree vicarious; he was always sexually timorous and literally insular, with no aptitude at all for real world adventure.[4]

Here is Harrison on Lawrence:

> Lawrence did not oppose the war on strict pacifist principles; he could hardly be said to have opposed the use of physical violence. He simply did not like being prodded with a stethoscope and told to put his lights out. His letters during the First World War amount to a bad-tempered rejection of humanity in general . . . 'I wish one could be a pirate or a highwayman in these days. But my way of shooting them with noiseless bullets that explode in their souls, these social people of today, perhaps it is more satisyfing.'

Larkin loathed the fitness tests for the service he evaded in the next war, and detested also the atmosphere of patriotic enthusiasm. Lawrence's character Somers in *Kangaroo* is a Larkinesque figure, full of bile against 'mob spirit', and though Larkin's version of Lawrentianism was an insipid one – adoration for Mrs Thatcher instead of prostration at the feet of 'splendour, gorgeousness, pride, assumption, glory and lordship' (Lawrence's *Apocalypse*) – the latent connection is evident. It's amusing in this context to note how Larkin identifies the end of sexual inhibition, in his poem 'Annus Mirabilis', with 'the end of the *Chatterley* ban'.

Larkin never commented, after the tide of war had turned, on the defeat of Hitlerism, the revelations of Nuremburg, or any other grand question. He chose to affect a frigid indifference. He was hardly out of university, then, when his whole intuitive and inculcated 'politics' had become generally unsayable, not to mention unspeakable. 'Internal exile' might not be the most inapposite term for what he disguised as reclusiveness. He did not resume the making of overt, or strident or, indeed any, remarks on public affairs until the 1960s, and it may not be too strenuous to see the relentless, private 'negativity' of those comments as an impotent sublimation of an old 'imperfectly-interred attachment'.[5]

On the Jewish question, for example, Larkin was largely silent. But

in 1970 he sent a poem to his friend and lover Monica Jones, which
ran:

> The flag you fly for us is furled,
> Your history speaks when ours is done,
> You have not welcomed in the scum,
> First of Europe, then the world.

And in 1981, writing to Noel Hughes, he referred to Israel as 'the land
of Kagan and Sidney Stanley' – both of them men of business who had
taken advantage of the Law of Return to evade scrutiny of their
accounting practices. These are small signals, but they represent all
that he ever said about Jewish people. It was to Noel Hughes, too, that
Larkin had the painful experience of writing in 1982, beseeching him
to omit any mention of his own father's Nazi sympathies from the
'Festschrift' of that year *Larkin at Sixty*. (The appeal to Hughes was
successful.)

It is also noticeable that there is a great exception in Larkin's
thesaurus of bigotry. No spleen is displayed against homosexuality. We
know that Larkin had some difficulties with boys until at least his
Oxford years, and there is one 1976 letter announcing the discovery,
in Cardiff of all places, of 'a newsagent with a good line in Yank homo
porn'. Larkin differs, also, from all his peers in 'The Movement' (Wain,
Amis, Conquest), in having written both gay and lesbian fiction, at least
as an experiment. His correspondence has a strong element of the
excremental vision, and also displays an abiding interest in corporal
punishment. Disgust is consistent – has there been anything bleaker
than Larkin's likening of sexual intercourse to 'getting someone else
to blow your nose'? But the correlation between sexual repression and
fascism, hatred and self-hatred, though often very strong, is not definite
enough in this instance to be very much more than suggestive.

Many of Larkin's sympathisers point to his love of jazz as a mitigating
quality – both as concerns hatred of modernism and hatred of black
people. Here, though, the evidence is unambiguous. Larkin's love of
jazz was an explicit function of his general attitudes, which seem
incidentally to have become very plain to him when he wrote about
music:

> If in the course of desegregation the enclosed, strongly categorised pattern
> of Negro life is broken up, its traditional cultures such as jazz would be
> diluted. The negro did not have the blues because he was naturally melan-
> choly. He had them because he was cheated and bullied and starved. End
> this, and the blues may end too.

If that wasn't clear enough:

The term 'modern', when applied to art, has a more than chronological meaning: it denotes the quality of irresponsibility peculiar to this century, known sometimes as modernism, and once I classified modern jazz under this heading I knew where I was.

Larkin, in other words, had no use for 'the other' except as victim. With Lawrence, he agreed that: 'for the mass of the people knowledge *must* be symbolical, mystical, dynamic. This means we must have a higher, responsible conscious class; and then in varying degrees the lower classes, varying in their degree of consciousness.' Thus while Larkin's detestation of strikers and of unions – and for Arthur Scargill personally – became notorious, he did in 1970 write a fine poem called 'The Explosion', which might well find a place in an anthology of mining disaster literature edited, as it might be, by John Saville. Yet scrutiny of the poem shows that Larkin had no real sympathy with the oppressed once they ceased to be underdogs and became agents on their own account.

So – unless we lose all interest in contradiction – we are fortunate in being able to say that Larkin's politics are buried well beneath, and somewhat apart from, his poems. The place he occupies in popular affection – which he won for himself long before the publication of his fouler private thoughts – is the place that he earned, paradoxically, by an attention to ordinariness, to quotidian suffering and to demotic humour. Decaying communities, old people's homes, housing estates, clinics . . . he mapped these much better than most social democrats, and he found words for experience. Physical decline is most often expressed as 'going down hill': it was Larkin who saw that age and dying are hard work for working people, and spoke of 'Extinction's Alp' as well as 'the private joke of existence'. The distance between his work and his life is one tenuous definition of the artistic. The poetry of Pound and Eliot is polluted by their respective politics and suffers badly as a consequence, and the most humanist revolutionary triumphs of Auden – Larkin's most admired poetic model – were later to be mutilated or smothered by their originator in what amounts to an *auto da fé*. Postmodern inquisitions do not help to clarify this complexity.

The uncertain resonance given off by Larkin is the consequence of a deep, ancient crack in the great British belfry. To trace the flaw is to ask why a part of our literary tradition – the register itself – is so much attuned to harsh, tribal clangour. Those who lead disappointed and stunted lives can form, as we have been forced to realise, an almost masochistic relationship to their familiar rulers. In looking for creative dissonance, we should attend to the long rhythms and traditional echoes. This essentially radical and critical task is made no easier by those who prefer a philistine display of the appropriate credentials. An authentic engagement with the sources of reaction ought to begin now, when even the dullest soul can experience the British condition as being that of Larkin without the poetry.

First published in *New Left Review*, no. 200, July/August 1993

Notes

1. *Philip Larkin: Selected Letters*, edited by Anthony Thwaite, Faber 1993; Andrew Motion, *Philip Larkin*, Faber 1993.
2. Paulin might have profited from a calm reading of Seamus Heaney's essay on Larkin in *The Government of the Tongue*, where Heaney (who had declined to appear in an Oxford Book of *English* Verse edited by Andrew Motion and Blake Morrison) wrote that Larkin might be compared to Joyce, but only on condition that his 'collected work would fit happily under the title *Englanders*'.
3. John Newsinger, 'Dead Poet: the Larkin Letters', *Race and Class*, vol. 34, no. 4, April–June 1993.
4. Heaney points out that in his own introduction to *The North Ship*, Larkin admits to being rebuked by friends for his infatuation with Yeats: '*When such as I cast out remorse, so great a sweetness flows into the breast.*' This favourite verse drew ire from Bruce Montgomery, and Heaney surmises that 'Larkin tells the anecdote to illustrate his early surrender to Yeats's music and also to commend the anti-Romantic, morally sensitive attitude which Montgomery was advocating and which would eventually issue in his conversion to the poetry of Thomas Hardy.' A conversion the completeness of which may be doubted.
5. In this very clarifying study *The Movement: English Poetry and Fiction of the 1960s* (Oxford 1980) which considers the school of Wain, Amis, Larkin, Enright and Davie, Blake Morrison intuited the same without benefit of later diaries or recollections. Concentrating chiefly on Larkin's stubborn 'nostalgia', he nonetheless noticed that 'In the 1950s and 1960s, it was difficult to tell what political opinions Larkin held' but adds that 'in the late 1960s and early 70s' Larkin began to emerge as more reactionary than nostalgic.

The Egg-Head's Egger-On

Novelists can be lucky in their editors, in their friends, in their mentors and even in their pupils. Sometimes they are generous or sentimental enough to fictionalise the relationship. In *Keep the Aspidistra Flying*, George Orwell gave his friendless, dowdy and self-pitying protagonist Comstock one true pal: the editor and patron Ravelston, proprietor of the small yet reliable magazine *Antichrist*. This Ravelston – some composite of Sir Richard Rees and John Middleton Murry – was a hedonistic yet guilt-ridden dilettante, good in a pinch, and soft on poets, but too easily embarrassed by brute exigence. Saul Bellow – who has already shown a vulnerability to exigent poets in his wonderful *Humboldt's Gift* – now presents us with Ravelstein, a hedonistic kvetch who manifests patience towards none. As is known to all but the meanest citizens of the republic of letters, the novel is an obelisk for the late Allan Bloom, author of the 1987 shocker *The Closing of the American Mind*. This book, which was a late product or blooming of the University of Chicago Committee on Social Thought, argued that the American mind was closed because it had become so god-damned *open* – a nice deployment of paradox and a vivid attack on the relativism that has become so OK on campus these days. Bloom's polemic swiftly became a primer for the right-wing Zeitgeist; a bookend for the shelf or index sternly marked 'all down-hill since 1967'. And even then, there were those who detected a Bellovian lending, or borrowing as the case might be.

When *The Closing of the American Mind* first came out, Robert Paul Wolff, then a professor at Amherst, wrote a short review in *Academe*, the journal of the American Association of University Professors. Let me quote from his prescient opening staves:

> Aficionados of the modern American novel have learned to look to Philip Roth for complex literary constructions that play wittily with narrative voice and frame. One thinks of such Roth works as *My Life as a Man* and *The Counterlife*. Now Saul Bellow has demonstrated that among his other well-recognized literary gifts is an unsuspected bent for daring satire. What Bellow has done, quite simply, is to write an entire coruscatingly funny novel in the form of a pettish, bookish, grumpy, reactionary complaint against the last two decades. The 'author' of this tirade, one of Bellow's most fully-realized

literary creations, is a mid-fiftyish Professor at the University of Chicago, to whom Bellow gives the evocative name 'Bloom'. Bellow appears in the book only as the author of an eight-page 'Foreword', in which he introduces us to his principal and only character.

Right away one thought of Herzog, the super-kvetch of all kvetches. But here again, in his foreword to Bloom or 'Bloom', Bellow kept us guessing. As he phrased it (teasingly?):

> There are times when I enjoy making fun of the educated American. *Herzog*, for instance, was meant to be a comic novel: a PhD from a good American university falls apart when his wife leaves him for another man. He is taken by an epistolary fit and writes grieving, biting, ironic and rambunctious letters not only to his friends and acquaintances, but also to the great men, the giants of thought, who formed his mind. What is he to do in this moment of crisis, pull Aristotle or Spinoza from the shelf and storm through the pages looking for consolation and advice?

Rather archly, perhaps, Bellow went on to smile at the simplicity of some of his public:

> Certain readers of *Herzog* complained the book was difficult. Much as they might have sympathized with the unhappy and comical history professor, they were occasionally put off by his long and erudite letters. Some felt that they were being asked to sit for a difficult exam in a survey course in intellectual history and thought it mean of me to mingle sympathy and wit with obscurity and pedantry. But I was making fun of pedantry!

Well, taking things all in all, I think we had better be the judge of that. Because now we have an ostensibly full-out novel, this time under Bellow's real name, which reveres pedantry and is all about the life and death of Allan Bloom. Indeed, with its many real names and actual locations, it constitutes a novelistic and realistic memoir of him. And it is related, partly in anguish, by a Herzog character – 'a PhD from a good American university' whose wife has just left him for another man, or at any rate for other men.

For some reason that I cannot pretend to decode, this Boswell is named 'Chick'. He it is who proposes that Ravelstein write the egghead bestseller ('It's no small matter to become rich and famous by saying exactly what you think') and who in return accepts Ravelstein's commission to become his – probably posthumous – biographer. So far, so accurate: Bellow was the egghead's egger-on, and also his angel in the publishing world, and here we find the second half of the debt redeemed. The story is authentic too, as far as it goes, about Ravelstein/Bloom's egghead allegiances. Bloom was an adept or disciple of the Chicago philosopher Leo Strauss, a German-Jewish émigré who was, according to your bias, sinister or arcane. Modelling himself on Aristotelian and Machiavellian theories of the covert formation of princes, Strauss never sought public renown and insisted on close explication of the occult element in classic and classical texts. His American disciples, of whom Francis Fukuyama is probably the most celebrated, achieved a brief nearness to real power during the Reagan and Bush Administrations, one of them (William Kristol, son of Irving) being the Aristotelian mentor of Dan Quayle. The giveaway in Straussian critiques is the employment of the term 'regime' to denote styles of rulership. Bellow captures this neo-cultist element quite deftly:

> But Ravelstein knew the value of a set. He had a set of his own. Its members were students he had trained in political philosophy and longtime friends. Most of them were trained as Ravelstein himself had been trained, under Professor Davarr, and used his esoteric vocabulary. Some of Ravelstein's older pupils now held positions of importance on national newspapers. Quite a number served in the State Department. Some lectured in the War College or worked on the staff of the National Security Adviser. One was a protégé of Paul Nitze. Another, a maverick, published a column in the *Washington Times*. Some were influential, all were well informed; they were a close group, a community. From them Ravelstein had frequent reports, and when he was at home he spent hours on the telephone with his disciples. After a fashion, he kept their secrets. At least he didn't quote them by name.

That's the first and almost the last we hear of the crucial and seminal Felix Davarr, who as Leo Strauss is mentioned only once in *The Closing of the American Mind*, where he makes the oddly trite observation that the moderns 'built on low but solid ground'. Bloom's reticence, though, is appropriate: it is that of the close-mouth and knowing initiate, while Bellow treats Strauss as if he were like Anthony Powell's Sillery: no more than a don with a number of influential ex-pupils. When Alexandre Kojève is mentioned a few pages later, he is drawn in the same rather lifeless terms as 'the famous Hegelian and high official who had educated a whole generation of influential thinkers and writers'. Someone who had really done that could once have expected a more lapidary (or do I just mean less tired?) sentence from Bellow's pen. The cynicism of Strauss's theory and practice was summarised in his antithesis between Athens and Jerusalem. I am certain to vulgarise the recondite here, but Straussians believe in religion and not in God. Philosophy is the high calling of the élite: a strenuous and contemplative effort directed at the moulding of a cultural and political leadership. Obviously, superstition and piety are mere encumbrances in the discharging of this elevated task. But the masses, of whom no such effort can be expected, must draw their ethical and disciplinary rations from the commissary of the supernatural. 'Chick'/Bellow shows no grasp at all of this dialectic, which he repeatedly expresses as Ravelstein's fascination with Athens *and* Jerusalem, as if Plato and the Talmud were equal treasures from the bran-tub of antiquity.

That of course was the *ad hoc* conclusion of the autodidact and omnivore Augie March, Bellow's most superbly rendered fictional creation. March passes long stretches on the periphery of the University of Chicago, and at one point makes a sort of jackdaw living by stealing 'great books' on commission for scholars like the lanky Hooker Frazer. His first major haul is 'a big Jowett's *Plato*' but he soon diversifies: 'Two volumes of Nietzsche's *Will to Power* I had a hell of a time swiping, for they were in a closed case at the Economy Book Store; I also got him Hegel's *Philosophy of Right*, as well as the last volumes of *Capital* from the Communist bookshop on Division Street, Herzen's *Autobiography*, and some de Tocqueville.' The influence of the University on the city, especially on its outcast or indigent element, can be felt all the time in *The Adventures of Augie March*. There is Padila, the impoverished Mexican who gets a scholarship to develop his genius for mathematics, and there's Clem, amassing erudition in a fly-blown rooming-house.

In *Augie March*, too, we sense Bellow's interest in gurus and savants and mentors. Here's the disabled local fixer and broker William Einhorn:

> The first superior man I knew. He had a brain and many enterprises, real directing power, philosophical capacity, and if I were methodical enough to take thought before an important and practical decision and also if I were really his disciple and not what I am, I'd ask myself: 'What would Caesar suffer in this case? What would Machiavelli advise or Ulysses do? What would Einhorn think?' I'm not kidding when I enter Einhorn in this eminent list. It was him that I knew, and what I understand of them in him. Unless you want to say that we're at the dwarf end of all times and mere children whose only share in grandeur is like a boy's share in fairy-tale kings.

When Einhorn's father dies, his self-educated and slum-bred son reaches for the 'deep-water greatness' of the ancients and strains pathetically but nobly for an elevated note and a high calling. In his dignified filial death-notice for the neighbourhood paper he writes without embarrassment: 'My father was not familiar with the observation of Plato that philosophy is the study of death, but he died nevertheless like a philosopher, saying to the ancient man who watched by his bedside in the last moments . . . "That was the vein of it."'

I can't resist adding two more themes from Bellow's triumph in 1953. One is a hatred of workhouse condescension towards the underclass: 'Something in his person argued what the community that contributed the money wanted us poor bastards to be: sober, dutiful, buttoned, clean, sad, moderate.' And the other a real demotic admiration for the Greeks, for their ancient willingness to face things as

Augie tries to face the humilations of jail and the Stygian gloom of Erie, Pennsylvania and other wasteland spots:

> Only some Greeks and admirers of theirs, in their liquid noon, where the friendship of beauty to human things was perfect, thought they were clearly divided from this darkness. And these Greeks too were in it. But still they are the admiration of the rest of the mud-sprung, famine-knifed, street-pounding, war-rattled, difficult, painstaking, kicked in the belly, grief and cartilage mankind, the multitude, some under a coal-sucking Vesuvius of chaos smoke, some inside a heaving Calcutta midnight, who very well know where they are.

By contrast, Ravelstein, and *Ravelstein*, are shadows on the wall of Augie March's cave. The great city of Chicago is now represented as a heaving Calcutta midnight, awash in feral delinquency. Ravelstein segregates himself in an apartment building, with the pretentious name of 'The Alhambra', where his only contact with the world of the streets is a superannuated black skivvy: 'As nearly as any honky could, he took into account her problems with her prostitute daughter, her jailed criminal son, and with the other son whose HIV troubles and scrambled wives and children were too complicated to describe.' Why does one get the impression that Bellow would rather these people were 'sober, dutiful, buttoned, clean, sad, moderate'? Ravelstein, meanwhile, looks on his students as the raw material of a future conservative hierarchy owing a debt to himself. (In a moment of lucid callousness we are informed that 'if they weren't going to make it he didn't hesitate to throw them out'.) Also, we soon discover that this new *maître*, who possesses none of the coarse vigour of Einhorn, has 'HIV troubles' of his own.

Chaos, most especially the chaos identified with pissed-off African-Americans, was the whole motif of *The Closing of the American Mind*. Bloom had taught at Cornell during the campus upheaval of 1968, and never recovered from the moment when black students produced guns to amplify their demands. (He also never reconciled himself to the ghastly fondness of the young for rock music. 'Whether it be Nuremberg or Woodstock,' he wrote in a passage of extreme dyspepsia comparing everybody to the Brownshirts, 'the principle is the same.') However, there was hope. A small group of classics students copied out and xeroxed a passage against ochlocracy from Plato's *Republic* and passed it out as a leaflet. Bloom sounds just like Bellow when he recalls this moment: 'They had learned from this old book what was going on and had gained real distance on it.'

Actually, Glaucon's evening with Socrates would have been a poor shadowy guide to an American 'regime' which was then engaged in confronting a revolt of the helots, and in fighting a war far more cruel and unjust and irrational than the Peloponnesian. But what Bloom liked was the attachment to form. At least, he liked it most of the time. The worst thing he could think of to say about one of his academic antagonists was that he was 'an assiduous importer of the latest Paris fashions'. By this of course he meant an interest in Sartre or Althusser or perhaps Foucault; it makes it all the funnier that when we first meet 'Ravelstein' he is in Paris on a vulgar spree of consumerism: Lanvin jackets, costly scarves, Lucullan restaurants and hotel suites; if you've got it, baby, flaunt it. Before too long there is a fast car with all the fixings being ordered for 'Nikki', the travelling companion, and we further learn that Abe (Ravelstein's seldom used first name) is *en rapport* with at least some young blacks for his fashion sense alone. By these signs, and a few others, Bellow makes it easy to know what 'Bloom' never admitted in his paeans to the Greek style: that for all his contempt for the counter-culture he was a live-dangerously homosexual.

As depicted by Bellow, this is perhaps the most attractive and sympathetic aspect of the man. But, as the novel fails to register, it was also a negation of his whole public stance. Allan Bloom thought, and Abe Ravelstein thinks, that sex – any sex – is a poor expression of Eros, but better than nothing at all. Heavy weather is made of this simple point:

> Naturally there was a Greek word for it, and I can't be expected to remember every Greek word I heard from him. Eros was a *daimon*, one's genius or demon provided by Zeus as a compensation for the cruel breaking-up of the original androgynous human whole. I'm sure I've got that part of the Aristophanic sex-myth straight. With the help of Eros we go on, each of us, looking for his missing half. Ravelstein was in real earnest about this quest, driven by longing. Not everyone feels that longing, or acknowledges it if he does feel it. In literature Antony and Cleopatra had it, Romeo and Juliet had it. Closer to our own time Anna Karenina and Emma Bovary had it, Stendhal's Madame de Rênal in her simplicity and innocence had it. And of course others, untaught, untouched by open recognition, have it in some obscure form.

The 'obscure form' in which 'Bloom' really experienced it was of this kind:

> One day he said to me: 'Chick, I need a cheque drawn. It's not a lot. Five hundred bucks.'
>   'Why can't you write it yourself?'
>   'I want to avoid trouble with Nikki. He'd see it on the cheque stub.'

In the first proof of the novel that I read, Bellow went on to be explicit about the sexual elements that were masked by this accountant version of anonymity. He has since excised that paragraph, perhaps or presumably in deference to the unease produced by his candour about Bloom's escapades. (Pre-publicity for the book drew some moans of pain from the old-school Chicago hands.) However, the chief point is allowed to survive its euphemisation: Allan Bloom died of AIDS, as was finally and reluctantly admitted by his admirers. Nor is this a detail. Bloom never mentioned the gay movement in his series of assaults on promiscuous Modernism. Throughout his posthumously published book *Love and Friendship*, a rather superior effort to analyse Eros and agape from Alcibiades to *Emile*, he hoarded his own views on pederasty well on the other side of the closet door. No ordinary reticence was involved here. The philosophical movement associated with Leo Strauss regards 'sodomy' as sterile and nihilistic, and as an unmanly betrayal of tribe and family. And the Straussian intellectuals have undergone a schism, every bit as sulphurous and Talmudic as the Trotskyist faction-fights that were known to Augie March and indeed the young Bellow. Professor Harry Jaffa, Strauss's most ardent disciple and Bloom's one-time collaborator in a volume on Shakespeare's politics, has authored a stream of polemics against homosexuality as a violation of 'natural law'. This very trope currently forms the moral cement of the American Right. There may or may not be a suggestive and contradictory connec-tion between 'Ravelstein's' secretive sex life and his attachment to arcane doctrines – between the erotic and the esoteric – but Bellow can't seem to be bothered with it.

This is perhaps because his narrator has problems of his own. Domestic traumas – heterosexual and banal ones, to be sure – are eating him up, and like Herzog he finds little release in pulling Aristotle or Spinoza from the shelf. Indeed, when he tries to scan anything at all, this happens:

> One day when I was reading a book (my regular diet of words) she wandered into the room entirely nude, came to my bedside and rubbed her pubic hair on my cheekbone. When I responded as she must have known that I would she turned and left with an air of having made her point. She had won hands down without having to speak a word. Her body spoke for her, and very effectively too, saying that the end was near.

Bellow has always had a fierce instinct for the blunt messages that female pudenda can convey, especially in closure. The much younger and tougher Augie March had to endure the following:

> In heat like this she preferred to go naked in her room. When I wanted to recall how she was, naked, I found I could do it very well. She saw my eyes on her lower belly and her hand descended to hold the edge of the robe there. Seeing that colourful, round-fingered hand descend, I bitterly felt how my privilege had ended and passed to another man.

The pubis-flaunting female in the present case – enough to drive anyone nuts, if not necessarily queer – is the coldly scientific and dedicated Romanian wife we last met in *The Dean's December*. By degrees, as Ravelstein sickens and dies, 'Chick' shuffles forward to become the subject and object of his own novel. He realises that his wife has outpointed him emotionally and also legally. Lamenting his own dullness, and also lapsing into terrible colloquialism, he kvetches: 'You deaden your critical powers. You stifle your shrewdness. Before you know it you are paying a humongous divorce settlement to a woman who had more than once declared that she was an innocent who had no understanding of money matters.' The spring-heeled and amoral Ravelstein is probably the near-perfect friend to have in such a fix; he mocks the wife's robotic ways and her frigidly perfectionist style, and suggests that her Romanian pals are probably Iron Guard fascists anyway. (He punctuates his monologues with the tic phrasing 'thee-ah, thee-ah', which Bellow records skilfully without noting that such mannerisms are designed to make the speaker uninterruptible, and are thus an unfailing sign of the closet authoritarian.) Still, Chick's best-ever pal turns out to be his next wife, who realises that he is not just sick but actually in mortal peril after he eats the wrong fish on a Caribbean holiday, and who exerts herself to pluck him back from the lip of the grave. I'm sorry that the narrative breaks off before the latest big news in Bellow's life, which is his fathering of a daughter at the age of eighty-plus, with the same staunch and estimable woman who did the plucking.

Thin though this novel may be, and perfunctory in keeping its commitment as the unwritten memoir that Bellow promised to Bloom in a moment of weakness, it does exemplify some of the stoicism of the neo-conservative mentality. 'Ravelstein' doesn't whine as the end approaches. We don't actually see him die (Bellow's own near-death experience follows, perhaps, too hard upon) but we witness him in the humiliating shipwreck of his last illness and he remains a wise-cracking atheist and materialist. 'Chick' chooses to see this as a pose, and to take literally Ravelstein's expiring gags about a reunion beyond the grave, which strikes me in the light of a slight but significant breach of faith. Say what you will about the Straussians, they aren't hypocrites or weaklings and they don't burble about heavenly rewards to make up for when the mind has gone. Indeed, they have made rather a pointed study of the dignified hemlockian terminus. Bloom should have been allowed this last nobility.

Bellow's own attitude to Jerusalem is given a mild work-out in these pages. In the past few decades he has had a fluctuating relationship with the neo-conservative movement. He first endorsed the bogus work of the pseudo-demographer Joan Peters, who argued that there had been no Palestinian population to be dispossessed in the first place, and then honourably withdrew his encomium when the facts about the book became known. He signed up with the grandiosely titled Committee for the Free World, run by Midge Decter and Norman Podhoretz, and then let his sponsorship lapse when the same outfit published hysterical slanders against Norman Mailer and Gore Vidal. In the argument about standardised courses in 'Western Civilization', he intervened with the now notorious remark that the Papuans had no Proust and the Zulus had no . . . was it Zola? He wrote a crabbed and resentful account of a visit to the Holy City, which seemed to some of us to be an Arab v. Jewish allegory of the fears and resentments – about black populism and demagogy in New York and Chicago – which have been more cheaply annexed by Tom Wolfe but which found an outlet also in *Mr Sammler's Planet*. In *Ravelstein* he presents the Jewish experience principally and unexceptionally as one of survival. With a tinge of self-pity, though, he also advances it as something that non-Jews can't be expected to understand. Even great humanists like Maynard Keynes, when you con the list of 'great books', disclose their rodent prejudice. 'I had a Jewish life to lead in the American language, and that's not a language that's helpful with dark thoughts.' There's a quavering note here which, ironically in its way, contrasts with Abe Ravelstein's robust and amoral and defiant and very American style; a style redeemed from being merely reactionary by its understanding of the ancients, and the understanding (to which it incidentally or accidentally assists us) that intellectuals never sound more foolish than when posing as the last civilised man.

First published as 'The Egg-Head's Egger-On' (a review of *Ravelstein* by Saul Bellow) in *London Review of Books*, 27 April 2000

Bloom's Way

Those who follow these things have long known that Allan Bloom, the neo-conservative panjandrum who helped spice up the Reaganite intellectual atmosphere by producing *The Closing of the American Mind* in 1987, was a homosexual, and that when he died in 1992 the report about 'liver failure' was a cover story. He died of AIDS. It's also known that the character Abe Ravelstein, eponymous hero of Saul Bellow's newest novel, is not just modelled on Bloom but is Bloom, so to speak, to the life. One or two critics have also noticed that Bellow's final published version is a little toned down from the original proof that was dispatched to reviewers. The subject's homosexuality is still mentioned, and so are some treatments for the AIDS virus, but the connection between the two has been somewhat blurred. For example, D. T. Max, writing in the Sunday magazine of the *New York Times*, noted that the sentence 'Abe was taking the common drug prescribed for AIDS' had diminished to 'Abe was taking the common drug prescribed for his condition'.

I am astonished that nobody has pointed out a much more suggestive bowdlerisation by Bellow. In the original, this appeared on the same page as the quotation above:

> Even towards the end Ravelstein was still cruising. It turned out that he went to gay bars.
>
> One day he said to me, 'Chick, I need a cheque drawn. It's not a lot. Five hundred bucks.'
>
> 'Why can't you write it yourself?'
>
> 'I want to avoid trouble with Nikki. He'd see it on the cheque stub.'
>
> 'All right. How do you want it drawn?'
>
> 'Make it out to Eulace Harms.'
>
> 'Eulace?'
>
> 'That's how the kid spells it. Pronounced Ulysee.'
>
> There was no need to ask Ravelstein to explain. Harms was a boy he had brought home one night ... Eulace was the handsome little boy who had wandered about his apartment in the nude ... physically so elegant. 'No older than sixteen. Very well built' ...
>
> I wanted to ask, what did the kid do or offer that was worth five hundred dollars ...

Well, of course I would like to know the answer to that, too. (Such questions Chick has!) But the more pressing matter at least for now is – why did Bellow choose to repress the fact that Bloom liked barely legal boys of African-American provenance?

I don't want any grief from anybody about my making that second assumption: I know what Bellow means to convey by 'Eulace' with the same certainty that I know what he intends by the name 'Harms'[1]. And in fact, the now-excised passage followed immediately upon an outburst by Ravelstein, in which he quarrels with his official boyfriend Nikki for saying that a black nurse should be understood as coming 'from the ghetto'.

> 'Ghetto nothing!' Ravelstein said. 'Ghetto Jews had highly developed feelings, civilized nerves – thousands of years of training. They had communities and laws. 'Ghetto' is an ignorant newspaper term. It's not a ghetto that they come from, it's a noisy, pointless, nihilistic turmoil.'

Bloom, you will recall, devoted much of his famous *Closing of the American Mind* to an attack on black militants on campus in the Sixties; he kept up a similar high pitch against the same decade by comparing Woodstock to a Nuremberg rally. And the term 'nihilist' is one of the giveaway words by which one can recognise a member or supporter of the school of Leo Strauss, Chicago godfather of the neo-cons and mentor of Bloom, Fukuyama and many others. So it's of more than passing interest that Bloom should have sought solace on what was to him the wrong side of innumerable tracks.

The Straussian school places homosexuality ('sodomy', as it insists upon terming it) under a rigorous ban. Not only does homosexual practice attack the root of family values but it erodes patriotism and the other manly virtues. Harry Jaffa, who collaborated with Bloom on a books about Shakespeare's politics, later denounced Bloom as a gay proselytiser for the sapping of the American morale. This helps explain why so many conservative intellectuals – who had come to look on Bellow as a fairly reliable ally – have reproached him so bitterly for relating an important truth (or some attenuated part of it) about their departed friend.

It all shows what a long way we still have to travel. Whether you are a creationist like Pat Robertson, or a Catholic like Pat Buchanan, or a materialist believer in 'Natural Law' like Jaffa and others, you can't avoid the salient fact that the creator, or the Divinity, or Nature, or Evolution, has evidently mandated that there be a certain quite large number of homosexuals. The proportion may seem to fluctuate, as do attitudes towards it, which is why the classical and traditional schools have so much trouble with their attitude toward Greek antiquity. But there it is, like a lion in the path of the anti-humanists. They cannot, without admitting to the chaos of their worldview, seriously affirm that men and women are simultaneously designed to be sick and commanded to be well. So they take refuge in various confected 'laws', and, when these inevitably break down, they resort to simple-minded denial.

Bloom was one of the many living proofs of this contradiction. I didn't care for his bestseller, and I don't like the ethos – partly paranoid and partly self-pitying – that Bellow has lately come to represent. But *Ravelstein*, even in its expurgated form, made me wish I'd been able to meet Bloom. His other writings, notably *Love and Friendship*, are quite moving even when they are pathetically closeted, because they explore with fascination the endless tension between eros and agape. It would have been instructive to ask him why he himself always sneered at the efforts of other cultural minorities; no less instructive to inquire why his own ideological cohort refused to see that the prefix 'homo' denotes not just a form of sex but a form of love.

First published as 'Bloom's Way' in *The Nation*, 15 May 2000

Notes

1. In *The Adventures of Augie March*, almost the only black character is named Ulace Padgett: a coal-yard employee found shot dead in a morgue.

III

'Themes . . .'

Hooked on Ebonics

In the course of 'the trial of the century', on July 12 1995, to be exact, a witness named Robert Heidstra was called to the stand and asked about his dog-walking experience in the vicinity of Nicole Simpson's home. He had, it seemed, been exercising the pooches and heard voices raised at or about the material time. Christopher Darden wanted to know if Mr Heidstra had indeed told a friend that one of these voices sounded like that of a 'black man'. This was altogether too much for Johnnie Cochran, who objected strenuously and said, 'You can't tell by somebody's voice whether they sounded black.' In case anyone may have missed his drift, he added that 'the very idea was entirely inappropriate . . . in America, at this time, in 1995'.

Mr Cochran's grammar was as confused as his thought, if we agree to give him the benefit of confusion. Anybody who owns a telephone in America and has average hearing can tell 'by somebody's voice', not if they 'sound' black, but if they are black. (Not all corollaries hold. You can't automatically tell that someone isn't. But you can damn sure tell that someone definitely is.) What are we noticing here? It's an accent, an inflection, a set of usages, and sometimes a grammatical or syntactical giveaway. In the public-school system of the city graced by Mr Cochran, it is effectively recognised as a separate dialect. Farther north, in Oakland, it has recently become famous under the name of 'Ebonics'. In Hollywood not so long ago, the makers of *Airplane!* put subtitles under a conversation between two 'jive' speakers. Nobody complained that the joke went over anybody's head.

If this point is as simple as it seems, then what's the problem with December's resolution of the Oakland School Board? Describing Ebonics as 'genetically based' and derived from the tongues of the Niger-Congo, it advocated recognition of the distinct language of local black schoolchildren 'for the combined purposes of maintaining the legitimacy and richness of such language and to facilitate their acquisition and mastery of English language skills'.

Well, there are actually three problems. The first is that the resolution itself is composed in no known language though there are traces of bureaucratese, therapese, legalese, and business English to be found within it. The second is that 'Ebonics' is a made-up term stressing two things – colour and phonetics – which have absolutely nothing to do with the structure or definition of a language. The third is that language by its nature cannot be 'genetically based'. If the black kids in Oakland are in fact speaking a different tongue, then it's because of *their* real lives and not because of any notional ancestral connection to the Niger-Congo. The essence of language is its transmissibility, which cannot be through the bloodstream. So that's that for the Oakland School Board, which seems to have been interested in picking up some 'bilingual' subsidy dough and which has since hastily reversed itself, stating for the record that Black English will only be honoured as part of a campaign to make it disappear.

The truth of the matter is that a number of unemployable cultural nationalists from the 1960s have found a form of employment in the educational bureaucracy of our less Athenian inner cities. One West Coast activist is Ron Karenga (now known as Maulana, which he believes to be Swahili for 'master teacher'), whom I remember distinctly as the leader of an Africanist nut group called Us – later found to be partially supported by the FBI – and who in 1966 gave us the exciting concept of Kwanzaa. Mr Karenga's slogan in those days was 'Anywhere we are, Us is!' I liked the slogan then, and I like it even more now. But if only the whole question could be disposed of with such ease.

In my native British islands, homeland of this great universal language, there dwells a population that is famously 'branded on the tongue.' I can 'place' anyone as soon as he or she begins to utter. James Baldwin once phrased it very well:

> To open your mouth in England is (if I may use black English) to 'put your business in the street': you have confessed your parents, your youth, your school, your salary, your self-esteem, and, alas, your future.

Which isn't exaggerating by very much. Margaret Thatcher had to take several courses in elocution to rid herself of bumpkin and awkward tones and to become the queenly figure that I left England to get away from. (To get away from whom, I mean to say, I left England.) And you would not have been able to see *Trainspotting* at your local multiplex last summer had it not been painstakingly dubbed. But it's a striking fact that black people born in England are not branded on the tongue, or at least not as blacks. They speak Cockney or South London or Manchester, or the BBC English which is charmingly known as 'Received Pronunciation', or 'RP'. There are a few Caribbean vernacular imports in the language, and that's it. So there must be a reason why this is not true for these United States, and it certainly won't be a 'genetic' one, but it may not be found just by having a free laugh at the expense of some mediocre officials in Oakland.

Baldwin made the above observation in an essay entitled 'If Black English Isn't a Language, Then Tell Me, What Is?' His defence of the separate integrity of the language was a very striking one, though I think that, as a man whose favourite author was Henry James, he would have winced at terming it 'Ebonics'. He once wrote, in *Notes of a Native Son*: 'I hazard that the King James Bible, the rhetoric of the storefront churches, something ironic and violent and perpetually understated in Negro speech – and something of Dickens' love for bravura – have something to do with me today; but I wouldn't stake my life on it.' Now you're talking. For Baldwin, recognition of the language he didn't speak was a duty paid to history. Black people, he said, came to America 'chained to each other, but from different tribes: Neither could speak the other's language. If two black people, at that bitter hour of the world's history, had been able to speak to each other, the institution of chattel slavery could never have lasted as long as it did.' Baldwin, as it happens, was entirely correct about the deliberate policy of splitting up slaves by language group. In the mid-eighteenth century, in his awful book *A New Voyage to Guinea*, the slave master Captain William Smith wrote that by 'having some of every Sort on board, there will be no more Likelihood of their succeeding in a Plot, than of finishing the Tower of Babel'.

Once landed in America, the slaves who had survived the Middle Passage had a bit of nautical pidgin English, the memories of their own varying tongues, and many encounters with different sorts of English speakers. Cleanth Brooks, the great scholar of William Faulkner and of southern speech, argues that the habit of saying 'dis' and 'dat' originates with the peasants of Kent and Sussex in southern England, who did indeed speak in that fashion and who came to colonise Virginia and the Carolinas. By this reckoning, as he puts it, poor and illiterate southern blacks 'held on to what their ancestors had learned by ear and which had been passed on to them through oral tradition. In short, they rather faithfully preserved what they had heard, were little influenced by spelling, and in general actually served as a conservative force.'

'Conservative', too, are the Sea Islanders, off the South Carolina coast, who as I write are still speaking in Gullah. Across the harbour from Charleston, perhaps a quarter of a million African-Americans use a dialect, or patois, that, according to Lorenzo Turner's celebrated book *Africanisms in the Gullah Dialect*, contains up to 6,000 African words and expressions. ('Baraka' is the word for 'thanks', and its origin is Mandingo; 'efi' is the word for 'smoke', and its origin is Yoruba.) Unlike the children of Oakland, California, the Gullahs can claim a direct philological relation with the mother continent. But this turns out not to clarify much, since the mother continent is a place where languages and dialects metamorphose with the crossing of a river. I have been in the Niger-Congo, and I didn't meet a single person who spoke only one language. To speak three is quite common, very often with a European colonial one as a kind of top layer or lingua franca. Inarticulacy is not the problem. Black English, then, is a product of the Babel effect of slavery, of pidgin and Creole, and of what Baldwin rightly calls 'the unprecedented tabernacle' of the black Church. Without it, we would be shorn of innumerable vigorous and humorous expressions. But it is only a tributary of English and can never substitute for it. That's why the cadences of black American oratory are imperishable, and why its greatest pulpit practitioners drew from the same well that Baldwin described, and eventually silenced their white audiences into thoughtfulness.

Take the example of Yiddish, the mother tongue of many impoverished immigrants and former victims. When I say 'What's not to like?' I am using a different syntax and one I wouldn't be without. (Without which, I mean to say, I would not be.) But it's English Yiddish, not Yiddish English. Can you imagine Jewish neighbourhoods mandating 'Hebronics' as a way of boosting morale? I don't think so. Nonetheless, I'm still a little melancholy at the total eclipse of the language of Isaac Singer, and I don't look forward to the day when all New Yorkers routinely say 'with regards to' and 'as far as'. At least Yiddish was a language in which things could be written. There's effectively nothing in print that's written in Black English, and the nearest approximation – the 'Uncle Remus' narrative of Joel Chandler Harris – was the work of a white man with a good ear. Baldwin, in other words, could write a stirring justification of black speech and black code, but he could not do so by employing that code itself. And this is the Information Age, buster, in case you hadn't noticed. An age that doesn't sit well with the 'oral tradition'. Anyone instructing a child that this is irrelevant, or anyone prating about Homer and the Bible being 'oral' too, is doing violence to that child's prospects.

Of course, violence is being done already. Not many years ago, it was predicted with confidence that Black English would die out because everyone would be watching the same television programmes. (National broadcasting networks have contributed hugely to the erosion of Piedmontese in Italy, Provençal in France, and Ruthenian in the Ukraine and the Czech lands.) The use has declined, but in some areas it has also intensified. This is testimony to the persistence – or, rather, the re-emergence and consolidation – of segregation in American cities. Those who rush to say that Oakland teachers are failing the kids had better acknowledge that they had been 'failed' well before now.

Whether we agree to call it a slang, an idiom, a vernacular, or a debased survival, the fact is that Black English does exist and is spoken, and does define (and circumscribe) the world of many Americans. I would not want to be an inner-city teacher and have no ear for it. Would it be good to have a manual for educators? Quite possibly. Can physics be taught in it? Quite obviously not. Does it have suggestive crossovers with the mainstream? Sure. Should it be taught? No – it's already been taught before the child gets to school. Would it, and its survival, make a good subject for a PhD dissertation? Undoubtedly. Can its recognition help toward its abolition? That must be the hope. But not complete abolition. I once had the amazing privilege of having Wynton Marsalis play in my apartment. (Play an instrument, I mean.) We talked later about rap and reggae, and he gave me a brilliantly lucid explanation of the no-goodness and second-rateness of it all. Finishing this up, he lapsed from the language of Chaucer and Milton for an instant and, pausing for finality, said, 'It is some *bullshit*.' That last pungent cadence drove the whole thing squarely home.

I called a few trusted friends in the week of the Ebonics brouhaha. Noam Chomsky, the founder of modern linguistics, said that while there's no difference in principle between 'I be' and 'Je suis', and while pre-modern and pre-technological languages can be extremely dynamic and complex, the chances of evolving one in a ghetto were distinctly slim. 'If it's taught, it has to be like the way that Standard English is taught to unintelligible white kids in eastern Tennessee – as a means of making them fluent.' Adolph Reed, professor of politics at Northwestern, said that he had two reactions to the Oakland news. 'The first reaction was: Oh man, I'd better check that I still have my American passport. The second reaction was to go and have a consoling drink.' Baldwin made a point of including irony as one of the necessary ingredients of the black vernacular style. And 'irony', as the great Polish-American Laureate Czeslaw Miloscz once put it, 'is the glory of slaves'. There is tragedy and history and emotion involved in the survival of a black speech in America, and giggling at its expense is not good manners. But the worst irony of all would be to congratulate, hypocritically, the 'richness' of something that threatens to imprison its speakers in the confines of a resentful, baffled, muttering serfdom.

First published as 'Hooked on Ebonics' in *Vanity Fair*, March 1997

In Defence of Plagiarism

How well I remember the sweetness of it. I was sitting on a plane, reading a copy of *The Spectator*. Taki Theodoracopulos had written one of his 'High Life' columns, taking off after 'the sodomites of the Big Bagel' (as he thoughtfully described the gorgeous mosaic of gay life in Manhattan). It was a spirited piece, made no less so by my growing conviction that I had read it before. By the time the plane landed, I had attained the 'Gotcha' moment that is the Nirvana of the vengeful reader. It took me only an hour to get a fax of the 'original article' (by Norman Podhoretz in the *New York Post* a few weeks previously), compare the sentences word for word, and fire off an extremely contented and self-righteous letter to the editor of *The Spectator*. I knew that he would have no choice but to print it, and Taki and I were not getting on very well at the time, so it was one of the most chore-free pieces of unpaid writing that I have ever done.

Dear reader, mark the sequel. Not many years later I wrote a strangely neglected book on the sculpture of the Parthenon. Reviewing this learned yet passionate text, *The Spectator*'s critic was good enough to notice a paragraph of mine about the arrangement of certain ancient stones. With a maddening loftiness, he compared it to another paragraph, written by quite another author in quite another book, and found it disconcertingly similar. Well, I mean to say, that was an entirely different matter.

Once again I found myself writing (and once again, revoltingly, without any *suggestion* of payment) a letter to the editor of this irresponsible magazine. The case was quite clear and the misunderstanding laughably self-evident to any serious reader. Both I and Mr William St Clair – this was the name of the other author – had obviously drawn on the same original eyewitness description of the Acropolis. What could be more natural than that both of us, committed scholars in our different ways, should have summarised the same source in much the same fashion? I need hardly say that that was the end of the story, except that I still wake up whimpering about it.

Plagiarism. A nasty little word. In the world of classical antiquity (not that I have any great desire to bring *that* up all over again) the word *plagiarius,* which to Cicero meant manstealer or kidnapper, was used by Martial to denote a literary thief. Ever since, the crime has haunted writers of all calibres.

Only a few weeks ago, Julian Barnes received a rather tepid review in *The Times Literary Supplement* of this new short-story collection, *Cross Channel.* The reviewer compared its style unfavourably with a 'resonant image' in Barnes's earlier novel *Flaubert's Parrot:* 'A pier is a disappointed bridge.' Then came one of those fearful letters, pointing out (doubtless to the discomfiture also of the reviewer, who hadn't noticed it) that the line was from James Joyce's *Ulysses.* So the question is: did Barnes pick up this happy phrase subliminally, did he 'annex' it for his own purposes, or did he simply assume that any literate reader would spot the reference? I should say that this is one of the public questions most dreaded by writers of fiction, the other being the equally knowing one about how much of their work is 'autobiographical'.

An enterprising editor could probably appoint a special correspondent to cover plagiarism, and see the poor guy or gal worked nearly to death. Think only of monitoring Ruth Shalit, whose secret until recently was that she filched sentences from writers – such as Fred Barnes and David Broder – whom she could be reasonably sure nobody else was bothering to read. Clever, but, as events have proved, not quite clever enough. *The New Yorker*'s February appreciation of Joseph Brodsky said that he had had a heart attack coming as surely as next Christmas, a memorable line appropriated (honestly enough I thought) from Philip Larkin's *All What Jazz.* Arianna Stassinopoulos Huffington, author of *Picasso: Creator and Destroyer,* put herself memorably in the debt of Ms Lydia Gasman, who seems to have written an earlier study of Picasso which the divine Arianna did not acquire by transcendental means. And while we are on the subject of My Sweet Lord – a favored Huffington invocation – we find that not even the world of music is immune. George Harrison had to pay a tidy sum to the Chiffons, whose 1963 smash 'He's So Fine' was ruled by a court to be the melodic ancestor of George's 1971 chartbuster. Experts have been retained on all sides to debate whether Sir Andrew Lloyd Webber ran out of inspiration and went with good old Puccini for some moments in *The Phantom of the Opera.*

Many people believe that they could easily hold down that job on the plagiarism desk. But if you think you know what plagiarism is, you are making a very large claim – the claim that you know originality when you see it. Apart from being the small change, and occasionally the major currency, of arguments within the worlds of letters and journalism, what we call plagiarism is a subject with deep roots in our literature and huge implications for the crafts of writing and speaking. Let me start with a relatively shattering example:

> I looked at the man; I saw him plain;
> Like a dead weed, gray and wan,
> Or a breath of dust. I looked again –
> And man and dog were one,
> Like the wisps of a graying dawn . . .

This comes from a poem called 'Waste Land', published in 1913. With the addition of a definite article to the title, T. S. Eliot published a rather more famous verse effort in 1922. Eliot's poem, which it would be trite to describe as the birth pang of poetic modernism, contained the imperishable line 'I will show you fear in a handful of dust'. It also speaks of 'the brown fog of a winter dawn'. See above. That's what Robert Ian Scott, a Canadian scholar, has done. He has found a number of other 'resemblances'. Aside from the title and the imagery, there is the matter of Eliot's access to the earlier poem. Madison Cawein was a Cincinnati pool-hall cashier who died one year after his 'Waste Land' was published. It was printed in a Chicago magazine of which Ezra Pound – Eliot's friend and mentor – was European editor. Eliot had submitted a poem of his own to this very magazine. Moreover, in the self-same issue in which Cawein's 'Waste Land' appeared, there was also an essay by Pound on poetry in London, which it is highly unlikely that Eliot would not have wanted to read.

Hold whatever thought you have for a moment. Here is a quotation from Dr Martin Luther King:

> In the course of its development western civilization has shifted from a colonial naivete of the frontier to the far-reaching machination of nationalism and from an agrarian pattern of occupation to the industrial one.

This comes from a seminary essay King wrote entitled 'The Sources of Fundamentalism'. It compares with reasonable smoothness to an earlier text, which instructs the curious reader that:

> In the course of its development western civilization has shifted from a colonial naivete of the frontier to the far-reaching machinations of nationalism and from an agrarian pattern of occupation to the industrial one.

The missing s in the King version could even have been a misprint.

Moving right along, we come to the great Scottish bard Hugh MacDiarmid. Here is his much-admired poem 'Perfect', published in 1939:

> I found a pigeon's skull on the machair,
> All the bones pure white and dry, and
> chalky,
> But perfect.
> Without a crack or a flaw anywhere.

At the back, rising out of the beak,
Were twin domes like bubbles of thin
bone,
Almost transparent, where the brain had been
That fixed the tilt of the wings.

And here is a passage from a book, *The Blue Bed*, by the Welsh writer Glyn Jones, published two years previously:

On her palm lay the small frail skull of a seagull, white, and complete as a pebble. It was lovely, all the bones pure white and dry, and chalky, but perfect without a crack or a flaw anywhere. At the back, rising out of the beak were twin domes like bubbles of thin bones, almost transparent, where the brain had been that fixed the tilt of the wings . . .

These all look like pretty damning, not to say open-and-shut, cases. Reputations in politics and journalism have been drastically compromised for much less. (Think of poor Senator Joe Biden caught lifting a speech from the born loser Neil Kinnock.) But a second look discloses a lot of ambiguity. Take Eliot first. Did he derive 'a handful of dust' from Madison Cawein? Or did he steal it instead from Charlotte Mew, who in a poem written in 1916 spoke of 'a handful of forgotten dust'? Or did he perhaps purloin the said handful from Virgil, Horace, Ovid, John Donne, Walter de la Mare, Alfred Tennyson, or Joseph Conrad, each of whom had employed the same phrase or something very close to it? And where had *they* taken it from?

One might also want to make the point that Eliot's verse is much more beautiful and powerful:

And I will show you something different from either
Your shadow at morning striding behind you
Or your shadow at evening rising to meet you;
I will show you fear in a handful of dust.

Contrast that to the Cawein stanza above.

What, then, about Dr King? His various academic dissertations have been found to be honeycombed with other people's property, and he seems to have had some very indulgent professors in college. It has even been alleged that part of the peroration of the 'I Have a Dream' speech – the part about 'from every mountainside, let freedom ring' – is lifted from, of all things, an address to the 1952 Republican convention by a black minister named Archibald Carey. But, of course, that line comes from 'My Country, 'Tis of Thee', which King quoted more or less completely.

And do you know how the closing passage of King's speech was supposed to have begun? If he'd followed the typed script provided by a virtual committee of do-gooders King would have said, 'And so today, let us go back to our communities as members of the international association for the advancement of creative dissatisfaction.' With the whole world watching, King realised that it wouldn't do, threw away the text in mid-stream, called on all he'd ever read, including the prophets Amos and Isaiah, and changed everything for the better – and for good. He may have done a lot of borrowing in his life, but he synthesised the borrowings into something higher.

MacDiarmid isn't such an easy case. He didn't dare advance the defence made by some friendly critics, such as Edwin Morgan, who argued that deft rearrangement of prose was itself a form of poetry. He took refuge instead in an old stratagem: 'I either automatically memorised it and subsequently thought it my own, or wrote it into one of my notebooks with the same result.' When that didn't work and he continued to be teased in print, he resorted to the argument from authority: 'As Mr T. S. Eliot said: "Minor poets borrow, major poets steal."' Actually, MacDiarmid got even that wrong. What Eliot had said was that 'immature poets imitate; mature poets steal'. And Eliot may well have knocked that off from Coleridge, who had observed after a lifetime of cormorant-like theft that 'the Eighth Commandment was not made for bards'.

A good rule of thumb for young plagiarists starting out in life might well be the one set down by George Moore. 'Taking something from one man and making it worse is plagiarism.' To 'making it worse' one could add 'or leaving it exactly the same'. Nexis and various computer systems may be making the problem more acute, but nobody who takes either their own writing or their own plagiarism seriously can afford to go about the place saying that they 'find' they have written something composed by somebody else.

When Princess Michael of Kent, one of the Queen's dimmer relatives, was shown to have nicked some material word for word for her biography of the Empress Eugénie, she got a spokesman to tell the press, 'It seems that, when she read her notes a long time after making them, she forgot that she had written down actual phrases from one of the books she was using.' Seems, madam! Nay, it is; I know not 'seems'. We have a certain respect for the professionalism of the forger and the counterfeiter. For kleptomaniacs we entertain no such feeling, but rather resentment at their sloppiness – and the suspicion that in some pathetic way they hope, or need, to get caught.

'Great literature', wrote Robert Benchley, 'must spring from an upheaval in the author's soul. If that upheaval is not present, then it must come from the works of any other author which happen to be handy and easily adapted.' Matching this, Dorothy Parker remarked after some time on the West Coast that the only ism that Hollywood cared about was plagiarism. Where would most of our culture be without borrowing, adaptation, and derivatives? Cineasts even have a fancy word for lifting, *hommage*. Why else would we require the copyright industry?

Originality is a quality so rarely met with in humans that when it does occur it is often disputed. Sir Isaac Newton, for example, took great credit for propounding a law of planetary motion. This was to the outrage of his rival Robert Hooke, who maintained that Newton had drawn on his work as well as that of others. At that date – 1678 – the modern world of the scholarly journal and the patent was not yet formed. Newton made no direct admission, but did tactfully say that 'if I have seen farther it is by standing on the shoulders of giants'. This is commonly known as Newton's Aphorism, though it had appeared as recently as 1651 in a collection of proverbs by George Herbert. According to the magisterial Robert K. Merton in his labyrinthine book *On the Shoulders of Giants*, other claimants to the coinage of the phrase include Bernard of Chartres in about 1126, John of Salisbury, Henri de Mondeville, and Robert Burton (he of the *Anatomy of Melancholy*). And this is to cite only some medieval and postmedieval candidates, since the remark was probably first made in classical times. Among later imitators were Coleridge – as usual – John Stuart Mill, Friedrich Engels, Frank Harris, and Sigmund Freud, all of whom in their different ways had a right to it, and some of whom (though not Mill, who had read everything and had a conscience) may have believed that they were uttering it for the first time. Thus Newton's most subtle and guarded admission of a possible 'debt' is itself one of the phrases most frequently 'borrowed'.

A decade ago, watching Ronald Reagan give his famous speech on the night of the *Challenger* calamity, and wanting as ever to resist his sentimental appeal, I became convinced that I had heard his closing lines somewhere. If you remember, he spoke of the dead astronauts as having 'slipped the surly bonds of earth', to 'touch the face of God'. The White House declined to help me in my search for the origins of this couplet. I finally discovered that the words came from a sonnet, 'High Flight', by John Gillespie Magee Jr, which was read out as the regular closedown on Washington's Channel 9 TV station.

Not a bad little story, I thought: Ron falling asleep in front of the TV, dimly catching some rather saccharine verse, adapting it in a hurry for a major address, and quite forgetting that the *Challenger* crew had, thanks to those O-rings, entirely failed to slip the surly bonds of earth. But then I realised that this would be a cheap 'Gotcha'. The only grandeur that Reagan's speech possessed was furnished by this purloined finery. No property had actually gone missing, so there had been no theft. A minor poet had become useful on a major occasion.

So I leave you with the words of that famous dopehead Thomas de Quincey, himself no mean plagiarist and the very man who first published accusations of Coleridge's thievery: 'It is undeniable, that thousands of feeble writers are constantly at work, who subsist by Plagiarism, more or less covert. It is equally undeniable ... that thousands of feeble critics subsist by detecting plagiarisms as imitations, real or supposed.'

Just as writers should beware of joining the first category, so readers should not be too eager to enlist in the second. Now, spot the unattributed quotation in this column. At least, I hope there's only one.

First published as 'Steal this Article' in *Vanity Fair*, May 1996

Ode to the West Wing

The 'Washington novel' is bound and confined by a number of relatively strict conventions, and by one limiting fact. The limiting fact is that the United States, alone among developed nations with the possible exception of Australia (and the recent anomaly of Germany), chooses to locate its capital city in the provinces. The effect of this on the national letters cannot be calculated; but let us just agree that an aspiring writer in Texas, say, or Wisconsin does not number among his aspirations the desire to relocate the garret to the District of Columbia. In *The Company of Critics*, Michael Walzer writes semi-humorously that he, like most of his friends and colleagues, has never really even been to Washington except to protest. For Updike, Bellow, and Roth, the action is elsewhere. Norman Mailer has, admittedly, attempted the city by way of nonfiction or its close relative, the historical reconstruction of old skullduggeries for fictional purposes. But only Gore Vidal has really annexed the capital as a novelist, and he enjoys the advantage – among many others – of being in some sense 'from' Washington and of therefore possessing the right combination of familiarity and contempt. This was the same advantage possessed by Henry Adams, whose *Democracy* is the foundation of the genre.

It is slightly surprising to see how much fealty is still demonstrated to the Adams model. Most 'Washington novels' still have the same cast: a President (inescapable), a British ambassador, a prominent hostess, a lobbyist or journalist, and a senator. Adams (who published *Democracy* anonymously and hoped that people would think the author was John Hay) even had a Clinton and a Gore among his characters. And he capitalised the question of motive. Mrs Lightfoot Lee is alive to the objection of her metropolitan and cosmopolitan friends that in moving to Washington she is condemning herself to live 'among the illiterate swarm of ordinary people who . . . represented constituencies so dreary that in comparison New York was a New Jerusalem, and Broad Street a grove of Academe.' Nonetheless:

> What she wished to see, she thought, was the clash of interests, the interests
> of forty millions of people and a whole continent, centering at Washington;

guided, restrained, controlled, or unrestrained and uncontrollable, by men of ordinary mould; the tremendous forces of government, and the machinery of society, at work. What she wanted, was POWER.

What she gets, of course, is corruption and cynicism and a near-insupportable climate, plus some unwelcome attention from an over-mighty senator. Already, the elements are in place. Allen Drury's *Advise and Consent*, published almost eighty years later, has Lord Claude Maudulayne instead of Lord Skye as British ambassador, and Mrs Phelps Harrison as the hostess. In this story, and in its numberless imitators, senators have 'manes', rooms are filled with smoke, party allegiances are strong and distinct, regional characteristics are heavily stressed among members of Congress, and newspapers are ruthlessly committed to breaking stories at any cost. The sexual temperature is set fairly low, because everything is sublimated by POWER, but animal magnetism is allowed. (A more recent sub-genre, written by Mrs Benjamin Bradlee and Mrs John Dean, turns up the thermostat a bit here and was indeed characterised by Christopher Buckley, one of the most deft local practitioners, as 'cliterature'. In this narrative, a lot of heavy drinking gets done and a crisis is often precipitated by the expiring, in the arms of the illicit, of some high officer of state.

In general, those responsible for this output are either journalists or retired practitioners of the power game. Hence the attachment to formula, which is also expected by the reading public and demanded by the sorts of publisher and Hollywood executive for whom it is actually composed. There are three crippling general disadvantages. The first is that virtually no one has ever invented a successful or believable President. (John Updike, who himself brought off quite a serviceable President Buchanan, points out that this also spoils almost all Washington screenplays.) With, again, the grand exception of Gore Vidal – who has had the nerve to fictionalise actual presidents and succeed at the task – fiction's chief executives are all craggy, troubled populists or faint Kennedy derivatives. Few authors have the nerve to do what Adams did, and represent the president as an impotent, transient stick insect; a plaything of the influence of others.

Second disadvantage: Washington is not a town awash with drink and smoke and sex, peopled with white manes and gruff regional charac-ters, and obsessed with power and partisanship. Nor is it a place where the remorseless press stalks the corridors in search of a story, any story, with which to embarrass the great and swell its own circulation. It's a near-teetotal, thank-you-for-not-smoking city, with an early bedtime and a National Prayer Breakfast and a stunted libido. There hasn't been a mane since Gene McCarthy, and the most striking senatorial hair ('belonging' to Strom Thurmond, admittedly a distinctive regional character) is a laughable dye-job. The tameness and complicity of the press, meanwhile, is something that has to be seen up close in order to be believed. The favourite word of this press – favourite, I mean, in point of approbation – is 'bipartisan'. That is also the favourite word on the Hill and in the White House. Consensus is the highest value. Fund raising, which both determines bipartisanship and is determined by it, is the principal practice of the city as well as its chief recreation.

Third disadvantage: when real crises and scandals occur, such as the exposure of Richard Nixon's court or Ronald Reagan's state within a state, they are so arresting as to make fiction superfluous. It would be a bold thriller writer who topped Kennedy's smuggling of a gun moll into his bedroom, or Reagan's telephonic musings on the End of Time, relayed in late-night calls to the head of the America-Israel Political Action Committee, or Nixon's chats with Chuck Colson about blowing up the Brookings Institution.

Nor does this city, so self-obsessed at one level, care to look much at itself in the fictional looking-glass. Larry McMurtry, who was once Washington's chief bookseller as well as its senior novelist-in-residence, wrote a book called *Cadillac Jack* in 1982. It is his only Washington fiction. In an early chapter, it features an amasingly recognisable Washington pundit holding forth in a pulverising manner in the drawing room of an amasingly recognisable Washington hostess. (The subject is South Yemen, pointed like a dagger at the heart of North Yemen.) McMurtry once told me that he had later been in that very drawing room, in the presence of that very hostess and that very pundit, when they decided to flatter him. 'Time to turn your talents to the capital, Larry. You should essay the dragons of Washington.' As he put it: 'What was I supposed to say? That I had already done it, and that they were both in it?'

Given the oppressive weight of these predecessors, these conventions, and these limitations, it is essential to choose between the tediously authentic model, symbolised by *Advise and Consent*, where at least everything depicted *could* have happened and where the only problem lies in making the reader care, and the frankly fantastic option (Tom Clancy, Jeffrey Archer), where the city is just a backdrop for melo-drama. One or the other. Not both. Charles McCarry's eighth novel, a six-hundred-pager marketed, inevitably, as the work of a 'Washington insider', is a failure because it is pedantic and didactic for whole furlongs of its immense length, *and* utterly, artlessly fantastic for the remainder. Try, if you will, to imagine C. P. Snow giving himself ample time to summarise a plot devised by Ian Fleming:

Mallory had never imagined that Lockwood would call him at eleven o'clock and offer to hand over the presidency. The advice he had given Lockwood the night before was excellent, and following it would certainly be in the best interests of the country and of Lockwood himself. But Lockwood was a politician to the depths of his being, and his office was all he had. Like most political figures of his generation who embraced progressive convictions, Lockwood had never in his adult life been anything but a politician. The only life he knew was public life. Unlike his heroes, Jefferson, Jackson, and Lincoln, he had never taken a mistress, fought a duel, or stood up for an unpopular cause. Every idea he had ever espoused was politically correct and brought him praise and approval among the opinion makers. The only money he had ever earned was government money: he had gone through a state college on an athletic scholarship, served for a while in the Army, where he played football and basketball instead of leading a platoon of rifles in Korea like many of his classmates now dead.

Back home, after marrying a rich girl from the Bluegrass whose family had influence in rural politics, he started running for office on the basis of his lovable personality, his humble childhood (he came from the hollows of the eastern Kentucky mountains), and his celebrity as an athlete. He had nothing to go back to, no life to lead.

The only energy is supplied by the same source as that which powers Mr McCarry himself: a very strong and very confused emotion of class resentment, in which only rich Republicans and certain kinds of soldiers can really empathise with the American poor, or with the rank and file in general.

About the novel you must know that it turns on the computerised theft of a presidential election at some time in the imaginable future; that this theft was committed by overzealous subordinates who may not have had the winning man's interests uppermost in mind; that this same winning man was already in trouble for ordering the assassination of a Middle Eastern sheik to prevent the detonation of stolen nuclear devices; that in the end a canker at the heart of the state is rooted out by an improvised 'bipartisan' alliance.

About the novelist you must know that he is a former spook from Langley, Virginia, that he has written many other thrillers which feature a character named Paul Christopher (CIA man with thwarted literary streak), and that he was chief speech writer to Henry Cabot Lodge when the latter ran with Nixon in 1960. In earlier adventures of Paul Christopher, like *The Tears of Autumn*, the original sin of modern American politics is held to be the theft, by the Kennedy dynasty, of that very election. (In *The Tears of Autumn*, North and South Vietnamese special forces join up to eliminate Kennedy and avenge the assassination of Diem, and it is stated: 'Kennedy wasn't elected President. Nixon was.... The Democrats are in the White House by fraud.')

Regularly drenched as we are – especially by the Clinton team – in

Ersatz Kennedyisms, it might be quite pleasurable to suspend such disbelief as remains in this hypothesis. There is persuasive evidence that the Kennedys rigged a decisive precinct or two, especially in Illinois, in 1960. And there is a mystery about the failure of that worst of bad losers Richard Nixon to complain about the fact. (Likeliest explanation: the words 'full election inquiry' would have had an unwelcome ring to his ear.) There's no mystery at all about the interim conclusion that Nixon drew, which was that he would never be out-smarted again. The covert interventions in the 1968 and 1972 campaigns are often 'explained', usually sotto voce, by his sympathisers as part of a rough-justice revenge for the fraud in Cook Country in 1960.

It would, in other words, be rather exciting if a real thriller writer decided to backdate Watergate to mayor Daley and let the chips (this style is infectious) fall where they may. Yet when Lockwood's rival, the stainless Republican Cincinnatus Franklin Mallory, is told by a cynic that 'elections have been stolen before', he can only reply:

> Yes, and look what happened afterward. Assassination, war, scandal, cover-up, the wholesale falsification of history. The people behind this kind of thing are always idealists.

So we know right there and then that this will be a work of rancor, and that it demands only one variety of disbelief-suspension. The political level never rises above that of a Herblock *Washington Post* cartoon, where donkeys and elephants are shown, with labels on their flanks for the easily instructed, hitting each other over the head in apparently genuine and passionate disagreement.

The novel doesn't actually feature a British ambassador, though it is peppered with knowing, 'special relationship'-style quotes from Kipling and various English monarchs. It is, however, Anglophile to the point of Anglophobia; not an uncommon trope among members of the 'intelligence community'. In order to believe the story, you have to believe that there exists an occult Shelley Society, based on a vile coven of Yale men, which is sworn to enact the poet's dream of an egalitarian Utopia. It reaches into Congress, the Supreme Court, the media, and Wall street, though not (a singular omission in the circumstances) into the armed forces or the police. So great are its reach and power and strength, and so avid is it for a constitutional coup, that it can persuade the tainted President Lockwood (see above) to nominate its most extreme and most identifiable member to be Chief Justice. This is as if we were to open the papers, find William Kunstler being nominated by Sam Nunn to head the court, and read every 'liberal media' editorial applauding the sapience of the proposition. One of McCarry's sympathetic characters explains for us the moral and intellectual squalor of Shelleyism:

Prometheus Unbound reads like a dream Stalin had in an opium den. Shelley describes heaven on earth as a place where people fall asleep and when they wake up they're not human any longer. They've taken off their human nature and condition like a disguise; therefore they're happy because now they're all alike, thinking beautiful thoughts. Utopia always turns out to be an eternal prison camp with people like Shelley in the commandant's office.

To which a secret Shelleyan who happens to be present replies as follows:

'What absolute sick nonsense!' Hammett cried, recoiling.

Since Hammett is the Kunstler figure, and since he is elsewhere represented as being preternaturally cold, fishlike, reserved, ruthless, and stoical, it seems peculiar that he should fall below the disciplinary standard of Skull and Bones, and just at the point, too, where the merest 'gadzooks' might give the whole game away, recoil or no recoil. But McCarry can't help himself writing like this.

In order to foil the fell designs of the dead poet's society, he has assembled the most extraordinary roster of stock characters. There is, of course, the pugilistic Shamus private eye with the rumpled look and the deceptive, shrewd way with him:

His lantern-jawed Celtic face was freckled and battered – skewed broken nose, thick eyebrows interrupted by thicker white scars, more scars around the brightgreen eyes. Red hair grew on the back of his bony, large-knuckled hands.

This son of Erin is a puzzle to the evil patrician Julian Hubbard, who as a confirmed Shelleyan is scheming against the honest men in the District of Columbia, and has wormed his way quite near the throne. He is baffled by the stripes on the Hibernian's tie until:

As Julian stepped closer in order to shake hands, he saw that the stripes were actually made up of a printed motto that read – he squinted to make it out – '*Non carborundum bastardum est*,' which Julian remembered was beer-joint Latin for 'Don't let the bastards grind you down.'

This illustrates the hazards of slumming for an author like McCarry, who sounds just as awkward, in his hearty condescension to the other ranks, as did his mentors like Kipling, Sapper, and John Buchan. (Incidentally, the actual beer-joint Latin reads '*Nil illegitimi carborundum*': McCarry's version would mean, if anything, 'the bastard is not ground down'.)

Who can be on next, if not the imperturbable and devoted black retainer, who appears on cue as the prop and stay to drunken, bleary, but decent Speaker Tucker Allenborough, the Texan populist with the heart of gold,

> Albert Tyler (Lockwood had always called him Albert), an aged black waiter and boyhood friend of Attenborough's from West Texas who had worked in the House for thirty years.

'Yes, sir, Mr Speaker', Albert is actually made to say when the speaker lapses alcoholically into Scripture. 'Mighty fine passage.'

Not all of freedom's allies are folkloric cutouts. Mallory, the once and future President who has been cheated of his election, has several safe houses in Washington, Maryland, and Virginia, as well as the control of a vast private corporation and the use of a top-notch private security force. This force is composed of sexless boy-girl teams, operating in pairs. Every month, we learn on page 63, each of these agents has to pass a fitness test in which he or she must

> run five miles, bike ten miles, swim two miles, and then, in less than two seconds, while stil standing chest-deep in the water, fire eighteen vinyl-tipped explosive/expansive rounds from a 6mm pistol into a three-inch bull's-eye from a distance of fifty yards.

It's just as well that McCarry mentions these exacting qualifications so early on, because on page 546, nearly five hundred pages later, all of them are required to fire the burst that puts the narrative out of its misery. His linking of the stipulations to their eventual deployment is the very essence of his concept of a plot device.

Other pockets of traditional Washington are also immune to the Shelleyan virus, and are reassuringly populated with the sorts of salon-fodder and Georgetown reliables who customarily swell a progress and fill a scene in storybooks of this kidney. At one such soirée:

> After looking Zarah up and down, Bitsy, a still-voluptuous former first runner-up for the title of Miss Oklahoma who was many years younger than her white-maned, corpulent husband, smiled a dazzling contestant's smile and moved protectively closer to the senator.

A relief in a way, for McCarry as well as the reader, to have got the senatorial mane out of the way. Or, as McCarry has his journalist-character confess, while he 'wrote all this out in green luminescent letters':

> The computer screen, so like another consciousness in its eager response to every thought and word, had an almost hypnotic effect on him.

This piece of work – bad writing about bad writing – is an oblique clue to McCarry's style of composition, or better say compilation. It also introduces one of McCarry's animating grudges, which is the one he holds against the press. Interviewed recently by *The New Yorker*, William Kristol had this to say about the most pelted target of the conservative and neoconservative vernacular:

> I admit it – the liberal media were never that powerful, and the whole thing was often used as an excuse by conservatives for conservative failures.

This is a piece of magnanimity in victory from a former Reagan and Quayle man, and a current Murdoch man, but it is nonetheless welcome for that. Considering the insipidity of the press since at least the Watergate hearings, it is also an overdue recognition. Charles McCarry in fiction cannot even contemplate the concession that Kristol makes in fact. He goes at the thing foot, horse, and guns. The reporter Macalaster, so essential to the turgid narration and thus indispensably present throughout, is nonetheless a member of a subversive profession, and so:

> He would never have gone to college if he had not been inducted into the Army at nineteen and sent to Vietnam in the place of some rich kid who dodged the draft. His social background won him assignment as a rifleman in the First Infantry Division and he was wounded twice by enemy fire, both times superficially, in battles around the Iron Triangle.
>
> While attending Williams College in the early 1970s as a representative of the deserving poor, he had been bullied in class and undermarked by leftist professors while being regarded as a babykiller by members of the antiwar movement, who constituted the majority of the student body. At the same time, Movement chicks from Bennington College who imagined themselves to be undercover members of the Viet Cong crawled through his window at night, as if he were a prisoner of war who excited their sexual fantasies. As Williams Macalaster discovered in himself a deep, undiscriminating curiosity and a gift for writing, and after serving an apprenticeship on a Buffalo newspaper, he got a job with a paper in Washington.

Here is all the self-pity of the American right, along with some of its prurience, condensed into one clichéclotted passage. (The stuff about class, sex, and the veteran might be easier to take, though not by much, if it had not come from the pen that once produced phrases to be intoned by Cabot Lodge.) One wants to ask: How did Macalaster find a niche in the degraded business of Washington journalism if he was so gung-ho and wholesome. McCarry solves this by having him ostracised within the profession and confined to 'writing books, appearing on talk shows on cable television, and writing a twice-weekly syndicated column'. Nobody lives in Washington and does those three things and occupies a political position to the left of Walter Mondale. (Let's not be so tasteless as to 'reopen the wounds of Vietnam' and inquire how a twice-wounded rifleman gets himself bullied at Williams College.)

The question now arises: Is this a nasty book, or just a stupid one? We are, remember, supposed to be in an unprecedented constitutional interregnum, with no lawful president in the White House and cabals afoot and nuclear weapons on the loose, to say nothing of the Shelleyans closing in with their weird Whiffenpoof oaths. Yet dozens of pages trudge by, and whole swaths of conversation and explanation occur, without so much as a single microsecond of tension. Subplots and characters break the surface only to vanish utterly; points in the evolution of the story are established only to be entirely forgotten. For example, in a moment of all-American sentiment or whimsy, McCarry elects at first to show both rivals for the presidency as friends beneath the skin:

> In Lockwood's mind, everything that had happened between them in their struggle over the presidency was just politics. He was a throwback to the age when American politicians were Christians first and ideologues second. [When *was* that, by the way?] Such men forgave and forgot: to them politics was a game, not a religion. Lockwood had been Mallory's friend for more than twenty years, and Mallory had been his.
>
> In spite of all the fouls on both sides, he was Mallory's friend even now. Nothing could change this . . . [etc., etc.]

In support of this redundancy-laden paragraph (one can presume that if someone has been someone's friend for twenty years, the other someone will have been his friend also) McCarry has Mallory and Lockwood meet in the White House for a man-to-man and a one-to-one. The *longueurs* of this encounter would make Lord Snow himself wonder if he wasn't holding up the action. Yet for the remainder of the story, the plot is needlessly and repeatedly convoluted by the insertion of 'intermediaries' who have to perform feats of disguise and evasion in order to relay simple messages between these two old and intimate friends.

Irritating distractions have their counterpart, in this masterpiece of inattention, in obvious omissions and inconsistencies. The sinister radical lesbian named Slim, who is a pliant tool of the Shelleyans and who is commissioned to research and discredit poor boozy Speaker Attenborough, is unaware at the dénouement of whether or not he is married. Julian Hubbard is described on one page as being sexually impotent because of his blood-pressure pills but then, only a few pages later:

> Like the giant he was, he plucked her from the floor and bore her, kissing and groaning, toward the bed. And as his great ursine weight fell upon her with a brutality that made her gasp with pleasure . . .

Yes, yes. After a while, I stopped listing the contradictions. Why should I care, if McCarry does not?

What he does care about, and does prosecute with some energy and consistency, is the rehabilitation of Richard Milhous Nixon. As the impeachment of President Lockwood looms, the near impeachment of President Nixon is recalled. One of the good-guy lawyers opines:

> Richard Nixon seems to have been condemned not for what he did, for which there was no documentary evidence until the Supreme Court, in effect, ordered him to incriminate himself by releasing the famous tapes, but for what a majority of the House of Representatives and the news media perceived him to be – a bad man.

(Bear in mind, incidentally, that the above is an unusually lively sample of McCarry's dialogue.) The plain fact – that Nixon got off scot-free – nonetheless dilutes the pure self-pity that his partisans desire to feel on his behalf. It must be dealt with somehow. So McCarry has President Lockwood say, of his disgraced predecessor:

> The fact is, he resigned the presidency because he knew he didn't have the votes in the Senate to be acquitted. He thought of the country, of what would happen if the government was paralyzed by a trial he couldn't win.

(McCarry here seems to have forgotten that he has already described Lockwood as an unflinching spokesman for the politically correct.)

The role model for this book seems to be *The Spike*, an atrocious thriller penned jointly by Robert Moss and Arnaud de Borchgrave, and published at the dawn of the Reagan era. *The Spike*, too, was based on preposterous assumptions (a determinedly liberal and gullible media, an unswervingly partisan and leftist Democratic Party, a cadre of determined Washington internationalists), but it did have some brio as a yarn, did have some oomph in its bedroom scenes, did feature intelligible motives, and did bear in mind the relationship between one action and another. Partly as a result, it succeeded in influencing the local *Zeitgeist* and in creating the atmosphere for a man like William Case. No such luck, I would venture, for this effort. McCarry is from the same milieu as Moss, de Borchgrave (and Casey), but he doesn't know plot from shinola and his timing is off. Seeking to express the fullest possible contempt for the William Kunstler type whom the Democrats desire to make Chief Justice, McCarry has one of his characters say:

> But then, what does anybody really know about the son of a bitch except that he's a friend of any poor suffering underdog that knows how to make a bomb out of fertilizer and diesel oil?

This, I predict, will not be the keynote novel of the age of speaker Gingrich, and of Congressman Steve Stockman.

First published as 'Ode to the West Wing' (a review of *Shelley's Heart* by Charles McCarry) in *New York Review of Books*, 13 July 1995

IV

'For Their Own Sake . . .'

O'Brian's Great Voyage

On any approximately proportionate view of history, of the kind that may become more gradually available to us as the long day of the twentieth century wanes, the Napoleonic conflict would deserve to be called the First World War. Never before had two great powers and their volatile allies mobilised their societies so extensively to contend for mastery over so immense a reach of the earth's surface. Great engagements were fought at the gates of Moscow, in the Baltic, at the mouth of the Nile, in Italy, Turkey, and Spain, but the reverberations extended, by way of proxy fighting, to China, Australia, and other barely charted latitudes. Both North and South America, and the intervening Caribbean basin, were drawn in, and found their internal politics conditioned by French and English rivalries and allegiances. Hitherto obscure archipelagoes and islands such as the Falklands and Mauritius became decisive. Local nationalisms were inflamed and manipulated from Chile to Ireland. Macaulay later wrote of Frederick the Great that, as a consequence of his perfidies, scalpings occurred by the Great Lakes and butcheries on the coast of Coromandel. How much more true is this of the long struggle between imperial and Georgian Britain and Jacobin and Bonapartist France. Conflicts to which tradition has awarded other customary names – the Peninsular War, the War of 1812 – were in actuality subplots of this great contest. Stendhal, Tolstoy, Wordsworth, Beethoven, and Goya all spent themselves trying to set down some of it.

This astonishing global tumult, which also involved important battles over religion and ideology, and which gave rise to convulsive changes in the technological and scientific apparatus available to men and to governments, is the macrocosmic context that was chosen, with great daring and address, by the late Patrick O'Brian. His fictional settings and allusions range – to use rather a paltry term – from the towns of Andalusia and Albania to the convict settlements in Botany Bay, the colonial outposts of Hong Kong and Calcutta, and the forts and monasteries of the Andes: from China to Peru as was once said by another author. But precisely because the deciding element in this war was that of sea power, he also summons the decidedly microcosmic atmosphere of the decks, holds, and cabins of a seagoing fighting machine.

It was the sloops, frigates, and men-of-war of the Royal Navy which first blockaded revolutionary France and then, by supplying her enemies and terrifying her friends, wore her down. A certain autonomy had to be given to commanders so far from home base, and this epoch marks the transition of British oceanic tactics from something quite like piracy into something more nearly resembling a professionalised if still highly mercenary imperial discipline. A person holding official seal and warrant in such a gigantic war could still appear in the character of a free-lance or aquatic knight-errant, though he would have been prudent to bear in mind, as Captain Aubrey must do in *The Mauritius Command* (1977), that members of the Board of Admiralty were also important shareholders in the East India Company. In the figure of Jack Aubrey, and that of his co-conspirator Stephen Maturin, O'Brian contrived over the space of twenty novels to present this first world war in all its grandeur and scope, yet meticulously shaped to human scale. A warship 'cleared' for action is a vessel in which the men's hammocks are swung into the rigging, and in which the partitions separating the officers' cabins are removed. Thus we have a chance to meet – as naval officers did and as army officers did not – the members of the lower orders. Barrett Bonden and Thomas Pullings, promoted by pluck and ability, become recognisable players as the chapters (they are in some ways chapters rather than books) knit themselves into a sequence.

Beseeching the delegates at the Democratic convention in 1980 to remember a recently departed so-called happy warrior, President Jimmy Carter outdid even himself for prodigious bathos by bidding them keep a moment of silence for 'Hubert, Horatio – Hornblower'. The absurd slip was impressive subliminal testimony to the work of C. S. Forester, whose earlier set of novels had magnetised readers by the same combination of historical narrative and individual drama. (Ernest Hemingway once said that he recommended Forester to every literate person he knew.) Aside from his authorship of such classics as *The African Queen*, Forester produced eleven novels to make up the Hornblower saga. The periods are slightly discrepant – Hornblower joins the navy in 1793 while Aubrey and Maturin meet in the early 1800s – but not the least sense in which O'Brian may be called daring is the extent to which he invites comparison.

Indeed he does rather more than invite it. Rereading the first fifty pages of *A Ship of the Line* (1938), I found Hornblower consumed with worry about a shortage of able-bodied crew for his commission, concerned about the coast of Catalonia, overwhelmed with love for a senior officer's wife (while assailed with unworthy second thoughts about his own), gnawed with anxiety about promotion, highly offended at the role played by parliamentary and political corruption, obsessed with the real gold in his epaulettes, proud of the engraved sword presented him by the Patriotic Fund (which he has to put straight into pawn), preoccupied by the slow rate of fire from his broadsides, and haunted by the pressing need of capital that can only come from a successful capture of an enemy merchant vessel or 'prize'. He makes regular use of expressions like 'handsomely, there', and 'give you joy'. He has a rather irritating manservant aboard ship, but feels a deep peace when he can be alone and look out of the stern windows in his private cabin. The opening also features a stupefying official banquet with many toasts, at which he does not shine socially. And all of this, as I say, in fifty pages.

Anybody who has experienced even partial immersion in the O'Brian odyssey will instantly recognise that this, in every detail and respect, is the world of Captain Jack Aubrey. Moreover, Forester's sequence followed Hornblower up the ladder of promotion from *Mr Midshipman Hornblower* to *Admiral Hornblower in the West Indies*, a struggle for advancement in rank which O'Brian emulated with almost pedantic fealty from *Master and Commander* (1970) right up to last year's concluding *Blue at the Mizzen*, where Aubrey achieved admiral's status with an entitlement to the pennant described in the title. The only salient differences, on a first inspection, are that Hornblower is thin and phlegmatic while in respect of the humours Aubrey is rotund and jovial, Hornblower suffers dreadfully from seasickness while Aubrey does not, and, though both men dislike having clergymen aboard, Hornblower is a stern agnostic and student of Gibbon, whereas Aubrey thinks that a dose of religion is at least good for morale.

O'Brian gains an edge, however, with his appetite for stark realism. 'The traditions of the Royal Navy', that 'former naval person' Winston Churchill is supposed to have said while stationed at the Admiralty, 'are rum, sodomy and the lash'. Like Hornblower (and like Lord Nelson himself) Jack Aubrey is no fanatic applicant of the cat-o'-nine-tails and the ritual flogging, a topic that has generated a whole specialist literature for certain aficionados in the English market. But he does have a robust attitude toward the making of babies and he does attend, in a way that would discountenance Hornblower fans, to the promptings of his male generative member. So does his accomplice, the good Dr Maturin. So indeed do the inhabitants of the lower deck.

O'Brian avoids anything too lurid or graphic, but he takes the facts of life very much as they come, and these narratives are salted, as one might say, with illustrative incidents of every sort of carnality (including the bestial, since animals had to be shipped for milk and protein) and also of the gross reality of attending to bodily functions in a confined and hazardous space. We are spared neither the scent of the bordello, nor the pox-ridden customers of the ship's surgeon, nor the reek of the head and the privy. As for rum, we come to appreciate how shrewd were the severe British Sea Lords who mandated a stunning daily draft of it as the only indulgence permitted afloat.

There is another respect in which O'Brian repeatedly outclasses Forester, and that is the political and cultural. 'I knew no harm of Bonaparte, and plenty of the Squire', once wrote G. K. Chesterton, who even as a Tory quite understood that the government of Pitt had been fighting social revolution as well as 'the Corsican usurper'. (It was the Duke of Wellington who, after Waterloo and the Congress of Vienna, became the great postwar antagonist of the Reform Bill.) Not since Thomas Flanagan produced *The Year of the French* (1979) to open his Hibernian trilogy has any novelist so well evoked the subculture of radical and millenarian sects, the boiling-up of revolutionary and Utopian ideas, that formed so strong a current in the English life of that period. (One says English, though in fact the concept of a Briton, or of the British, was being forged out of stubborn Welsh, Scottish, and Irish materials at that very time.) Dr Stephen Maturin is the sensitive register of these political pressures and temperatures.

By the time we are introduced to him, he has already outlived by luck his sympathy for the rising of the United Irishmen – Flanagan's great subject – in the quixotic French-backed revolt of Wolfe Tone and Lord Edward Fitzgerald in 1798. He is, moreover, a Catholic in a time of English penal laws against Papacy, and of part-Catalan bastardised parentage during the changes of alliance between Castilian Spain and the Parisian Directory. His protean Celtic/Pyrenean identity supplies the ideal counterpoint to Jack Aubrey, who is a bluff and unreflecting Tory in the service of a navy dominated by Whigs, utilitarians, and other sophists and calculators.

O'Brian is not always easy to cite, because his many terse moments of wit and aptitude require context for their explication, and because he allows himself so much time and room for the development of his tale, but here for example is what Jack Aubrey finds when he is returned to English shores in *Blue at the Mizzen*, during one of the several truces that punctuate the long war to which he devotes his life:

> It is true that Jack's game dwindled strangely; but on a nearby estate, which had been subjected to rigorous enclosure – no common land with rights of grazing, cutting fern, taking turf – there was not so much as a single rabbit to be seen. Then again, although the Corn Laws endeavoured to keep the price of wheat at £4, taxing imports accordingly, a great deal of American and Continental food now came in, legally or illegally, and farming was no longer a very profitable business. The landowners suffered, of course; and most of the farmers suffered even more; but the people who were really ground right down into misery were the men, women and children who

worked the land – those who had not so much as a decent garden left after enclosure.

Meanwhile Maturin encounters the home base of the sect that commands the allegiance of so many crew members of HMS *Surprise*. One needs an edition of E. P. Thompson at hand to follow his nose for the scent of plebeian nonconformism.

> 'There is the Sethians' chapel,' he said, nodding in the direction of a white building with enormous brilliant letters of brass on its face. 'Seth,' they read. 'What is Seth? Who is Seth?'
> 'He was one of Adam's sons, brother to Cain and Abel.'

In a few strokes, then, O'Brian has thickened and deepened his text by reminding us that this was the era of William Blake and his Muggletonian transcendental faction, and of the bitter and melancholy rural poetry of John Clare. The good ship *Surprise* is described as 'an ark of dissent' in *The Wine-Dark Sea* (1993), containing as it does 'Brownists, Sethians, Arminians, Muggletonians and several others, generally united in a seamanlike tolerance when afloat and always in a determined hatred of tithes when ashore'. Later, when a radical French officer escapes Aubrey's custody en route to Argentina, it is freely acknowledged that Mennonite sympathies among the hands have allowed him to do so.

It is Maturin who makes all the difference here. For a sidekick, Hornblower had only the dogged Mr Bush, a character of John Bullish stoicism. Jack Aubrey ships out with the Georgian equivalent of a Straussian intellectual, a man of many parts but with a good many of them hidden. To Jack he shows his command of medicine and natural history and the classics, but beneath the waterline he is also an intelligence expert familiar with complex codes, and a closet revolutionary. In the very first novel of the series, *Master and Commander*, Maturin is shocked to find himself on the same ship as a former subversive associate, and fears exposure. When the two men are left alone at last, they recall the recruiting oath of the United Irishmen, a test that begins:

> 'Are you straight?'
> 'I am.'
> 'How straight?'
> 'As straight as a rush.'
> 'Go on then.'
> 'In truth, in trust, in unity and liberty.'
> 'What have you got in your hand?'
> 'A green bough.'
> 'Where did it first grow?'

'In America.'
'Where did it bud?'
'In France.'
'Where are you going to plant it?'

The answer to the last question, not disclosed until later, is 'In the crown of Great Britain.' Without quite forsaking his radical republican past, and while cleaving very strongly to the cause of Catalan independence, Maturin has come to detest Bonapartism and he sails, pro tem, under King George's flag. He puts me in mind of Conor Cruise O'Brien's analysis of Edmund Burke: an Irishman wearing English patriotic colours against France, the better to plead by indirection for the cause of Ireland, India, and the American colonies.[1]

Front-line fighters and espionage agents may need, and display, entirely different styles, but they possess one essential piece of hard-won experience in common, which is that they are both in great danger from their superiors. Confined as he is in a wooden shell, Jack Aubrey may still count himself a king of infinite space while he is out on the ocean. Nonetheless, a twitch upon the thread held by the Admiralty and he can be court-martialed and dishonoured, or reduced to penury and shame by a malign superior. As for Stephen Maturin, an indiscretion may be enough to expose him and his network of European informants to ruin, while any treachery in the sinuous world of the London spymasters will condemn him to torture and/or death. We get a hint of that universe in *The Fortune of War* (1979), where a Mr Wallis is described as 'an old, tried colleague, with no vices but the parsimony, meanness, and cold lechery so usual in intelligence'. Not one of the twenty novels fails to discover our heroes fatally jeopardised by their 'own' side. In *Desolation Island* (1978), the fifth in the series, we find the following:

> In former days Jack had cuckolded the Admiral, an unscrupulous, revengeful man who would not hesitate to break him if he could. During his naval career, Jack had made a great many friends in the service, but he had also made a surprising number of enemies for so amiable a man: some had been jealous of his success; some (and these were his seniors) had found him too independent, even insubordinate in his youth; some disliked his politics (he hated a Whig); and some had the same grudge as Admiral Harte, or fancied they did.

This is actually a recapitulation – O'Brian is the only author I know of save P. G. Wodehouse to include so many of them – of the state of affairs four books earlier, in *Master and Commander*, when a medical colleague explains to Maturin how matters stand for Aubrey:

'Our friend is famous for his dash, his enterprise and his good luck rather than for his strict sense of subordination: and some few of the senior captains here feel a good deal of jealousy and uneasiness at his success. What is more, he is a Tory, or his family is; and the husband and the present First Lord are rabid Whigs, vile ranting dogs of Whigs. Do you follow me, Dr Maturin?'

'I do indeed, sir, and am much obliged to you for your candour in telling me this: it confirms what was in my mind, and I shall do all I can to make him conscious of the delicacy of his position. Though upon my word', he added with a sigh, 'there are times when it seems to me that nothing short of a radical ablation of the *membrum virile* would answer, in this case.'

'That is very generally the peccant part', said Mr Florey.

(This fine Latinity, some sly Boswellian allusions, and some general physical accounts of his scruffiness and bookish disorder always make me visualise Dr Maturin as Samuel Johnson.)

Maturin has his own vicissitudes. In *HMS Surprise* (1973), the third of the series, he has his fingernails torn out by vindictive French interrogators in the Balearic Islands, while in *Treason's Harbour* (1983), the ninth volume, he is dangerously compromised by a Bonapartist mole planted deep in the British Admiralty itself. As each story begins, it is customary to find Jack fighting a rearguard action against the naval bureaucracy and Stephen in the toils of a deep-laid conspiracy that is being bungled by British intelligence. Though this puts the middle and later books somewhat into the category of the formulaic, it also helps one to understand the addictive, cultish following that has crystallised around the O'Brian 'Gunroom' site on the World Wide Web. One sign of mastery and command is the ability to create a familiar world-within-world for the reader: O'Brian had this faculty in lavish measure. Even the repeated expressions and ritualised orders – 'Give you joy of it', 'A glass of wine with you, Sir', 'Hoist the topgallants', 'Where away?' – come to acquire a soothing and reassuring patina.

These features, one must also say, are a weakness of the series. Since we 'know' that Aubrey and Maturin will outlive each scrape, there is often a relaxation of tension and several of the books conclude with the flatness of a 'to be continued . . .' serialisation. There are large pieces of unfinished business: in *Desolation Island* Maturin discovers among the convicts a 'Mrs Hoath, the procuress and abortionist [who] seems to me to have thrown off what little humanity she may have been born with, and by long perseverance to have reached a depth of iniquity that I have rarely seen equalled, never surpassed'. One instantly longs for a further introduction which never takes place. In *The Fortune of War* two incidental seamen on two different vessels are both given the single name of Raikes. O'Brian's lulling, almost hypnotic reiteration of his set pieces (Jack and Stephen's cello and violin duets, the sextant observations at noon, the rousing out of the special bottle of wine, gunnery drills, changes of the tide, loading of stores) are so automatic that they occasionally dull his own pen.

In a Calvino-like manner, O'Brian seems to make his anticipatory self-criticism in *The Nutmeg of Consolation* (1991), fourteenth of the novels and dedicated to Robert Hughes's pioneering work on Botany Bay. The two botanisers Martin and Maturin find themselves reflecting upon what one can only term the sense of an ending:

> 'As for an end,' said Martin, 'are endings really so very important? Sterne did quite well without one; and often an unfinished picture is all the more interesting for the bare canvas. I remember Bourville's definition of a novel as a work in which life flows in abundance, swirling without a pause: or as you might say without an end, an organized end. And there is at least one Mozart quartet that stops without the slightest ceremony: most satisfying when you get used to it.'
>
> Stephen said: 'There is another Frenchman whose name escapes me but who is even more to the point: *La bêtise c'est de vouloir conclure*. The conventional ending, with virtue rewarded and loose ends tied up, is often sadly chilling; and its platitude and falsity tend to infect what has gone before, however excellent. Many books would be far better without their last chapter: or at least with no more than a brief, cool, unemotional statement of the outcome.'

I choose to think of this as still another instance of O'Brian's amplitude of trust in the reader: the fact remains that six books later he rather matter-of-factly hoisted Jack Aubrey's flag to the Admiral's rank, signed off, and then (on January 7 this year) died.

Nonetheless, Maturin's polymathic reach – multilingual, highly politicised, ethnically hybrid, and hypereducated – make him the ideal fictional compass. His skill as a physician gives him automatic access to the lower deck, which holds him in near-superstitious awe and affection for his virtue as trepanner and bone-setter and curer of pervasive venereal infection. He is capable of compressing a great deal into a short insight. 'Protestants', he notes in *HMS Surprise*, 'often confessed to medical men.' As a taxonomist and natural historian, he occupies that rather odd interlude between the expeditions of Captain James Cook and the voyage of the *Beagle*; he anticipates Darwin while revering Cook (and goes as far as Australia to classify marsupials, also helping to rediscover Captain Bligh of the *Bounty*, who we are inclined to forget had sailed with Cook and who survived four thousand miles in an open boat before making landfall in Timor). Jack, meanwhile, pushes ahead with his study of the then-mysterious subject of longitude, and collects salinity samples for Humboldt as late as the voyage in *The Truelove* (1992). He has no patience with any science that offers no immediate practical application.

From Dean King's enterprising but decidedly unauthorised biography we are to collect, as Jack Aubrey might phrase it, that there exists an emotional connection between Maturin and his progenitor. Patrick O'Brian changed his name from Richard Russ in an attempt to remake his life; acquired a second identity by removing himself to Catalonia and writing a biography of that nation's favourite son, Pablo Picasso; spent much time under sail; translated Simone de Beauvoir, among others, into English; composed a study of Sir Joseph Banks, the great naturalist who voyaged with Cook; and for some reasons of unexplained distaste would not discuss his wartime service with British military intelligence. In addition, he suffered distraught relations with family and lovers, more than once severing both ties altogether. It seems a defensible thesis. Here is Maturin being plagued with a fit of melancholy, in the closing passages of *Post Captain* (1972):

> Such potentiality, and so much misery? Hatred the only moving force, a petulant unhappy striving – childhood the only happiness, and that unknowing; then the continual battle that cannot ever possibly be won: a losing fight against ill-health – poverty for nearly all. Life is a long disease with only one termination and its last years are appalling: weak, racked by the stone, rheumatismal pains, senses going, friends, family, occupation gone, a man must pray for imbecility or a heart of stone. All under sentence of death, often ignominious, frequently agonizing: and then the unspeakable levity with which the faint chance of happiness is thrown away for some jealousy, tiff, sullenness, private vanity, mistaken sense of honour . . .

This, too, is a fairly exhaustive taxonomy. Yet when the doctor's spirits are recovered he takes immense delight in the albatross, the aardvark, the sloth, the turtle, and the whale, and never loses his sense of outrage at the foulness of slavery and oppression. It's true that he needs his laudanum and his coca leaves to keep going, but a dryish sense of humour often buoys him up also, offsetting the heavy puns and awful malapropisms that Jack Aubrey uses. ('*Autre temps – autre merde*', he muses at one juncture, while never failing to hug himself at the production of such sallies as 'the lesser of two weevils'.)

One might legitimately surmise that O'Brian's mood-swings and prejudices took something of the same form as do Maturin's. He allows himself two major slashes at the reputation of the peerless Lord Nelson – a man esteemed this side of idolatry by Jack Aubrey – once for supporting the African slave trade and once for his cruelty and perfidy in putting down the republican insurgents in Naples (the same episode that is depicted more fully in Susan Sontag's *The Volcano Lover*). Lord Byron is often mentioned with approval, as are the barely discernible future struggles for liberty in Greece, Malta, and other places where the British Empire colonised Europeans. In *Treason's Harbour* we read of a Mr Holden who

> had been dismissed from the service for using his ship to protect some Greeks fleeing from a Turkish punitive expedition: he was now acting for a small, remote, ineffectual and premature Committee for Greek Independence, and since the English government had to keep on terms with the Sublime Porte he was a most unwelcome visitor to official Malta . . .

– while in *The Wine-Dark Sea*, where the ship touches at Sierra Leone (founded before Liberia as a state for free slaves), Maturin is in a positive rage about the Middle Passage and its overseers:

> It is a retrospective passion, sure, but I feel it still. Thinking of that ill-looking flabby ornamented conceited self-complacent ignorant shallow mean-spirited cowardly young shite with absolute power over fifteen hundred blacks makes me fairly tremble even now.

The more pragmatic Jack ('perhaps it comes more natural if you are black') cannot quite approve his friend's unpunctuated Irish polemic, but we learn that this leathery old Tory has fathered a son with an African woman, and that he dotes on the boy.

O'Brian is also at some pains to undermine the 'Hearts of Oak' image of the Royal Navy of the period, pointing out repeatedly that a large number of those hauling on the ropes were not the sons of Anglo-Saxon yeomen and bowmen, whether forcibly impressed into the service or otherwise. Bengalis, Finns, Italians, Poles go to make up the ship's complement – this is not the least respect in which the influence of Joseph Conrad can be felt. And, speaking of the impressment of seamen, the acerbic Maturin registers very strong objections to the British habit of stopping American vessels and impounding their crews. In the confrontations with the USS *Chesapeake* and *Constitution*, in fact, the doctor feels his loyalty palpably engaged on the other side.

And in several of the novels – perhaps most notably in *The Far Side of the World* (1984), the tenth of the series – we get a clear prefiguration of the rise of another great maritime power, which has learned in the same way (and from the same empire) as would Admiral Mahan that command of the oceans is essential. O'Brian's accounts of American whalers and their nautical prowess evoke and equal Melville; on another hand the conduct of British and American seafarers when wrecked on the same island suggests Defoe, and also, perhaps, William Golding. In *The Fortune of War*, having seen the New World in action, our gallant captain makes the largest concession that is allowable to him:

> Nelson had never much cared for the use of fighting-tops in battle, partly because of the danger of fire, and until recently everything that Nelson said

was Gospel to Jack Aubrey. But on the other hand, he had seen the *Java* carried into battle in obedience to the great man's dictum, 'Never mind manoeuvres: go straight at 'em,' and it occurred to him that although Nelson was always right where the French and Spaniards were concerned, he might have had other views if he had been at war with the Americans.

(It comes back to me that I met Patrick O'Brian at a reception in the Decatur Rooms off Lafayette Square in Washington: he showed the liveliest admiration for the memory of the American commodore.)

Some readers affect to be repelled by the astonishing amount of technical and archaic language (what on earth are those 'fighting-tops' mentioned above?) charting the movement of the ship and of the winds. The diagram of the sailing tackle of a square-rigger, thoughtfully appended in the most recent editions, is more intimidating than otherwise: a glossary of terms would be of greater assistance.

> 'Almost ready, sir,' said the sweating, harassed bosun. 'I'm working the cunt-splice myself.'
>
> 'Well,' said Jack, hurrying off to where the stern-chaser hung poised above the Sophie's quarter-deck, ready to plunge through her bottom if gravity could but have its way, 'a simple thing like a cunt-splice will not take a man of war's bosun long, I believe.'

This is all very well, until the futtock-shrouds come in a few pages later on, or until we read the command to 'scandalise the foretop-sailyards'. As a navy brat myself, brought up in Portsmouth and Plymouth and Malta and on tales of the 'wooden wall' which had been 'England's sure shield', I know most of the words to the songs that appear in these pages, and I understand that bosun is shorthand for boatswain, but in the passage above the only term that is absolutely clear to me is 'bottom' (though I dimly apprehend that a 'stern-chaser', louche as it sounds, is a brass cannon). However, I recommend persistence. For an instance, take this paragraph from *The Far Side of the World*:

> It took fifty-seven men to haul the foresheet aft, to tally and belay; and as the strain increased so the *Surprise* heeled another strake, another and yet another, until she showed a broad streak of copper on her windward side, while the howl in the rigging rose shriller and shriller, almost to the breaking-note. And there she steadied, racing through the sea and flinging a bow-wave so high to leeward that the sun sent back a double rainbow.

This is almost invisible writing, but it brings even a landlubber to the feel of a crucial rope tautening under his hand, imparting velocity and direction. In *The Surgeon's Mate* (1979) there is a brief lovely sentence worthy of the *Iliad*, where Maturin feels 'a change in the brig's progress, a greater thrust that raised her general music by half a tone'. This everlasting tuning explains without sentiment why life afloat was so harsh and exhausting and subject to such horrific, absolute authority. One false guess about the weather and it was all over. Many terms we employ unreflectingly – from 'first-rate' to 'piping down' to 'bitter end' – acquired their use in these circumstances and are given their original provenance in these accounts. One also recalls that the British Admiral Byng, executed by firing squad on his own quarterdeck for insufficient zeal, is the occasion for the laconic French maxim *pour encourager les autres.*

Perhaps I have not said enough about the microcosmic. O'Brian gives us minute accounts of human relations on land and sea. His trusty scheme is of course the time-honoured one of the buddy movie or the literary double act, and he milks it to the utmost. Aboard, Jack saves Maturin from drowning, from falling into the hold, from dangerous innocence and from all manner of shot and shell. On land, Maturin rescues the gullible Jack from French patrols (once farcically disguising him as a dancing bear), from English card-sharpers and swindlers and other urban predators, including ominously modern versions of the political police. The two men come close to a falling-out over a woman, the fatally solipsistic Diana Villiers, a lady brilliantly realised as undone by her physical splendour, her intelligence, her pride, and her lack of means. Her violent death in *The Hundred Days* (1998) is read by some as a tribute to O'Brian's own wife, who died in the same year. One of the novels (*Post Captain*) is indeed set largely on shore and negotiates the shoals of English social relations.

O'Brian we know was a tremendous admirer of Jane Austen: in the figure of Jack Aubrey's mother-in-law he created a woman so profoundly false and irritating that she could well have been of the party at Mansfield Park. The tedium and hypocrisy of contemporary courtship is captured to a satisfying degree (those infinitely laborious removals from one torpid country house to another dull spa): the reader shares with the narrator's subjects the mounting desire to smell gunpowder and rigging again. I do not think, however, that Miss Austen would have allowed herself some of the broad yet private jesting in which O'Brian indulged: not every gentle reader will know that some of his quaint English village names (Swiving being the roughest example) are in fact common obscenities of the period.

Within the microcosm of the service, however, O'Brian succeeds in something that Kipling, say, could never attempt without embarrassing himself. He is able to give an unaffected account of demotic talk; accurate one feels sure, and uncondescending. Here is an extract, admittedly in reported speech, in which a second mate enlightens Maturin about climatic conditions on the Grand Banks:

As to the fog, it was caused by the cold Labrador current setting south, then rising over the Banks and meeting the warm air of the Gulf Stream – the Doctor had heard tell of the Gulf Stream? – and so brewing up a fog almost continual. Some days you would say the whole sea was steaming like a pot, it brewed so fast: and that was why the wind did not blow it away – it was brewed afresh continual.

It is O'Brian's lack of cant that makes up for his occasional overreliance on coincidence, his tendency towards repetition, and his lapses into boyish seafaring homespun (most marked on those occasions when our heroes run into female warriors in torrid zones). He keeps before him the essential realisation that men *like* warfare and relish plunder, and pine away for the lack of it. In *The Thirteen-Gun Salute* (1989) Jack Aubrey remembers with 'a fulness of being, like no other every detail of blows given and received'. In almost every book there is either an outbreak of peace or a rumour that hostilities have been suspended, and in each instance the response is a moan of disappointment, because the chance of enrichment or advancement has been thereby snatched away. In *Desolation Island* a Turkish crew member – a castrated man to boot – is convicted of thieving and sentenced to be tied to a grating, stripped, and flogged:

The bosun's mate brought the cat out of its red baize bag: nine hearty strokes, nine appalling falsetto screams of a shrillness and a volume enough to mark the day as quite uncommon, and to gratify that part of the ship's company which took pleasure in bull-baiting, bear-baiting, prize-fighting, pillories, and executions – perhaps nine-tenths of those present.

This is not sadistic or prurient, but a blunt recognition of the callousness without which the muster could not have been called, nor the sails spread. The presence of women aboard ship is never depicted as anything but toxic and calamitous. The fortunes of war are shown to be a matter of caprice; when Jack Aubrey winces at the foundering with all hands of an enormous Dutch battleship he is thought by his brother-officers to have become temporarily unhinged. The fate of men dragged from dank rural jails to fill the naval quota is sometimes described but usually in such a way as to leave the vilest parts to the imagination: the fate of transported convicts – including political and labour union prisoners who appear in *The Ionian Mission* (1981) and *The Nutmeg of Consolation* (1991) – is described in such a way that you can almost smell it (though the pathos of Maturin's lost Irish servitor Padeen in the latter volume is O'Brian's only lapse into outright sentimentality).

And, once Bonaparte has been defeated, both Aubrey and Maturin (in *The Wine-Dark Sea* and *Blue at the Mizzen*) sign up for a fresh set of contingent hostilities in Spanish America. Maturin may have the excuse of taking the side of liberty – his contacts with sub rosa Masonic orders are very finely traced, and form a credible continuation of his surreptitious political commitments – but for Jack the motive is simple mayhem with the chance of an admiral's pennant at the end of it. This, you feel with the same growing pressure that tautens the sheets and masts of the narrative, is how it really was.

The Wine-Dark Sea is of course meant to put us in mind of Homer, and in *The Far Side of the World* a young officer confesses to having looked into Chapman's version while stationed in Gibraltar. Maturin, naturally, has read Pope's edition, and has conned Virgil and Horace. It was evidently O'Brian's intention to transcend the naval yarn and to show for another generation 'the man of many resources' (or 'many wiles', as Pope has it) who 'saw the cities and learned the thoughts of many men, and on the sea suffered in his heart many woes'.

First published as 'O'Brian's Great Voyage' (a review of *Blue at the Mizzen* by Patrick O'Brian, and *Patrick O'Brian: A Life Revealed* by Dean King) in *New York Review of Books*, 9 March 2000

Notes

1. See Conor Cruise O'Brien's introduction to Edmund Burke's *Reflections on the Revolution in France* (Penguin, 1986). See also his *The Great Melody* (University of Chicago, Press, 1992).

The Case of Arthur Conan Doyle

T. S. Eliot's most successful feline – the depraved Macavity in *Old Possum's Book of Practical Cats* – is well known as a straight lift from Professor Moriarty, the saturnine villain in Sir Arthur Conan Doyle's 'The Final Problem':

> He is the Napoleon of crime, Watson. He is the organiser of half that is evil and of nearly all that is undetected in this great city . . . Is there a crime to be done, a paper to be abstracted, we will say, a house to be rifled, a man to be removed – the word is passed to the Professor, the matter is organised and carried out . . . But the central power which uses the agent is never caught – never so much as suspected . . . [He] is, I dare say, working out problems on a blackboard ten miles away.

Thus Sherlock Holmes, in portentous form. And thus Eliot, making sport of him:

> And when the larder's looted, or
>   the jewel-case is rifled,
> Or when the milk is missing, or
>   another Peke's been stifled,
> Or the greenhouse glass is
>   broken, and the trellis past repair –
> Ay, there's the wonder of the
>   thing! Macavity's not there!
>
> And when the Foreign Office find
>   a Treaty's gone astray
> Or the Admiralty loses some
>   plans and drawings by the way,
> There may be a scrap of paper in
>   the hall or on the stair –
> But it's useless to investigate –
>   *Macavity's not there!*
> And when the loss has been
>   disclosed, the Secret Service say:
> 'It *must* have been Macavity!' –
>   but he's a mile away.
> You'll be sure to find him resting,

or a-licking of his thumbs,
Or engaged in doing complicated
    long division sums.

Having in passing satirised the plots of two other Holmesian escapades, Eliot closes by saying that there are other foul toms in London
but that they

Are nothing more than agents for
    the Cat who all the time
Just controls their operations: the
    Napoleon of Crime!

This is all in jest, but see how Eliot phrases a grave moment in his
Murder in the Cathedral. A 'tempter' has been sent from King Henry to
Thomas Becket, offering him secular power in exchange for an
acknowledgement of royal supremacy over the Church. Becket engages
the emissary in a cryptic exchange of call and response:

'Who shall have it?'
'He who will come.'
'What shall be the month?'
'The last from the first.'
'What shall we give for it?'
'Pretense of priestly power.'

In an early Sherlock Holmes case, entitled 'The Musgrave Ritual', a
piece of mysterious doggerel holds the clue:

Whose is it?
His who is gone.
Who shall have it?
He who will come.
What was the month?
The sixth from the first.
What shall we give for it?
All that is ours.

Since the subject of *Murder in the Cathedral* is the martyrdom of the
Archbishop of Canterbury, and the occult or arcane topic of 'The
Musgrave Ritual' is the retrieval of the crown of King Charles I – 'King
and Martyr' to the Tory faction, and upholder of divine right – one
can surmise that, this time, the Anglo-Catholic Eliot was annexing
Conan Doyle for more than just cartoonish material.

Conan Doyle is one of those popular authors who create – to borrow
a telling phrase from Harold Isaacs – 'scratches on our minds'. W. H.
Auden, in his essay 'The Guilty Vicarage', says that the mystery tale is a
species of fantasy in which 'the job of the detective is to restore the

state of grace in which the aesthetic and the ethical are one', and that 'Holmes is the exceptional individual who is in a state of grace because he is a genius in whom scientific curiosity is raised to the status of a heroic passion.' There is no doubting that Conan Doyle would have been baffled and embarrassed by such tribute, but then there is no question that his deerstalker-and-bloodstain pastiche is one of the most salient examples in literature of an unintended consequence.

The creator of the ascetic and introverted sleuth – highest instance of what Jacques Barzun termed 'the romance of reason' – was himself a hearty, athletic, patriotic type: an exemplar of Victorian values. Born to a 'good' family that was nonetheless compromised by alcoholism and indigence and (probably) insanity on the part of his father, Conan Doyle tried all the avenues that were open to those without capital: Arctic and African expeditions; colonial and military postings; the medical profession. (The option of taking holy orders – often reserved for the fool of the family or for the least promising younger son – did not appeal to him. He experienced an early revulsion from Christianity as a consequence of being sent to a harsh Roman Catholic public school.) Forced to settle for the life of a general practitioner in Southsea – the scene of childhood for Charles Dickens and Rudyard Kipling – he found in himself the *cacoethia scribendi*, or the urge to scribble, and hoped to become a historical novelist on the model of Sir Walter Scott. Personally, I think his romances of high medieval England, especially *The White Company*, to be grossly underrated. And his tales of the Napoleonic wars, related through an attractive if slightly farcical French gallant named Brigadier Gerard, are something better than well crafted. It was his fate, however, to invent a stop-gap fictional 'character' with whom to pay the bills, and to have his second-order creation take over, golem-like, his life and reputation.

Why does the mystique of Sherlock persist? Auden supplies only part of the answer but, I think, the most important part. Comparable authors in the middlebrow English market – John Buchan, say, or 'Sapper' with his Bulldog Drummond – have dated badly because they made uncritical assumptions about the British Empire, and because they encoded social and racial prejudices that were questionable even in their own time. (In the case of Bulldog Drummond, one might add that there was a shocking element of sadism, while the bigoted and semi-literate pulp produced by Agatha Christie raises only the uninteresting mystery of its own success.) With Holmes and Watson, however, Conan Doyle achieved something closer to the ageless if not the transcendent. The two men can be ranked fictionally with Don Quixote and Sancho Panza, or Jeeves and Wooster, and (since many people subconsciously refer to them as if they were, in fact, real) with Samuel

Johnson and James Boswell. They are wholly anchored in time and place, to be sure. But the gaslight and the fog and the hansom cab are not enough on their own to explain the almost numinous appeal.

The two essential elements, common to almost all the stories, are, first, a commitment to science and the forensic as positively healing powers – almost on a par with medicine itself – and, second, a thirst, or perhaps better to say an instinct, for justice. Holmes is not exactly Robin Hood. On more than one occasion he acts with lofty discretion for illustrious or potent clients, and in one rather regrettable instance ('The Priory School') seems postively to solicit money from a venal duke. But his exertions are generally rendered on the side of the powerless or the wronged and there is usually no mention of any fee.

Though violence is used and neither Holmes nor Watson is in the least bit pacific, it is sheer power of mind that does the trick, and that turns the tables not just on evil but – by letting in the light – on superstition and nameless dread as well. It must be for this reason that Umberto Eco, in *The Name of the Rose*, awards the name Sir William of Baskerville to the lucid, deductive investigator who dispels the cloud of monkish obfuscation.

Contemptible though he found his own literary success – 'The Final Problem' was not the first time he had contemplated shoving Sherlock into the caldron of the Reichenbach Falls – Conan Doyle was proud of the associations that it brought him. Recalling his 'breakthrough' as a celebrated author, he wrote:

> At that time I was practising in a small way as a doctor, and in a draper's shop close by H. G. Wells was an assistant. There was also a raw-boned Irishman rolling about London. His name was Bernard Shaw. There was another named Thomas Hardy, and there was a young journalist struggling for a living in Nottingham, whose name was Barrie.

Anthony Hope, author of *The Prisoner of Zenda*, observed that Conan Doyle looked like a man who had never heard of a book, and one can imagine the bluff and beefy rugby-playing provincial doctor regarding this as no insult. Daniel Stashower's rather jaunty biography returns us to the days of George Gissing and *New Grub Street*, the age of an awakening mass literacy and of popular fiction magazines like *The Strand*, the perhaps latent connection between Victorian optimism and the stirrings of science fiction. (Conan Doyle tried his hand at that, too, in the stories about the eccentric but rationalist Professor Challenger: the debate between the partisans of Darwin and the last-ditch creationism of Bishop Wilberforce was still resounding at that period.) In the world of the London stage, Henry Irving was unchallenged, with the help of his adroit business manager Bram Stoker. It was to the future author of *Dracula*, indeed, that Conan Doyle sent his most successful play – a sentimental but well-wrought piece about the last survivor of the Battle of Waterloo.

Extensive though his newly won acquaintance was, it must still have seemed incongruous to Conan Doyle to find himself seated one evening next to Oscar Wilde. The occasion was a dinner given by Joseph Marshall Stoddart, the editor of *Lippincott's Monthly Magazine*, who had come from Philadelphia to recruit new talent. The year was 1889 and, although Wilde's exposure and persecution lay ahead of him, he had already been lampooned for his aestheticism by Gilbert and Sullivan in their philistine production *Patience*. However improbably, Conan Doyle found himself much impressed by Wilde's depth and courtesy and wit, and also by his 'curious precision of statement'. Imagining how a future war might be conducted, Wilde had simply said: 'A chemist on each side will approach the frontier with a bottle.' This remark could hardly have been better calculated for the *Zeitgeist* or for its amateur-scientist hearer. But *Lippincott's* did the best out of the evening, by proposing that both authors produce a short novel for the magazine. Conan Doyle turned out *The Sign of the Four* (originally entitled *The Sign of Four*). Oscar Wilde came up with *The Picture of Dorian Gray*.

Conan Doyle defended that story from the obloquy that fell upon it when published, and it's of great interest that, in after years, he continued to manifest praise and sympathy for Wilde. Though he felt, as many did in those days, that homosexuality was a disease, he at least did not regard it as a crime. (One of Holmes's most repeated maxims is that prejudice is fatal to the proper approach in a case.) Nor was his decency in the Wilde matter a single instance, or an example of his being star-struck. Having taken a voyage down the coast of Africa as a ship's doctor, he formed an unfavourable opinion of white settler life and was highly impressed to meet Henry Highland Garnet, the abolitionist son of a slave who was then American consul in Liberia.

There was a certain coarseness in the way Conan Doyle wrote of his experiences – the natives, he said, 'begin to get their stew-pans and sauce-bottles ready when they see a Stanley or any other modern explorer coming down on them'. But, like Conrad, he had seen the demoralisation and misery inflicted by slavery and empire, and when the time came he wrote an extremely powerful pamphlet against King Leopold's appalling empire in the Congo. His ally and friend here was Sir Roger Casement, another promiscuous Irish homosexual. It speaks well of Conan Doyle that, when Casement was sentenced to death for his part in the Irish rebellion of 1916, he organised an exceptionally dogged campaign to have him reprieved. Nor was he deflected from this by the British government's cynical release of Casement's lurid private diaries. (The use of sexual frame-ups by the British against the Irish – from Parnell to Wilde to Casement – is perhaps a subject on which Holmes would not have chosen to write one of his celebrated monographs.)

Conan Doyle's 1891 novel *The White Company* had been dedicated 'To the Hope of the Future, The Reunion of the English-Speaking Races', and speaks feelingly of the common ancestry of these races in the Anglo-Saxon yeomen and bowmen. There was a fashion in that period, very closely identified with Cecil Rhodes and Rudyard Kipling, for reunifying North America with the British Empire. (The founding statutes of the Rhodes Scholarships made this aim an explicit one.) Conan Doyle was a stout partisan of the idea, but he did not have the Rhodes or Kipling attitude toward the lesser breeds. Indeed, there is an unconscious or unacknowledged loophole in the concept of 'English-*Speaking* Races'. Might this not apply to Bengalis, Gaels, Zulus? Like many such contradictions, this remained unresolved in Conan Doyle's mind. But it also remains the case that, in the large cast which populates the Sherlockian universe, there is no shifty and cunning Jew, no brutish and prognathous blackamoor, no drunken Hibernian lout.[1] In the context of the times, this counts as a sort of humanism. Of course, in the late Victorian period it was very much easier to guess a man's background or occupation by mere physical inspection – as Dr Joseph Bell, Conan Doyle's celebrated mentor at Edinburgh University medical school, had shown him how to do. Nowadays, the distinction between 'profiling' and 'stereotyping' can in itself be an obstacle to good police work.

Holmes has one thing in common with every fictional detective since, which is an innate lack of respect for the official gendarmerie. The forces of law and order are not represented as corrupt or cruel, but they are depicted as if they are not up to their job. Law-and-order man as he was, Conan Doyle became involved in a number of nonpolitical cases of justice miscarried. The most renowned of these campaigns was his exhausting but finally successful effort to clear the name of George Edalji, an unpopular and ill-favoured Parsee Indian, living near Birmingham, who was falsely accused of a series of cattle mutilations. On other occasions – sometimes approached by admirers who believed that he must possess Sherlockian skills, but also in his capacity as a gentleman and a conscientious public figure – he was able to identify a serial killer, to reopen the case of a victim of mistaken identity named Oscar Slater, and to reprieve a collie dog named Rex, who had been set up for savaging a sheep.

The intense Englishness of some of these episodes did not prevent his being referred to in the public prints as a Dreyfusard. Anticipating what is now sometimes called 'the blue wall' of police complicity, and foreshadowing some even more harrowing conspiracies to pervert the course of justice that have lately surfaced in British–Irish relations, Conan Doyle put it as plainly as it has ever been put by commenting that

> What confronts you is a determination to admit nothing which inculpates another official, and as to the idea of punishing another official for offences which have caused misery to helpless victims, it never comes within their horizons.

Fashions in punishment and retribution change, of course, and though the authorities would unhesitatingly put Oscar Wilde on a jail regime that alternated between solitary confinement and the treadmill, they would not have thought then of interfering with the following victimless crime:

> Sherlock Holmes took his bottle from the corner of the mantelpiece, and his hypodermic syringe from its neat morocco case. With his long, white, nervous fingers he adjusted the delicate needle, and rolled back his left shirt-cuff. For some little time his eyes rested thoughtfully upon the sinewy forearm and wrist, all dotted and scarred with innumerable puncture marks. Finally, he thrust the sharp point home, pressed down the tiny piston, and sank back into the velvet-lined arm-chair with a long sigh of satisfaction.

Thus the opening of *The Sign of the Four*, the very novel that Doyle wrote for *Lippincott's* as a bookend for *Dorian Gray* (which last he described as written 'upon a high moral plane'). It's true that Watson protests energetically about the abuse of his friend's powers, if only for the look of the thing, but Victorian England was sunk in opium- and coca-based remedies at that date, and Mr Stashower is certainly right when he says:

> To Conan Doyle's way of thinking, however, the syringe would have been very much of a piece with the violin, the purple dressing-gown, and the interest in such abstruse subjects as the motets of Lassus . . . He needed to cast his detective as an artist rather than a simple policeman.

This is not the only sense in which Doyle used Holmes as his alter ego. The cold-bath school of sexual sublimation – even misogyny – in Baker Street was partly necessary for Doyle's audience and editors, who could read of seven-percent cocaine solutions without blanching yet would have recoiled from an undraped ankle or calf. But it was also necessary in his own private existence. With a bedridden and tubercular wife, and a doting, not to say domineering, mother, and a younger woman with whom he was certainly in love, he could write unironically of the need to 'steady myself down' by concentrated work on Ernest Renan, adding almost self-parodically that his stern regimen, 'with plenty of golf and cricket, ought to keep me right – body and mind'. It is notable that he didn't turn to the bottle or to the array of consolations that a doctor's medicine cabinet might lawfully have supplied. On the other hand, though many critics have noticed Conan Doyle's dependence on the detective plots of Edgar Allan Poe – a dependence which he proudly acknowledged – I did not appreciate until reading Mr Stashower that there is another influence to be traced via the work of the French author Emile Gaboriau. His Parisian sleuth Monsieur Lecoq, like Dupin of the Rue Morgue, has a dull-witted chum, and a brain too fine to be appreciated by the dunderheaded *flics*. His amiable but dense Sancho Panza, though, is named Father Absinthe ... In *A Study in Scarlet*, Holmes himself expresses scorn for the bumbling methods of Monsieur Lecoq, but perhaps out of deference to the sensitive Watson, omits mention of the useless Father Absinthe – who sounds like a presage of a Graham Greene character.

The most astonishing disjunction between Conan Doyle and Holmes is the one which occurs in the realm of the supernatural. In 'His Last Bow', the only tale which is written in the third person, the time is the doom-laden month of August 1914. Holmes the undercover agent has infiltrated the Kaiser's embassy (posing, one notes, as an embittered Irish-American Anglophobe) and has outwitted the diabolical von Bork. In all respects, the story resembles a John Buchan plot more than a Holmes one, and recalls both *Greenmantle* and *The Thirty-Nine Steps*. Their task over, and the outbreak of war only a matter of hours away, the two old friends repair to a view of the sea:

> 'Stand with me here upon the terrace, for it may be the last quiet talk that we will ever have ... There's an east wind coming, Watson.'
> 'I think not, Holmes. It is very warm.'
> 'Good old Watson! You are the one fixed point in a changing age. There's an east wind coming all the same, such a wind as never blew on England yet. It will be cold and bitter, Watson, and a good many of us may wither before its blast. But it's God's own wind none the less, and a cleaner, better, stronger land will lie in the sunshine when the storm has cleared. Start her up, Watson, for it's time that we were on our way ...'

This little parable of the jingo and 'preparedness' movement – the story was published in 1917 – reminds us that, whatever the appeal of the stories may be, it does not always lie in the writing. More than this, within a year or so of the appearance of 'His Last Bow', Conan Doyle was to receive news of the deaths of his brother, his son, his brothers-in-law, and his two nephews. The loyal, uncynical England that he had loved was to be laid waste, and his fantasy of Anglo-American and Anglo-Saxon imperial rapprochement was to evaporate.

Some defenders argue that his conversion to spiritualism – the most feebleminded of all the cults that sprang up in the 1920s – was not the outcome of trauma, or of a half-acknowledged desire to establish 'contact' with the lost and the beyond. And it is true that Conan Doyle had evinced some interest in tableturning, Ouija boards, haunted houses, and ectoplasmic emanations before the First World War. However, it was only after the calamity of the Western Front that he became the patron and captain of that sad, deluded faction which sought to peer through the curtain of separation. (Since almost one third of the British casualties in that war have no identified resting place to this day, the phenomenon in itself is no great cause for wonder.)

At all events, prior to 1914 Conan Doyle had shown no more than a sympathetic curiosity. He was slightly overimpressed by Daniel Dunglas Home, a celebrity adept of the midnineteenth century and original of Browning's 'Mr Sludge', who was said to be able to levitate and to make heavy objects do the same. Home made a vast impression on Elizabeth Barrett Browning, who wrote excitedly to her sister on the occasion of the master conjuror's nuptials: 'Think of the conjugal furniture floating about the room at night, Henrietta.'[2] As against such abject credulity, Conan Doyle was able to set the militant skepticism of his friend and hero Oliver Wendell Holmes (after whom the great detective is named). This Holmes denounced the spiritualist movement as a 'plague'.

It is painful to read about Conan Doyle's declining years. Even his great fan T. S. Eliot wrote regretfully of the 'mental decay' that was apparent in the writing. Once the reserves of scientific doubt were gone, his sails would swell at the last zephyr of anything fraudulent or inane. He fell for everything, from photographs of fairies to spirit mediums. He quarrelled with everyone, from Harry Houndini – the greatest charlatan-buster of his day – to the poltergeist-fancying Society for Psychical Research, which in his view had become too self-critical. His last public action was a campaign to repeal the Witchcraft Act, a statute dating from James I and prohibiting various forms of sorcery. But it is notable that he never allowed his main character to succumb. In one of the very last stories, 'The Sussex Vampire', published in 1924, Holmes expresses contempt for necromancy and kindred foolishness:

> Are we to give serious attention to such things? This agency stands flat-footed upon the ground, and there it must remain. *The world is big enough for us. No ghosts need apply.* [Italics mine.]

And indeed, in short order, the puncture marks on the victim's neck are shown to be susceptible of a rational explanation. This must come as something of a blow to Mr Stephen Kendrick, a Unitarian enthusiast who, in *Holy Clues: The Gospel According to Sherlock Holmes*, looks for hidden luminosities – a new-age version of the Reverend Casaubon's *Key to All Mythologies* – in the fact that Holmes fails on seven occasions, or in his claim to have passed some time in Tibet after faking his own death at the Reichenbach Falls. As he puts it:

On a research trip to London on a cold February morning, my son Paul and I stood on Baker Street with friends Dawn Tibbetts and Dermot Walker. In front of the Abbey National Building, we were reading the respectful marker at the place where 221-B, holy of holies for Sherlockians, is supposed to have been. Dermot turned to me and asked, 'Stephen, don't you think it is odd that we are visiting an imaginary address of an imaginary person?'

Not such a searching question when you think about it: many of us have the same sensation at the thresholds of churches or ashrams. Conan Doyle claimed to have been contacted by the shade of Joseph Conrad, who asked him to finish the writing of his uncompleted novel *Suspense*. This handsome offer was succeeded by another one from the spirit of Charles Dickens, who said that if he made a good job of the Conrad he might consider himself entitled to try and round off *The Mystery of Edwin Drood*. 'I shall be honoured, Mr Dickens', Conan Doyle reported that he said (in the *Journal of the Society for Psychical Research*). 'Charles, if you please,' the great man supposedly responded. 'We like friends to be friends.' Conan Doyle never executed either of these potentially great exercises in mediumship but then – even more remarkable when you think of it – neither did Mr Conrad or Mr Dickens use their presumable powers to do the job themselves. Thus we may be grateful that, when he took himself over the precipice and into the maelstrom of babble and superstition, Conan Doyle left his main man behind on the ledge, there to bear witness to the beauties of deduction, and to the consolations of philosophy, mentation, ratiocination, and hard drugs.

First published as 'The Case of Arthur Conan Doyle' (a review of *Teller of Tales: The Life of Arthur Conan Doyle* by Daniel Stashower and *Holy Clues: The Gospel According to Sherlock Holmes* by Stephen Kendrick) in *New York Review of Books*, 4 November 1999

Notes

1. The lamentable exception occurs in a very late story, ('The Three Gables'). But more than one Sherlockian has surmised that this episode, together with some others of the concluding ones published in the 1920s, was either 'ghost-written' (if the phrase may be allowed) or not written by Conan Doyle at all. The final court of appeal here is the nine-volume *Oxford Sherlock Holmes*, edited by Owen Dudley Edwards (Oxford University Press, 1993) and annotated with great thoroughness and brilliance.
2. The recently published *Complete Works of George Orwell* (London: Secker & Warburg, 1998) contains a scornful review of him of an overly respectful biography of Home entitled *Heyday of a Wizard*. See vol. 19, p. 388.

The Road to West Egg

The Great Gatsby was originally published in April 1925, which means that those who first read it were much nearer in time to Henry James and even Charles Dickens than we are to Scott Fitzgerald. And that reflection brings a shock. For just as the book survives in our minds partly as a period piece – the encapsulation of the splendours and miseries of 'the Jazz Age' (an expression which Fitzgerald coined as well as symbolised) – so does it seem distinctly modern as well as, in certain passages, almost contemporary.

Why does this novel retain such a firm grip on our up-to-the-minute today, even as it is borne back ceaselessly into the past? First, because it represents a declaration of independence by American writing, a noticeably native style and subject owing little to the old European school. Fitzgerald was named for Francis Scott Key, author of 'The Star-Spangled Banner' (he even thought of titling his novel *Under the Red, White, and Blue*), and though we glimpse him now through a mist of booze and debauchery and latter-day Hollywood posturings, it's important to remember that he was, at bottom, a patriotic young man from the Midwest who always wished he had seen active service in the First World War. Having decided with *The Great Gatsby* to chisel out nine short and finely wrought chapters that would demand everything he had, Fitzgerald found he'd taken on all the great American themes, from the original 'dream' itself to the corresponding loss of innocence.

That phrase, 'loss of innocence', has become stale with overuse and diminishing returns; no other culture is so addicted to this narcissistic impression of itself as having any innocence to lose in the first place. I have seen Mark Twain's *Innocents Abroad* described as the literary 'declaration of independence' (though Mr Twain never wrote about sexual obsession). And I have seen the famous 'loss' attributed to Watergate, to Vietnam, to Hiroshima, to the Spanish–American War of 1898, and to the assassinations of the Kennedy brothers. Robert Redford dates it, in discussing his movie *Quiz Show*, to the moment in the respectable 1950s when Americans discovered that the egghead games on TV were fixed. That's a more plausible suggestion than the one made in the *New York Times*'s front-page obituary for Frank Sinatra, which solemnly argued that Frank's croons were the 'loss of innocence' for a generation.

A virginity so casually renewable can easily be mislaid again and again, just as many Jazz Age narcissists must have hoped it could be. However, the year 1919 did see a genuine loss of innocence and a serious, if hopeless, attempt to regain it. In that year, 'Shoeless' Joe Jackson of the White Sox was widely believed to have been asked, by a crushed and plaintive little boy, to preserve and protect some childhood illusions and 'say it ain't so'. The rigging of the World Series really did come as a blow, innocence not so much lost as stolen or defiled. And the context? Why, the United States had just engaged in a war on the killing fields of the bloodstained old Europe it had been created to escape. Disillusionment was setting in, and the boys from 'over there' had brought back some racy and cynical new ideas. Sensing the coming of a brash new world, the traditionalists of Puritan America mounted their last great stand in 1919 by passing the 18th Amendment, or Prohibition. Their target was not just the demon drink but really the whole phenomenon of modernism, with its sexual freedom, motorcars, and migration from the small and simple town to the big and clever city – most especially pagan and glittering New York City: star of the novel.

Early in *Gatsby* we encounter Meyer Wolfsheim, the man with human teeth for cuff links who has, according to sick and fascinated rumour, fixed the 1919 World Series. The narrator, Nick Carraway, is back from the war, and when he first meets his rich neighbour on Long Island discovers a common bond in the experience of combat. Every page, practically, bears the scent of gin and rum and whiskey: the characters marinate in illegal hooch and moonshine, and the cops are paid off. Innocence – what innocence? It's in the course of a drunken and spiteful moment in the Plaza Hotel that Nick realises something:

> 'I just remembered that today's my birthday.'
> I was thirty. Before me stretched the portentous menacing road of a new decade . . . Thirty – the promise of a decade of loneliness, a thinning list of single men to know, a thinning briefcase of enthusiasm, thinning hair.

Recall that Tom Buchanan is described in the opening pages as 'one of those men who reach such an acute limited excellence at twenty-one that everything afterwards savours of anticlimax'. They are not long, the days of wine and roses . . .

As the other characters – Daisy and Gatsby in the lead, and driving badly – are embarking on the 'portentous menacing road' back to East Egg and calamity, Nick is oppressed by another sense of the 'Lost Generation' of those years. Youth is gone; there may be some comfort to be found in sex and alcohol, but . . . youth is gone all the same, and is irretrievable. Needless to add, innocence departed before youth did. There will never be glad, confident morning again.

In its evocation, *The Great Gatsby* is the American *Brideshead Revisited*. Or perhaps one should say that *Brideshead*, produced two decades later, is the English *Gatsby*. In both novels young people are caught in a backwash of postwar blues and anomie, and everybody drinks too much. In both novels, too, the old order is visibly deteriorating, and an insecure yet grand mansion is a centrepiece. The dreaming spires of Oxford play a strange, background role in each, but the fictional foreground is filled with jazz and flappers and infidelity and brittle, amoral talk. Rex Mottram, Julia Flyte's crude lover in *Brideshead*, is a newly rich and self-invented man from a shabby background, vulgar and ostentatious in his hospitality, suspected of crime and violence, and full of status anxiety. (I can't find any evidence that Waugh ever read *Gatsby*, and he affected to disdain American writers, but still . . .)

Both books outlive their abysmal weakness of plot and plausibility precisely because they attach themselves to our emotions and perceptions by condensing the evanescence of youth and the hateful, inescapable proximity of boredom and death. The epoch of *Gatsby* was also the period of the first, sensational publication of 'The Waste Land'. Waugh quotes very effectively from that crucial poem in *Brideshead*; Fitzgerald is known to have drawn his valley of ashes on Long Island from Eliot's haunting imagery. (And Eliot praised *Gatsby* extravagantly, calling it 'the first step the American novel has taken since Henry James'.) Not all the great modernists liked *Gatsby* as much – here's H. L. Mencken's annihilating review:

> This clown [Gatsby] Fitzgerald rushes to his death in nine short chapters. The other performers in the *Totentanz* [dance of death] are of a like, or even worse quality. One of them is a rich man who carries on a grotesque intrigue with the wife of a garage keeper.
>
> Another is a woman golfer who wins championships by cheating. A third, a sort of chorus to the tragic farce, is a bond salesman – symbol of the New America! Fitzgerald clears them all off at last by a triple butchery. The garage keeper's wife, rushing out upon the road to escape her husband's third degree, is run down and killed by the wife of her lover. The garage keeper, misled by the lover, kills the lover of the lover's wife – the Great Gatsby himself. Another bullet, and the garage keeper is also reduced to offal . . . The crooked lady golfer departs. The lover of the garage keeper's wife goes back to his own consort. The immense house of the Great Gatsby stands idle, its bedrooms given over to the bat and the owl, and its cocktail shakers dry. The curtain lurches down.

Mencken is inarguably right in one way: a man of Gatsby's supposed force and vitality just takes a house and waits for the girl to come, luckily discovering after brooding at length on a green light that the adored one's cousin lives next door! And one winces when Mr Wilson's body is found near Gatsby's blood-streaked pool and 'the holocaust was complete', because of the awful straining for effect and also because any definition of a holocaust would have had to take the life of Tom or at least Daisy. And yet, look back at what Mencken writes and see where he falls into obvious error. Fitzgerald doesn't 'clear them all off at last'. The only ones who die or are killed, from or by a combination of callousness and caprice, are – the innocent.

There are two key words in the book. They are 'pointless' (and its analogues) and 'careless'. They recur with striking and mounting emphasis as the narrative shakes off its near-permanent hangover. A dog biscuit at Tom Buchanan's adulterous and nasty gathering is represented as 'decomposed apathetically' in a saucer of milk; Myrtle on the same horrid occasion 'looked at me and laughed pointlessly'. At Gatsby's bigger but even hollower party, there's a cocktail table – 'the only place in the garden where a single man could linger without looking purposeless and alone'. After 'a somehow wasteful and inappropriate half hour', Jordan Baker wants to leave. In New York one hot evening, Nick notices 'young clerks in the dusk, wasting the most poignant moments of night and life'. Driving through Central Park, Gatsby 'came alive to me, delivered suddenly from the womb of his purposeless splendor'. Is there a line more expressive of vicious tedium than Daisy's petulant demand: 'What'll we do with ourselves this afternoon, and the day after that, and the next thirty years?' If there is, it's the earlier pettishness when she insists on knowing whatever it is that people do when they make plans. Even the great cars are bored and affectless: 'The dilatory limousine came rolling up the drive.' When Tom talks about getting gas, 'a pause followed this apparently pointless remark'; when the stop for gas is made, the expression on Myrtle's face at first seems 'purposeless and inexplicable'. In West Egg, Daisy dreads 'the too obtrusive fate that herded its inhabitants along a shortcut from nothing to nothing'. As Nick takes his penultimate leave of Gatsby, he quits him 'standing there in the moonlight – watching over nothing'. Here is the full-out horror of torpor and morbidity and futility and waste, saturated in joyless heat and sweat. *Gatsby* came out in April of that year of grace 1925: the cruellest month seems right.

But then what of care, or caring? It's the antithesis of the spoiled and the bored and the nihilistic: it shares an impulse with charity and *caritas* and, well, love. People come uninvited to Gatsby's mansion, which is as lonely and desperate as Hearst's castle, and he doesn't care. He is indifferent. So is Jordan Baker, a rotten and insouciant woman of whom Nick inquires, if only about her terrible driving, 'Suppose you met somebody just as careless as yourself.' And then I'm sure you remember: 'They were careless people, Tom and Daisy – they smashed up things and creatures and then retreated back into their money or their vast carelessness or whatever it was that kept them together, and let other people clean up the mess they had made.'

(I sometimes think that the word 'car-less' is lurking here in some subliminal, Jungian way, given the role played by the nonsentient, automatic, and then entirely new and exciting status symbol of the fast limo or coupe. What poor, degraded Mr Wilson wouldn't give to be buying a car instead of just repairing one.) Anyway, the ultimate and startling point about Gatsby is that he does care, deeply and secretly and inarticulately and naïvely and vulnerably, and he cares for someone who could hardly care less. And he *is* innocent, in spite of all his worldliness. This is the lineament of tragedy.

Fitzgerald used to say that he had a 'presentiment of disaster' that inflected all his stories. Another reason for the hardihood of his finest novel may be the foreshadowing that it contains of a brutish and inhuman modernity succeeding the dance music and the affectless flippancy. Fitzgerald had been reading Spengler's dismal and reactionary *Decline of the West*, and many people had been peering at a popular and poisonous volume on eugenics called *The Rising Tide of Color Against White World-Supremacy*, published by a quack named Lothrop Stoddard in 1920. When we first meet Tom Buchanan he has been reading

'*The Rise of the Coloured Empires* by this man Goddard . . . It's a fine book and everybody ought to read it. The idea is if we don't look out the white race will be – will be utterly submerged. It's all scientific stuff; it's been proved . . . we're Nordics . . . and we've produced all the things that go to make civilization – oh, science and art and all that.'

One wants to smile at a total philistine who could make no other reference to science and art, let alone 'all that' – just as one smiles today when silly people pretend to ask For Whom the Bell Curves – but Tom Buchanan is a prefiguration of the ugly pseudo-scientific and pseudo-intellectual types who would mutate into fascism over the horizon of 1929. References to Jews and the upwardly mobile are consistently disobliging in the book – Fitzgerald also has this in common with Waugh, coming up with absurd names for arrivistes such as Stonewall Jackson Abram – but it gives one quite a turn to find Meyer Wolfsheim, he with molars for cuff links, hidden Shylock-like behind the address of 'The Swastika Holding Company'. Pure coincidence: the symbol meant nothing sinister at the time. Still, you can get the sensation, from *The Great Gatsby*, that the twentieth century is not going to be a feast of reason and a flow of soul.

Other notes are struck that keep the novel stingingly fresh. Fitzgerald sardonically foreshadowed the epoch of self-generating celebrity with the same skill he employed capturing the tone of the non-event: 'We all turned and looked around for Gatsby. It was testimony to the romantic speculation he inspired that there were whispers about him from those who had found little that it was necessary to whisper about in this world.'

And as for the dawning of the corresponding myth of publicity, how can one equal the frenzied pointlessness of this episode, almost post-modern in its effect?

> About this time an ambitious young reporter from New York arrived one morning at Gatsby's door and asked him if he had anything to say.
>
> 'Anything to say about what?' inquired Gatsby politely.
>
> 'Why – any statement to give out.'
>
> It transpired after a confused five minutes that the man had heard Gatsby's name around his office in a connection which he either wouldn't reveal or didn't fully understand . . . [His] notoriety, spread about by the hundreds who had accepted his hospitality and so become authorities upon his past, had increased all summer until he fell just short of being news.

'Her voice', says Gatsby of Daisy when he finally finds his own, 'is full of money.' And Nick picks up on this metaphor right away – 'the inexhaustible charm that rose and fell in it, the jingle of it, the cymbals' song of it . . . High in a white palace the king's daughter, the golden girl.' Fitzgerald really believed, with Somerset Maugham, that money is the sixth sense that makes the other five senses tingle and come alive. He also believed that in America you could remake yourself and get others to judge you by the identity and reputation you had fought to make your own. Yet in *Gatsby*, his artistry won't allow this drossy romanticism to be vindicated. Gatsby looks and sounds a fool when he says, 'Can't repeat the past? Why of course you can!', as if opportunity were boundless, or a matter of the triumph of the will. His gold turns to ordure. He might as well not have changed his name from Jimmy Gatz, or written out that Horatio Alger schedule for getting ahead by sheer effort and merit, which his sad father discovers on the flyleaf of an old Hopalong Cassidy book. His strenuous reinvention makes him look pitiable. The snobs win; this is a class society, and those who work hard and play by the rules, like the wretched Mr Wilson, are treated like ordure, too. And is there anything in American fiction more frigid and careless than Daisy's treatment of the little daughter she appears to have? Despair is never very far away, so it's no exaggeration to say that *Gatsby* also achieved and held its strangely contemporary status by anticipating, in an age of relative if aimless cheerfulness, the concept of the existential, the causeless rebel, and indeed the absurd.

Such themes deserve the name of timeless; the beautiful metaphysics of the novel (the 'yellow cocktail music' and the young woman who appears 'like an angry diamond') are echoed in Fitzgerald's devastating rendition of the pangs of disprized love. Of the many such passages: 'He stretched out his hand desperately as if to snatch only a wisp of air, to save a fragment of the spot that she had made lovely for him. But it was all going by too fast now for his blurred eyes and he knew he had lost that part of it, the freshest and the best, forever.'

These days, the Eggs and the Hamptons and Montauk are still an adventure playground on 'that slender riotous island which extends itself due east of New York', but Mencken was also right when he went on to say that Fitzgerald's prose redeemed his story. The grand houses on the Sound may be called 'inessential', yet the young and the vivid, the loving and the yearning and the sexual chords above are answered by:

> The old island here that flowered once for Dutch sailors' eyes – a fresh, green breast of the new world. Its vanished trees, the trees that had made way for Gatsby's house, had once pandered in whispers to the last and greatest of all human dreams; for a transitory enchanted moment man must have held his breath in the presence of this continent, compelled into an aesthetic contemplation he neither understood nor desired, face to face for the last time in history with something commensurate to his capacity for wonder.

Fitzgerald's work captures the evaporating memory of the American Eden while connecting it to the advent of the New World of smartness and thuggery and corruption. It was his rite of passage; it is our bridge to the time before 'dreams' were slogans. He wanted to call it *Among the Ashheaps and Millionaires* – thank heaven that his editor, Maxwell Perkins, talked him out of it. It was nearly entitled just plain *Gatsby*. It remains 'the great' because it confronts the defeat of youth and beauty and idealism, and finds the defeat unbearable, and then turns to face the defeat unflinchingly. With *The Great Gatsby*, American letters grew up.

First published as 'The Road to West Egg' in *Vanity Fair*, May 2000

Rebel in Evening Clothes

In the fall of 1914, as Europe was marching over the precipice, Miss Dorothy Rothschild of New York wrote a poem entitled 'Any Porch' and sent it off to *Vanity Fair* editor Frank Crowninshield. It was a nine-stanza lampoon, satirising the hotel-porch babble of spoiled upper-crust ladies in Connecticut, and its acceptance, for an emolument of $12, marked the first time that the future Dorothy Parker got anything into print:

> 'My husband says, often, "Elise,
> You feel things too deeply, you do – " '
> 'Yes, forty a month, if you please,
> Oh, servants impose on me, too.'
> 'I don't want the vote for myself.
> But women with property, dear – '
> 'I think the poor girl's on the shelf,
> She's talking about her "career".'

Crowninshield – the granduncle of Benjamin Crowninshield Bradlee, late of *The Washington Post* – soon after hired Miss Rothschild for Condé Nast and thereby enabled her to quit her day job as a pianist at a Manhattan dance school. This was an odd alliance, between the cultivated and immaculate super-WASP Crowninshield, who combined fashion-plate tastes with an interest in Picasso, and the daughter of an ambitious sweat-shop manager in the New York Garment District. From then on, young Dorothy divided her time agreeably enough between writing suggestive fashion captions for *Vogue* and incendiary verses for *Vanity Fair*. The fashion lines had an edge to them – 'Brevity is the soul of lingerie', she wrote, and also 'There was a little girl who had a little curl, right in the middle of her forehead. When she was good she was very very good, and when she was bad she wore this divine nightdress of rose-coloured mousseline de soie, trimmed with frothy Valenciennes lace.'

This sort of thing was a revenge for the detested convent school to which her upwardly mobile parents had insisted upon sending her. The poetry, though, was sometimes so subversive that Mr Crowninshield had to publish it under the pseudonym 'Henriette Rousseau'. Composed in free verse rather than conventional stanzas, they included 'Women: A Hate Song' ('I Hate Women, They get on my Nerves'). There was also a pungent prose article, 'Why I Haven't Married', in which it was the turn of the male sex to get the treatment. There was another poem with the 'Hate Song' title, from 1919, subtitled 'An Intimate Glimpse of *Vanity Fair* – En Famille'. It began and ended with the italicised cry '*I hate the office, / It cuts in on my social life*'. Here one encountered such figures as

> . . . the Boss;
> The Great White Chief.
> He made us what we are to-day, –
> I hope he's satisfied.
> He has some bizarre ideas
> About his employees getting to work
> At nine o'clock in the morning –
> As if they were a lot of milkmen.
> He has never been known to see you
> When you arrive at 8.45,
> But try to come in at a quarter past ten
> And he will always go up in the elevator with you.
> He goes to Paris on the slightest provocation
> And nobody knows why he has to stay there so long.

(To this, one can only add, how different, how very different, is the style of our own dear *rédacteur en chef*.) Crowninshield was a stuffy man in some ways, but we owe him a debt of gratitude because it was he who kept Mrs Parker – she married in 1917 – in work, he who introduced her to Robert Benchley and Robert Sherwood and caused them to become friends and colleagues, and he who had the inspired idea of giving her P. G. Wodehouse's old job as *Vanity Fair's* theatre critic, when 'Plum' took himself off to write musical comedies in collaboration with Jerome Kern and Guy Bolton. Mr Benchley once observed that the joy of being a *Vanity Fair* contributor was this: you could write about any subject you liked, no matter how outrageous, as long as you said it in evening clothes. (I have devoted my professional life to the emulation of this fine line.)

I never knew Mrs Parker, but I did know Jessica Mitford, whose life in some ways reminds me of Parker's: refugee from a perfectly ghastly family; champion of the oppressed; implacable foe of the bores. Once, during Mitford's days in the Deep South as a partisan of civil rights, 'Decca' was taken to an all-white garden party by her friend Virginia Durr. Introduced to the head of the local board of education, she sweetly confided that in Oakland, California, where she lived, the student honour roll was led by blacks. 'It don't seem to make no sense, do it?' said the sturdy segregationist. 'To me it do,' retorted Decca, sweeping away as the education boss wilted like a salted snail. The crisp one-line comeback is among the least ephemeral things in the world.

People revere and remember Mrs Parker's work to this day, for its epigrams and multiple entendres and for its terse, brittle approach to the long littleness of life. There's a tendency to forget, though, that the 'edge' and the acuity came from an acidulated approach to stupidity and bigotry and cruelty. Much of this awareness originated in her family life; as the youngest of two brothers and two sisters she was the keenest in observing the difference between their uptown life and the dismal condition of those who toiled in the apparel industry. As, in 1939, she was to tell the readers of *New Masses* – arguably the least brittle and witty magazine ever to be published on American soil:

> I think I knew first what side I was on when I was about five years old, at which time nobody was safe from buffaloes. It was in a brownstone house in New York, and there was a blizzard, and my rich aunt – a horrible woman then and now – had come to visit. I remember going to the window and seeing the street with the men shovelling snow; their hands were purple on their shovels, and their feet were wrapped with burlap. And my aunt, looking over my shoulder, said, 'Now isn't it nice there's this blizzard. All those men have work.' And I knew then that it was not nice that men could work for their lives only in desperate weather; that there was no work for them when it was fair.

The word 'fair' is beautifully deployed there, I think. Even when she was writing for *New Masses* (the Communist-dominated mutation of the old Greenwich Village *The Masses*, which had been associated with John Reed and Max Eastman) Mrs Parker did not forsake her habit of stretching like a feline and then whipping out with a murderous paw. (Of some superior-minded socialists she used to know, she wrote: 'Some of them are dead. And the rest are liberals, too.')

So that a life apparently consecrated to Broadway and the speakeasy and (Oh God, not all that again) the Algonquin Hotel, with its celebrated Round Table and matching circle of wits – George S. Kaufman and Alexander Woollcott predominating – was also a life, as she phrased it, 'wild with the knowledge of injustice and brutality and misrepresentation'. And in 1927 she married her two styles – deadly perfect-pitch eavesdropping and cold contempt for prejudice – in a story entitled 'Arrangement in Black and White'. It opens like this: 'The woman with the pink velvet poppies wreathed round the assisted gold of her hair traversed the crowded room at an interesting gait combining a skip with a sidle . . .'

Rather like her first poem, 'Any Porch', much of Mrs Parker's story is overheard dialogue, made up of mingled inanity and condescension. The vapid woman of 'assisted gold' hair is bent on meeting the 'colored' singer who is the social lion of the evening. Yet she worries what her husband may think:

> But I must say for Burton, he's heaps broader-minded than lots of these Southerners. He's really awfully fond of colored people. Well, he says himself, he wouldn't have white servants. And you know, he had this old colored nurse, this regular old nigger mammy, and he just simply loves her. Why, every time he goes home, he goes out in the kitchen to see her. He does, really, to this day.

There are some moments of superb dryness to offset the electrifying embarrassment, as when the woman gushingly asks her host, 'Aren't I terrible?' and he replies 'Oh, no, no, no. No, no'. Or when she asks:

> 'There are some bad white people, too, in this world. Aren't there?'
> 'I guess there are', said her host.

It's a fairly short story, but it seems longer – as moments of gross social *bêtise* always do – because the female character just cannot put a foot right. (When she eventually meets the black singer, she speaks 'With great distinctness, moving her lips meticulously, as if in parlance with the deaf'.) Viewed from more than seven decades later, it seems at moments a little obvious, until one remembers those seven decades and their passage, and the fact that Jim Crow – legally enforced segregation in everything from trains to the armed forces – was the unchallenged rule in 1927, and until one appreciates that Mrs Parker had anticipated every agonised, patronising person who was ever to speak of the African-American and his divine sense of rhythm. Indeed, she was four decades ahead of *Guess Who's Coming to Dinner*.

She was also four decades away from her own death. 'But I shall stay the way I am,' she wrote in 1925. 'Because I do not give a damn.' In consequence, partly, of her non-damn donation policy, her end wasn't as sweet as it might have been. Lonely, except for her dog, Troy, and a bit sour, and a touch too fond of the pre-noon cocktail, she hung on in the Volney residential hotel in New York – within dog-walking distance of Central Park and full of the sort of idle women she had always despised – and continued to make biting remarks to a diminishing audience. She was habitually hopeless about money, and her friends were surprised, after her demise, to find that she had bothered to make a will at all. But in 1965, feeling herself wasting away, she had summoned a lawyer named Oscar Bernstein and drawn up a very simple document. Her shares of common stock in *The New Yorker* (given to her by editor Harold Ross), her savings accounts, and her copyrights and royalties, she instructed him, were to go to the Reverend Martin Luther

King. In the event of his death, they would be bequeathed to the National Association for the Advancement of Colored People (NAACP). Oscar Bernstein's widow, Rebecca, later said, 'He understood completely what she had in mind. It seemed natural because she had no heirs, and racial injustice had always affected her very deeply.' Having made these simple provisions – and meanwhile appointing Lillian Hellman as her literary executor – she told Zero Mostel that the least she could do now was die.

But this she didn't do until June 7 1967. The Reverend Dr King was chairing a meeting of the Southern Christian Leadership Conference, in an Atlanta restaurant called B. B. Beamon's, when he received the news of the bequest. It didn't amount to all that much – $20,448.39 after deductions – but at 1967 prices it caused him to tell his executive that it 'verifies what I have always said, that the Lord will provide'. At the moment, he had less than a year to live himself.

Mrs Parker had stipulated that she be cremated, with no funeral service of any kind, and she nearly got her wish. Lillian Hellman organised a memorial at which she herself was the star attraction, and seems to have lost or destroyed her friend's remaining papers. The cremation, though, did take place.

'Excuse my dust' had been Mrs Parker's joke all-purpose epitaph. But the laugh was on her. Lillian Hellman sent her ashes to the law firm of Oscar Bernstein and Paul O'Dwyer, and Mr O'Dwyer, one of New York's greatest people's attorneys and labour defenders, receiving no instructions about their disposal or their disposition, kept them in a filing cabinet in his office for two decades. There is only one plausible explanation for this amazingly unaesthetic outcome, and that is the vindictiveness of Lillian Hellman – surely one of the least attractive women produced by the American 'progressive' culture in this century. Furious at not having been named owner of the estate, she contested the transfer of the rights from Dr King to the NAACP. A court ruled in favour of the organisation, causing Ms Hellman to explode with irritation and to speak with almost as much condescension as the frothy lady in 'Arrangement in Black and White'. 'It's one thing to have real feeling for black people,' she expostulated, 'but to have the kind of blind sentimentality about the NAACP, a group so conservative that even many blacks now don't have any respect for it, is something else.' To her playwright friend Howard Teichmann, according to Marion Meade's surpassingly good Parker biography, *What Fresh Hell is This?*, Hellman raged about Mrs Parker's alleged promise that 'when she died, she would leave me the rights to her writing. At my death, they would pass directly to the NAACP. But what did she do? She left them to the NAACP. Damn her!' (To the present day, those who want to reprint Mrs Parker have to go to the

NAACP and discuss royalties: a perfect posthumous revenge from two points of view.)

That period of spitefulness and neglect came to its close in October 1983, when Benjamin Hooks of the NAACP became aware that Mrs Parker's remains had no resting-place except for a dank filing cabinet. A small memorial garden was prepared on the grounds of the organisation's headquarters in Baltimore, and a brief ceremony was held at which Mr Hooks improved somewhat on the terse line about 'excuse my dust'. It might be better, he said, to recall her lines from 'Epitaph for a Darling Lady':

> Leave for her a red young rose
> Go your way, and save your pity.
> She is happy, for she knows
> That her dust is very pretty.

Mrs Parker had never been very affirmatively Jewish – she disliked her father's piety and always insisted that her hatred of Hitler and fascism was, so to say, secular – but Mr Hooks took the opportunity to stress the historic comradeship between blacks and Jews. The inscription at the little memorial reads:

> Here lie the ashes of Dorothy Parker (1893–1967) Humorist, writer, critic, defender of human and civil rights. For her epitaph she suggested 'Excuse My Dust'. This memorial garden is dedicated to her noble spirit which celebrated the oneness of humankind, and to the bonds of everlasting friendship between black and Jewish people.

This rather affecting gesture drew little publicity at the time. And black–Jewish relations were not exactly flourishing in the late 1980s. A few years ago, when I was in Baltimore to visit the H. L. Mencken Library, I heard about the Parker monument and made a brief detour-cum-pilgrimage. I was sad to find the garden slightly neglected, and some of the staff unaware that it was even there. But the NAACP was undergoing a dismal interlude then, with its executive director, the Reverend Ben Chavis, accused of diverting its hard-won funds to pay off his mistress. (He has since changed names and identities and sought relief in the 'ministry' of Louis Farrakhan.)

On my most recent visit, in June of this year, things were already looking up. I was greeted by Ms Chris Mencken, one of the NAACP's staffers, whose grandfather's second cousin was the sage of Baltimore himself. (H. L. Mencken, indeed, published several of Mrs Parker's early stories in *The Smart Set*, the middle-brow-baiting review that he edited with George Jean Nathan. But that didn't prevent her, when they met in Baltimore in 1924, from walking out when he took too many drinks and began to give off slurring jokes about black people.)

Ms Mencken, whose presence seemed like a sort of ideal recompense for that spoiled evening, had just finished sweeping up around the memorial. It stands in a small grove of pines, which could be mistaken for a circle of listeners. The plaque with the above inscription sits on a cylindrical urn which contains the ashes. The whole is set in three circular courses of brown brickwork. Harry G. Robinson, then dean of the School of Architecture at Howard University, was given the commission for the memorial and wrote that it was intended to symbolise the centre of a Round Table.

With America's most venerable civil-rights organisation until recently facing bankruptcy and other sorts of discredit, it has been a time for volunteers. Mrs Myrlie Evers-Williams, widow of the civil-rights martyr Medgar Evers, first stepped forward to assume responsibility. So did former congressman Kweisi Mfume, and so did Julian Bond, the brilliant Georgian activist and orator who was a student of Dr King's. As the NAACP itself 'came back' from an interval of decline, and as Bond and others began to speak back boldly against the black separatist demagogues (and the mealymouthed senators and congressmen who would not disown the so-called Council of Conservative Citizens), I had a tiny idea. I wrote to Julian Bond, proposing that Mrs Parker's memorial garden be refurbished and rededicated. (One hopes that she, who so despised the Church, would 'excuse' the fact that the NAACP building is a converted nunnery.) By this means, I thought we could do honour to one of *Vanity Fair*'s founding minxes, and also to the brave causes that she upheld so tenaciously. Julian Bond right away agreed it was a sound scheme, so we're going to have a little party to celebrate said scheme. I would modestly propose adding a line of Mrs Parker's from 1939, about the misery and bigotry she saw around her: 'I knew it need not be so; I think I knew even then that it would eventually not be so.' These are only words, and this is only a gesture, but as Mrs Parker proved somewhat to her own surprise, there is power in words, and in gestures too.

First published as 'Rebel in Evening Clothes' in *Vanity Fair*,
October 1999

The Long Littleness of Life

Christopher Isherwood and W. H. Auden left their country of birth – effectively forever – on January 19 1939. Their departure for America was widely construed as an act of desertion if not of cowardice. In his Munich-era novelette *Put Out More Flags*, Evelyn Waugh lampooned the pair as 'Parsnip and Pimpernell'. He went slightly further than the insinuation of funk: 'What I don't see is how these two can claim to be contemporary if they run away from the biggest event in contemporary history. They were contemporary enough about Spain when no one threatened to come and bomb them.' (For additional taunt value, Waugh put these words into the mouth of all ill-favoured female Trotskyist of advanced opinions.)

These diaries begin on the day that the ship left the dock, and they show Isherwood engaging with precisely those sorts of suspicion. Was his pacifism based merely on fear, and on the misery he felt at the horrible death of his adored father on the Western Front in 1915? And how could it be squared with his anti-fascism? On the matter of physical courage he had come to feel more secure since making his voyage to China with Auden the previous year (the voyage that resulted in their co-authored *Journey to a War*). As he recollects that trip, in his very first entry:

> True, it wasn't really very dangerous; I think there were only three or four occasions on which we were likely to be killed by bombs or bullets. But a very little danger will go a long way psychologically. Several times I had been afraid, but healthily afraid. I no longer dreaded the unknown.

Reassured on this score, he reflected on his hatred of Nazism. Throughout the 1930s, Isherwood had been a dedicated and conscious anti-fascist (which is more, I cannot resist adding, than could be said for Mr Evelyn Waugh). But now his longtime lover, Heinz Neddermeyer, had been captured by the Gestapo, severely punished, and put into uniform. So had many other German boys of Isherwood's acquaintance. Could he acquiesce in doing to them what had been done to his father?

> Suppose I have in my power an army of six million men. I can destroy it by pressing an electric button. The six millionth man is Heinz. Will I press the button'? Of course not – even if the 5,999,999 others are hundred per cent Jew-baiting blood-mad fiends (which is absurd).

But anti-Nazism was qualified, in Isherwood's mind, by more than just this rationalisation:

> One morning on deck, it seems to me, I turned to Auden and said: 'You know, I just don't believe in any of it any more – the united front, the party line, the antifascist struggle. I suppose they're okay, but something's wrong with me. I simply can't swallow another mouthful.' And Auden answered: 'No, neither can I.' In a few sentences, with exquisite relief, we confessed our mutual disgust at the parts we had been playing and resolved to abandon them, then and there. We had forgotten our real vocation. We would be artists again, with our own values, our own integrity, and not amateur socialist agitators, parlour reds.

As more and more baggage went over the side, Isherwood realised that he was going to need some sort of ballast even so. Auden, he reflected, 'had his Anglo-Catholicism to fall back on. I had nothing of this kind, and I didn't yet clearly realise how much I was going to need it.'

The first third of this diary is preoccupied almost exclusively with the working out of these themes. It proved harder than anticipated for Isherwood to remake himself as a homosexual and artistic free spirit in the New World. For one thing, he hadn't completely succeeded in convincing himself that it was right to leave England. The diaries continue to worry at the point. In early 1940 he receives a letter from the 'William Hickey' columnist of the London *Daily Express*. It contains the following verse:

> The literary erstwhile Left-wellwisher would
> Seek vainly now for Auden or for Isherwood:
> The dog beneath the skin has had the brains
> To save it, Norris-like, by changing trains.

'Why', asks Isherwood, 'does this sting me so? Simply because it is really clever. I am not in the least ashamed of myself: but I feel foolish.' (How, I wonder, would Isherwood have felt if he had known that 'William Hickey' was the pseudonym for Tom Driberg, a leading member of the gay and Left underworlds and a man later to be accused of keeping unseemly company with Guy Burgess?) However outwardly defiant of such teasing, Isherwood now tells us that he went to the length of writing to the British Embassy in Washington and 'offering, if necessary, to return to England and serve in a noncombatant capacity'. The Embassy took the news calmly, not to say indifferently, and Isherwood felt that he had at least tried to clean the slate.

Katherine Bucknell's exemplary editing and arrangement of these journals has divided them into three parts. Part One, *The Emigration*, takes the reader from January 19 1939, to December 31 1944. Part Two, *The Postwar Years*, runs from January 1 1945, to December 26 1949, and from April 11 1948, to April 13 1956. Part Three, *The Late Fifties*, stretches from April 14 1956, to May 25 1958, and from May 26 1958, to August 26 1960. The dates conceal a hiatus of almost two years between 1945 and 1947, during which Isherwood underwent a species of mid-life crisis and made no entries at all. Otherwise, however, he was true both to the boyhood habit of writing daily in a journal, and to the more elaborate maintenance of a record of private fantasies, first evolved in Cambridge with his lifelong friend Edward Upward and distilled into the half-sinister and half-playful world of the 'Mortmere' stories they wrote together.

The Emigration shows Isherwood establishing the contacts and filiations which were to determine the rest of his life in America. He decided to leave Manhattan to Auden and to begin anew on the West Coast and within reach of Hollywood: not to be a camera but to work for the camera. He fell in with the hermetic world of Swami Prabhavananda with whom he associated in what he himself described as a 'guru and disciple' relationship for three decades, and with whom he was to produce a translation of the *Bhagavad-Gita*. And he joined a loose-knit world of mainly English, Russian, and German artists and writers – ranging from the Stravinskys to the Brechts and the Thomas Manns and including Aldous Huxley and Gerald Heard – who were either exiles or émigrés. One month into the Second World War he is at Tujunga Canyon with Huxley, Bertrand Russell, Krishnamurti, Anita Loos, and Greta Garbo, Russell having 'the air of a father joining in a game to amuse the children'. To judge by the account he gives of this somewhat strained occasion (Garbo and Krishnamurti were rather afraid of each other; Isherwood himself was rather too forward with Garbo), it's a mercy that Fleet Street cynics were not on hand to immortalise it.

A number of asides make it plain that he either wanted or expected his diaries to be read later on by other eyes. His initial reactions to the world of mescaline and Ojai and Llano and Om and enlightenment and California mysticism form a kind of period piece. He recorded them at first in the same wry fashion with which he had observed the foibles of Berliners:

The place is run by a Mrs Behr, one of those art-corsairs of the desert, in bold gaudy clothes, who speak of their guests as 'my little family'. The guests were third-rate film notables, some nice college kids, with sound teeth, clear empty eyes and consciences, and a young man dying of TB who publishes a weekly newspaper supposed to be written by his dogs.

In a solemn talk with Gerald Heard about the three stages of 'the enlargement of consciousness' he sets down, in what I suppose might be termed a deadpan fashion, the following reminiscence:

> Gerald told me how, the other day, he was looking into the bowl of the toilet: a green light fell on the porcelain, through the leaves outside the window, and it appeared to him 'as it really was'.
>
> 'Nothing else mattered to me at that moment. I could have gone on looking at it for ever.'

One almost wishes that he had; as the diary progresses we encounter Heard as that most dangerous of types, the micro-megalomaniac. Content to dominate and impress a small flock, and a living example of the precept about a little learning, he had a mental sail so rigged as to be swelled by any little zephyr of bogus philosophy or pseudoscience. Isherwood seems to have forgiven him much, including an early fascination with UFOs, for his strength of personality and for his appearing to lead that 'intentional life' that he always so envied in others.

As the war progressed, Isherwood's pacifism became tougher and less apologetic. He even attacks Erika Mann's 'hate lectures' against the Nazis. And he is terribly upset when his old friend E. M. Forster comes out for the Churchill side in a pamphlet called *Nordic Twilight*:

> Certainly, life would be ten thousand times worse under the Nazis. Churchill, from his point of view, is absolutely right when he says this, and absolutely right to fight Hitler. But from Morgan, our philosopher, we expect something more. There are plenty of people able and willing to sound the call to battle. To stand up for the half-truths and the relative values. To preach the doctrine of the Lesser Evil. That is not Forster's function.

(And now I wonder about that crack-up in 1945, where the diaries break off. Having mentioned the eerie figure of 'six million' in his argument about not killing Heinz under any circumstances, did Isherwood have another crisis when the crimes of the Third Reich were fully exposed? He never alludes to the subject here, though in later memoirs, such as *Christopher and His Kind* (1976), he restated the dilemma but dropped the words 'six million'.) However that may be, it ought to be said for Isherwood that he fought his corner hard, and had terrible rows with the Brechts when they might have done him some good in Hollywood, and ignored Berthold Viertel's advice not to offend the Germans and Jews from whom he might have to earn his bread. Still attempting to prove something about himself, he quit California in October 1941, and went to work as a Quaker volunteer among German refugees who had recently arrived in Pennsylvania. Here, in that odd part of the state where all the place names are Welsh, he made another stab at 'intentional living' combined with self-sacrifice and spirituality.

These pages are among the most touching, as well as the most amusing, in the entire book. It suited Isherwood in many ways to be dealing with the victims of Hitler; the work was obviously worthwhile for one thing, and his Berlin street-wisdom came in handy. But he must have realised quite early on that the intense worthiness and dowdiness of Quaker life were not for him. (Among other things, it elevated the sacrament of marriage to an oppressive degree.) Before long, he is giving us the sorts of vignette that he had once culled from observing the clientele at Fräulein Schroeder's pension:

> I quite liked Timbres, who was a trained nurse and had been in Russia with her husband on some project when he died of typhus. She was a big woman with eyeglasses who made herself look like an elephant by unwisely wearing light blue. Hanstein was rather pretty and rather a bitch.

The sheer scale of certain female types always made a great impression on Isherwood:

> She was a whale of a girl, with breasts like an Alpine meadow, and a great pouchy purple face surrounded by nondescript hair like sofa stuffing, worn in a sawed-off bob. Betty Schloss had the largest behind in the world.

Meanwhile the war news is getting worse, and Isherwood's contempt for those who follow it eagerly is intensifying. Shortly after Pearl Harbor 'came news that San Francisco had been bombed; a journalistic rumour. A stout belligerent woman in the Haverford drugstore opined, "Well – I guess we can take it."' There's an authentic thrill of disgust in that glancing notice. Three other things can be remarked of this period. First, Isherwood starts to use American locutions ('pinch-hit') as if to the manner born. Second, he broods a lot on the ego, sometimes rendering it in upper case – when he is thinking about the Swami – and sometimes in lower case, when he is speaking of his own daily battles against selfishness. Third, he affords us a few glimpses of his homosexual life. In general the book is rather oblique about this, dwelling only on how things are going with X or Y, but in the war years Isherwood was still very much on the lookout. After an evening in Philadelphia he comes up with a marvelous metaphor – interpolated later into the diary – for the gay underworld:

> The others went back by a late train to New York: Pete and I spent the night at our favourite haunt, the Camac Baths.
> (It has always seemed to me that there is in fact only one Turkish bath – an enormous subterranean world, a delicious purgatory, a naked democracy

in which the only class distinctions are anatomical. And that this underworld merely has a number of different entrances and vestibules in all the cities of the earth. You could enter it in Sydney and emerge from it to find yourself in Jermyn Street.)

And then to stand straight-faced in front of a solemn group the next morning thinking something like: 'Bet you wouldn't believe what yours truly was up to last night.' But not content to be the odd man out merely in this sense, Isherwood also felt the urge to be the gadfly at Friends' discussions:

He also spoke about the Quaker theory of meditation: contact with the Inner Light. 'The Quakers', said Steere, 'have only one dogma: God is available.' Of course, the connection between this and Vedanta is obvious. To hear what he'd say, I asked him, 'Does a Quaker necessarily have to be a Christian?' Steere looked very sly and mysterious; I think he realised what I was driving at. 'Well', he answered, after a moment's hesitation, 'perhaps not necessarily. No.'

Still seeking a moral equivalent to Auden's Anglo-Catholicism, Isherwood goes again to argue with Bertrand Russell and Julian Huxley. They are most concerned about Aldous. He describes the encounter in his best Mr Norris style:

'Did he – I mean – er, that is – do you mean to say he actually, er, really – prays?' 'And why', asked Bertie, 'does Aldous talk about Ultimate Reality? Surely one kind of reality isn't any more or less real than another.'

The exchange becomes a *dialogue des sourds*:

'You mean' – Julian was helping me out, now – 'that what Aldous is after is some kind of psychological adjustment?' 'Well, yes,' I said, 'if you like to put it that way: everything's a psychological adjustment: marriage, for instance, or learning Spanish, or becoming a fascist.' But they only nodded indulgently. 'A psychological adjustment – ' they murmured to each other, no longer giving me their full attention, 'Well, in that case, of course, one quite sees – '

Very well caught: two dry old Cantabrigian rationalists stuffing another pigeonhole. But it isn't long before one starts to pine for a bit of pedantically rigorous materialism.

On his return to California, Isherwood keeps on recording things without comment – the internment camps for the Japanese, a headline in the *Los Angeles Times* reading 'Uniform Veal Ceiling Near'. The ego and the Ego continue to oscillate.

If there's anything I'm sick of, it's personal relationships, on which I and the rest of my friends used to expend a positively horticultural energy. Ah, what a coldness there was, underneath those 'darlings', those kisses, those hugs, those protestations! Here, I'm happy to say, all that seems meaningless.

'Here', in this entry, is the Swami's establishment on Ivar Avenue. But if Isherwood hoped to escape from petty personal relations in this setting, he was to be sorely disappointed. The place seems to have been a hellhole of rivalry, precedence, and sanctimony. Only a few weeks later he is writing:

> As Arniya says, it's the little things which are hard to take. No good making up all sorts of excellent and perfectly valid reasons why I should no longer be deprived of my room by Hayne, or annoyed by George's chanting, Web's alarm clock, Asit's radio, Apama's beads. I missed the prayer for the liberation of earthbound spirits and all the precautions against psychic obstacles.

One can only be subjective here. If you find this sort of thing tedious and irritating and shallow, then there is plenty of it to get you down:

> July 28, 1943. Salka brought Garbo up to lunch at Ivar Avenue. The girls were all a-flutter, and Garbo didn't disappoint them. She played up outrageously, sighing about how wonderful it must be to be a nun, and flirting with Swami, telling him about his dark, mysterious, oriental eyes. Sarada, of course, was convinced that Garbo's soul is halfway saved already, and Swami says that now I have to bring him the Duke of Windsor – his other great object of admiration.

Good grief! And one doesn't know whether Isherwood quite appreciates the absurdity or not. What is of interest, at this precise moment, is his decision to record the fact that: 'I don't really like Indians as a race; Swami is an exception.' Nor does this seem to have been the impulse of one day's entry. In *Palimpsest*, Gore Vidal writes that in Rome, in 1962:

> Isherwood stayed with us. He had just returned from his first trip to India. The culture shock had been extreme. 'There are so many of them,' he said. 'And how few there are of us, the white race. We must create special reservations for people like the Danes, to protect our exotic blond wildlife.'

Extraordinary to dislike Indians 'as a race'; more extraordinary to make such an avowal without having troubled to visit India; more extraordinary still to exempt only Prabhavananda. And this is only the first time that a distinctly sour and misanthropic tone begins to be heard.

Isherwood seldom forgets to mention the anniversary of his beloved father's death. And he tells us that the old boy had become interested in Buddhism before he was killed. With serene lack of affectation, and without ever making the connection on the page, he repeatedly refers to the Swami as a loving papa. As this first section draws to a close,

Isherwood is becoming more introspective and repetitive, and less amusing. There are a couple of hilarious Audenesque and anal moments ('Oh God, make me into a public convenience.' 'I developed a pile. I called Peggy and suggested that Bill Kiskadden should come down and cut it open for me – thinking, in the kindness of my heart, that this would be a nice treat for him, since he never gets any surgery to do in the army.') And it is fascinating to discover, even as the war is ending, that Isherwood still hasn't quite absolved himself of the charge of desertion. Hearing of the heroic death of a German anti-fascist he asks: 'What have I done today, to express my solidarity with such people? Nothing. Only one hour of meditation.' In a late 1944 letter to Cyril Connolly, who had criticised him in a much more fraternal fashion than Evelyn Waugh, he writes: 'This is not in any way to defend my conduct in leaving England in the first place – that, I repeat, was irresponsible.'

Even as he writes this, he is feeling the tension between his duties to the ashram and his involvement with 'X'. 'X' was Bill Harris, with whom things ended badly. During the unrecorded years which mark the transition to Part Two and the postwar, Isherwood began a long affair with William Caskey. He abandoned the Swami's tepid but stifling monastery nine days after the end of the war. The diaries don't discuss the defection, but the experience is touched upon in two of the rather slight books upon which he worked at this time, *Prater Violet* and *The World In the Evening.*

In *Prater Violet*, he compares the prospect of a lofty spiritual annihilation to 'the high far glimpse of a goat-track through the mountains', clear and even tempting. 'Then the clouds shut down, and a breath of the glacier, icy with the inhuman coldness of the peaks, touches my cheek. "No", I think, "I could never do it – . I should no longer be a person. I should no longer be Christopher Isherwood."' This is very like the moment in *The Ascent of F6* where Odell sees Malory and Irvine clinging to the icy crag before 'the cloud hid them for ever'. As for *The World in the Evening*, which dwells more on the sexual trials of worldly renunciation, suffice it to say that the overwrought narrator is named Monk.

In Part One, Isherwood scarcely talks about his writing and seems not to have attempted much. In Part Two, he tries to start work again. Collaboration may have suited him when the writing partner was Auden, but the record of his script-partnerships as given here is not an encouraging one. Too much time spent in meetings and at the planning stage; too little finished material; too much socialising under the pretext of business. Hardly any of the screenplays were actually consummated as motion pictures. Meanwhile, Isherwood is noticing a decline in his body's efficiency, including passages of impotence to which he recurs often in the diary, and leading to repeated resolutions to give up or cut down on smoking and drinking. These (with their immediately following accounts of tremendous relapses) do not make for very absorbing reading. The Swami, with whom he worked on a book about Vedanta, still exerts an influence. A sample entry from June 1952:

> When I typed out the title page of the Patanjali this morning, I put 'by Swami Prabhavananda and Christopher Isherwood', and Swami said, 'Why put and, Chris? It separates us.' It's impossible to convey the sweetness and meaning with which he said this. It's his complete assurance, and his smiling, almost sly air of having a private source of information.

To say nothing of his not knowing the purpose or meaning of a conjunction. One wonders what they did put, in the end.

Another gap in the diary, in the same year, deprives us of any account of Isherwood's return trip to Berlin. We know that he did succeed in finding Heinz Neddermeyer, who had survived the war and become a paterfamilias. We also learn that, until the crisis in Poland and Hungary in 1956, Neddermeyer opted to stay in the German Democratic Republic. Later mentions of him are few and terse, and feature him as a potential bore who might turn up unexpectedly or start asking for money:

> Heinz has written, suggesting that I sponsor the immigration of Gerda, Christian and himself to the States, and that we shall then all live together in a house that I'm to buy. He offers, of course, to pay all the money back by degrees. And now I must answer his letter – explaining tactfully that this scheme is impossible; that is to say, I'd rather die than agree to it.

And for this youth he would once have spared the entire Wehrmacht. . . In the year after the Berlin trip, Isherwood met Don Bachardy, thirty years his junior, and began the relationship which was to endure for the rest of his life. This put an end to a period of chaotic promiscuity, which had included at least one narrow-squeak bathhouse arrest. It also helped to confirm the new stability that had been conferred on Isherwood by the vast success of *I Am a Camera*, John van Druten's stage adaptation of *Goodbye to Berlin*.

From this time forward, it has to be said, there is a noticeable contraction of Isherwood's horizons. Political remarks, though often acute, become fewer (General Douglas MacArthur is described as a 'veteran diva'; the British aggression at Suez is touched upon quite shrewdly with a prediction that Eisenhower won't let it succeed). Dylan Thomas does a drop-by and behaves just as every other published recollection of him suggests that he should. Shortly before his fiftieth birthday, Isherwood records the following:

> As you get older, it's as if a sort of film covers your perceptions of the outer world, most of the time. But there are faces which have a sharpness, a vital sharpness, like that of an instrument, which cuts through this film – so that they seem more real than anything else.

Compare this to 'I am a camera with its shutter open, quite passive, recording, not thinking. Recording the man shaving at the window opposite and the woman in the kimono washing her hair. Some day, all this will have to be developed, carefully printed, fixed.'

Rereading the Berlin novels recently, I was impressed again by the quality of careful, witty, humane curiosity about the lives of others. This is the quality that is absent from great desolate stretches of the middle and late sections of the diary. Moreover, when Isherwood attempts to compose any new fiction, which he does at an agonisingly slow and joyless rate, he finds himself forever pressing on the same nerve of pre-war authenticity, but with a tendency to diminishing returns. In describing Bernhard Landauer in *Goodbye to Berlin*, furthermore, he was alert enough to notice something he called 'the arrogant humility of the East'. This is hugely preferable to the abject credulity he manifests in the presence of the Swami.

Observations about prose and poetry become less frequent. He re-reads an old favourite novel, *The Counterplot*, by Hope Mirrlees, which was once a standby but which on reconsideration 'represents so much that I used to imagine I hated and was fighting to the death – Cambridge cleverness and the whole Waste Land technique of describing moods by quotations from the classics – in fact, indulging in moods that were nothing else but the quotations themselves'. But even flashes of this quality are rare. More typical is something like a description of a pointless 1955 festivity where:

> I gave Harry the manuscript of Auden's 'Spain' in one of those cellophane-page albums with embossed leather covers which are designed to hold the pictures of Beverly Hills moppets. Harry cried.

Describing this gruesome-sounding party, which ended with practically everyone in tears before bedtime, Isherwood expresses distaste for the nasty atmosphere by introducing the word 'niggery'. It's a strange usage in more than one way (only white people are recorded as being present) and it crops up again in similar situations, adding its mite to the growing tone of misanthropy. One wonders where he picked up the term.

Isherwood retained enough self-awareness to know that he was dissipating his time and his talent. He even came up with a phrase, 'the as-if life', which still has a contemporary ring to it. Mescaline turns out to be a disappointment. 'Japam', the practice of repeating a mantra while telling a rosary, is honoured more in the breach than the observance, appears to be largely fruitless, but leads to spasms of irritable guilt when not kept up.

The only redeeming aspect is the strong and consistent love he shows for Don Bachardy. And Mr Bachardy, who holds the copyright in this trove of paper, deserves our thanks for his unflinching candour in allowing it to be published without redaction. The ceaseless rows and spats between the two men are set down in their raw, morning-after state, and make Angus Wilson's novels seem quite reticent by contrast. Sexual disclosures are fairly rigorously avoided, though it becomes clear that Isherwood had given up cruising, while allowing Bachardy the occasional night off for extramural adventure. On a visit to Somerset Maugham's villa, however, Isherwood records a moment of electrifying embarrassment when the great man's valets 'unpacked everything – including Don's movie magazines, our powder to kill crab lice and our K.Y.'. (Uninstructed readers may not automatically recognise the brand name of a popular sexual lubricant.)

At times, as Parts Two and Three merge, a new Isherwood despairingly sets down the futility and repetition that he feels himself powerless to resist. On his birthday in 1957:

> Then we had a ghastly boring party at Gavin Lambert's, and a much dreadfuller party at the Hackett's to welcome Patrick Woodcock from England, and a mismatched emergency dinner at home for Dick Hopper and his friend John, to which we were compelled to ask Gavin Lambert so he and I could discuss the new script idea for Gingold, and a disaster dinner for the [Joseph] Cottens, Gore Vidal and Howard Austen, at which Gore insulted the Cottens' darling friend Bouverie, the widower of his friend Alice Bouverie – calling him a crook, a fortune hunter and a cocksucker.

'Nina,' as Waugh put it in *Vile Bodies*, 'such a *lot* of parties.' And thank heaven for a breath of fresh air from Mr Vidal. Otherwise we would have to content ourselves with many entries like: 'Don sulked last night because the bathroom light dropped on his head and he thought my attitude was callous.' Comparatively seldom are the sardonic moments of distance or self-awareness ('Johnnie told me, with the air of a president declaring a state of war, that he and Starcke have split up'). There begins to be a convergence between the commitment to Vedanta and the trite need to be soothing at the domestic hearth: 'I told Don about the Swiss scientist who snipped off a bit of ectoplasm and kept it alive – and about the clairvoyant experience in which two women relived the Dieppe Raid. He said this made him feel frightened. I reminded him that he is now protected by Ramakrishna. Ramakrishna has touched him.'

It was in a slightly pre-Isherwood Cambridge that Frances Cornford wrote, contemplating Rupert Brooke, about 'the long littleness of life'. The phrase recurred to me as the diaries drew to a close. Using one of his frequent public-school injunctions to himself ('Let's see you make the effort' – 'Snap out of it' – 'Try again') Isherwood reflects:

> But I must pull myself together. Look at it like this – the effective part of one's life, barring sickness, falls into three thirds – twenty-five to forty, forty to fifty-five, fifty-five to seventy. My impression is that I packed a terrific amount into the first third, and that I've wasted a good deal of the second.

Striving for a correspondence between life and work, he goes on:

> (In the first third, I produced twelve works – including two translations and three collaborations: the plays. In the second third, I have so far produced four works – including two translations. Maybe I can pack in the novel and the Ramakrishna book before the August 1959 deadline – but I doubt it.)

The two non-translation works here must be *The World in the Evening* and *Prater Violet*, while the one which just missed the impending deadline is presumably *Down There on a Visit*, the distilled residue of a never-completed macro-novel of the Thirties, provisionally entitled *The Lost*. The fault that many found with *The World in the Evening*, and is certainly there to be found still, consists in a certain wooden artifice that sits oddly with a noticeable sentimentality. This cannot all be laid to Isherwood's charge, since he was prevented by friends and by publishers from writing anything that was confessedly or candidly homosexual. He rehashes (the term is not too unkind) his wartime and pacifist experiences, but he does so at a certain stilted remove. The diary entries covering the same time span are much fresher and more humorous. Katherine Bucknell points out in her brilliant introductory essay that Isherwood originally threw in some provocative scenes, precisely in order that his publishers should notice them, excise them, and thus leave the 'rest' of the work unmarred in its integrity. Any beginning writer wishing to try this tactic in the future could profit by studying his failure.

Prater Violet is a great deal more finished and intense. It is a satirical miniature about the absurdity of the early movie industry, with that same absurdity thrown into even sharper relief by the imminence of war and fascism. It has a certain tang of the young Evelyn Waugh to it, and I am obviously not the first person to have made this observation since, in *Down There on a Visit*, Isherwood vented his distaste for any such comparison:

> 'Oh, but I know Mr Isherwood,' cried Maria, shaking hands with me. 'Only lately, I read your delightful novel. It is the only novel written in a long time, I find. Most of the new ones are so stupid. But yours – truly delightful! This

young man who is a schoolmaster and becomes imprisoned for the traffic in the white slaves – *quel esprit!*'

'I'm afraid that's by Evelyn Waugh', I said, not charmed.

The annoyance at Waugh's farewell bouquet in 1939 obviously never quite wore off. *Prater Violet* is, however, an excellent study in not taking oneself too seriously or, perhaps better say, in coming to terms with one's own limitations. Isherwood – once again taking his own name as that of the fictional narrator – simply admits that he has neither the energy nor the courage to be more than a faint ally of Friedrich Bergmann, the gargantuan Viennese director who at one point expostulates: 'Very well. We also can play at this game of rat and mouse.' Rat-and-mouse would actually make a very good metaphor for the world of bullies and toadies that constitutes the studio universe as summoned by the book, but what's admirable about the line in this instance is the way that Isherwood lets it fall, without drawing attention to it as an example of unintentional hilarity. One appreciates more the care he took with the anti-Nazi refugees on whom he based the tale, and also the modesty he felt in the face of the risks they had run and he had not.

The 'Christopher Isherwood' character in *Prater Violet* is again sexually 'neutral' as between homo and hetero, and the novel also has the irritating Isherwood fictional habit of, when in doubt, naming female characters 'Dorothy'. (Not as decisive or intended, one feels, as the naming of Sally Bowles after the much-admired Paul.) But there are absorbing cross-overs between its reflective world and that of the diaries:

> I must confess, I want to be looked after. I want the background of a home. I see now how well the arrangement at Pembroke Gardens suited me, during the last year or so in England (much as I complained about it). I could go out as much as I wanted to, but I had the snugness of a room and breakfast. What I really want is solitude in the midst of snugness.

Kathleen Isherwood, Christopher's mother, had kept her home in Pembroke Gardens. In *Prater Violet*, published in 1945, Friedrich Bergmann brought all his Viennese batteries to bear on Isherwood as a flighty example of the 'declassed intellectual' type. 'He is unable to cut himself free, sternly, from the bourgeois dream of the Mother, that fatal and comforting dream. He wants to crawl back into the economic safety of the womb.' The diaries are the superego for much of the fiction.

By the time of *Down There on a Visit*, a novel of vignettes, Isherwood was able to be candid about homosexuality, but not yet, or not quite, about his own. Three decades earlier, John Lehmann had helped to publish *The Memorial,* Isherwood's second novel, and the first sample chapter of *Down There on a Visit* was also printed by him in *The London Magazine.* The stories and portraits preserve the continuity of subject, as they do the continuity of first-person narrator. 'Down there on a visit' proves to be a phrase that summarises the attitude of the dilettante, the amateur and the tourist – an impression of his own unseriousness and lack of commitment that Isherwood took with him wherever he went. In the foursome of 'Mr Lancaster', 'Ambrose', 'Waldemar' and 'Paul' one may choose to have fun spotting the real-life models, and one can also notice that Isherwood really did feel happier as a camera, just as certain photographers are tongue-tied until they can get behind their apparatus and have a reason for being at the party. It is through such detachment that Isherwood learns the more demanding trick of turning the lens upon himself: discovering at the end of the 1950s something that he would not even tell his own diaries at the end of the 1930s – namely, that, all feelings about Heinz to one side, he had been relieved if not positively pleased by the signing of the Munich agreement:

> I have made another discovery about myself, and I don't care if it's humiliating or not. I am quite certain of this now: as far as I am concerned, nothing, nothing, nothing is worth a war.

Which, written at the close of the Fifties, is where we came in two decades before. Ahead lie works of the more mature period, like *A Single Man,* which – as well as being proudly and finally gay, as well as containing revenge fantasies that might be called Mortmere Revisited – also call upon the experience set down in the diaries. Ahead, too, are some more winnowed and considered memoirs, notably the manifesto-like *Christopher and His Kind.* The picture of 'Christopher Isherwood' will gradually take the fixing and printing fluids, swim up from the developing tray, and acquire a grain, a focus, and a perspective. The evolving series of sketches and portraits by Don Bachardy tells a similar story in parallel. The gaze that meets the camera's eye – or the eye of the painter – is one of self-knowledge dearly bought and somewhat haggled over. His adjusted estimate of the three ages of man was true at any rate for the years set down and recorded here.

First published as 'The Long Littleness of Life' (a review of *Christopher Isherwood: Diaries, Volume One: 1939–1960* edited and introduced by Katherine Bucknell) in *New York Review of Books,* 20 February 1997

V

'Enemies List . . .'

Running on Empty

Like every writer before him who has ever scored a triumph . . . Fallow was willing to give no credit to luck. Would he have any trouble repeating his triumph in a city he knew nothing about, in a country he looked upon as a stupendous joke? Well . . . why should he? His genius had only begun to flower. This was only journalism, after all, a cup of tea on the way to his eventual triumph as a novelist.

The Bonfire of the Vanities (1987)

Take it for all in all, *The Bonfire of the Vanities* was a blockbuster. It rewrote the whole career description of commercial-cum-literary success. And it got people where they lived, if they lived on or near Park Avenue. These days, New York City is becoming a ramified variant of St Louis, Missouri or Des Moines, Iowa: a great big 'thank you for not smoking' town, with 'buckle up' messages played on automatic tapes in the yellow cabs, and the cheery, kitsch sovereignty of Walt Disney exerted over what was once Times Square and 42nd Street. The golden arches of McDonald's are to be seen winking near the Bowery, and cops look out for jay-walkers as if patrolling some dire Jim Carrey utopia. The mayor of the city, and the governor of the state, are two mirthless white ethnic conservatives named Giuliani and Pataki. They have restored capital punishment, and encouraged franchising of all sorts while discouraging loitering and littering. Not long ago, a Haitian immigrant named Abner Louima was grabbed outside a funky nightclub, roughed up in the police van, hurled into a cell at the stationhouse and held down while a guardian of the peace forced a rupturing lavatory plunger all the way up his ass. The foul object was then violently withdrawn, only to be shoved into his mouth (breaking many teeth) and down his throat. This was a hot case, for about ten days.

There has probably never been a less prescient journo-novel than *The Bonfire of the Vanities*, which subliminally heralded a New York that was given over to wild and feral African politics at one end (reading from north to south of Manhattan Island) and dubious market strategies at the other. The market strategies continue. Indeed, Wall Street has almost deposed the opinion polls as the index of national well-being. The ethnic spoils system, meanwhile, is manipulated by the same class as ever. If either of these elements ever undergoes a dramatic metamorphosis, it won't be Tom Wolfe who sounds the alarm.

Yet, even as he tries to move to another city, and to make the leap from former journalist to actual novelist, Wolfe keeps *The Bonfire of the Vanities* constantly at hand. It worked once. Why should it not work again?

> She wore some sort of go-to-hell white pants that were very floppy in the legs but exceptionally tight in the crotch. *Exceptionally*! There was an astonishing crevice. Sherman stared and then looked at her face.
> *The Bonfire of the Vanities*

> The way she flaunted it all – the way her stretch riding pants hugged her thighs and the declivities of her loins fore and aft – how could you help it?
> *A Man in Full*

> This entire apartment, known as 3½-room in New York real-estate parlance, had been created out of what had once been a pleasant but by no means huge bedroom on the third floor of a townhouse, with three windows overlooking the street. The so-called room he now stood in was really nothing more than a slot that had been created by inserting a plasterboard wall.
> *The Bonfire of the Vanities*

> They were living in a duet, a form of cheap housing Conrad had never heard of before he and Jill moved in a year ago . . . Duets were rows of small one-storey houses about twelve feet apart, with patchy little strips of yard between them. In each house a wall ran right down the middle, the long way, dividing it into two narrow apartments.
> *A Man in Full*

> Steiner had been swept off his feet by a series on country life among the rich that Fallow had done . . . It had been full of names and titles and helicopters and perplexing perversions ('that thing with the cup').
> *The Bonfire of the Vanities*

> Charlie Croker, master builder – Croker Concourse – checking into a motel on the Buford Highway with a 23-year-old girl – but he had lost his mind to her demented form of lust. Danger! Imminent exposure! That thing with the cup!
> *A Man in Full*

From Masters of the Universe to 'master builder'. From class-and-race New York to race-and-class Atlanta. From a wrong turn on a Bronx exit ramp to – in the first pages of this new novel – an unsettling traffic jam in the wrong part of town. From 'boxes of doughnuts, cheese Danishes, onion rolls, crullers, every variety of muck and lard known to the takeout food business', in *The Bonfire of the Vanities*, to 'a huge, cold, sticky, cheesy, cowpie-like cinnamon-Cheddar coffee bun' in *A Man in Full*. This last item is an early and seductive scene-setter in the set-piece that all critics have so far simply adored, where Charlie Croker is humbled into perspiration by a gang of sadistic creditors ('*Saddlebags!*') Yet even this episode is a device for un-springing – or perhaps better say 'telegraphing' – the plot. Croker is supposed, when we meet him, to have all his humiliations in the future. He's supposed to be a mensch. But he submits too meekly; acts the victim too soon; isn't clothed in sufficient male arrogance to make his subsequent declension into a real thing. The scene-shifters are too visible as the curtain rises.

As the book progresses, the scene-shifters don't even bother to ease themselves off-stage. They hang about, picking their noses and nudging each other to give warning of the action to come. And this is not all that frightfully difficult, since black people en masse can still be recognised, whether in New York or Atlanta, by their signature noise of *Unnhhh . . . unnhhh*, while the susceptibilities of the well-to-do are summoned with equal ease as follows:

> 'All of black New York rises up . . . Do you really think this is your city any longer? Open your eyes! The greatest city of the 20th century! Do you think *money* will keep it yours?'
> *The Bonfire of the Vanities*

> 'Oh, these black boys and girls came to Atlanta . . . tying up traffic, even on Highways 75 and 85, baying at the moon, which turns chocolate during Freaknic, freaking out White Atlanta, scaring them indoors, where they cower for three days, giving them a snootful of the future.'
> *A Man in Full*

Do I accuse Wolfe of dealing in stereotypes; even of recycling the stereotypes he deployed in his last chartbuster? As it happens, I don't need to do so. He does all the work himself, in the same cartoonish fashion with which he used to illustrate his own 'status radar' essays of the Sixties. Not only does the term 'status radar' recur here, along with the time-honoured Wolfean word 'shuck' (used for discarding a super-fluous wife), but he charmingly advertises his own dependence on cliché and received image. Thus the football coach Buck McNutter is 'a prototypical Southern white boy', and a grim steward on the Croker estate is 'the archetype of what the overseers had been'. This certainly economises on characterisation. And, just as Wolfe used to describe keg-sized sportsmen, he repeatedly depicts slab-cut Southern tycoons and other masculine authority figures in this story, often using the metaphor of a welded torso and very, very frequently alluding to the neck that is wider than the cranium. In his mind, mass counts for something. The converse holds, because if a character is named Peepgass he will also be scrawny and ineffectual. Irony, in other words, is not king in these pages.

Wolfe's declared chief ambition is to have himself described as Dickensian, but it's not only the names that let him down. (In *The Bonfire of the Vanities* an old firm is called Dunning, Sponget and Leach; in *A Man in Full* we encounter a legal oufit entitled Clockett, Paddet, Skynnham and Glote, which reeks of midnight oil, and also of insufficient midnight oil.) It's a considerable distance from Bauhaus to *Bleak House*, and one of the proofs – apart from the rib-tickling names – is that, unlike any Dickens novel, *A Man in Full* is fairly easy to summarise. Charlie Croker is a redneck entrepreneur and former football champ living wildly beyond his means. His bankers coldly decide to foreclose. Meanwhile, elsewhere in the city of Atlanta, anxiety is climbing because a loutish black sports-superstar may or may not have date-raped the daughter of another white tycoon. The black city fathers, in an attempt to keep their street cred, propose that Charlie act as a character witness for the sports star, and offer in return to ask the bankers for lenience. With his other hand, Croker orders layoffs at a food-processing plant in his empire, and thus indirectly ruins the life of Conrad Hensley. This young loser, pitched into hell, redeems himself by his exertions and Charlie Croker by his example.

It must be said that there are four or five scenes that really lodge in the memory. The first one ('*Saddlebags!*') suffers from its inept set-up but is strong nonetheless. Two episodes involving beasts – the capture of a giant rattlesnake and the mating of two bloodstock horses – are marvellously written and help ram home, as it were, the point that nature is both earthy and pitiless. Conrad Hensley's two transfiguring moments, of being exploited and victimised in a frozen-food warehouse and of being set upon in a California penitentiary, are equally vivid. All of these passages, however, involve the same macho chemistry, which defines full manhood as some combination of bluff, bulk, cruelty and defiance. Many of those who relished the paean to Chuck Yeager in *The Right Stuff* had not scanned its antecedent essay 'Duelling with Sam and Charlie', where Wolfe gloatingly celebrated the testicularity of pilots who, between recreational breaks, bombed Vietnam from an aircraft-carrier. All considerations of small, foppish, white-suited, vicarious admiration for violence and for men of action to one side, this version of chivalry and gallantry also has a certain Confederate element to it. Wolfe's Richmond, Virginia is far enough north of Atlanta for him to have some fun at the expense of good ol' boy Georgians, but when he tries to capture the black pulpit-speech of the Reverend Blakey, he does no more than reprise the Reverend Bacon of *The Bonfire of the Vanities*. His purported eavesdropping on black conversation is beyond embarrassing; perhaps beyond embarrassment. Here is the cynical mayor of Atlanta, Wes Jordan (get it?), as he shoots the shit with the upwardly mobile black attorney Roger White II, who is known to homeboys (get it?) as Roger Too White:

> 'But you, Wes? As I remember, you used to *laugh* at all this Afrocentric business. I remember one night – when was it? – '87 – '88 – you made so much fun of Jesse Jackson and his 'African-American' pronouncement at that press conference – you remember? – wherever it was – Chicago, I think – that press conference where he started everybody using 'African-American' instead of 'black'? – you remember that night – you had Albert Hill laughing so hard, I thought he was going to die, and he *liked* Jesse.'
>
> 'Well,' said the mayor, cocking his head and smiling more knowingly than ever, 'times change. Times change, times change, and the polls change.'
>
> 'The polls?'
>
> 'The polls and the focus groups.'
>
> 'You use focus groups?'

Yup, that's how *these people* talk all right, when they think nobody's listening. (If there was anyone listening, a smart lawyer wouldn't be telling a smart politician what they both already knew, nor would he pretend to that smart politician that he was flummoxed at the mention of such jujus as polls and focus groups.) A few hundred pages later, the two darkies meet again, and broach the forbidden subject of 'shade' among blacks in the following forthright manner:

> Roger sat bolt upright on the couch, opened his eyes wide, and flashed a big grin. 'I've figured it out!'
>
> 'Figured out what?'
>
> 'What's different! About *you!*'
>
> 'Really? You gonna let me in on it, too?'
>
> Roger Too White slapped the side of his leg and grinned some more and started laughing.
>
> 'You're *darker*, Brother Wes, you're *darker!* What'd you do? How'd you do it?'
>
> '. . . Been playing a lot of golf recently, Brother Roger.'
>
> '. . . Well, you sly old dog, you!' exclaimed Roger Too White. 'You're getting . . . a *sun*tan – for the election campaign! You're getting . . . *darker!*'
>
> Wes Jordan winked and chuckled deep in his throat. 'It just naturally happens to us golf lovers, just naturally happens. And besides, everything is relative. I've always been blacker than thou, Roger Too White.

Eyes wide, big grin flashing . . . why not just lob a big slice of watermelon onto the set and have done with it? There's a certain amount of sanctimony and hypocrisy involved in the new 'Olympic' Atlanta. It used to market itself with the cringe-making and boosterish slogan 'The City Too Busy to Hate'. A splash of satire would certainly be in order. But Amos 'n' Andy is not satire.

Nor is it realism. In a now notorious open letter published in *Harper's* magazine just after the success of *The Bonfire of the Vanities* ('Stalking the Billion-Footed Beast: A Literary Manifesto for the New Social Novel') Wolfe put everyone right about actuality in fiction. Call him a dandified poseur if you liked, but the planter-suited chap from Richmond was here to say that Emile Zola was the *man*. Wolfe had emitted earlier diatribes, against modern architecture and – most klutzily of all – against the Vietnam Veterans' Memorial in Washington, which he described as a ditch of shame. (He still can't manage to be 'realistic' about Vietnam, incidentally: the Indochinese characters in *A Man in Full* are rendered as toothy, babbling, half-sinister and half-farcical immigrants, a condition they might have escaped if their society had not been so frazzled by those brave extreme-right-stuff bomber pilots and their political masters.) But the call to a gritty new fiction was the weirdest of all. Let's do some *research*, people! Let's get out there and get real! In his acknowledgements to the latest, Wolfe bows to one who has assisted him with 'the telling details of contemporary American life', and one wants to say: Hey! *We'll* be the judge of that!

The giveaway phrase in the 1989 screed came when Wolfe announced that the great American subject was 'status modified by personality'. It sounded then, and it sounds now, like rags-to-riches or riches-to-rags; the corniest imaginable scheme, and also the actual scaffolding of this new effort, as indeed of the last one. (You must understand, to appreciate the full effect of Wolfe's Tiny Tim Toryism, that his Horatio Alger realism was sneeringly counterposed to 'that longtime French intellectual favourite, the psychological novel'). Thus, tribulations may come, but men of character can bear them and rise, as Jeeves used to remark to Bertie, on stepping-stones of their dead selves to higher things. Sentimentality has many guises, but this is, surely, its essential one. Charlie Croker is wealthy, and loses all. Conrad Hensley is dirt-poor and modest, and is hit by tragedy. Indeed, like Sherman McCoy in *The Bonfire of the Vanities*, he is arbitrarily cast into the penal system, itself reserved for the lowest of the low. But he will not submit. How long until the two men, one rich and one poor, linked by a tenuous thread of fate and destiny, actually meet, and kindle a tiny but affecting mutual spark of deeply human recognition? Not all that long, unless you have to read through it.

In his manifesto of enthusiasm for Zola's notebook tactics and shoe-leather research (the sort of 'research' that he himself so laboriously demonstrates in the agonising White–Jordan dialogue above), Wolfe did not find room to recommend Upton Sinclair's novel *The Jungle*. He cited Sinclair Lewis, who is often confused with his near-namesake, but did not even allude to the author who briefly revolutionised American reading habits, and who also made the longed-for 'crossover' between journalism and literature. Yet there are some intriguing points of similarity and congruence. *The Jungle* was initially written as a serial (for the Midwest socialist paper *The Appeal to Reason*) and has that much in common with some of Dickens and with Wolfe's palate-testing experiments in the pages of *Rolling Stone*. It set out to describe the intestines of Chicago, and has that in common with Zola's *Le Ventre de Paris*. Its intention was to change public opinion, which it did by means of unintended consequence, because Sinclair thought readers would be stirred by the depiction of working conditions and millions of readers were indeed stirred, not to say sickened, by the accounts of how food was produced in the stockyards. ('I aimed at the public's heart,' he ruefully said, 'and by accident I hit it in the stomach.' Here was an accidental discovery of the consumer society at which Wolfe has aimed from the start.)

The resemblances, or do I mean correspondences, are astonishing. In *The Bonfire of the Vanities* Wolfe referred to the subjected lumpen defendants, delivered daily in police wagons to the Bronx courthouse, as 'the meat'. In *A Man in Full* he decides to do meat as a subject in itself. At a gruesome packing plant on the wrong side of the San Francisco Bay, working men fight the zero temperature and the lack of safety regulations and the want of job security. No man knows the other's wage-scale, and the fear of 'termination' turns up as regularly as the pay-packets do. A man who loses his job may well forfeit his home, his family, his pride and his health, all at the same time. Caprice and callousness being the rule, the author can do as he bloody well likes to any wretch caught in this situation. Wolfe certainly gives Conrad Hensley a workout. But when, in a vile dungeon, the victim discovers the Stoic works of Epictetus, he suddenly rises to his full height as a man, or chap.

Whereas, in *The Jungle*, the Lithuanian immigrant Jurgis Rudkus works in a packing plant for horrible meat, is cheated out of livelihood and home, is subjected to the grossest humiliations, exists on the whim of the foreman and the boss, is terrified by the spectre of unemployment and the jealousies that exist between different grades of worker, and at last achieves redemption by reading the classics of the socialist movement. Not entirely unlike Conrad Hensley, furthermore (one wouldn't want to spoil such an intricate plot by disclosing any more details), he spends some time as an accidental or coincidental guest in the big home of the big boss. Upton Sinclair at one point describes tough old Jurgis as 'Prometheus'. Wolfe prefers Epictetus, perhaps because Stoicism is more a matter of individual choice. But, as Morris Dickstein once wrote in a magnificent essay on Sinclair,

> in his research and interviews he was able to accumulate masses of clear information not only on the workplace and living conditions but also about

machinery, transportation, profit margins, sewage, hygiene, prisons, hospitals, the courts, the political clubs – all the institutions needed to keep a modern city running. He shows not only how the meat industry and the steel industry operate but also how the machinery of power is greased, how the system of graft and patronage functions, how the bosses, the politicians, the contractors, the criminals and the police work hand in glove.

To say of Wolfe that he even attempted such a standard of realism – let alone reformism – would be an insult to the Zola whose name he so casually drops. We overhear some whispers about the real authorship and ownership of the big bad 'system' that enfolds Conrad and his employer Charlie Croker, and that makes them (of all things) brothers under the skin. Conrad's parents were 'hippies', which naturally gave him a poor start in the race, and Atlanta is run by cynical Knee-Grows. Thus is the occult mask of power torn away! It's the Sixties that are to blame, again. (Meanwhile, in Wolfe's actually-existing New York, the forces of order do as they like, and that bankrupt real-estate monarch Donald Trump can treat the skyline as his own without any hint of a nasty creditors' meeting at any of his numerous and lenient banks.)

There's only one genuine similarity between Upton Sinclair and Tom Wolfe. Neither had, or has, much time for those who immigrated involuntarily to these United States. Writing in the days when 'white socialism' was still thinkable for Jack London, himself and others, Sinclair said of the dark-skinned underclass in Chicago: 'The ancestors of these black people had been savages in Africa, and since then they had been chattel slaves, or had been held down by a community ruled by the traditions of slavery. Now for the first time they were free – free to gratify every passion, free to wreck themselves.' Wolfe never misses an opportunity to underline the same point, with staves of barbaric rap music, awful grunts, and wild sexual Saturnalias lurking at every turn of the story. He remembers every now and then to lob a bone of 'compassion' into the cannibal stew. But then, who doesn't these days? He isn't considerate or realist enough, however, to enlighten us about how to perform 'that thing with the cup'.

Wolfe got lucky, once, by eavesdropping a Late Sixties party given by conscience-stricken Jews for not very conscience-striken blacks. He has, at least as a realist but I would say also as a stylist, been running on empty ever since. His self-esteem tank, in bold contrast, has been filled to overflowing. As he instructed us all, in 'Stalking the Billion-Footed Beast',

No one was ever moved to tears by reading about the unhappy fates of heroes and heroines in Homer, Sophocles, Molière, Racine, Sydney [sic], Spenser, or Shakespeare. Yet even the impeccable Lord Jeffrey, editor of the *Edinburgh Review*, confessed to having cried – blubbered, boohooed, snuffled and sighed – over the death of Little Nell in *The Old Curiosity Shop*. For writers to give up this power in the quest for a more up-to-date kind of fiction – it is as if an engineer were to set out to develop a more sophisticated machine technology by first of all discarding the principle of electricity, on the grounds that it has been used ad nauseam for a hundred years.

There he stands, in all his vulgarity. (It's even possible to believe that Wolfe hasn't read of Wilde's most laboured joke about Nell.) The carnival barker sweeps off his rakish and jaunty panama: 'If you won't weep for Hecuba, surely you'll shed a tear for Mister Dickens here. Roll up, you fine ladies and gentlemen, for Lord Jeffrey, known to one and all as 'The Impeccable!' Snuffle away – don't be shy – here's a hankie! This very show has been performed in front of the crowned heads of Europe! It's all real: the genuine article!' Let him paint an inch thick: to this favour he has come.

And that's before you have the chance to mangle yourself in the mechanistic clauses of his ill-wrought analogy. It's not just the scene-shifters who are on view in a Wolfean scene. The wires and the flies and the groaning contraptions and contrivances are all on display as well, so that those who find him diverting are quite probably the same people who fancy their Shakespeare without tears.

First published as 'Running on Empty' (a review of *A Man In Full* by Tom Wolfe) in *London Review of Books*, 7 January 1997

Unmaking Friends

Evelyn Waugh, discoursing on the etiquette of book reviewing, observed that one must always give favourable treatment to the work of close friends. Quite apart from anything else, he explained, it was the height of bad manners to give a poor review to a book one had not read. Waugh's remark may have been cynical, but it had a certain lightness and paradox to it. Whereas Norman Podhoretz has no levity – unbearable heaviness is his preferred métier – and never strays into paradox, and gives a series of chiefly posthumous but always spiteful reviews to several authors whom he may have read but certainly has not understood. This is bad manners cubed, boorishness wrenched almost into a literary form.

True, the former editor of the supposedly solemn *Commentary* magazine has always himself sought to ease the life of the book reviewer. He does this small but welcome favour by making all his faults crashingly apparent from the very first page, sometimes even from the opening paragraph. Here are the initial two sentences of *Ex-Friends*:

> I have often said that if I wish to name-drop, I have only to list my ex-friends. This remark always gets a laugh, but, in addition to being funny, it has the advantage of being true.

If he does say so himself. To be invariably witty and unfailingly truthful is a claim many of us might wish to make or perhaps (shall we hint?) to have made on our behalf. To reduce the claim to an assertion, frequently advanced – as we are assured by the author himself – and no less often mirthfully received, is to force the question. Who is the audience for this sapient gag? How often does it meet, and where? Who pays for the dinner? Then again, if Podhoretz stands alone in a forest, and falls over as a result of laughing at his own mordant humour, and there is nobody to hear or to see, does he still look and sound such a fool?

But seriously, folks, Norman doesn't want you to think that he is a mere Catskills jester, nor yet a pure and ascetic intellectual. Let us proceed, drying our eyes, to page two, where it is confided with perfect gravity that:

It will seem even stranger to my more recent acquaintances that in my younger years I was also full of fun, as Norman Mailer confirmed when he said that I was 'merrier' in the 'old days'. The same word was once used by Max Lerner, the historian and columnist (now among the almost forgotten), who after spending a few days in my company described me (to general agreement) as 'the merry madcap' of the group.

Must have been quite a party. The Pod setting the table on a roar and bearing Lerner on his back to the land of infinite jest. In the corner, perhaps, Irving Kristol screaming, 'Stop! You're killing me!' But as I contemplated this lugubrious fiesta, the image of Yorick faded from my mind to be deposed by that of Polonius himself, endlessly finger-wagging to the young and making himself useful around the court. He gave way in turn to Justice Shallow, cackling senescently about the chimes of midnight and the tales he might have told of a laddish youth.

A melancholy lesson of advancing years is the realisation that you can't make old friends. This is redeemed somewhat by the possibility of making new ones, and in his late maturity – some might say that like the medlar fruit he went rotten before becoming ripe – Podhoretz has found companionship and solidarity with some new chums. He mentions them shyly, as if he were back in his lonely childhood and his mother had secretly bribed them to play with him:

> Here, in what is for me a rare submission to the principles of affirmative action, which dictate that I should strive to achieve greater name-dropping 'diversity', I will single out Henry Kissinger and William F. Buckley Jr.
>
> In spite of our failure to form ourselves into a cohesive family, we have managed to join forces as a dissenting minority of 'heretical' intellectuals who are trying to break the virtual monopoly that the worst ideas of my ex-friends hold (even from beyond the grave) over the cultural institutions of this country.

The purpose of recruiting these new chums is clear: to enlist them in the urgent task of pissing on the graves of the old ones. This makes them more like cronies, or accomplices, than actual friends. But perhaps that's better than nothing. Is it Henry and Bill, perhaps, who get together and agree to laugh at Norman's jokes? Whatever the case, the man who can describe this gleesome threesome as a trio of heretical dissenters is certainly eager to please.

For the purposes of comparison, here's what happens when Podhoretz encounters an authentic dissident:

> When on a visit of my own to Prague in 1988 I was taken to meet Vaclav Havel, . . . the first thing that hit my eye upon entering his apartment was a huge poster of John Lennon hanging on the wall. Disconcerted, I tried to persuade Havel that the counterculture in the West was no friend of anti-

Communists like himself, but I made even less of a 'dent' on him than Ginsberg had made on me thirty years earlier.

Good of Podhoretz to have spared so much time to put Havel straight. But that's the sort of guy he is – always willing to oblige. Also, the fact that Havel was under house arrest may have helped both men to concentrate.

The above anecdote occurs in the chapter on Allen Ginsberg, the most recently dead of Podhoretz's exes. (As a literary critic, he rather resembles an undertaker scanning the obits for trade.) You can take whatever view you like of Ginsberg's poetry, or of his vague teachings about hedonism, or of his fierce commitment to *penetratio per anum*. Podhoretz thinks that Ginsberg was a serious and gifted poet, that his views on family and society were destructive, and that (great wailing walls of glossy video in every heterosexual porn shop notwithstanding) anal sex is something that fascinates only homosexuals. The last point is an obsessive one in the neo-conservative school, incidentally, and requires professional attention from someone better qualified than the present author. But the fact remains that the two men were once friends, and that they quarrelled bitterly over Vietnam and the war on drugs and everything else, and that the cruellest words in the dispute were probably uttered – if only because he had the superior command of language – by Allen Ginsberg. In 1986, however, Ginsberg began to speak more softly about his old antagonist:

> He then followed up – I forget exactly when – with a handwritten note very warmly inviting me to a seminar. . . . *This* invitation, unlike the one some thirty years earlier to his apartment in the Village, I unhesitatingly declined, knowing that the new Ginsberg's loving kindness would put me even more uncomfortably on the defensive than the young Ginsberg's rage had done.

On Ginsberg's seventieth birthday, he gave an interview in which he again sought to repair the breach:

> Another invitation then arrived, not from Ginsberg himself but from a television producer who wanted to put us on the air together. But once more I passed up a chance to see him again. Six months later he was dead.

So let us recapitulate. At Columbia, Ginsberg had published Podhoretz's long poem about the prophet Jeremiah in the college literary magazine. Podhoretz had later written favourably about Ginsberg and compared him to Pound and Whitman. Then there was, for intelligible reasons, a major falling-out. And then, not once but twice, Ginsberg extended the hand of reconciliation, and Podhoretz, writing for the first time since his former friend's funeral, takes an obvious pride – a pride in his own integrity – in having slapped that hand away. Small wonder, then, that when he needs a friend these days he has to rely on Henry Kissinger, who probably bills him for meetings.

The Russian exile writer Vassily Aksyonov – another example of the real as opposed to the bogus dissident – once wrote that Podhoretz reminded him of all the things he had left the Soviet Union to escape. He had, said Aksyonov, the mentality of a cultural commissar. As the Ginsberg essay demonstrates, he has the soul of one as well. And the literary sensitivity and imagination: most of the chapters here are regurgitated in great chunks from previous jeremiads such as *Making It* and *Breaking Ranks.* Here is what Podhoretz wrote about Norman Mailer in *Making It* in 1967:

> Like most famous writers, he was surrounded by courtiers and sycophants, but with this difference: he allowed them into his life not to flatter him but to give his radically egalitarian imagination a constant workout. He had the true novelist's curiosity about people unlike himself – you could see him getting hooked ten times a night by strangers at a party. . . . He would look into the empty eyes of some vapid upper-class girl and announce to her that she could be the madam of a Mexican whorehouse.

If you consult page 193 of the present offering, for which The Free Press is charging a tidy sum, you will be informed that

> Like many famous people, Mailer liked to surround himself with a crowd of courtiers, many of whom had nothing to recommend them that I could see other than their worshipful attitude toward him . . . [H]e could be positively intolerable – posing, showing off, bumping heads (another of his favorite sports), bullying, ordering about, and, underneath it all, flattering.
>
> The flattering was especially in evidence with women, not only or even primarily as a means of seduction but mainly as a way of romanticizing and thereby inflating the significance of everything that came into his life. He would inform some perfectly ordinary and uninteresting girl that she could have been a great madam running the best whorehouse in town.

This is not just boring and tenth-rate. It is *sinister.* Like Andrei Zhdanov, Stalin's literary enforcer, Podhoretz doesn't content himself with saying that a certain novelist is no longer in favour or no longer any good. That would be banal. No, it must be shown that he *never was* any good, that he always harboured the germs of anti-party feeling, that he was a rank rodent from the get-go. Then comes the airbrush, the rewritten entry in the encyclopaedia, the memory hole. But even some of Zhdanov's hacks would have made the effort to employ some new phrases and new disclosures. I once noticed a column in the London *Spectator,* written by someone named Taki Theodoracopulos and devoted to a hysterical attack on anal sex borrowed whole cloth from an earlier diatribe by Norman Podhoretz in Rupert Murdoch's *New*

York Post. I wrote a letter to the editor of the *Spectator*, asking if no more elevated source for plagiarism could be found. I now feel I owe Theodoracopulos an apology. Podhoretz, in stealing from himself, has found a real mug for a victim. He's also found some real new friends for reviewers – William F. Buckley Jr, writing, or typing, in the *New York Post*, now compares the congealed regurgitations of Podhoretz to Lytton Strachey's *Eminent Victorians*.

The other essays, on Hellman and Trilling and so forth, are also sterile reworkings and recyclings of ancient grudges, and you should go to the library to reread them, if you must, and not reward The Free Press for its marketing of old rope. For old hands, there is the occasional and unmistakable Podhoretz touch, like the knot of imperfection in an authentic Turkish rug. 'Having reportedly spent eighteen years in psychoanalysis', he slyly says of Diana Trilling, as if unable to make an unambiguous assertion to her face, even now. 'Reportedly'. There's a fine word. Nor is it the only breastplate of courage donned by our critic. Indeed, his instinct for a place of safety is something that he still can't resist delineating in detail. Faced with a conflict between two of his early patrons – F. R. Leavis and C. P. Snow – he decided that Lionel Trilling should be his human shield:

> As an additional bonus, since the article would be coming from America's leading critic, I would not be held responsible (as I would have been if I had commissioned a lesser writer) for any thing he might say that would offend either of the two warring parties.

But it didn't work out, because all parties to the dispute decided that Podhoretz had acted in a surreptitious manner, and so we are treated to moans of self-pity and recrimination, as if the sentences just quoted did not already manifest the cowardice of its own convictions.

There is such a thing as a disagreement on fundamentals between old friends. Fallings-out do occur in real life. One way of measuring the depth and intensity of such divisions is intuitive but sound: does either party maintain that there was no real comradeship to begin with? Or does either party repudiate, with glacial attitudes masquerading as principles, a genuine attempt at a later composition of the quarrel? There's a relevant instance in this very book. Podhoretz parodies the views of the late Irving Howe, who generally sought for civilised relations with his former City College associates, many of whom had traded up and become apostles of the market, 'free' or otherwise, and of the military-industrial complex, however defined. Yet for saying what was perfectly true about Irving Kristol – that in 1952 he had written in highly euphemistic terms of Senator Joseph McCarthy – Howe is indicted for taking a cheap shot. This may not be 'the politics of personal destruction', as Mr Clinton's many hired slanderers refer to arguments that go against them, but it is certainly the reduction of essential dispute to petty rancor.

A suggestive counterexample is touched upon in this book but is skated over, in a single paragraph, as if it had not really occurred. When Joseph Heller published *Catch-22* in the early 1960s, Podhoretz rushed to praise it in a glossy sheet called *Show*. As a consequence, Heller and he became social friends. But as the years passed, and as Podhoretz began to fawn more openly on Richard Nixon and the Israeli general staff (as if rehearsing for the engulfing, mandible-straining blow job that he would later bestow on Ronald Reagan), Heller hauled off and dealt him a sock in the jaw in a letter to *The Nation*. He rammed this home, as it were, with a sprightly caricature of our Norman in his novel *Good as Gold*. One can now see the cruelty of Heller's tactic. He not only repudiated his old friend but stabbed him in the front! And he did so at a time when the tide was running in Podhoretz's favour. I ran into Heller, by a happy chance, while I was cogitating this review. 'Yeah,' he said. 'I never gave him the chance to dump *me*.'

What Heller saw coming is what we now term 'neo-conservatism'. This is a protean and slippery definition, and very inexact as a category, but not all that hard to parse. If you take the version offered by its acolytes, you discover a group of New York Jewish intellectuals who decided that duty, honour, and country were superior, morally and mentally, to the bleeding-heart allegiances of their boy-and-girlhoods. If you take the versions offered by its critics, you stumble on an old Anglo-Saxon definition of the upper crust: 'A load of crumbs held together by dough.' They just might have set out to do good, but there is no question that they end up doing well. Podhoretz, of all the old gang, is in the weakest position to rebut this charge. His book *Making It* is perhaps the most vulgar paean to pure and simple arrivisme that has ever been penned. He still broods over the yellowing reviews that made sport of him, in particular over the shudder of distaste that both Trillings evinced at the sheer crumminess of his aspirations. Norman Mailer, if you will credit this, told Podhoretz to his face that he quite liked the book, and then trashed it in the pages of *Partisan Review*. Treachery defined! Yet Podhoretz calmly tells us that he stayed on good terms with Lillian Hellman in just the same way, so as to remain on her party list. When, in the 1980s, the country-club Republicans found that there were tame New York intellectuals to be had for the asking, and from places like Brooklyn College at that, their polite surprise was evident. They had not been paying attention to the many attention-getting rehearsals, at which these old tarts had been dropping veils as if they were going out of style.

Podhoretz is accidentally right, as it happens, in maintaining that there is also a special *ad hominen* venom on the Left, and an extreme willingness to attribute the very lowest motives to those who transgress its codes. Not long ago, having had a series of very public disagreements with an old political friend, I clinched matters by making public something that, although it was public business, could have been described as privately held. Immediately, all evidence of my own strictly private shortcomings was placed on view by former comrades, an operation that I am half-ashamed to say required the spilling of much ink. Having come across this syndrome more than once, I have learned to regard it with resignation, as yet one more aspect of radical impotence in America. But the sufferers from said syndrome can acquire no worthwhile lessons from a crass power worshiper whose only regrets are for himself, and who can conceive of no cause larger than his own esteem. 'The sweet solipsism of youth', says the poet. The solipsism of embittered old age is a lot harder to bear, if not for the writer then at least for the reader.

First published as 'Unmaking Friends' (a review of *Ex-Friends* by Norman Podhoretz and *Making It* by Norman Podhoretz) in *Harper's Magazine,* June 1999

Something for the Boys

The dedication page of this behemoth carries a lapidary, capitalised inscription. 'To Ronald Wilson Reagan. Fortieth President of the United States: The Man Who Won the War.' And this is only fair. In 1984, the Naval Institute Press paid Tom Clancy an advance of $5,000 for *The Hunt for Red October*. It was the first fiction that the Naval Institute had knowingly or admittedly published. There matters might have rested, except that someone handed a copy to the Fortieth President, who (then at the zenith of his great parabola) gave it an unoriginal but unequivocal blurb. 'The perfect yarn', he said, and the Baltimore insurance agent was on his way to blockbuster authorship. Putnam this past August issued a first printing of 2,211,101 copies of his newest novel, *Executive Orders*, and, on the Internet site devoted to Clancy, mayhem broke out as enthusiasts posted news of pre publication copies available at Wal Mart. Clancy's nine thrillers, as well as exemplifying an almost Reaganesque dream of American success, have catapulted him into that section of the cultural supermarket which is always designated by the hieroglyph #1. And this, too, is apt. Remember when America itself was #1? Are we not #1 today? Must we not be #1 tomorrow?

There are other superficial resemblances between the Reagan phenomenon and the Clancy one. Tom Clancy, the true-grit chronicler of air combat, has an aversion to flying and will not get on a plane unless he absolutely has to. Ronald Reagan became phobic about flying in 1937 and did not board another aircraft for almost thirty years. (While grounded, he played heroic airmen in *Secret Service of the Air, Murder in the Air, International Squadron* and *Desperate Journey*.) When he wrote *Red October*, Clancy had never been on a submarine unless it was tethered to the dockside. Ronald Reagan, who never got further than the Hal Loach Training Studio on a Los Angeles backlot, told Yitzhak Shamir and Simon Wiesenthal that he had been present in person at the liberation of the Nazi camps, and often referred fondly to the wartime years he had spent 'in uniform'. Tom Clancy talks like a leatherneck when interviewed by the press, and keeps a large green M4A1 tank parked on the main lawn of his 4,000-acre estate on

Chesapeake Bay. (There is a shooting range in the basement of the main house.) So the nation's two leading fans of vicarious combat make a good pairing. We cannot therefore be sure which 'war', in the dedication, Reagan is supposed to have 'won'. It may be one of the wars that took place only in his head. I think that the millions of Clancy-consuming vicarious-war fans are supposed to assume, however, that it was that 'cold' war, in which Tom Clancy was proposed by Vice-President Dan Quayle as a member of the National Space Council.

Clancy's fictional projection of his rather rotund and unadventurous self is Jack Ryan, who has now been animated on screen by Harrison Ford and Alec Baldwin. A child of the national security apparat, Ryan has captured a Soviet nuclear submarine (*The Hunt for Red October*), done battle with IRA gunmen (*Patriot Games*), outpointed the KGB (*The Cardinal of the Kremlin*), taken the war to the foe in the matter of the Colombian cartels (*Clear and Present Danger*), foiled a world-domination plot by the Indian Navy and a Japanese business consortium (*Debt of Honor*). On the cusp between *Debt of Honor* and *Executive Orders* he becomes Vice-President and President of the United States, all on the same day. Since Ryan has always been represented as an uncomplicated patriot with a distaste for politics and politicians, this transition might seem to offer a difficulty. But Clancy resolves it with a tremendous plot device, whereby a Japanese airliner crashes into a joint session of Congress, killing the Chief Executive, most of the members of the House and the Senate, most of the Cabinet, the Joint Chiefs, and all of the Justices of the Supreme Court. Ryan has been appointed as a stopgap, can-do, pinch-hitting Veep, in the wake of the resignation of a scoundrelly incumbent. By nothing short of a miracle, he escapes the hecatomb of the Joint Session and finds not only that he is Leader of the Free World, but that he has a huge number of vacant appointments in his gift.

It rapidly becomes clear that Tom Clancy's political beau ideal is not really Ronald Reagan so much as it is Ross Perot. Ryan decides to hire a new Treasury Secretary and goes straight to a friend on Wall Street. He tells him:

> Buy a mop. I want your department cleaned up, streamlined and run like you want to make a profit someday. How you do that is your problem. For Defense, I want the same thing. The biggest problem over there is administrative. I need somebody who can run a business and make a profit to cull the bureaucracy out. That's the biggest problem of all, for all the agencies.

There's a great deal more in this style of what I call 'gruff stuff': husky admonitions and *semper fi* shoulder-punches and injunctions not to stand on ceremony or go by the book. Is this, for one thing, a great country or is it not? As one young aide reflects, squeezing his eyes shut in a manly fashion:

> Only in America could a working-class kid who'd scratched into Harvard on a scholarship get befriended by the great son of a great family.

Read with any care, this assertion is only true to the extent that Harvard is in America. But care is just what Clancy doesn't exercise. As he once told an interviewer about an earlier volume in his oeuvre:

> I was never thinking about whether this was a good book or a bad book. I was thinking of the mission, and the mission is finishing the book, and everything else is a sideshow to the mission.

Here is the authentic voice of a man who must sometimes wish that he had not been excused from the draft on the grounds of his myopia. How he loves the argot, of 'doing what you have to do to get the job done'. Regrettably, in *Executive Orders* he sets himself too many missions and succumbs very early to what might be called imperial overstretch.

The outside world is, as is now notorious, a dangerous place. President Ryan is not to be allowed his honeymoon. In far-off Iran, a scheming ayatollah sees his chance. In distant, throbbing Zaire, a young Iranian physician starts to culture the Ebola virus. The glacial Stalinist mandarins of Beijing decide to test 'this Ryan'; a very Fleming-like locution, incidentally, often employed to characterise the speech of a devious and fanatical foreigner. Even the nasty female who heads the government of India is in on the convoluted Sino-Iranian conspiracy, though it turns out to be a conspiracy with no objective beyond itself. The humiliation of the naïve unsuspecting Americans is the general idea. They are so – heh, heh, heh – *enfeebled* by their attachment to democracy . . .

Nor are things at home all that propitious. Some bucolic fascists in Montana decide that their hour has struck. There may be a mole in the President's security detail. And of course, political and journalistic enemies never sleep. This salad of sub-plots, plucked alternately from the marquees of the Cineplex and the filler copy at *US News and World Report*, is narrated by means of inter-cutting, but will present serious problems of continuity for the studio which options it.

For a while, it seems that Jack Ryan doesn't have a friend in the world. But he does, he does. There is Prince Charles, who of course we remember from Ryan's heroic rescue of the royals in *Patriot Games*. And there is the Israeli Mossad, without which no writer in this genre since Frederick Forsyth has dared move a step. At the memorial of those massacred on Capitol Hill:

'Mr President,' said the man in the Royal Navy mess jacket. His ambassador had positioned things nicely. On the whole, London rather liked the new arrangement. The 'special relationship' would become more special, as President Ryan was an (honorary) Knight Commander of the Victorian Order.

'Your Highness,' Jack paused, and allowed himself a smile as he shook the offered hand. 'Long time since that day in London, pal.'

'Indeed.'

I'm citing this not as a sample of Clancy's abysmal dialogue, because in point of fact it's much better crafted and more economical than most of the exchanges that he types, but because it illustrates two recurring Clancy tropes, which are his matey populism and his deference and snobbery. The two are as indissolubly linked, in this as in all Clancy narratives, as his taste for sadistic ruthlessness and his sentimentality.

These qualities are summarised for me in the way in which Clancy names his characters. 'Jack Ryan' is a nothing name to start with, and the character is just an attitudinal cipher, with a tendency to long and sanctimonious monologues, who is naturally devoted to the children he never sees and who gets in bed with his wife only in order to go to sleep. We are informed at one point that he is 'a student of human behaviour', as who indeed is not? His associates and subordinates are called Pat Martin and Dave James and Bob Fowler. There's a John Clark and a Robert Jackson. And think of the ingenuity tax that must have been levied when Clancy had to come up with some tough but tender FBI veterans to be Ryan's only friends in the world (apart of course from the Windsors and the Israelis) and named them Patrick O'Day and Tony Caruso. It's like watching one of those macho 'unit' movies from the Second World War, where there is a Kowalski and an O'Rourke and a Gambino in every platoon.

The geopolitics are evoked with the same skill. The Middle East, that renowned caldron, is described as 'a part of the world known for its inter-locking non-sequiturs'. I will say that I enjoyed that effortless oxymoron more than the immediately following revelation: 'Like most Russians, Golovko had a deep respect for history.' There is, then, inevitably, some talk about wolves and steppes and the uncomfortable conclusion that 'lying on the ground, the horizon could be surprisingly close'. I dare say it could, if one were dangling. We meet a handsome pro-American Saudi prince called Prince Ali Bin Sheik – a name as absurd in Arabic as it is in English. At one point, the saturnine Iranian doctor in the outback of Zaire makes a decision, lifts the phone, and calls the Iranian embassy in Kinshasa. Mr Clancy's travels obviously haven't taken him to Zaire. The telephones there are down. You can't call the Iranian embassy – even if there is one – even if you are already in Kinshasa.

Having commissioned the assassination of Saddam Hussein, the Iranian leadership is able to unite Iraq and Iran, on the basis of Shi'a solidarity, in a matter of days. The newly fused army is ready to reinvade Kuwait at once. Switzerland, on the other hand, hasn't changed since it was visited by Paul Erdman and Robert Ludlum. It is still, you will be reassured to hear, 'a cold country in terms of both climate and culture, but a safe one, and for those with money to invest, an anonymous one'. Books like *Executive Orders* depend on a species of paradox: vast changes in the natural order which leave the landscape of conventional wisdom unchanged. This is why Clancy, in a yarn of 874 pages, invents a few shocks but cannot bring off a nanosecond of real tension.

There comes a point when, chopping one's way though the hopeless tangle of Clancy's thoughts and Clancy's prose, one is compelled to ask who, if anybody, edits this stuff? Is it assumed that the customers will simply buy anything that bears the TC#1 franchise label? Even if so, both they and he are ill-served. That sinister Iranian physician 'walked out of the room ... removing his protective garb as he went, and dumping the articles in the proper container'. A few pages later, 'he left the room, stripping off his protective garb as he did so, depositing it in the proper containers'. Sometimes the inattention creates miniature hilarities. 'For the first time in a very long time, Clark went pale as a ghost.' 'Barry, I've never committed public suicide before.' Sometimes, though, it results in a syntactical pileup from which there is no extrication:

> At every stop, the information was handed over raw, sometimes with the local assessment, but more often without, or if it were, placed at the bottom so that the national intelligence officers in charge of the various watches could make their own assessments, and duplicate the work of others. Mostly this made sense, but in fast-breaking situations it very often did not. The problem was that one couldn't tell the difference in a crisis.

Apparently not.

I believe that I can guess exactly the point at which Mr Clancy gave up on his 'mission' but kept going blindly on. Having been at some pains to show us the Ebola virus being bottled with diabolical care in vials of blood, he allows this blood to spill and permits the ultra-vigilant physician to notice that something sticky and liquid has escaped, only to dismiss the thought. The next person to encounter the spillage finds that 'his seat was wet, with what he didn't know, but it was sticky and ... red? Tomato juice or something probably'. The man making this suggestive blunder is an Iraqi Ba'athist secret policeman, who might be expected to know the difference between blood and Bloody Mary.

Clancy is forgiven much by his fans because he can deliver the high-octane military-industrial prose that is his hallmark. Writing of this calibre is essentially non-fictional, as is shown by Clancy's latest boy's-own guidebook, *Marine*, a breathless history and description of the real-life past and present of America's #1 military *corps d'élite*. But even *Marine* has a closing section in which fantasy is given its head and we are asked to accompany our boys on a future mission against those described as 'rag-heads' in *Executive Orders*:

> Two minutes behind the B-2s came eight B-1B Lancers from the 7th Wing at Dyess AFB, Texas, also launched from Anderson AFB and refuelled from KC-10As at Diego Garcia. Their targets were two battalions of troops in barracks adjacent to Bushehr airport. Each unloaded twelve AGM-154 Joint Standoff Weapons (JSOWs) from their weapons bays, well outside Iranian airspace. Following a two-minute gliding flight, the ninety-six JSOWs, guided by onboard GPS receivers, unloaded their payloads of BLU-97/B Combined Effects Munitions (CEMs). They blanketed over a hundred acres of troop billeting and vehicle-parking areas with thousands of CEMs, and the effects were horrific. The two minutes since the bombs from the B-2 strike had given the troops time to throw on their boots, grab weapons, and rush outside to be shredded into hamburger by exploding cluster munitions.

Here is another pileup, this time acronymic, culminating in a moment of sub-Mickey Spillane. It is the on-page equivalent of the 'smart' videos from the Gulf War. (With this difference. After the Gulf War, staff officers who had viewed the non-virtual effects of cluster and fragmentation weapons decided not to put these triumphs on the air. The videos are still classified by he Department of Defense, whether out of squeamishness or not. But Clancy the gloating civilian is subject to no such inhibition.)

Descriptions like this bear the broken-backed weight of *Executive Orders*, too, and carry the badly injured plot toward its final foxhole. It's interesting to notice the amount of product endorsement that Clancy throws in to enhance the industrial side of his uncomplex military industrial writing. Tributes to the excellence of Merck chemicals, Gulfstream aircraft, and Merrill Lynch brokers are plentiful, as are fulminations by Jack Ryan against the capital gains tax. The acknowledgements to *Marine* include the good people at Bell Textron, Boeing, Sikorsky, Texas Instruments, General Dynamics and Hughes Aircraft. Are we entering the age of sponsorship in airport fiction?

Jack Ryan manages to battle successfully against the multiple and simultaneous subplots that conspire against him, but he succeeds chiefly because most of them just peter out. The Montana militiamen's scheme is discarded (by Clancy, not by the conspirators) and the Indians and Chinese seem just to change their minds. The ever-menacing Japanese are left out altogether on this occasion, while entire Ebola outbreaks, including one in Chicago and a nasty one in the

Sudan, just vanish from the story. Having found a couple of tycoons to serve at Treasury and Defense, Ryan never does get around to any Supreme Court appointments. He even forgets to have a vice-president, which is a requirement of the very Constitution that he repeatedly tells us he is sworn to defend. Actually, Clancy only comes to life at all on those occasions when he can describe either a president trashing the Constitution or a field officer exceeding orders and kicking ass:

> Ryan's problem was that he really didn't have a political philosophy per se. He believed in things that worked, that produced the promised results and fixed whatever was broken. Whether these things adhered to one political slant or another was less important than the effects they had.

Will you adhere to my slant? But when it's a question of proclaiming martial law to combat Ebola, or of violating the prohibition on the assassination of foreign leaders, Ryan's pragmatism reveals itself for what it is; an authoritarian populism set out with more energy than grammar by its fictional author. The same goes for cutting out red tape on military expeditions:

> 'How many can we kill before they make us stop, sir?'
> 'If it's a tank, kill it. If it's BMP, kill it. If it's a truck, kill it. If it's south of the berm and it's holding a weapon, kill it. But the rules are serious about killing unresisting people. We don't break those rules. That's important.'
> 'Fair 'nuff, Colonel.'
> 'Don't take any unnecessary chances with prisoners, either.'
> 'No, sir', the track commander promised. 'I won't.'

The implication of the passage is quite subtle by Clancy standards, but it shares in the same down-and-dirty tough-guy pornography of which this is the soft version.

The usual throaty justification for such nastiness is, of course, the existence of women and children. As far as I can see, Clancy has fitted out Ryan with a spouse and some offspring simply so that he can experience paroxysms of justified male wrath when physical attacks are made on them. ('Why my kids, Jeff? I'm the one – here. If people get mad, it's supposed to be at me. Why do people like this go after children, tell me that...?') Strong, drivelling men like this are also traditionally very fond of committing minor infractions and then asking their subordinates not to tell the lady of the house or she'll have his guts for garters. Clancy does not spare us this convention. I lost count of the number of times that Ryan bummed a cigarette and then, likeably and democratically, cautioned the underling not to let 'Cathy' know. This makes the mighty appear so much more ... human, really.

Even though Clancy often seems bored by his own devices, there is one other subject – apart from political and military bullying – that gets him excited. Like many people who know absolutely nothing about Washington, and who reveal the fact by talking portentously of 'this town', he believes that the press is out to 'get' the man in charge. If a Jack Ryan had actually become President in the manner described here, and had then had to face a challenge from a newly united Iran–Iraq federation, he would have had the mass media at his disposal from early morn to dewy eve. 'Bipartisanship' would not have been the half of it.

Instead, Clancy shows us a president who meekly submits to atrocious rudeness at press conferences, who is harried by reporters wherever he goes, who does five unrehearsed network interviews one after the other (on the same topic, in his private quarters) and who is subjected to a last-minute 'set-up' grilling by a crafty presenter. Moreover, the Pentagon flies hostile correspondents directly to the scene of combat, while reporters call and get the National Security Advisor on the telephone at all times. A clue to Clancy's resentful caricature of the Fourth Estate is probably to be found in one such scene, where 'a very liberated lady' reporter asks an impertinent question about Roe v Wade. But I never want to read again that, say what you will about Clancy's losing arm-wrestle with the English language, he is at least good on the details.

Details can be suggestive, however, and some absorbing ones are to be found in *Marine*. We find that Clancy praises his favourite corps for capturing John Brown at Harper's Ferry (under the command of Virginia Army officers Robert E. Lee and J. E. B. Stuart); for subverting Mexico at Vera Cruz in 1847; for putting down Filipino rebels in 1899 and invading Nicaragua in 1913; for intervening in Haiti between 1915 and 1934; and for 'pacifying the Panama Canal Zone' between 1901 and 1914, to say nothing of enforcing the Platt Amendment in Cuba. For Clancy, these are not disfigurements of a record that after all includes Iwo Jima, but glorious pages in and of themselves. As the novel began to recede in my memory, it was deposed and replaced by the image of Oliver North, a disgraced Marine officer for whom Clancy used to 'do' fundraisers. There are obviously many 'guys' out there, some of them perhaps living near bases threatened with closure, dwelling in the lost world of 'choke points' and 'arcs of crisis' and 'daggers pointed at the heart of'. For them, Clancy is a novelist and North is a hero. With no official enemy on the radar screen (and even the foul Iranians better-armed thanks to North and Reagan), Clancy has become the junk supplier of surrogate testosterone. His books bear the same relation to reality as Oliver North's lachrymose and bragging speeches do to patriotism, and his writing is to prose what military music is to music.

First published as 'Something for the Boys' (a review of *Executive Orders* by Tom Clancy) in *New York Review of Books*, 14 November 1996

The Cruiser

Few things are harder to write than a sincere treatment in the style of 'more sorrow than anger'. The sincerity is bound to get in the way of both the sorrow and the anger, and vice versa. One will be suspected, perhaps, of masking (beneath the regret) a covert relish. The fulsome style of the obituarist may creep in, causing one to be sanctimonious about the virtues in order to appear generous about the backsliding. Hypocrisy waits at every intersection. But it remains the fact that Conor Cruise O'Brien has been one of the great stylists of our time, whether writing about France, Britain, Ireland or Africa. It further remains a fact that his has been a voice attuned to the discourse of reason, and that when he has been 'mobbish' (his own preferred term for a bit of polemical exaggeration; no harm in it; no malice; the fellow needed a bit of a start anyway) then even this mobbishness has been generous, and a pleasure to read. O'Brien has been an internationalist, a wit, a polymath and a provocateur. I can still remember the excitement with which I discovered a copy of *Writers and Politics*, in a provincial library in Devonshire thirty years ago. Nobody who tries to write about either of these subjects can disown a debt to the Cruiser. I hope that this is enough by way of sorrow and sincerity, though I could certainly have amplified it. Because the plain fact is that his latest book is a disgrace. Even if it doesn't make one angry, it is a cause for disgust and depression. He fouls his reputation both for writing and for reasoning.

Ostensibly, what we have here is an extended rumination on the next horizon of our species: the oncoming hieroglyphic of the year 2000. O'Brien fears that there will be an increase in mania and fanaticism as this appointment draws nigh, and though he eschews the pun, he also fears that this increase will be secular. It's not that he ignores the religious dimension: more that he correctly fears the overflow of the superstitious into the quotidian. This is a good subject for a man of his range (even if one is slightly fed up in advance at the prospect of how much one may have to read, and even perhaps to write, about the onset of the millennium). But O'Brien has made the mistake of confusing the condition of the cosmos with the state of his own liver.

He begins with – what else? – Yeat's 'Second Coming'. Then he recapitulates the writing of Jules Michelet, who recalled the panic and terror of the year 1000 in his *History of France.* O'Brien has written well in the past about both Yeats and Michelet. But in this instance he is content to lard his tired prose with a few 'rough beasts' and 'mere anarchies', much as any hack might do. And he ignores the large body of more recent work by medievalists, which argues that Michelet was simply repeating some sixteenth-century fabrications about the last millennium.[1] This serves as a weak introduction to his attack on the present Pope. Of course it is true, as O'Brien says, that John Paul II is an authoritarian and an obscurantist. (It could almost be said that these qualities come with the territory.) It is likewise the case that the Vatican and the Muslim extremists made common cause at the world population conference in Cairo. Yet there is no linear progression, of the sort he suggests, between these findings and a sort of reverse-ecumenical counter-enlightenment brought on by the millennium. And there is no reason at all to suppose, as O'Brien preposterously argues, that while 'John Paul II is not about to embrace Islam' nevertheless 'he is not averse to giving the impression that he may be about to do so.' Remind me. When did he start giving this impression? By overstressing the importance of the year 2000 in his explication (the Pope 'hopes, as he has told us', O'Brien notes significantly, 'to be presiding over the destinies of the Catholic Church when the great turning point is reached') he goggles at the date just as one of Michelet's imagined peasants might have done. A safer prediction might be that the Pope will not make it to the turn of the century, and nor will his National Security Adviser, Mother Teresa, and that nothing in any case can save their Church from the crisis of allegiance being undergone by its faithful. An instance of this – the divorce referendum in O'Brien's native Ireland – occurred too recently to be considered by him.

At first I thought that this was just a shaky start. But in the second chapter (this book originated as a series of lectures) came a point of decline which rapidly disclosed itself as inaugurating something irreversible. Discussing Europe on the eve of 1914, O'Brien correctly says that Lenin did not foresee the coming of the European war:

> When the chain of events that led to the war was set in motion by the assassination of Archduke Franz Ferdinand at Sarajevo, Lenin was sceptical: 'I cannot believe that Franz Joseph and our Nikolashka will give us that pleasure.'
>
> Pleasure: Russia's revolutionary destines were now in the hands of a man who thought of the coming First World War as a pleasure.

Say what you will about O'Brien, his work has been infused with irony and paradox. That he should so heavily and sarcastically miss the point of a black joke is a sorry thing. And note the leaden, ordinary prose. ('Chains of events' is a cliché, and you can't easily have a chain of any sort 'set in motion'.)

Not only is O'Brien being crass here, he is also being reactionary. He sounds like one of those paranoid pamphleteers against the man Ronald Reagan unfailingly called 'Nikolai Lenin'. Lenin, incidentally, also couldn't believe the news that the German Social Democrats had voted for the war – a truly vertiginous moment in modern history – but if you go on mentioning the number of things that he couldn't credit then it becomes harder to go on about his supernatural 'ruthlessness' and 'coldness'. The traditional next stages in polemics of this kind are a. some incantation about 1984 and b. some growls about 'appeasement'. O'Brien does not disappoint. Arguing that the present ceasefire in Ireland 'will bring Ireland closer and closer to civil war every day that it continues', he says as if coining the thought for the first time that 'the year 1994 is more like Orwell's *Nineteen Eighty-Four* than the real 1984 was. In 1994, we are beginning to understand the full force of the Orwellian slogan, "Peace Means War".'

Oh, please. In the first place, the famous Ministry of Truth slogan was 'War is Peace'. In the second place, we are now (as could have been predicted) in 1996, which means that the lucky coincidence of one digit is of no literary use. Does that make O'Brien reconsider his argument? Not at all. Does it make him question the usefulness of numerology in his analysis? Fat chance. Indeed, when he comes to consider Haiti – and to take another crack at the Clinton who has offended him by meeting Gerry Adams, and so can do nothing right – he has his deadly thrust at the ready: 'The year 1994 is a lot more like Orwell's *Nineteen Eighty-Four* than the chronological 1984 was. Operation Restore Democracy is a masterpiece both of Newspeak and Doublespeak.'

Anyway, on to appeasement. Hitting on the analogy of Munich as if he has stumbled across a wholly new historical metaphor, O'Brien employs it to impugn any government which seeks to gratify the assumed popular fondness for 'peace'. (Not much 1914 here.) To his dead-obvious recitation of the record of Chamberlain and Daladier he adds at least one new factoid:

> Throughout the Thirties, Nobel Peace Prizes went to pacifists, mostly British and French pacifist whose activities were consistently – although altogether inadvertently – beneficial to Hitler ... The peace process, from 1936 on, meant that the West had to fight, three years later, a Germany grown immensely formidable, through the yearning of the West for peace.

Bet you didn't know that. But then O'Brien doesn't seem to know that the Nobel Peace Prize in 1935 went to Carl von Ossietsky, a German

anti-militarist whose award outraged the Nazis and got him sent to a
camp. (There were no French winners. The three British ones were a
mixed bag.) And he seems to have forgotten what he once knew, which
is that Munich represented not so much a weak-kneed capitulation to
Hitler as a spirited attempt to make an agreement with him. The later
'spin', the 'inadvertently' lenient one of invertebrate naiveté, was
furnished retrospectively in order to suit the requirements of the Cold
War. Of course Hitler, like Lenin, must always be presented in these
sorts of minatory discourse as if he was the only person who had any
idea of what he was up to: 'Hitler, that great propagandist, knew what
he was doing when he announced his Thousand Year Reich. He
understood the magical resonances that adhere to the idea of a
thousand years: the heady echoes of the Book of Revelation which
linger even in consciously secular minds.' Enough to make your flesh
creep, with its 'heady echoes' and all. No doubt Churchill was aiming
for the same effect when he spoke of the thousand-year empire in his
'Finest Hour' address.

What is true in O'Brien's argument is not original, and what is
original is not true. Proceeding with his bilious view of the state of
democracy, he makes the point that the American founding documents
represent a civil religion. Some truth, I'd say, in that oft-repeated
observation. But is it the case that

> the Declaration of Independence is the supremely sacred scripture of the
> American civil religion. Jefferson's role as the man who wrote down the
> scripture is analogous to the role of the Prophet Muhammed taking down
> the Blessed Koran at the dictation of an angel of God . . . The effect of the
> cult of Jefferson, therefore, is to invest the secular and ostensibly wholly
> rational Enlightenment with an aura of revelation and the numinous.

Nobody believes the proposition advanced in the second sentence
above. And the only people who applaud the general argument are
those in the Christian Right movement who tried, a few years ago, to
have 'secular liberalism' denominated as a religion so that they could
demand 'equal time' with it in the schools. This sinister nonsense was
seen off with hardly any trouble at all and (though it can be imprudent
to underestimate these Protestant fundamentalists) it hasn't been
resurrected. In writing with heroic exaggeration that Jefferson is 'the
secular patron saint of modern liberal intellectuals', O'Brien makes the
astounding discovery that Jefferson owned slaves and insinuates that
there has been a liberal cover-up here. Well, I find it's tolerably well-
known that the Sage of Monticello had some unpaid help on his estate.
I. F. Stone, indeed, who used to describe himself as a 'Jeffersonian
Marxist', was always expecting trouble on the Marxist bit, but got
himself roundly abused for identifying with a holder of people as

property. Finally, O'Brien correctly notes that Jefferson chose 'Author of the Declaration of Independence' as his epitaph but fails to add that he also chose (instead of 'Twice President of the United States') his authorship of the Virginia Statute on Religious Freedom. This last, which institutes the separation of Church and State and prevents the establishment of any government-endorsed faith, is unlikely to have been dictated by an angel of any kind and thus leaves O'Brien's analogy looking perfectly stupid.

Of course, O'Brien doesn't especially care about the slavery business or any of the other distractions he intrudes into the discussion. What matters to him is that Jefferson was a life-long antagonist of Edmund Burke. And this, you must know, is not to be pardoned. Now (and here I return to my more-in-sorrow mode) we all know more about Burke – how to think about him and how to read him – as a result of O'Brien's labours. In school we were taught about Burke the Tory versus Paine the incendiary, where the only text was the *Reflections*, but from O'Brien we learned about Burke's solicitude for the Thirteen Colonies, his outrage at the depredations of Warren Hastings in India, and his willingness to spend time on matters of principle. We also learned of the fascinating, occluded, red-haired Irishman, who hoped by careful husbandry of his counsel to be allowed to plead for his stricken homeland. In the ironic and ambivalent figure of Burke, indeed, it didn't seem too fanciful to detect something of O'Brien himself. As he wrote in his own Preface to the *Reflections*:

> The contradictions in Burke's position enrich his eloquence, extend its range, deepen its pathos, heighten its fantasy and make possible its strange appeal to 'men of liberal temper'. On this interpretation, part of his power to penetrate the processes of a revolution derives from a suppressed sympathy with revolution, combined with an intuitive grasp of the subversive possibilities of counter-revolutionary propaganda, as affecting the established order in the land of his birth. . . . For him, the forces of revolution and the counter-revolution exist not only in the world at large but also within himself.

As George Orwell did say in another context, it would almost be worth being dead to have something like that written about you. And in *The Great Melody*, O'Brien expanded upon some of these themes, without actually expanding them very much. Yet here we have Burke presented as a straight, unambiguous Tory; either the adamant foe of Jefferson or the moaning defender of Marie Antoinette. This is a real and sad declension.

One of the signal achievements of the French Revolution was the abolition of slavery, and one of the horrors of Bonapartism was its restoration. This drama took place largely on the soil of Haiti, which is the site of another O'Brienish rant. As his dull attribution to Orwell made plain, O'Brien is no fan of the Clinton policy, which he takes to be another exercise in hypocrisy. There's a lot to be said (believe me) on that side of the case. But to argue as O'Brien does that the removal of the Cedras junta had but one objective, and that objective the ignoble one of stemming the flow of Haitian emigration, is to be reductionist. (At one point, he refers to it as 'a black political force': the best but not the only misprint inflicted on him by the yawning editors at the celebrated Free Press.) Like the US intervention in Bosnia, the restoration of the elected President Aristide – never mentioned by the Cruiser – was compounded of a mixture of realpolitik, imperialism, democratic rhetoric, moral promises and political opportunism. (It was also part of the price that the United States pays for being 'top nation' at the UN; again something you might think the author of *The United Nations: Sacred Drama* might have found room to discuss.) But here is what it was not, and here is what O'Brien, stupefyingly, says it was: 'an example of degenerative processes affecting the intellect: processes which, if they continue to develop as they are now doing on the eve of the third millennium, may well destroy our Western civilisation by around the third century of that millennium'. Let nobody say that O'Brien does not take himself, or his own argument, with due seriousness. On the very next occasion that he mentions Operation Restore Democracy (not many pages away) he asserts: 'That way madness lies, quite literally. If that level of wishful fantasy should become the norm, and then perhaps even be surpassed, our whole Western culture will be going out of its collective mind, probably within the first quarter of the third millennium.'

Pray, why so vague? (And yet, so exact? Dost know hawk from handsaw?) Why need we wait three hundred years for the vindication of a judgment so self-evident in the present? On other matters, O'Brien is not even this temperate. He worries about the future of Britain without a Crown and says, in full chiliastic mode but with a shorter time-line, that 'I doubt whether the monarchy can survive until the end of the next century. And I fear that its disappearance may wrench the fabric of British society in such a way as to endanger British democracy and even – in conjunction with other forces – endanger democracy in the West in general.'

Which would be in nice time for the subsequent collapse, post-Haiti, of civilisation itself. O'Brien obviously likes this idea well enough to be brooding on it, because in a flash of inspiration a few pages later he confides: 'For these reasons, I think it unlikely that the British monarchy can survive to the end of the next century. Its fall will have very serious implications, not only for Britain, but also for the whole of the West.' In speaking of 'degenerative processes affecting the intellect', O'Brien has given a large hostage to fortune. I scarcely need to add that he blames the monarchy's trouble on 'the tabloid press', and dilates on the need for some kind of restraint, for all the world as if C and D (I'm sorry, I just can't give them either their titles or their familiar names) had not each enlisted a gutter on either side of Fleet Street. There, if he cared to look for it, the Cruiser might unearth a clue about the Ancien Régime. As it is, he really does vindicate Paine by mourning the plumage and forgetting the dying bird.

What else might one expect from the autumn of such a patriarch? Well, an attack on pornography and a hard-hitting critique of political correctness would be in order. These duly arrive – porn being blamed for the destruction of the Bourbons, and PC being courageously and uniquely defined as 'that fascinating late development of Orwellian Newspeak which is known as "politically correct"', I might add that our boy fears that this, too, 'may be a symptom of a wider degeneration within the Western mind, and related to other symptoms, such as those indicative of deep malaise within the democratic system.' Which takes care of all that. (The real symptom of a PC bore, by the way, is a tendency to stress the fact that Thomas Jefferson was a slaveholder.) There is barely a 'quotable' passage in the whole book, as you may guess from what I have unselectively quoted, though one might make an exception for this: 'British diplomats, constantly exposed to American political-ethical rhetoric, find their professional skills tested to the limits by the need to keep a straight face. For illustrations of what I mean, study the photographs of the expressions worn by Mr Douglas Hurd at any international conference involving all the Western allies.' This recalls O'Brien's statement, delivered just between his sacking from the UN and his writing of *Murderous Angels*, that 'as a result of the policy of Macmillan's Government, Great Britain presents in the United Nations the face of Pecksniff and in Katanga the face of Gradgrind'. Otherwise, these pages crumble before the eye like yesterday's (or today's) effusion from Paul Johnson.

And this would be all knockabout stuff if it were not for the fact that – like the writing of the aforesaid Johnson – it has calcified around an increasingly nasty little core. The early chapters of this book are mostly and merely stupid, mostly and merely boring. But a gruesome little light is switched on behind the glaucous eyes when O'Brien comes to his closing passage, which is a veiled tribute to Nietzsche. Quoting himself from an earlier incarnation, he writes in a synthesis of the worst of Camus and the worst of Sartre:

> The advanced world may well be like, and feel like, a closed and guarded palace, in a city gripped by the plague. There is another metaphor, developed by André Gide, one of the many powerful minds powerfully influenced by Nietzsche. This is the metaphor of the lifeboat, in a sea full of the survivors

of a shipwreck. The hands of survivors cling to the sides of the boat. But the boat has already as many passengers as it can carry. No more survivors can be accommodated, and if they gather and cling on, the boat will sink and all be drowned. The captain orders out the hatchets. The hands of the survivors are severed. The lifeboat and its passengers are saved.

Even when I read this ABC of utilitarianism in 1970 (when O'Brien to the delight of all was holder of the Albert Schweitzer Chair in the Humanities) I was compelled to notice the choice of the word 'passenger' in the fifth and last sentences. Guess, in other words, who is in the boat and who is in the water. You can't help but observe that the person so ostentatiously chewing the moral knuckle is also the 'tough-minded' person who is, in imagination and reality, well inside the boat. Try it the other way about. The steerage and cooks have got to the boats first, and the paying customers are flailing in the foam? I don't think so. Had he only written 'the lifeboat and its occupants' we might have been faced with an exercise in strict moral neutrality. (And then, perhaps, have inquired whether anyone had thought to jettison the golf-clubs or the safe-deposit boxes.) As it is, O'Brien is playing the pseudo-Swiftian role of asking us to face difficult choices, while actually taking a modest proposal – to lop off the limbs of fellow creatures – as literally as he takes Lenin and Hitler. In his update of this argument, the enthusiasm for what he suggestively terms 'bracing fierceness' is barely masked by any affectation of repugnance. As he phrases it, this time uttering his own thoughts without mediation: 'In reality, the Third World ghettoes – such as the townships of South Africa – are the centres of an intensified and accelerated process of natural selection.' Worth knowing, if you are bracing yourself for fierceness. You flick back to the earlier O'Brien attack on the Pope, and suddenly notice that his argument is entirely, or better say simply, Malthusian. Birth control, in other words, is not to be advocated because it increases the sum of health and freedom, and teaches people how to limit family size in a decent and voluntary way, but only because there are too many of *them*. And we know, do we not, who *they* are. (Who cares that planetary resources are used up far more promiscuously, and very much more rapidly, by the citizens of rich countries? We're talking *lifeboats* here.)

How was such a noble mind o'erthrown? One becomes less intrigued by this question as the long day wanes, but it seems clear that by the time of his book *The Siege* the Cruiser had surrendered to the termites within. Conor Cruise O'Zion was one thing; empurpled defender of the proprietary rights of Jewish settlers in Palestine. Camera Crews O'Booze was also a discrete entity, bracingly fierce in his guarding of Derry's Walls against Popery and terrorism. But Afrikaner Cruise

O'Brien was a bit much. Having identified these three minorities as encircled members of the community of the oppressed, O'Brien had mastered the trick of presenting overdog causes in underdog rhetorical yowls. He wrote of Mandela's ANC that it was 'a political movement whose sanction, symbol and signature is the burning alive of people in the street'. (There's a warning there, and not just against infelicitous alliteration.)

At least, in presenting these lost causes in those ways, O'Brien could posture as one who swam 'against the current'. He also knew a lot, in those days, about the bad intellectual habit of coming up with pretty names for violence and cruelty. How he must mourn the fact that he could not, then, have depicted himself with due rectitude as 'politically incorrect'. How he must deplore the incautious conduct of the South African National Party, and the Israelis, in having deferred to the existence of another people on 'their' besieged national territories. And how he chirrups for the Orangemen when they prove his point by denying this salient fact. Never have the Romantic and the Rejectionist been compounded in such a frightful macedoine. Seldom can witless sneering and empty cynicism have been so hastily wed to a show of idealism. At the close, O'Brien writes – much more, no doubt, in sorrow than in relish – that 'Fascism, like its ancestor Nietzscheanism, is unfortunately an appropriate ideology for a guarded palace in a city gripped by plague.'

One has to love and respect that placing of the word 'unfortunately', by one who has just exhausted himself in trying to suggest that we do inhabit such a 'palace'. O'Brien can speak for himself. I will not elect to be Pangloss just because he has chosen to be Spengler. But one can't help noticing that those with axe in hand are the Michael Portillos and Alan Clarks and Pat Buchanans and Ross Perots (who don't choose to share any of their palaces with me or anyone else) and that those with their hands on the gunwale are the Ken Saro-Wiwas and others. A difficult choice? Not all that difficult. Lest I be thought queasy and irresolute, however, I can make a modest proposal of my own which could yet give the vessel a breathing space. The Cruiser should be made to read this book, which would quite possibly be for the first time. Then he should be asked to eat it. Then he should agree, without sentimentality or sickly compassion, to make a utilitarian sacrifice for suffering humanity, and pitch himself over the side.

First published as 'The Cruiser' (a review of *On the Eve of the Millennium: The Future of Democracy Through an Age of Unreason* by Conor Cruise O'Brien) in *London Review of Books*, 22 February 1996

Notes

1. See especially *Century's End: An orientation towards the year 2000* by Hillel Schwarz (Doubleday, 1999).

Acknowledgements

Call no man lucky until he is dead, as the Greeks properly said, but a writer may still without hubris claim a share of fortune. To say that I have been lucky with my editors is the very smallest bow I can make in this direction. 'Editor', indeed, seems to me a paltry word for those who have encouraged me; conceived of topics and subjects that might engage or interest me; printed me; corrected or rescued me; and finally (in the sense of last but not least, rather than tardily) paid me.

I owe an immense gratitude to Barbara Epstein at the *New York Review of Books*, Graydon Carter, Aimee Bell and Elise O'Shaughnessy at *Vanity Fair*, Colin MacCabe at the *Critical Quarterly*, Mary-Kay Wilmers at the *London Review of Books*, Brian Morton at *Dissent*, Steve Wasserman at the *Los Angeles Times Book Review*, Lewis Lapham at *Harper's*, Ferdinand Mount at the *Times Literary Supplement* and Katrina vanden Heuvel and Victor Navasky at *The Nation*.

The fraternity of *New Left Review* and Verso has sustained me now through several books and defended me in numerous combats, orthodox and unorthodox. So I should especially thank Perry Anderson, Colin Robinson and Robin Blackburn.

I'd like also to register my gratitude to James Miller, head of my department at the Graduate Faculty of the New School for Social Research in New York, and to the bright and patient graduates of my class on Unacknowledged Legislation, who know who they are and have contributed more than they know.

Index